SAGE was founded in 1965 by Sara Miller McCune to support the dissemination of usable knowledge by publishing innovative and high-qual ty research and teaching content. Today, we publish over 900 jourrals, including those of more than 400 learned societ es, more than 800 new books per year, and a growing range of library products including archives, data, case studies, reports, and video. SAGE remains majcrity-owned by our founder, and after Sara's lifetime will become owned by a charitable trust that secures our continued independence.

Los Angeles | London | New Delhi | Singapore | Washington DC | Melbourne

Caste, Social Inequality and Mobility in
Rural India

Caste, Social Inequality and Mobility in
Rural India

Reconceptualizing the Indian Village

K. L. Sharma

Los Angeles I London I New Delhi
Singapore I Washington DC I Melbourne

First published in 2019 by

SAGE Publications India Pvt Ltd
B1/I-1 Mohan Cooperative Industrial Area
Mathura Road, New Delhi 110 044, India
www.sagepub.in

SAGE Publications Inc
2455 Teller Road
Thousand Oaks, California 91320, USA

SAGE Publications Ltd
1 Oliver's Yard, 55 City Road
London EC1Y 1SP, United Kingdom

SAGE Publications Asia-Pacific Pte Ltd
18 Cross Street #10-10/11/12
China Square Central
Singapore 048423

Published by Vivek Mehra for SAGE Publications India Pvt Ltd, typeset in 11/14 pts Bembo by Zaza Eunice, Hosur, Tamil Nadu, India.

Library of Congress Cataloging-in-Publication Data

Name: Sharma, K. L. (Kanhaiya Lal), - author.
Title: Caste, social inequality and mobility in rural India:
   reconceptualizing the Indian village/K. L. Sharma.
Description: Thousand Oaks: SAGE Publications India Pvt Ltd, 2019. |
   Includes bibliographical references and index.
Identifiers: LCCN 2018050189| ISBN 9789353282011 (hardcover: alk. paper) |
   ISBN 9789353282028 (e pub 2.0) | ISBN 9789353282035 (e book)
Subjects: LCSH: Caste—India | Equality—India. | Social mobility—India.
Classification: LCC HT720.S398 2019 | DDC 305.5/1220954—dc23 LC record available at https://lccn.loc.gov/2018050189

ISBN: 978-93-532-8201-1 (HB)

SAGE Team: Rajesh Dey, Guneet Kaur, Syeda Aina Rahat Ali and Nishant Dhawan

Dedicated to my beloved and caring life partner Geeta Sharma, son Professor Rajendra Sharma, daughter Dr. Rachna Sharma and younger son Er. Ravindra Sharma for their utmost respect and concern.

I also dedicate this book to my elder brother Shri Jagdish Prasad Sharma for his generosity, love, inspiration and hard work in helping to restudy the six villages in Rajasthan.

Thank you for choosing a SAGE product!
If you have any comment, observation or feedback,
I would like to personally hear from you.

Please write to me at **contactceo@sagepub.in**

Vivek Mehra, Managing Director and CEO, SAGE India.

Bulk Sales

SAGE India offers special discounts
for purchase of books in bulk.
We also make available special imprints
and excerpts from our books on demand.

For orders and enquiries, write to us at

Marketing Department
SAGE Publications India Pvt Ltd
B1/I-1, Mohan Cooperative Industrial Area
Mathura Road, Post Bag 7
New Delhi 110044, India

E-mail us at **marketing@sagepub.in**

Subscribe to our mailing list
Write to **marketing@sagepub.in**

This book is also available as an e-book.

Contents

Part IV: Emerging Patterns of Stratification and Change

Part V: Theoretical and Empirical Concerns in Village Studies

Foreword

Professor K. L. Sharma stoutly refuses to miss the trees for the forest and the forest for the trees. This book is an excellent example of his continuous attention to both empirical reality and theoretical explanation. In every chapter, one finds Professor Sharma introducing some of the most enduring theoretical and conceptual constructs and interweaving these with a wealth of field material and factual details. Nothing is too small to miss his attention and nothing is too large to be out of his canvas.

In one way, Professor Sharma has reconciled the contradictions between theory and ground reality and that is by refusing to let traditional authorities overwhelm modern scholarship. For anybody who is entering the domain of Indian studies as well as for someone who is an old hand at it, this volume offers many variegated lessons. When the book is read and the covers are closed, both the newcomer and the veteran will feel amply rewarded. Those who are already distinguished practitioners of sociology will find a lot in here that they had either overlooked or never known. The novice will exult in brand new knowledge, about that there is little doubt. But many professional Indianists too might also feel humbled by the knowledge gaps they never knew they had till they read this book.

That sociology of India and in India has made huge advances is indubitable, but what remains surprising is how doughty and resilient popular prejudices and conceptions of Indian reality are. Perhaps, this book will help put many of these erroneous impressions of Indian society to rest, and there is good reason this might happen, provided readers take the arguments in here seriously. India is well past its colonial and oriental past, but the mind has still not emptied itself of the many fallacies that earlier periods had instilled in it. Why this should be so is a good sociology of knowledge question and Professor Sharma's untiring efforts can go a long way in sorting out this issue as well.

Indian villages have long ceased to be isolates; India's caste order has long ceased being a system; Indians too have demonstrated that they are not just culture bearers but individuals too. Yet, time and again, in popular journals and dailies, as well as in political commentaries, one finds repeated visits to these ancient shrines that have long been overgrown by the undergrowth. True, most lay people are informed by these sources, but what aggravates it is when scholars too give in to such popular impressions, thus widening our knowledge fault lines. Both the specialist and the generalist have enough in this book to ponder over and, hopefully, Professor Sharma's persuasive work will lead them to a more scholarly consensus.

It is a fact that India's villages, while still there as an empirical and geographic reality, have been hollowed out from the inside. There are several reasons for this, but the overriding one is the fact that the rural economy is no longer a closed one. The phenomenal increase in rural non-farm employment, the extent of migration and the collapse of patronage structures have changed the countryside dramatically. While such phenomena can be examined as separate entities, the truth is that the genesis of all these is the breakdown of the earlier village economy. The most significant contributor to this outcome has been the dissolution of zamindari and old feudalism. This hastened the advances that have today made the village a more fractured than a cohesive reality.

Naturally, this impinges upon some other big facts such as caste and family. Professor Sharma has adroitly demonstrated how the earlier renditions of caste hierarchy no longer work and that a serious rethink is required in this regard. Likewise, the family too has been buffeted by multiple forces, such as those arising from urbanization, fragmentation of holdings, altered gender relations and new-found aspirations too. Therefore, unlike previous scholarship that saw the village as a passive sponge of urban influences, today one should factor in the reverse flow as well. It is for this reason that the concept 'country–town continuum' must be replaced with the concept of 'country–town nexus'. Read this book to know more about it.

Professor Sharma eminently succeeds in demonstrating how Indian villages are changing, and changing rapidly; but he also has an eye for detail and lists out the many resistant forces within. It is this tension that provides the basic epistemological key for understanding the many layers in Indian society. India is modern and yet tradition has smudged it with prints of the past; India is getting urbanized, but the dung and dirt are ever present. If there is a direction of change that some can plot, one can see this trajectory suffering a kind of drag as well.

One must congratulate Professor Sharma for bringing out a very thoughtful book on India which is accessible to people of different backgrounds. This volume will be a great help, to both teachers and students. It informs the layperson and wises up the professional too. Professor K. L. Sharma's latest offering should enjoy a very wide readership, for it deserves nothing less.

Dipankar Gupta

Preface and Acknowledgements

This study of social stratification and change in contemporary rural India was envisaged as a mirror of the ramifications of the Indian rural society and its economy and polity, keeping in view the emerging patterns of inequality and social mobility. We have made a modest attempt to put together a large number of studies, analyses and commentaries, available particularly since Independence. At the same time, several studies have been left out, not because they are less significant but because our eclectic approach was constrained by the limitation of time and space. Despite such a limitation, a sincere effort has been made to make it an interdisciplinary study and analysis on the theme of social stratification and change.

Some very important points have clearly emerged. The Indian village was never an 'isolate', as it was projected during the pre-Independence period, and it is quite different after 1947 as it has witnessed tremendous change. Country–town nexus existed earlier, though it was shaped by the factors prevailing during the British period. Today, it is quite pronounced with a new face. Some villages have grown as 'towns', and some have merged with the nearby cities and towns, and the interior/remote villages are no more 'remote' as the means of transport and communication have provided an easy access to towns/cities. Migration, mobility and education have transformed the country–town nexus immensely during the post-Independence period, hence the reconceptualization of the idea of Indian village, because there is an element of 'urbanity' in the village, and there is also an element of 'rurality' in urban India. Rural–urban networks have also resulted into a 'rural middle class'.

'Caste' persists without 'caste system'. Caste in everyday life has nearly disappeared. Caste councils are non-existent, except in some states where occasionally one comes to know about the atrocities inflicted by the Khap panchayats on the violators of the rules of marriage. Inter-caste marriages among the rural settlers in towns and cities are taking place, without inviting punitive actions. Untouchability is non-existent, and so is the jajmani system. In the absence of inter-caste dependence, castes have become segmentary, but when inter-caste brotherhood also becomes practically nonfunctional, even segmentary nature of caste is rarely observable due to cooperation among different castes having specific ends-in-view. Thus, caste-based inequality is not found as such, but some people appropriate 'caste' for accessing resources, extracting favours and benefits. Some even claim 'casteless-ness' for gaining a political mileage; and some appropriate 'casteness' to seek support and help from the members of their own castes/sub-castes. In such a situation, caste is no more a bedrock of social relations in everyday life.

However, despite a big jolt to the caste hierarchy, there is an enhanced social inequality in which the caste system has played a minimal role. Structural changes in village India have not benefited different sections of the society equally. Special provisions for the backward sections have created a small sub-section of elites and a miniscule middle class.

Those who have moved out of the village are better off. The people who have successfully appropriated social networks and have established nexus with urban institutions and people are the new dominants and influential people. Even mobility has created inequality for those who have remained deprived of it. Simple migration or formal education alone (without quality) have not reduced inequality considerably. The role of the State is quite minimal, keeping in view the role of caste, education, migration, mobility, etc., and their consequences in terms of equality, emergence of middle class and new forms of inequality. Our revisit to 'Six Villages' in Rajasthan has also substantiated these observations.

I am grateful to the Indian Council of Social Science Research (ICSSR), New Delhi, for the award of National Fellowship to undertake the present study over a period of two years (2014–2016). My particular thanks to Professor S. D. Thorat, the then Chairman; Professor Ramesh Dadhich, the then Member Secretary; and

Dr Ajay Gupta, Director, who were always considerate about my endeavour. I also thank the present Member Secretary Professor V. K. Malhotra for his help and support.

I wish to thank Professor Naresh Dadheech, the then Director of the Institute of Development Studies (IDS), Jaipur, for granting me affiliation to IDS, and an office space, and access to its library. The librarian and his colleagues were always helpful in providing access to books, journals and documents. The faculty and the staff of IDS provided me a cordial ambience, which motivated me for completion of the study. Mr G. L. Mittal looked after the timely payment of fellowship and maintained documents, systematically. I am thankful to Mr Mittal. I am also indebted to the present Director, Professor Shanker Kumar Bhaumik for his genuine support at IDS.

The presence of Padma Bhushan Professor V. S. Vyas, former Chairman and Director of IDS, and currently Emeritus Professor, has been a source of inspiration and strength for me during the National Fellowship. Occasional discussions with Professor Vyas reflected his academic excellence and wisdom. I feel honoured for having interaction with Professor Vyas.

I am grateful to my well-wishers at Jaipur National University, Jaipur, particularly Chancellor Dr Sandeep Bakshi, and Vice-Chancellor Professor H. N. Verma for their concern and encouragement in my academic pursuit.

I wish to express my thanks to Mr Pramod Shanker Mathur, for meticulously typing the manuscript, while also being a constant source of support during the last 10 years.

During the tenure of the fellowship, I have written papers, delivered keynote lectures and inaugural and valedictory addresses. These have also enriched the present study. I am thankful to several institutions which extended me invitations to participate in their academic activities.

Professor S. L. Sharma, Dean, University of Rajasthan, was always available for extending academic and logistic support during this period.

At home, Dr. Sanju Sharma provided help and support as and when required. I am thankful to her.

The study would have not been completed without the genuine concern and emotional engagement of my wife, Geeta Sharma. My wife and her sister-in-law, Suman, were always in attendance with hot meals and innumerable rounds of hot cups of tea and coffee. I thank them for all those favours. I sincerely wish to dedicate this work to my life partner Mrs Geeta Sharma and my other family members— Rajendra, Lavleena, Rachna, Bhanu, Ravindra, Deveshi, Annika, Piu and Aryan.

Introduction

No Indian village is representative of the village India. Not only differences in rural India can be found between villages of different provinces, regions, districts, etc., but one can also see differences even between two neighbouring villages, and a lot of differences among castes/sub-castes, families and individuals one can note in a given village. As such, caste is no more an overriding and encompassing system, as it was in the past, to a certain extent, binding people within a caste, between castes and also the village people in general, through some institutions and practices. It would be unwise to see the Indian village as an 'isolate' or even 'isolable' today. In fact, even in the past, country–town nexus existed, though it was of a different nature, compared to the present one, due to constraints and forces at work at that time. Country–town nexus has persisted, with a semblance of continuity and change. The nexus varied from village to village, depending upon its location, proximity to the town, and also upon socio-economic fabric and political set-up.

I

In the background of divergent rural dynamics, a 'holistic' village structure is an unrealistic or a fictional imagination. The Indian village had its social arrangements, like other human settlements, though the arrangements differed in terms of the needs of the people. The village has/had no 'ambiguous' social formation. There were definite patterns and practices of social interaction, equality and inequality, freedom and interdependence, and cooperation and competition/conflict. Such a system of social relations prevails even today, though with a new ethos, needs, interests and understanding. Village is not an 'ambiguous' entity as perceived by Gurucharan Das (2012, 187–203).

As stated above, portrayal of the Indian village as 'unchanging' and 'idyllic' was more of a misconception (Gupta, 1975, 751–758). The use of derogatory and denigrating expressions about the jajmani functionaries, undermined the 'realistic view', characterized by jajmani relations, withdrawal or denial of jajmani based services, caste and village councils, inter-village ties, village exogamy, non-agricultural means of livelihood, etc. Though vast changes have occurred in these institutions and practices, and agriculture and related practices have been considerably substituted by non-farm pursuits and contractual ties, yet the Indian village has not 'vanished' as it has happened to a great extent in the West in the wake of industrialization and the present-day communication revolution. The Indian village remains a 'village' to a considerable extent. A village which has become, practically and even legally, a part of a town/city, retains its identity, inter-family ties and common interests that bind it. As caste has become a resilient and non-systemic institution, so is the nature of the Indian village (Beteille, 2012, 41–48; Shah, 2007, 109–116).

Both structural and cultural changes occurred throughout the Mughal and the British periods by way of land tenure systems, administrative set-up, education and cultural practices. B. S. Cohn (1968) reports that in the Banaras region, during the British period, the cultivators, the controllers of the cultivators and the state shared the product of the land. The three groups had constant conflict and negotiation regarding their respective claims and shares. Agrarian hierarchy, cutting across the caste-based hierarchical relations, was an established fact. The land control system was such that 'new men', commercial families, aristocrats and religious institutions were dominated by government service men, who came from communities, such as Muslim, Brahmin, Kayastha, Bhumihar, Bania and Eurasian. India was, thus, not a closed system, and change was discrete, and not holistic. Change was not uniform for different castes. For example, in the princely state of Rajputana (Rajasthan), the lower caste men, who served the princes, *thikanedars* and *jagirdars,* were given land grants and wages (in both cash and kind), and they enjoyed higher status, compared with even higher caste men (Sharma, 1998a, 26–43). The practice of 'contra-priest' (Gould, 1967), that is, performance as 'priests' by lower caste functionaries, was valued a lot. Bargaining for rightful wages and benefits for the services rendered to the jajmans (patrons) by the functionaries, such as barbers, carpenters, potters and blacksmiths, was an accepted practice, and that compelled the patrons to do justice with those who served them generation after generation.

Village as a spatial entity and as a transformed social milieu exists, despite huge migration to towns and cities and mobility within and outside it. Perhaps *jatis* used to cooperate, compete and quarrel earlier, today families and individuals do it within and outside their castes and families. Today, the 'actors' in the village are not the same people. Some of the families and individuals who were not quite capable in the past are not only today capable but also aspire for high status and positions of power and authority. The earlier entrenched people have either withdrawn from the race for status and power or have moved out of the village for greener pastures. We have noted this in our study of the village (Sharma, 1974) as reported here in this study. The people who acquired hold over land, infrastructure and non-farm income compete for power within the village. The families and individuals who aspire to dominate the village affairs are generally from those principal intermediate agricultural castes and communities, who have been benefited from land reforms, green revolution, Panchayati Raj, extra-village connections, etc. Education has not been a major factor in this process of social transformation, though migration and mobility are mainly due to education and support from one's relatives and friends.

We have noted that over the years, merchants, markets, money lending and migration have changed in rural India due to new economic and political situation, resulting in a 'push' factor for those who have moved out of the village. Networks have played a significant role in migration and mobility (Sharma, 1997a, 174–194). Such a process has created a 'village' in the town, and, in turn, a 'town' sort of ambience has emerged in the village. This exemplifies a renewed pattern of country–town nexus. Country–town nexus is multifaceted and multidimensional. It is both a historical and a contextual reality concerning relations between village and town (Sharma and Gupta, 1991, XI–XVIII).

Migration, mobility and education have given a new twist to rural–urban relations. Village traders, shopkeepers, drivers, factory workers, middlemen in the towns and government functionaries working in the village coming from the town have strengthened and reshaped the country–town nexus. Rural–urban divide has changed and become weak in certain respects, but 'village' is not moving towards its assimilation, nor town is overpowered by rural ethos and organization. Such is the shape and face of rural India. It has created new parameters of status and power. Caste-based status and inheritance play a marginal role in determination of status and power. Yogendra Singh (2009, 178–195) talks of two levels of social praxis in a village in eastern Uttar Pradesh: (a) the state policies of development and (b) a new resurgence of entrepreneurial ventures. We have observed elsewhere: 'The caste in everyday life is no more a source of anxiety or happiness. The way it is used/misused or not used has made caste a very different phenomenon' (Sharma, 2014b, XXIV).

Besides understanding the Indian village in its new avatar, two other aspects need to be analysed with far more seriousness, namely, social inequality and mobility. Both have to be seen beyond caste/community and religion. Yogendra Singh (2009) highlights the significance of social praxis as a major factor in the formulation of the conceptual categories, such as community, caste and class, for a wholesome understanding of the Indian village. Singh writes:

> Social praxis includes all forces, indigenous and exogenous to the system, that energises and activate the historical forces, structural contradictions, and movements within the system, generating pressure for change, both adaptive and entrepreneurial or innovative. Social praxis also includes deliberate intervention to bring about desired changes in the system through induction and implementation of policies of planned social change and development. (Singh, 2009, 183)

Singh (2009, 193) also observes: 'Social praxis is from where social change begins'. Entrepreneurial innovations and the state-sponsored policies of development and change are the dominant forces of social change and mobility.

II

It is an established fact that when an individual and a family are at the centre stage in society rather than group/caste, society is less rigid, is more open and has less inequality and more mobility. The simple reason is that the entire group finds it quite difficult to move up, whereas it is easier for an individual and/or a family to move up in social ladder. The second point is: Can an individual or a family do so independent of its group? Or ultimately, is it that both individual and family matter? In rural India, now caste system does not matter as it used to matter on the eve of India's Independence. Land reforms, reservations for the SCs, STs and OBCs, adult franchise, Panchayati Raj, education, migration, urban employment, rural non-farm sources of income, etc., have reduced the caste system as a non-encompassing entity. We may say here that individual and family were always 'actors' in the caste system even in its heydays, though often in a not so open manner; but at times, when caste rigidities became intolerable, protests and voices of dissent were expressed, which were heeded too.

Following D. P. Mukerji (2002 [1958], 2014), we do not look for an 'individual' and 'individualism' as philosophical constructs in the Western sense, but we look for *purush,* a concrete person, performing his duties for himself, his family and entire society. Louis Dumont (1986), unlike Mukerji, prefers the idea of hierarchy and holism to individualism. Men–men relations or men–things relations can be better understood from the perspective of hierarchy. But this makes the ideology of hierarchy supreme by suppression of individuality of a man/person. Pradip Kumar Bose (2014, 185–205), while examining 'individualism' in the sociology of D. P. Mukerji, and comparing it with the ideas of Max Weber and Louis Dumont, makes the following observations:

The important problem of our days then is not to try to liberate the individual from the state and state's institutions, but, as Mukerji's search for alternative to the individual and individuation shows, the social and philosophical compulsion is to find ways to liberate the humans both from the state and from the type of individualization which is linked to the state. In fact, what is needed is a process of 'de-individualisation' through collectives and diverse combinations. As Mukerji would argue, there is a need to promote new forms of subjectivity through the refusal of this kind of individuality and this he attempts to do with his theory of personhood.

Bose further writes:

Persons are products of socio-cultural conditions; individuals exists in spite of them. Persons may be understood as those who realize the given and embody the categories which are prescribed by the tradition and the social order. Person is continuously in process of elaboration, and producing herself or himself through social action and interaction. (Bose, 2014, 203)

Thus, a person is, no doubt, a sociocultural product, a reasoned human being, in a social setting, having her/his autonomy and freedom. A person's success lies in her/his capability in striking a balance between personal ends and sociocultural ambience.

A glance at the recent studies and analyses clearly indicates that the caste system does not matter to a great extent; however, 'caste' matters discretely, and that too rarely, in matters relating to violation of rules of marriages and preference for one's caste candidates in election, not always, but sometimes. What matters is one's own nuclear family to a considerable extent. There is a fast decline of an individual in engagement with joint/extended family, both lineal and lateral. Size of the family has also become quite small, two to three children. Preference for son is no more a sacred choice. Daughter is being valued, and education and employment for girls are considered quite desirable. Stray incidences engineered by Khap panchayat(s) are no indication of persisting caste-based hierarchy and rigid norms and regulations. Even in the 1960s (Sharma, 1969), individual and family were observed as active agents of occupational mobility, in violation of the norms of hereditary occupation, jajmani system and caste ideology.

Today, caste-based inequality is hardly perceptible. What matters is inequality, and not caste hierarchy. How much caste hierarchy is embedded in inequality is the right question. Despite immense weakening of the caste system, why 'caste' persists? In case inequality is independent of caste, what is wrong with the process of change and development related to egalitarianism in Indian society?

In rural India, inequality is linked to unequal sharing of resources, partly due to lack of required capability among people to make a claim and grab the resources, and partly because the very nature of the distribution of resources is such that some entrenched families and their members take away the lion's share. Such people do not necessarily belong to the upper castes. A large number of them are beneficiaries of the state-sponsored policies and programmes and as such have become quite strong. They often do not allow the poor and deprived people to have substantial benefits from the developmental programmes. Hence, people suffer from poverty, malnutrition, ill-health, etc.

It is a new situation of inequality, where caste has hardly any role to play and the very nature and process of development are the cause of inequality. Inequality of 'consumption', of 'results' and of 'opportunities' is a main concern analysed by Radhika Kapoor (2013, 58–65). Inequalities related to gender or caste and access to key social services are also there. However, Kapoor (2013, 65) rightly observes: 'To achieve a higher rate of poverty reduction, India will need to address the inequalities in asset and income distribution and in opportunities that impede poor people from participating in the growth process'. Caste cannot be a cover-up tactic to hide inequality, which has been there due to failure of the policies and programmes of the Indian state.

It is a paradoxical situation as the caste-based inequality has nearly disappeared, and a new form of inequality has taken roots, emanating from the institutions, policies and programmes created by the Indian state after Independence. The beneficiaries of the post-Independence state in rural India are those who have been benefited from land reforms. Many of them are also petty shopkeepers and entrepreneurs, petty contractors, school teachers and other government functionaries, and those who are controlling the Panchayati Raj institutions and cooperative societies. Such a hold over sources of income and institutions of power and authority has created a situation of 'inequality of opportunity'.

III

There is ample evidence of social mobility in rural India. Migration from rural areas to towns, cities and metropolises is a strong indicator of social mobility. Migration is often due to hardships of survival in the village, in case of the poor, but those who aspire for a far better quality of life by having access to lucrative jobs and venture entrepreneurship also migrate. Generally, male members move out initially, and in course of time, their families join them, depending upon sustainability of their incomes and opportunities for other members to get employment. Such a practice has been followed for a very long time. It is also a fact that in many cases only the male members have moved out, leaving behind their womenfolk, elderly people and children.

Over the past seven decades, the Indian village has changed a lot due to social mobility and also as a result of new inequalities. For example, an inroad of 'urbanity' in rural India is an established fact, evidenced by roads, means of transport and communication, education, social services and sources of non-farm income. Visibly, there is a 'new middle class' in rural India, though somewhat different from the urban/industrial middle class. Such a select section of people are drawn from a cross-section of rural society, that is, the SCs, the STs, the OBCs and the General category. The formation of such a class of people is selective as many people from the needy families have been left out. The village institutions are ruled by such a class of people along with those who preside over panchayats and cooperatives. Such a situation gives an impression that assets, wealth and prosperity have increased in the Indian village, undermining gross disparities and inequalities.

The beneficiaries have not only entrenched into the village economy and polity, but they have also created a situation of 'reproduction' of status and power in favour of their family members and kinsmen. Apparently, it seems that they are incapable of having access to resources and positions of power and authority based on their competence and capability, but in reality, there is a marked role of ascription (not necessarily caste), parentage and inheritance in intergenerational transmission of inequality. Amartya Sen (1995) argues that besides 'equality of opportunity', the acquisition of capability is quite important in overcoming of some specific barriers/constraints in regard to social mobility. Those who have acquired capability have moved up and it is they who, along with the state's soft policies, have been slowing down the pace of mobility of the poor and deprived. A new oligarchy and a new set of dominant people have emerged through a faulty process of change and development.

IV

In this volume, we have focused on the reconceptualization of the Indian village, reinterpretation of caste as a system, role of individual and family, rural economy (peasants, artisans and weavers), political institutions (elections, Panchayati Raj), education, middle class, and inequality and social mobility. As per the planning of this volume, we have also visited 'The Six Villages' in Rajasthan, with a view to look at the nature and direction of social change over half a century, from 1965 to 2006 (Sharma, 1968a). Due to constraints of time, a specific analysis of gendering of social relations has not been attempted. However, throughout this work, gendered relations have been reported.

Our main focus is on the changing pattern of society, economy and polity in contemporary rural India. It is quite clear that the concepts and frameworks that were in vogue in the 1950s and 1960s need to be challenged and reconceptualized, as also suggested by some scholars. Ignoring the place and role of individual and family under the garb of the caste system has been a major flaw in the study of Indian village. This point has been constantly taken up in this study. Inequality and social mobility are other related aspects in their new forms and at the grass-roots level. Education and emergence of a new middle class are two distinct substantive realities of rural society. People often talk of these two new dimensions of status and power.

A process of reproduction of status and power has taken deep roots. Even reservations have contributed to such a process of centralization of status among select families. This has been happening despite vast infrastructural and cultural transformation of the Indian village. 'Caste' does not matter, but 'class' matters. Inequality of a sort has nearly disappeared, but a new form of inequality has emerged. Several traditional social arrangements have vanished, and a new bazaar has emerged, in most cases at the new sites, particularly on the sides of the metalled road, connecting the village with nearest towns. The notion of old bazaar, dominated by a bania(s) (merchant), does not exist anymore. The roadside shops are also very different today, compared to the old bazaar. However, there is more openness and less cultural distance among the people. Caste-based segregation is minimal and it is discretionary. Often it is avoided in public places. The bazaar has people drawn from several castes, owning shops and providing goods and services to the customers irrespective of their social background.

PART I

Social Contours of Indian Village

Chapter 1

Introducing the Indian Village

For a long time, the Indian village was characterized by the Asiatic Mode of Production (Marx, 1954). It was perceived as 'idyllic' and reflected despotism, barbaric egotism, rigid caste system and slavery (Maine, 1871). Such were the misconceptions in the 19th century on the nature of the Indian village. Besides these repulsions, the Indian village was also seen as a 'little republic' (Metcalfe, 1979), having self-sufficiency and isolation. Such a characterization continued even in the first half of the 20th century (Wiser and Wiser, 1936, 1964). Inter-caste interdependence and holistic structure were the main features as observed by Wiser and Wiser. Mahatma Gandhi (1962) also eulogized the village community through his idea of Ram Ra ya. To a considerable extent, the Indian village was considered a 'closed' and 'isolated' system (Baden-Powell, 1896, 1899; Maine, 1871; Metcalfe, 1979).

APPROACHES TO THE STUDY OF INDIAN SOCIETY VIS-À-VIS INDIAN VILLAGE

In the 1950s, a debate began on the approaches to the study of Indian society, and the Indian village was seen within those frameworks. Bernard S. Cohn (1987) outlined three approaches, namely, (a) the Orientalist, (b) the Administrative and (c) the Missionary. During the colonial period, the Orientalist approach focused on the Indian texts; the Administrative approach reflected on the interests of the British rule; and the Missionary approach was more, at least apparently, about reforms in Indian society. Cohn infers that the Indian society was seen as having 'caste' and 'village' at the centre stage. Here, it may be indicated that all the three approaches imply an 'official view' of the Indian society and the village community. It was more of a macro view. The 'realist view' was ignored to a considerable extent. Several studies, including the subaltern studies (13 volumes) (Guha et al., 1982 and onwards), focus on those sections of people who were never noticed, rather ignored and undermined, by the Indian rulers and dominant sections.

The Indian village was never 'static' and 'isolated' as it was projected in the colonial period. The nature of interaction and contacts were certainly very different compared to what we have since Independence. Intra-village and inter-village differences, inequalities and conflicts were quite pronounced. Village exogamy itself was an 'absolute' norm, thereby having inter-village social and cultural networks. Since the Indian village was a part of the wider society in the colonial period, and it has undergone tremendous changes after Independence, it is imperative to have a relook at the Indian village as an entity and as a mode of living and social relationships. Let us be clear here that the Indian village has not 'vanished' nor it is on the path of transforming itself into the 'town'. It has witnessed a new form of change and is quite different from the pre-Independence era; hence a reconceptualization is both a heuristic and a substantive requirement in the present context.

The orientalist view, as mentioned earlier, considered the texts as accurate guides to the understanding of culture and society, situating the Brahmins as the dominant group. The textualist view led to a picture of Indian society as being 'static, timeless and spaceless' (Cohn, 1968, 7). The Orientalists ignored the hiatus between the normative prescriptions and actual behaviour. The village community was seen as a microcosm of Indian civilization. The missionary view considered the Indian people as a race of men lamentably degenerate (Cohn, 1968, 8), having 'a feeble sense of moral obligations', 'obstinate', 'malevolent' and 'licentious'. The Indian people had corrupt manners and 'views'. Contempt and condemnation for the Indian people were the ethos of such a view.

Both the orientalist and the missionary views suffered from a lack of objectivity and apriorism (Sharma, 1985, 116). The 'official view', as reflected in the provincial and imperial gazetteers and census reports of India, reflected collection of information on land, settlement pattern, revenue, caste and social organization. Though such an exercise was motivated by the interests of the colonial rulers, yet it provided a quite different picture of the Indian village compared to the characterizations emanating from the orientalist and the missionary views. As a result of the 'official view', intensive survey of landholdings began in the 18th century, and the Indian village was compared with the English village. Such a paradigm shift put a stop on considering the Indian village as a 'closed' and 'isolated' system. However, the 'official view' of the Indian village persisted, considering India as a land of 'village republics', characterized by self-sufficiency and homogeneity. Louis Dumont (1966b, 67) refers to the term 'village community' as (a) a political society, (b) a body of co-owners of the soil and (c) an emblem of traditional economy and polity, 'a watch word of Indian patriotism'. As such, the Indian village had been a part of India's economy and polity.

David G. Mandelbaum (1968, 40) opines: 'A village is far from than a locale, more than just a collection of houses, lanes and fields'. For a village, such a setup is a prime social reality. However, Dumont and Pocock (1957, 68–69) do not consider the Indian village either as a corporate group or as a useful unit of analysis, because of its exaggerated notion of the Independence. As it has been stated earlier, the Indian village was romanticized by many as a 'republic' and as a 'self-sufficient' entity. Village exogamy and inter-village networks falsify such an exaggeration. We would like to admit here that despite very basic structural and cultural changes, the Indian village, even today, remains a cohesive territorial unit, having its specific identity, solidarity and loyalty, cutting across castes and factions. On this basis too, we need to redefine the Indian village as it is not the same entity as it was in the past, and it has not been vanishing, as has been mistakenly observed.

COLONIAL CONSTRUCTION OF THE INDIAN VILLAGE

Manish Thakur (2014) provides an excellent conceptual trajectory of the Indian village, with an emphasis on its colonial construction in particular, along with locating the Indian village in the nationalist discourse, in the discipline of sociology/social anthropology and in the development discourse. We have already cast a cursory look on the colonial rule vis-à-vis the Indian village. Thakur (2014, 15) observes that, more than a settlement of the land revenue, the colonial rule 'was also an exercise in how best to fit the disparate facts of India's social order into the proper modes of British explanation'. This was 'a new idiom of the village and signalled a new level of involvement of the (colonial) state in the village'. The British thus deliberately changed the socio-economic and political contours. The village was transformed to fit in with the colonial construction of the Indian society. Reshaping the Indian village strengthened the colonial rule. Thakur (2014, 17) writes: 'Thus, the specific meaning of the term "village" is seen here as part of the history of colonial knowledge about India and the use of that knowledge in official projects'.

The British tried to reshape the village in terms of its newly intro-duced land tenure systems and taxes. The indigenous economic and social structure of the village was not in tune with the British rule. The idea of the Indian village as a 'mini republic' was more of a stereotype rather than a socio-economic and political reality. The Indian village was thus viewed by the British more as an administrative entity, and not as a functioning social organization (Stocks, 1978). Stocks opines that the British administrators were responsible for propagating the repub-lican nature of the Indian village. The romantic image created by the British helped in keeping the Indian village 'static' and contained, and this was the motive of the British to ensure fixing of their roots in India.

Thakur (2014, 22) notes: 'The colonial stereotyping of the village community had two principal ingredients: (i) the portrayal of the village as an idyllic and utopian political community—a society of equals, and (ii) its characterization as a body of co-shares of the soil'. Thakur (2014, 22) further states that such a view tended to underplay the facts of dominance and hierarchy within the village. The village could not remain isolated and independent vis-à-vis the state and the market. Even if there was some autonomy of the village, the British rule violated it by way of its new land tenures and the system of land revenue. Caste, being a vital institution, was a symbol of patron–client relations, hierarchy and inequality. Breman (1997, 16) is of the view that by the 19th century, Indian villages had multiple meanings and connotations, such as theoretical, ideological and pragmatic. There was *the village colonized*. During the freedom struggle, the Indian village (Dumont, 1970b, 112–132) was eulogized by way of propagation that India's soul was in its villages. In the post-Independence period, the Indian villages have received a great deal of attention for social change and development to bring it at par with the towns and cities.

RECONCEPTUALIZATION OF INDIAN VILLAGE

In fact, we are more concerned about reconceptualization of Indian villages since Independence. It is our intention to have a critical look at village studies and the perceptions and views about socio-economic and political transformation of the village over the past nearly seven decades. The discourse after Independence has centred around the substance and relevance of the Indian village as a 'closed' and 'isolated' system, as observed by Metcalfe, Maine and Baden–Powell. Robert Redfield's idea of 'Little Community' (1955, 1956), a model for studying the Indian village, has also been under attack. Generally, it has been sensed that the Indian village was not a 'republic', 'self-sufficient' and 'autonomous' entity. There was no 'harmony' as depicted in some of these writings (Hutton, 1963). Moreover, there was no absolute divide between the village and the town, rather a 'nexus' existed between the two. At the same time, it was considered that all the villages in India or in different regions varied in terms of land-tenure systems, geographical conditions, social organization, etc.

Bernard S. Cohn (1987, 343–421) discusses at length the nature of 'structural change' in Indian rural society during 1596–1885, particularly in the Banaras region. Three main assumptions regarding the pre-modern India were, namely, (1) the stability of traditional structures, the village communities as little republics, (2) the similar internal composition of the village republics and the relations between village republics, and (3) the decline of the state and the centralized military and political control. Cohn finds these three sets of assumptions untenable based on substantive sources and data. For example, three distinct groups, namely, the cultivators, the controllers of the cultivators and the state, shared the product of the land. Cohn (1987, 344) writes: 'The three were in constant conflict and negotiation over rightful claim to the product of the soil and the results of the labour of the cultivator. In this system, legal title over the land itself was irrelevant'. As such, the Indian village was not 'static', nor a 'republic', and land was a saleable commodity. 'Under the British men who had been tax farmers, petty revenue collectors, bankers, moneylenders, and traders obtained control of the land, first at auctions of the rights of delinquent revenue payers and later through moneylending activities' (Cohn, 1987, 345). Cohn refers to a lot of structural changes regarding the new class of landlords, the cultivators and small intermediaries. Tenants-at-will increased. Weavers, potters, blacksmiths and carpenters became impoverished, and the village 'servants' lost their clientele. 'All of these supposedly linked changes are assumed to have turned the village community into a headless, disorganized body in which most of the population was poor, degraded, and helpless' (Cohn, 1987, 345).

Those who were revenue payers, paying more than ₹1,000, included 'New men', commercial families, 18th century aristocrats and traditional aristocrats and some were religious institutions. They were mainly in government service, and belonged to castes and communities, such as Muslim, Brahmin, Kayastha, Bhumihar, Bania and Eurasian. Cohn concludes that India was not a closed system, where change was discrete, and not holistic. In another essay, Cohn (1987, 88–99) talks of two parts, 'traditional' and 'historical', and these two parts are not the same for different castes, such as Thakurs, Chamars and Telis, based on his study of the village Senapur, in eastern Uttar Pradesh.

While agreeing with Dumont and Pocock (1957, 25–32; 1960, 88–89), David G. Mandelbaum (1972, 327–357) observes that *jatis* both cooperate and compete, the main locale of this being the village. For a villager, his village is far more than just a collection of houses, lanes and fields; it is a prime social reality (Mandelbaum, 1972, 327). Like many others, Mandelbaum also opines that village exogamy, market, religion, etc., are the main reasons for which rural people move out often to other villages and towns. 'A village is not a neatly separable social and conceptual package, but it is nonetheless a fundamental social unit' (Mandelbaum, 1972, 329). This is so despite prevalence of cleavages and daily avoidances overshadowing solidarity. Solidarity persists too to a great extent in regard to observance of rituals, festivals and inter-village ties. Mandelbaum, drawing upon several village studies, conducted in the 1950s and 1960s, analyses internal differentiation and common concerns and regulations, wider ties with towns and regional entities and with the wider economy, polity and religion (civilizational links).

CHANGING CONTOURS OF VILLAGE LIFE

Wiser and Wiser (1964), in their double synchronic study of a North Indian village (1930–1960), depict noticeable changes in rural life over a period of three decades. The village was no more tightly tied to imperial rule. However, the change was slow, and the outward aspects had little changed. Agriculture, animal husbandry, neighbourhood relations and status of women were more or less in the 1960s as they were in 1930s. Family, kinship and caste hierarchy ruled the village. So was the significance of religious activities in rural life. The change was more in the field of agriculture and cropping pattern. Medical care was also a new development. After Independence, Community Development Programme (CDP) was a new social invention. The presence of the government in the village was clearly visible in the form of the functionaries such as village level worker, school teachers, gram panchayat as a key agency and visibility of young men in action.

Merchants, markets, moneylending and migration have a long history, affected by economic and political constraints and desire for economic betterment and social well-being (Sharma, 1997a, 174–194). From Rajasthan, people of different castes and communities used to move out of their native villages to far off places to work as construction workers, masons, cooks, *munims*, merchants, etc. *Jagirdars* and *zamindars* had their houses/*havelis* at the headquarters of their princely states. No village was without such networks: economic, administrative and social. It was wrong to label the Indian village as 'unchanging' and 'idyllic'. Perhaps, the British administrators did it so from the viewpoint of the western world. To reduce the existence and functioning of the village to 'caste' and 'agriculture' was an exaggeration, as it ignored the role of 'contra-priest' (Gould, 1968), and non-agricultural pursuits despite caste hierarchy and predominance of agriculture. A couple of studies of the Indian villages have focused on the problems created by adverse effects of nature (rains, floods, droughts, epidemics, etc.), and also on the sociocultural and economic hardships, due to exploitation, ignorance, illiteracy and unemployment. Some studies have analysed intra-regional and inter-regional inequalities and differences (Epstein, 1962; Sharma, 1974).

Rural–urban dichotomy has become somewhat elusive due to expansion of towns and cities. The villages on the highways and in the urban periphery show an 'urban face'. However, there are a vast number of villages which continue to have a 'rural face', showing a slow process of change. The emergence of non-farm occupations, on the one hand, and the persistence of dependence on traditional means of livelihood, on the other, have blurred the dichotomy. Hence, a new country–town nexus has been necessitated to identify the dynamics of the rural–urban differences and its narrowing down in contemporary India.

PROMINENCE OF VILLAGE STUDIES

In the 1950s, particularly in 1955, four volumes were published on the Indian village, *Indian Village* (Dube, 1955), *India's Villages* (Srinivas, 1955), *Village India* (Marriott, 1955) and *Rural Profiles* (Majumdar, 1955), and these publications marked a watershed in the study of the Indian village. A vast range of data and ground realities were presented in these volumes, covering different regions of India. Monographic single village studies were in vogue in the 1950s. However, soon after these notable holistic studies, focus was laid on comparative analysis of multiple villages with a view to know more about structural change in the village as the main emphasis in the earlier studies was on cultural aspects of rural life.

Besides synchronic view of the village, double synchrony and diachrony were added as methods of study to map out the extent and magnitude of social change. The frameworks, such as the 'folk–urban continuum' and the 'little community', were put to an acid test to understand Indian rural society (Chauhan, 1967, 1974; Majumdar, 1958). A couple of comparative studies (Bailey, 1957; Dasgupta, 1975; Epstein, 1962; Mukherjee, 1957; Sharma, 1974) have vividly shown that the Indian village has witnessed tremendous structural change, far beyond cultural mobility in terms of 'sanskritization' (Srinivas, 1966) and 'parochialization' and 'universalization' (Marriott, 1955).

Kathleen Gough (1955) refers to two pertinent questions about the study of Indian village: (a) To what extent the Indian village is an isolable social unit? (b) To what extent it is changing? Gough analyses, in view of these questions, economic organization, local administration, ritual practices, inter-caste relations and the relations of the village to the wider community. Gough shows that radical change has occurred in the Tanjore village, the locale of her study. Traditional village institutions are fast disintegrating and there is growing interdependence on urban/national institutions. Decline of the economic and social power of Brahmins and rise of the depressed castes are clearly evident in the village as reported in the 1950s. Gough takes a class-view of caste. She talks of 'open' changing system, secular law, expanding economy and competition between castes as indicators of a new Indian village.

The volume *Village India*, edited by Marriott (1955), clearly demonstrates that villages in the states of Karnataka, Tamil Nadu, Uttar Pradesh and Gujarat are not the same. The same is true about *India's Villages*, edited by Srinivas (1955), covering nine states. Surendra Sharma (1985, 131) sums up the papers in two volumes by way of some common features, such as the unity of the village, caste solidarity, extensions of the village into the outside world and the penetration of the wider world into the village, kinship networks, affinal ties, village exogamy, etc.

Dumont and Pocock (1957) raise two pertinent questions about the above village studies: (a) Is the village indeed a social fact that it has for so long been assumed to be? (b) Is it feasible to compare villages as such or should it be considered through a different point of view? While commenting on holistic-micro studies of the Indian village in view of the above questions, Dumont and Pocock further raise the following questions:

1. How far is the village a representative of Indian civilization?
2. Is India made up of villages alone?
3. Is there a microcosm–macrocosm opposition?

As viewed by Dumont and Pocock, a village is taken for study as a convenient entity to confer upon that the village as a sociological reality exists. However, the fact is that a selection of the Indian village in such a manner lures us away from a structural perspective. Caste and kinship in a given village link it with other villages. Today, politically, the village is linked with wider arenas, through the institutions such as adult franchise, elections, governance and the bridges that have come in the wake of India's Independence.

In the first review of 'Rural Studies' by the ICSSR, Chauhan (1974, 82–114), brings out the following points:

1. The village as a unit of study,
2. Communities and traditions,
3. Sanskritization,
4. Peasant society,
5. Village-outward Studies: Action-sets and quasi-groups, and
6. A resume of concepts.

Chauhan looks at the Indian village through its economic, social and ritual norms and activities. In support of such a view, he refers to the village studies undertaken by Opler (1956), Dube (1955), Srinivas (1955) and Marriott (1955) in particular. Further, Chauhan works out a classification of rural studies in the context of caste. This includes: (a) One village and one caste; (b) One village and many castes; (c) One caste and many villages; and (d) Many castes and many villages (Chauhan, 1974, 88). In regard to the other points, Chauhan makes a reference to the studies by Redfield and Singer (1956), Vidhyarthi (1961), Marriott (1955), Srinivas (1962), Lynch (1966), Mayer (1962), etc.

Some studies were also conducted in the 1950s and 1960s on rural leadership, Panchayati Raj institutions and development process (Haldipur, 1974, 30–61, 62–165). Haldipur (1974, 34) focuses on the following points:

1. Village social structure;
2. Community organization, extension and communication;
3. People's participation and decision-making;
4. Leadership and its emerging trend;
5. Institutional development;
6. Problems and process of planned change; and
7. Building up of morale, motivation and levels of aspiration.

In the second part of the Trend Report by Haldipur, the main focus is on Panchayati Raj vis-à-vis social structure and change, the leadership pattern, political process and people's perception of Panchayati Raj. Based on several village studies, Biplab Das Gupta (1978) classifies village studies into (a) fact finding empirical studies and (b) problem-oriented.

Thus, most of the studies were influenced by structural–functional perspective as the village was taken as an integrated, holistic social structure. Even intra-family and intra-caste tensions and conflicts were undermined as everyday social realities. The ideas of 'little community', 'peasant society' and 'folk-urban continuum' were the main guiding currents in the 1960s and 1970s. During this period, historical perspective was a casualty due to an overarching impact of both British and American social anthropology and sociology. 'Issue specific' studies were neglected under the garb of village as a holistic formation.

RURAL DIVERSITIES AND COUNTRY-TOWN NEXUS

The Village in India by Vandana Madan (2002) has put together twenty papers, covering topics such as (a) themes and perspectives, (b) caste, kinship, locality, and gender, (c) economy and survivals, (d) power and politics, (e) religion, culture and ideology, and (f) development and change. In the 'introduction' to this volume, Vandana Madan (2002, 1–30) reflects on these six points. In most of the post-Independence village studies, emphasis is given on a shift from the 'book view' to the 'field view' (Srinivas, 1966). Village is seen as the microcosm of Indian society and civilization. There was co-existence of tradition and modernity (Majumdar, 1958). The Indian village was seen in terms of its networks with the society, including social, cultural and political relations (Bailey, 1957, 1963; Gould, 1967, 1988; Mayer, 1960). The Indian village was not a closed social system. Interaction of the village with the town always existed in some measure to meet the existential requirements of the people.

Isolation of the village was never absolute; it was a relative phenomenon. Based on some empirical studies, Sharma and Gupta (1991, XI-XVI) observe that the village and town are incorrectly depicted as polar opposites, or unmatching contrasts, in terms of population composition, density of population, professions, civic amenities, occupations, lifestyles, etc. The two are, in fact, necessarily interacting units, and the pattern of interaction is such that neither the country nor the town is privileged as the epicentre of social transformation. Sharma and Gupta (1991, XI) write:

> Both country and town mutually influence each other, but not on the basis of an ad hoc format, but rather on account of supra-local forces of transition. These supra-local forces need to be conceptually understood and appreciated so that a more refined approach towards the *country town nexus* may emerge which will have greater empirical validity for our times.

For example, A. M. Shah (1991, 11–42), in his paper in the volume edited by Sharma and Gupta, negates several age-old notions regarding exclusivity of village and town, caste and class, joint and nuclear families, corporateness and individualism. Based on his analysis of society and culture in Gujarat, Shah describes that the links between villages and towns are not confined to caste, kinship and marriage alone; there are links also in regard to religion, culture, trade and commerce. There is commonality with regard to institutions and villages and towns; however, there is a difference in relation to their functioning. Hence, there are varied patterns of change in villages and towns.

K. L. Sharma (1991, 43–60), in the above volume, puts forth the view that country–town nexus is both a historical and contextual reality concerning relations between village and town. The nexus is defined as a set of ties (in terms of connection) between village and town which explains both the structural and cultural changes in the two settings. Macro-structural changes, social stratification and specific conditions of given villages and towns determine largely the country–town nexus and the consequent structural and cultural changes in the two. Sharma suggests the country–town nexus as a viable conceptual tool for analysing social transformation, keeping in view the limitations of the prevalent frameworks, dichotomies and continua, for understanding of interaction between villages and towns.

Moneylenders, artisans, shopkeepers, salaried workers, non-agricultural wage-earners, priests, white-collar workers, etc., are an important element in the country–town nexus. Migration, mobility and education have reshaped the nexus in the recent years. Today, school teachers, revenue officials, village-level workers, peons and bank officials are the new agents of country–town nexus. New institutions, such as Panchayati Raj, healthcare system, employment agencies, means of transport and communication, and lifestyles are restructuring the ties between villages and towns. There is today a village in a town, and vice versa. We may have to see the extent and magnitude of the presence of the one in the other, through an appropriate application of the idea of country–town nexus.

Indian Sociological Society has been bringing out *Readings in Indian Sociology* for some time now, drawing papers published in its journal, *Sociological Bulletin*. A volume entitled as *Sociological Probings in Rural Society*, edited by K. L. Sharma (2014), classifies the incorporated papers under the following headings:

1. Rural Society and Rural–Urban Relations,
2. Social Stratification in Rural India,
3. Village Profiles,
4. Religion and Rituals, and
5. Social Change in Rural India.

All the papers focus on extensions and networks of the Indian village, and the nature and extent of social change in the countryside. Sharma (2014, XXI–XL), in the 'introduction', states that the villages, which were in the periphery, are now merged with the neighbouring urban centres. Sharma (2014b) writes: 'Today, such villages have acquired an urban face as the people who live there are no more dependent on traditional pattern of agriculture, handicrafts and *jajmani* system'. Salaried jobs have become the main source of livelihood. But on the contrary, the fact remains that nearly 60 per cent of the people in remote villages remain dependent on agriculture and allied economic activities. This shows a changed rural–urban divide and nexus between the two as well. Hence, a reconceptualization of the Indian village becomes inevitable to have a relook at both the divide and the nexus vis-à-vis rural–urban relations.

RURAL DEVELOPMENT

One can infer from various village studies that cognitive and ontological bases of village life have considerably changed as new issues and dilemmas have become pronounced. Multi-village, comparative and variable-based, historical, double synchronic and diachronic studies have opened up new vistas of our understanding of the ever-changing rural society (Sharma, 2014, xxiii–xxv). For example, discourse on development shifts to discourse on dignity and honour in a West UP village over a period of three decades (Kolenda, 1978, 1989). In many village studies, change-agents are land reforms, green revolution, Panchayati Raj institutions, urbanization, education, migration and communication networks rather than caste system, jajmani relations, pollution–purity syndrome, and transformed country–town ties. Sharma asks the following questions:

1. Was the Indian village ever a community?
2. Is the village a community now?
3. Does the concept of the 'individual' exist in the village?
4. Was there a group (caste) alone in the village in the remote past?

Our revisit to the Six Villages in 2016 (Sharma, 1974, 2016) shows that the three suburban villages have completely submerged with the respective towns, namely, Sikar, Jaipur and Bharatpur, which were quite distinct in the 1960s in terms of territory, jurisdiction, economy, and social and cultural life. The other three villages, which were in remote parts of the three respective towns today have connectivity with the towns and surrounding villages, tehsil and district head-quarters. They also have facilities like senior schools, public health centres, drinking water and communication links. Inter-caste differentiation has lessened and has taken a new form, due to weakening of the traditional principle of pure and impure in determination of social relations. Intra-caste differences have emerged due to enhanced recognition of the status of a family and merit of an individual. It is rare to find 'sanskritization' and 'dominant caste' as observed by M. N. Srinivas (1955, 1966). There is an 'individual' in the village, and so is the 'family', and the two are not just shadows of caste alone. Changes in economic and power relations are occurring more around individual and family, rather than having essentially caste/group as the epicentre. Extra-systemic changes have become pronounced as education, migration, mobility, modern occupations and entrepreneurship have occupied the centre stage in the Indian village. In the political context, adult franchise, elections, power and authority have lured people to assert their value and significance in the present-day situation. Concepts and frameworks such as country–town nexus (Sharma and Gupta, 1991), emergence of a new rural middle class (Shah, 1991), differentiated structures (1966) and downward social mobility (Sharma, 1973) indicate paradigm shifts from the ideas of sanskritization, dominant caste, parochialization and universalization. Besides these shifts, green revolution and the discourse on capitalist mode of production, empowerment of weaker sections and women, growth in non-farm income, new employment avenues and opportunities, environmental issues, etc., have provided new inputs in reconceptualizing the Indian village. Uneven development and inequality, government schemes and rise in prices of agricultural products are offshoots of recent changes affecting rural India. In such a situation, the following questions may be asked:

1. What is development?
2. Where is development?
3. Whose development?
4. Who are beneficiaries of the initiatives taken by the government?
5. How is non-farm income restricted?

There are voices of protest and dissent against atrocities and exploitation by the deprived sections of society. The Indian village is, therefore, not today as it was in the decades of the 1950s and 1960s. Gupta (2005, 751–758) talks of change of culture and agriculture, fearing the withering away of the Indian village. Agriculture is under severe stress. Traditional agrarian structure has given way to new categories of people engaged in agriculture. Agri-business is a recent addition aggravating the stress, at times culminating into suicides by farmers. New rural activism for larger state subsidies, high prices and more favourable terms of trade with the urban world has changed the economic and political map of rural India. Political power in terms of control over Panchayati Raj institutions and cooperatives have affected social and cultural contours in the countryside. Gupta (2005) observes based on his study of peasantry in Western Uttar Pradesh that caste and agriculture no longer exercise their vigorous hold. Fluidity in occupational choices, migration to towns and cities, and vote-bank politics overshadow the issues related to agriculture, jajmani system, inter- and intra-caste relations. The main considerations are access to economic resources and control over institutions of power and authority.

There are substantial segments of people in rural India who solely depend upon agriculture and allied activities for their livelihood. A significant fragment of rural population has both agricultural and non-farm incomes as means of livelihood. Yet, there are also some people who are mainly engaged in salaried jobs. Finally, we also see some rural people who are self-employed as small entrepreneurs, shopkeepers, weavers, artisans, etc. Besides these, some people have settled in towns and cities, but they continue to own land in the village, and manage it by giving it on contract for cultivation. Yogendra Singh (2009, 178–195) is of the view that the changing nature of social praxis in the village has brought about social change. According to Singh, there are two levels of social praxis: (a) the state policies of the government and (b) a new resurgence in entrepreneurial ventures.

Bonds of village as a community have weakened, as village-centric inter-caste relations have ceased to exist. The Dalits, the backward classes and other weaker sections have become more assertive and demanding for their share in the resources of the village. Thus, class cleavages have become much sharper across caste stratification. Caste in everyday life is no more a source of anxiety or happiness. It is discretely used/misused. Hence, reconceptualization of the notions of 'village', 'community' and 'caste' is required.

A. Vaidyanathan and R. Srinivasan (2015, 65–73), based on the census data of 1991, 2001 and 2011 of Tamil Nadu, paint a broad picture of the average Tamil Nadu village and variations in sex ratio, literacy rate, work participation rate, the proportions of agriculture and non-agriculture workers and cultivators to total workers and proportions of agricultural labourers to total agricultural workers. In different districts and taluks, there are villages in the bottom docile and top docile based on these characteristics. Spatial distribution has also been there in both types of villages.

Due to rapid urbanization, the annual population growth rate in rural Tamil Nadu is far less than that of the state. Tiny village hamlets are being abandoned, contiguous villages are being amalgamated, and the larger ones are being reclassified as towns. Average size of villages is increasing. Our revisit to the six villages in three districts of Rajasthan also shows a similar pattern.

Chapter 2

Reinterpreting Caste

The caste question has occupied a central space in social sciences as its organization and ethos have undergone a noticeable process of change and transformation, particularly since Independence. This is so because of the 'official' annihilation of the caste system, except the Scheduled Castes (SCs) as mentioned in the Constitution of India, and the subsequent inclusion of the Other Backward Classes (OBCs), granting them benefits in education and government jobs, and recently in Panchayati Raj institutions. The improved socio-economic and political status of the erstwhile deprived castes, and a decline of the dominant position of the upper and upper middle castes, have created a new quest for reconsidering caste as a system and as a discrete phenomenon. Caste as a determinant of sociocultural activities and economic pursuits has nearly ceased to exist, but it continues to persist in myriad ways as a means of recognition, identity and at times a mechanism of articulation and expression of values and expectations. Such a situation prevails despite violation of rules of caste endogamy and clan exogamy and commensality. In some parts of India, within some castes, such violations are also met with severe punitive action by the overlords of castes under the pretext of protection of the inviolable caste norms.

THE CASTE QUESTION

Both Marxist and non-Marxist scholars have conceptualized caste as structure. 'Caste questions' were central in D. D. Kosambi's historical probing. Kumkum Roy (2008, 78–84) writes: 'castes assumed a centrality in D. D. Kosambi's relentless quest for the origins of Indian society, since for him it was a category to understand socio-economic differences'. Caste as a structure brings out how caste identities were constituted, consolidated and even contested. Kosambi equated caste with class, as he stated: 'caste is an important reflection of the actual relations of production, particularly at the time of its formation' (Kosambi, 2002, 59). Roy has quoted from Kosambi (2002, 59) as follows:

> India has a unique social division, the (endogamous) caste system. Caste is class at a primitive level of production, a religious method of forming social consciousness in such a manner that the primary producer is deprived of his surplus with the minimum coercions. This is done with the adoption of local usages into religion and ritual, being thus the negation of history by giving fictitious sanction from 'times immemorial' to any new development, the actual change being denied altogether. To this extent and at a low level of commodity production, it is clear that an Asiatic Mode did exist, reaching over reversal stages; at least, the term is applicable to India, whatever the case elsewhere.

In ancient India, in the 2nd or 3rd stages, as mentioned by Kosambi, division of labour existed, and assumedly in the form of *varnas*, caste as a system was not known and the division of labour was characterized by 'classes', hence equation of caste (*varna*) with class. It is not clear in Kosambi whether the religious–ritual dimension was an offshoot of the division of labour (*varna*) or it was its base (determinant). There is evidently tension in Kosambi's formulation of 'caste', whether it was a stagnant system or a dynamic institution, and whether it was a semblance of both, and how did it function. Roy raises the question: 'Does Caste Equal Class?' (Kosambi, 2002, 79). Kosambi considered Shudras as a class as they were dependent labourers, with virtually no independent access to productive resources. He reflected on all castes (varnas), such as Brahmanas, Kshatriyas, Vaishyas and Shudras, as classes, in effect, and also related both varnas and classes to religious and social activities. Contrary to this, M. V. Nadkarni (2003, 4783–4793), based on evidence from the ancient scriptures, argues that Hinduism did not support the caste system; it rigorously opposed it in practice and principle. Occupational and social mobility has occurred despite strict sanctions in Hinduism. Caste system has survived because of socio-economic and ecological factors.

Notionally accepting Dumont's view on caste (1970a, 65–91), Nadkarni observes: 'The whole system along with its taboos and restrictions is authenticated by religion or canon, giving it a religious sanctity' (2003, 4783). He further writes:

> At the foundation of the whole system there is a production system, which is subsistence-oriented and locally based rather than oriented to large market, and production relations being of patron-client type, based on mutual dependence. Such a system is not necessarily generally for the generation of economic surplus and its appropriation, as it was not oriented to the larger market but to local needs.

Nadkarni lists the following points to demolish the correlation between Hinduism and caste system:

1. No spatial or temporal correlation between Hinduism and caste system.
2. Considerable social and occupational mobility under the caste system, particularly in the classical period.
3. Hindu canon and philosophy against caste system based on birth.
4. Creation of legends in Hinduism declaring caste system as immoral and invalid.
5. Under the umbrella of Hinduism, several caste movements.
6. Survival of caste due to non-interference of Hinduism.

Nadkarni, thus, sees no correlation between Hinduism and caste system. Moreover, 'caste' has existed among Christians and Muslims as well. Religious conversion and social and occupational mobility have also been a check on rigidity of the caste system. Occupations based on heredity have not been strictly adhered to. Ambedkar has mentioned several examples of social and occupational mobility during the Vedic and Upanishadic period. In the medieval period of Indian history, the Bhakti movement had several low caste saints and poets. Even the process of 'sanskritization', as described by Srinivas (1966), was in vogue during the pre-British and the British periods. Not just birth, but 'Guna' (merit/work quality) was also always considered as a virtue along with caste status. A number of movements against caste, such as the Shiva in

6th century, the *Basavanna* in 12th century, the *Veerashaiva* movement and Sikhism, speak about persisting challenge to the hierarchical order of the caste system. *Bhakti* movement in North India, Karnataka and Maharashtra shook the caste system. In the 19th and 20th centuries, the movement led by Shri Narayan Guru (1854–1928) aimed at liberation of the *Ezhovas* (a lower caste) and other depressed castes from the clutches of the upper castes. The lower castes were subjugated under the pretext of religious sanctity by the upper castes, whereas Hinduism was not supportive of the caste system in general, except the *dharma shastras* (*dharma sutras* and *smritis*).

The four *varnas* were created on the basis of character and occupation (Nadkarni, 2003, 4786). Denigration of birth as the basis of *varnas*/occupational divisions is evident in several texts and commentaries (Kane, 1990; Sharma, 1996). The point is that even as a scheme of division of labour, caste has changed considerably; in fact, caste-based division of labour has nearly disappeared, and the new division of labour is based on education, migration, urbanization, industrialization, market and myriad policies and programmes of the state. In such a multiplex situation, it is a herculean task to locate caste as the basis of division of labour and status determination. In this situation, more than caste, individual and to some extent family become actual actors/agencies of mobility and change.

CASTE AS A SOCIAL FORMATION

Ambedkar (1987, 336) vehemently argues that the principle of caste is overwhelmingly domineering in all aspects of social life. Suvira Jaiswal (1998) observes that the origin of caste is not a one-time creation as a system of social relations, and its functions have also evolved over the centuries. As such, the present morphology of caste is therefore the result of a long, dynamic trajectory. Caste has also not evolved on an even keel. Jaiswal also observes that origins of caste are embedded in the processes of patriarchy and state formation. Endogamy (Ketkar, 1979, 15) along with 'birth' are the main determinants of caste; however, for Jaiswal, endogamy is intrinsic to the process of stratification and establishment of a patriarchal society in terms of *anuloma* (hypergamy), which amounts to a lower status to women than men. In a well-documented work, Jaiswal examines the specific historical contexts (specificities) which led to the emergence of the *varnas* and their crystallization into castes. Varna had intra-segmented identities, which accommodated regional divergences and allowed sufficient flexibility to suit politico-economic requirements. Jaiswal makes it explicit that not so much the Brahamana caste spread and propagated *varna* as it was done by the dominant non-Brahamana community or the ruling elite, as they benefited from the notions of hierarchy (1998, X). Such an analysis of caste implies that economic and political necessities were the compelling reasons for emergence of social divisions, namely, *varnas*. The idea of 'pure' and 'impure' *varnas* and their sub-divisions was not prevalent. While commenting on some recent analyses of caste (Dumont, 1970a; Gupta, 1984; Klass, 1980; Kosambi, 1975), Jaiswal (1998, 6–7) writes:

> In fact the evolution of the caste system cannot be delinked from the emergence of patriarchy, class divisions, and state; and as this did not happen at the same time all over the subcontinent, one cannot speak of its simultaneous appearance in different regions of the country.

Jaiswal (1998, 6–7) further emphatically states that occupational specialization and hierarchical gradation along with the suppression of women as a class have played a no less crucial role than endogamy in the formation of caste society and in regulating its internal intercommunal relationships.

No doubt, caste had been a rigid hierarchical system of social relations based on birth, hereditary occupations, connubial and commensal rules and regulations and asymmetrical ties among different castes (*jatis*) characterized by higher and lower statuses and ritual power. Castes under such a rubric, despite alarming differences of status and rank, were required to cooperate with each other and also within castes, members were made to behave as a community of equals and brethren. Such an ethos and organization of caste has ceased to exist. Leach (1960, 1–10) is of the view that when castes begin to compete with each other rather than to cooperate, they cease to be castes, and become class-like entities.

COMPARISON OF CASTE AND RACE

Caste and race have been equated as systems of differentiation and hierarchization. Both are ascribed systems with pregiven perceptions, preferences and prejudices. Insulation is also unique to both caste and race. Cox (1970; 1987, 37) considers caste as 'ancient, non-conflictive, non-pathological and static'. On the contrary, Cox observes that race is putatively modern, conflictive, pathological and dynamic. As such Cox relates 'race' to materialist sociology, reflected in capitalist world of Western Europe and America. Caste remains an object of an idealist anthropology, rooted into cultural grounds with manifestations of hierarchy. Smaje (2000, 1–34) rejects Cox's view on such a demarcation between caste and race. Race is not to be so lightly dismissed as a 'pathological' consequence of capitalist development as Cox states, and caste is not quite as stable, normative or consensual, not quite as 'non-pathological'. Smaje is of the view that both caste and race refer to the social phenomena which are continuously recreated in relation to distinctive cultural repertories within which the analytical categories of sociological theory can themselves be located (2000, 2). Both have ideological similarities, as they are different kinds of 'natural hierarchy', as they involve the idea that people can be divided into ordered collectivities as *sui generis*. Smaje admits that caste and race are not the same things, they differ from one another because of differing ordering principles. To compare caste and race, Smaje suggests three factors as follows

1. The separation or identity between persons and things;
2. Conceptions of cosmic order and its relation to worldly diversity, particularly with respect to political boundaries; and
3. The character of the person and the 'substance' that they embody (2000, 2).

Smaje suggests that both caste and race need to be viewed from the 'essentialist' (mainly in case of race) and 'relational' view (in case of caste) as natural hierarchies. Smaje writes: 'Relations and essences are better seen as mutually entailed moments in ideologies of a particular kind—ideologies of natural hierarchy and it is worth appreciating that the sociological penchant for turning substances into relations, immensely revealing though it is, has its own specific cultural grounding' (2000, 3–4).

In 1960s, an intense debate on comparison of caste and race engaged several eminent scholars in working out differences and similarities between the two systems (de Reuck and Knight, 1967). The racist mentality arose around 1800–1815 in Europe (Poliakov, 1967, 223–234). Hostile attitudes to the Jews were justified theologically, and there was also a struggle against theological dogmatism, which paved the way for new beliefs. A century later the Nazis formulated their racial laws. The superiority of German blood emerged as a frenzy along with nationalism. Against such a backdrop, 'coloured races' were pronounced congenitally inferior. Even racism was associated with capitalism or capitalist interests. Racism acquired a deterministic and materialistic meaning. 'All is race, there is no other truth', 'Race is the key to history' (Poliakov, 1967, 229). Such expressions were quite common in the 19th century writings (Sorokin, 1927, 291–292). The idea and practice of superiority and inferiority was so much justified as a phenomenon of racism that it affected all the aspects of people's lives—their culture, occupations, aspirations and actions.

At the Durban Conference (2001), the main question was: Is caste race? (Thorat and Umakant, 2004, xxii–xxvi). The question was raised regarding discrimination in India, Nepal and Buraku (in Japan). A plea was made to recognize the discrimination based on caste and social origin and/or the descent-based discrimination. The view was that caste is not race and that caste is an internal matter of India. Andre Beteille (2004, 65–68) rejects caste discrimination as form of racial discrimination; hence caste is not a form of race. All discriminations cannot be an act of racial discrimination. Dipankar Gupta (2004) also substantiates Beteille's view when he says that the language of race cannot be used in the caste situation (quoted from Thorat and Umakant, 2004, 69–84). Equating caste with race is also unacceptable to D. L. Sheth (2004, 85–96). However, Gerald D. Berreman (2002) argues that race is no more a biological or genetic fact than is caste. Both race and caste are social construction; both hierarchize people. Thorat and Umakant (2004, XXV), relying on Berreman's view, observe: 'As race is socially constructed and acted upon in the form of racism, it is real and devastating—just as caste and casteism'. T. K. Oommen (2004, 97–109) substantiates both Berreman and Thorat when he says that race as a biological concept does not have any validity; and caste as a social category is constructed on the basis of imagined attributes. Thus, for Oommen, 'racism' and 'casteism' are main concerns as the basis of discrimination. Similarities between caste and race can be seen in terms of the practices of superior and inferior people, hence discrimination.

Ambedkar, without engaging himself in the debate on caste and race, as similar or different phenomena, clearly postulated that 'Caste Has to Go'. In 1936, Ambedkar (2014) vehemently argued for annihilation of caste, as he advocated that caste, *varna* and hereditary occupations had no place in an egalitarian India. Mahatma Gandhi, who had a soft corner for *varna*/caste system, often stated that 'an ideal' form of caste could be justified, and also said that 'the ideal' never existed in practice. Gandhi also said that any notion of superiority and inferiority was utterly wrong. As a result of Gandhi's debate with Ambedkar, Gandhi realized that publicly accepted rejection of caste, as strongly voiced by Ambedkar, was 'harmful' both to 'spiritual and national growth'. Gandhi, after this historical debate, pleaded for inter-dinning and inter-marriage among different castes. Even Jawaharlal Nehru asked Gandhi repeatedly, 'Why don't you hit out at the caste system directly?' Gandhi used to say that by tackling 'untouchability', he would be able to weaken the caste system (Gandhi, 2015, 35–44). For both Gandhi and Ambedkar, 'discrimination' in the Indian society was a common concern, though they differed in their approach to tackle the menace of discrimination based on caste and religion. Gandhi considered 'untouchability' as the basic justification for caste, whereas Ambedkar thought of 'caste' as the bigger evil, which paved the way for untouchability.

For Gandhi, 'caste question' implied the analysis of caste and its removal as its key concern (Palshikar, 2015, 45–50). 'Ambedkar looks at caste as providing spiritual and practical sustenance to untouchability. Therefore, unless caste goes, he could not imagine how untouchability could go' (Palshikar, 2015, 48). Ambedkar felt that the untouchables were the most deprived people as they did not derive any benefit from the caste system, and therefore, they could demand and work for its demolition. Ambedkar encouraged the untouchables in the anti-caste struggles. Gandhi, as mentioned earlier, was for the abolition of untouchability to attack/modify the caste system. Caste, with differentiation, and without hierarchy, would lose its *caste-ness*. It seems, much before Dumont's idea of 'pure and impure' as the basis of hierarchy, Gandhi understood 'untouchability' (pure–impure) as the basis of caste, and desired to weaken it by attacking the untouchability.

LOUIS DUMONT'S VIEW ON CASTE

Around this time (in the 1960s), caste was perceived as the 'sub-culture of class' (Leach, 1967, 8–12), a cultural phenomenon, characterized by caste endogamy and birth. Caste was also seen as the system of social organization (hierarchical arrangement of castes and sub-castes). At the same time, correspondence between caste and occupation (class) had been a noticeable feature and it continues to be so to a certain extent even today, though social mobility has always existed in the caste system by way of status-emulation and betterment of economic standing, particularly by the low castes. Dumont (1967, 28–38) mentions two approaches to the study of caste, one he calls as *Classifying Approach*, and the other is referred to as *Typifying Approach*. The first one stems from natural science. The classifying approach considers caste as a phenomenon of social structure or an aspect of social stratification. There are forms of 'social stratification', and 'caste' is one form abstracted from the whole. In the typifying approach, caste is specific to Indian society, in which it has emerged and persisted in varied contexts and ways; hence caste is unique to Indian society; it is an aspect of Indian culture. The question is: What is caste? Going by the preference of Dumont for typifying approach, caste system is viewed as a 'closed system of social stratification'. Dumont strongly argues that 'class' and 'caste' cannot be dealt with by the same common principle. However, Barth (1960, 113–145) writes: 'If the concept of caste is to be useful in sociological analysis its definition must be based on structural criteria, and not on particular features of the Hindu philosophical scheme'. He further mentions that caste is a system of social stratification only, and therefore, 'the principle of status summation seems to be the structural

feature that most clearly characterizes caste as a system of social stratification' (Barth, 1960, 145).

Dumont rejects Barth's view on caste as 'mistaken' as a part of social
stratification in general. The Swat system, which Barth has studied in
North-West Pakistan, is a system of patronage and clientele, and as
such it is not a caste system. Caste is not a general social sub-system.
According to Dumont, there is a purely cultural view of caste, that is,
typifying. Dumont says: 'I believe this is the real, or deeper, comparative approach. The main thing is to *understand*, and therefore ideas and
values cannot be separated from "structure"' (Dumont, 1967, 31).

Dumont's cultural-determinism is quite evident in his plea for typifying approach to caste in opposition to the structural approach, which
he names as *classifying* approach. Going by Dumont's view, question
is as follows: Is caste an extreme form of stratification? For Dumont,
caste is a hierarchical system, characterized by interrelatedness of its
components/units, seeing it as a concrete social whole. Caste cannot
be understood just in terms of religion and/or economy (division of
labour). Both ideology and hard facts of social life define caste as a
system. Dumont (1967, 33–37) makes the following observations in
this context:

1. A hierarchical relation is a relation between larger and smaller, or
   more precisely between that which encompasses and that which is
   encompassed.
2. One must oppose the orientation to the whole (holism) to the orientation to the element (individualism). Caste represents 'holism',
   and 'the whole' is something religious (or philosophical), while
   'economy' is a matter of the individual. The division of labour in
   the Indian society is not, strictly speaking, an economic fact: it is a
   'holistic' (hence, largely a religious) fact.
3. In principle, priest and king are absolutely distinguished in the caste
   system. The priest (Brahman) is highest in status even when he is
   poor and materially dependent. However, priesthood encompasses
   rulership; and at the same time, these 'twin forces' together encom-
   pass all the rest. There are two implications of this: (a) hierarchy
   (ritual) is independent of power and (b) rulership in devalued in

terms of the whole, it takes its place immediately after priesthood. Thus, there is a system of the *prescriber* and the *prescribed*, and also the twinning of the two.

A CRITIQUE OF DUMONT'S VIEW

Many scholars do not agree with Dumont's approaches of typology and classification in relation to caste. Dumont does not make a distinction between *analogous* structures and *homologous* structures, which are often used in the field of biology and in the study of animals and birds. Caste cannot be understood without understanding its functioning. Caste as an all-encompassing expression has value as typifying a form of relationship to be found in other social structures as well (De Vos, 1967, 39–40). In his study of the Swat society, Barth (1960) observes a correspondence of status among the political, economic and social-prestige dimensions. Status congruence was found in the Swat society. However, at the lowest level (untouchable group), readjustment of status positions was not allowed. Barth says that the Swat social system and the caste system have similarity only at the bottom level, as flexibility in the Swat society is quite possible at the higher level, contrary to the caste system.

Gerald D. Berreman (1967, 45–73; 1969) highlights the necessity of a comparative analysis of caste in terms of caste stratification in India, race in America, the Burakumin in Japan, the Ruanda society as reported by Maquet (1967) and South Africa as reported by Van den Berghe (1964, 69–70). Berreman quotes Nadel (1954, 8, 9–22), who says that there is 'caste' in Africa, and writes: 'I am comparing types of society and wish to show that the "same type" (namely, caste-stratified society) can occur in widely different cultures and areas of the world, given certain common conditions or processes' (Berreman, 1967, 45). Now the question is: Whether societies with one institution in common are sufficiently similar in other respects that the entire societies can properly be classified together? After having raised this question, Berreman prefers to use 'caste stratification' and 'caste systems' rather than to 'caste societies' (1967, 46).

Further, Berreman writes:

> I want to analyse what caste systems are, how they work, and what they do to people. This is, I shall look at caste as a structural principle and as a social and cultural fact, and I shall look at the social, cultural and psychological concomitants of caste systems. (1967, 46)

Such a perspective is based on Berreman's studies of two very different caste societies, namely, (a) in Montgomery, Alabama (1953–1955), and (b) in North India (1957–1958). The two societies do not have a common historical source, but share similarity between the social relations and psychological mechanisms of Indians and of Southerners in the United States. Berreman, thus, describes caste systems as systems of stratification, unusually rigid, birth-ascribed, permitting of no individual mobility and ranked aggregates of people. Berreman prefers a cross-cultural comparability without sacrificing cultural content (1967, 47). He suggests three dimensions, that is, stratification, pluralism and interaction for a comprehensive, comparative analysis of the study of caste systems. An abstract definition of a caste system is. 'A caste system occurs where a society is made up of birth-ascribed groups which are hierarchically ordered and culturally distinct. The hierarchy entails differential evaluation, rewards, and association' (Berreman, 1967, 48).

Castes are differentiated groups, interacting with each other and are interdependent parts of a larger society. Differential evaluation of castes is in terms of 'ranking' in different idioms, such as purity (in India), honour (in Swat), or genetically determined capabilities (in the United States). High and low positions (ranks) are based on such idioms or ethos. Referring to M. G. Smith (1960) and P. Bohannan (1963), Berreman (1967, 49) describes that 'caste systems rank birth-ascribed group membership rather than attributers'. Class systems, on the contrary, define the rank of their members according to their individual attributes and behaviour. 'In a caste system, an individual displays the attributes of his caste because he is a member of it. In a class system, an individual is a member of his class because he displays its attributes' (Berreman, 1967, 49–50). Individual mobility is by definition impossible in a caste system, and possible in a class system (Berreman, 1967, 50). Though, Berreman draws a clear-cut demarcation between caste systems and class systems, along with attributes, such as, group v/s individual and immobility v/s mobility, respectively. He perceives systems of differential power and rewards contingent upon caste membership. Incongruence between ritual status and power has been reported in India's caste system, and perhaps this has not been noted by Berreman as he states that caste status determines differential association or hierarchical interaction and access to distribution of resources—social, cultural, economic and political. Barth (1960) refers to such a system of hierarchical interaction as 'status summation'.

Berreman also observes that 'castes are discrete social and cultural entities; caste hierarchies are discontinuous, echelon hierarchies' (1967, 52). This shows the dynamics of caste systems. In a modified way, Dipankar Gupta (1984, 2049) talks of 'continuous hierarchies and discrete castes'. He writes: 'Any notion of hierarchy is arbitrary and is valid from the perspective of certain individual castes. To state that the pure hierarchy is one that is universally believed in, or the one which legitimizes the position of those who participate in the caste system, is misleading'. Gupta argues that inconsistencies and incongruities in behaviour of members of different caste groups in different spheres can be understood in terms of their discreteness.

India's caste system is both 'organic' and 'segmentary' because it is a system of interdependent units (castes), which makes it as a 'whole', and each caste is also a composite entity, having its own rules and regulations for social interaction, enjoying a certain degree of autonomy of its own, while remaining a part of the 'organic whole'. In this sense, caste system implies a 'plural society', and as such violations of the caste system have occurred in Indian society from times immemorial. Berreman says that 'the plural society is held together by power rather than consensus', and in the caste system ritual hierarchy has been appropriated as the structure of power relations. Diverse castes remain tied to a set of norms and values under the hierarchical caste system, despite their divergent statuses and functions as higher and lower people. Thus, hierarchy, pluralism, and discreteness characterize the caste system. While concluding the debate on the caste systems, Berreman (1967, 70) observes as follows:

Caste systems have been defined here as systems of birth-ascribed stratification, of socio-cultural pluralism, and of hierarchical interaction. Such systems, it is suggested, have characteristic and inevitable effects on the minds and behavior of those who live them. Rigidity of stratification, degree of pluralism, exclusiveness of interaction and pervasiveness of hierarchy vary from society to society, as do their effects. The degree to which power and consensus hold the systems together varies also. But their common features afford insights into the relationship between society, culture and personality which are impossible to derive without such comparative analysis.

CASTE AND STATE IN INDIA

Now it has been established that caste was transformed by the British rule to serve its own interests. A couple of writings, namely, *Caste in History* (Banerjee-Dube, 2008), *Caste, Society and Politics in India* (S. Bayly, 2000), *Castes of Mind* (Dirks, 2002) and *Caste in Modern India*, two volumes (Sumit Sarkar and Tanika Sarkar, 2015), are the recent ones to bring out how colonialism indulged in reshaping caste as a handmaid to serve its dictates. Dirks, unhesitatingly, argues that caste is not in fact some unchanged survival of ancient India, not some single system that reflects a core civilizational value, nor a basic expression of Indian tradition. Caste is a modern phenomenon, that is, specifically, the product of a historical encounter between India and the Western colonial rule. To quote Dirks:

> It was under the British that 'caste' became a single term capable of expressing, organizing, and above all 'systematizing' India's diverse forms of social identity, community, and organization. This was achieved through an identifiable (if contested) ideological canon as the result of a concrete encounter with social colonial modernity during two hundred years of British domination. In short, colonialism made caste what it is today. (2002, 5)

The British made caste the central symbol of Indian society. The language of caste pervaded in all walks of life, such as ritual, familial, communal, socio-economic, political and public theatres of quotidian life.

Dirks, while disagreeing with Nehru and Dumont, considers caste as a historical construction of the colonial rule. He writes:

I argue that the history in which caste has been constituted as the principal modality of Indian society draws as much from the role of British Orientalists, administrators, and missionaries as it does from Indian reformers, social thinkers, and political actors. Indeed, my argument is about the power of the colonial leviathan to produce caste as the measure of all social things, a feat that could not have been accomplished had caste not become one of the most import emblems of tradition.... (Dirks, 2002, 8)

Caste endures because it has been the precipitate of a powerful history, as the very condition of the Indian social (Dirks, 2002, 8). The colonial state saw caste as an obstacle to its rule in India. Caste was 'a kind of civil society', it regulated and mediated the private domain, particularly commensal and connubial ties through its elaborate norms and regulations. Caste opposed the modern state, and the modern state opposed the hold of the caste on the people. In such a situation, the British made caste far more pervasive, far more totalizing, and far more uniform, declaring it as a fundamentally religious social order (Dirks, 2002, 13). Caste was kept aloof from being a means of political struggles as it was in the past. Dirks observes: 'Caste had been political all along, but under colonialism was anchored to the service of a colonial interest in maintaining social order, justifying colonial power, and sustaining a very peculiar form of indirect rule' (2002, 14–15). Colonial rule colonized not only caste, it also did it in case of tradition, sources of knowledge, administration, mobilization and movements.

The question of caste is blatantly not of 'pure and impure' or of a functional social organization as projected by Dumont (1970a), Risley (1909/1969), Hutton (1963) and many others. Even in such ideological and functional interpretations of caste, one could see underlying layers of power relations along with caste hierarchy. However, one would not find one-to-one correspondence between caste ranks and economic and political standing. There was no absolute power at the top as it was shared by the *Dwij* castes, namely, Brahmins enjoyed ritual power, Kshatriyas ruled over the society and Vaishyas controlled economy (trade and commerce). The Shudras (agriculturists) and the *Ati-Shudras* (Untouchables) had no say in the affairs of the society. However, since the functionary castes (lower castes) performed some rituals, whom Harold A. Gould (1967) has named as 'contra-priests', at times bargained for appropriate rewards, gifts and concessions for the services which they rendered to their *jajmans* (patrons) on festivals and occasions like birth, marriage and death. In this sense, caste was a system of power relations as well, but it was not an absolute one, as despite hierarchy, different castes, through their respective *biradaris* (caste panchayats), what is known as *khap*, in some states, such as Haryana and Western Uttar Pradesh, voiced against oppression and deprivation inflicted upon by the patrons of the higher castes.

RESILIENCE OF THE CASTE SYSTEM

The question(s) of caste have attracted attention of social scientists in an immeasurable way, including historians, sociologists, anthropologists, political scientists, economists, and even administrators. The questions, often asked, are: How did caste originate? What has been its nature in different historical epochs? What forces have shaped and reshaped the caste system? Or how caste has shaped and reshaped polity and economy in history? No clear answers have been there to such questions. However, one striking point is, as Ishita Banerjee-Dube (2008, XV) observes: 'Caste, elusive yet enduring, retains a critical importance as concept and practice in India Today'. Caste has no linear progression, it has a chequered path, ups and downs, and diverse patterns of rigidity and flexibility in different parts of India.

Susan Bayly (2000) has extensively mapped out the trajectory of caste from the 18th century to the modern age in her seminal work *Caste, Society and Politics in India*. In the days of British rule, India was referred as a 'caste society', and in the post-Independence period, the idea of 'caste model' of Indian society has been in vogue, as a somewhat new version of the old notion of 'caste society'. The idea of 'caste society' and also that of 'caste model' has been questioned time and again as a creation of the British in the first instance, and of the scholars like Louis Dumont, in the post-Independence era. Bayly accords a value to 'constructions' of caste, but they cannot be equal to 'lived reality'. There were a lot of changes in the caste system prior to British rule, and during the colonial period, significant changes occurred in the caste system. Since Independence, assertion of caste identities for reservations, elections and opportunities has been a constant feature till today, Bayly observes that no single static system of caste has dominated Indian life since ancient times. However, certain generalized caste ideals have been extolled in some texts. In the medieval period, there were caste-like observances, but there was nothing like a caste society. Today, caste is far more generalized than in the past. Recent political and social developments have 'engendered, shaped and perpetuated' caste more than the ancient and the medieval periods of Indian history (Bayly, 2000, 4).

Why has caste persisted for so long? Bayly argues that by embracing caste principles, by imposing them on others, 'modern' men and women may gain an extraordinarily flexible resource in uncertain times. The assertions of caste, therefore, surpass many boundaries of religion, faith, language and economic status, and at the same time, caste principles are appropriated as means of excluding, disempowering or subjugating others (2000, 5). This is how Ambedkar has blamed caste as a means of deprivation of the lower castes by the dominant ones. In a 'caste society', 'class' and 'individual' become subordinate to *jati* (group). After a cursory survey of selected writings, Bayly seems to accept the concept of caste as given by R. S. Khare (1983, 85), who says that the concept of *jati* refers to the experience of caste in the 'concrete and factual domain' of everyday social life, as opposed to the 'ideal and symbolic' ... archetypes which are embodied in the concept of *varna* (Bayly, 2000, 9). This also implies to certain extent caste-class nexus, though regional variations could be there in terms of such a nexus. There is a 'rough match' between caste and other attributes of status and power. However, when caste and caste like norms are shared in a region, caste is used as an identity by the people in that region. Caste is more of a notion of attachment (Bayly, 2000). However, even this is not recognized by the new generation of educated men and women in big cities and by those who live abroad, particularly in the developed countries of the West. Many of them even would not know their own sub-caste or sub-sub-caste.

Bayly (2000, 10) writes: 'Above all, the concept of caste has come to imply both boundaries and collective or corporate rank'. However, this has often been contested particularly since Independence. Today, the way 'caste' is found in real everyday life in different settings and contexts and for different sections of society should be the basis of understanding of caste and its dynamics. The presence of the past in the present needs to be understood to know the caste dynamics. What are the markers of the caste today? Caste boundaries have become blurred to a great extent. A lip service is paid to fellow caste members at the time of a function by a given family. Inter-family ties cutting across caste boundaries have become frequent and intense due to extra-caste considerations, such as winning an election or for an economic end-in-view, or seeking a favour for one or other purpose. Thus, in place of caste-based status-congruence or incongruence of yesteryears, today, there is a new pattern of social relations, may be ad hoc, not so enduring, flouting caste limits. One needs to analyse dynamics of such status-alignments or distances in the present-day context. For example, extending hospitality to 'low caste' politicians and government officials has become a common practice, at least in the public gaze. A high caste person with poor economic standing and without political clout can be witnessed in abundance. On the contrary, one can see a lower caste man/woman as a *Sarpanch*, with sound economic standing and assertion of enhanced social standing, making the upper castes to realize and accept such a remarkable change in no uncertain terms. Women from the lower and middle castes, who have been elected for Panchayati Raj institutions, have been sharing dais with men, without covering their faces, and also participating in decision-making.

Ordinary people do not have a clear idea about the origin of caste or of the versions provided in the scripts. They are not able to relate their own life with the scriptural dictates. The real life is guided by mundane concerns and anxieties rather than by holy prescriptions. The distinction between the lower and the upper castes has not been simply that of ritual purity and impurity; it has been more of practical material realities. Bayly seems to adhere to Barth's view regarding caste. She writes:

> Caste in Barth's view was therefore not a unique moral or religious system. It was merely a more elaborate form of the social stratification to be found in many other societies: the true basis of the distinction

between those of low and high caste was differential access to political and economic resources. (2000, 12)

Several other scholars have endorsed such a view of caste. 'Caste-free' areas (Beteille, 1965, 1966, 1969b) and 'extra-caste considerations' (Sharma, 1974) have been noted indicating the enhanced space being occupied by 'family' and 'individual' in social relations and status determination. A couple of studies of social mobility in the caste system (Beteille, 1991, 1965; Kolenda, 1984, 1986; Sharma, 1973; Srinivas, 1965) speak that caste has been a mobile and flexible rather than rigid and static system. Obviously, as such caste has not been a unique and a coherent structure of 'core values' of Hindu society as viewed by Dumont. Material differences, in Dumont' view, do not constitute the ethos or essence of the ideology of pure and impure—which is a guiding principle of the caste hierarchy. According to Dumont, the facts of life for a Hindu village are not the simple material differences. Preoccupation with the pure and the impure pervades in Hindu Life. Emile Senart (1930), C. Bougle (1971) and A. M. Hocart (1950) had already overrated the ritual aspect of caste much before Louis Dumont. Even Srinivas (1952) had proposed a cohesive tie-up between caste and religion in his study of the Coorgs of South India before Dumont's analysis of caste as Homo Hierarchic (1970a). Everything, in Dumont's understanding, falls under the categories of either 'pure' or 'impure'. Such a 'cultural determinism' is of a limited significance in the wake of dynamics of the caste system over several centuries.

Bayly (2000, 16–19) while challenging Dumont's binary opposition as a mechanistic construction, ignoring diversity in real social life, analyses three viewpoints. (a) Burghart (1978, 1983a, 1983b) finds three ideals extolled as principles of supreme human and cosmic virtue and harmony. These are: (i) the standards of *dharmic* caste life; (ii) ascetic renunciation; and (iii) the exercise of power by righteous kings, and by those who share kingly qualities of initiative, assertion and command. (b) Veena Das (1982) identifies a whole series of interconnected conceptual pairings: Kings and their unkingly subjects; Brahmans and renouncers; renouncers and unkingly subjects; Brahmins and Kings. The idea of 'latent' principle, that of the renouncer, provides a scheme of tripartite classifications. (c) Marriott (1976, 1989) offers a highly complex formulation, treating the bonds of caste as a product of mutable, ever-changing 'coded substances' and offering a model of caste society in which status rankings are expressed and experienced as a multidimensional web of ordered ceremonial exchanges and transactions. Bayly (2000, fn 24) observes that for Marriott, Hindu culture is 'transactional and transformational', and of the Hindu person as a fluid, unbounded, continually transacting 'dividual' or divisible entity composed of coded substances or essences transferred to others through marriage and other inter-personal contacts.

India is a mosaic of castes, sub-castes, sub–sub–castes and communities formed out of the Hindu castes, such as Sikhs, Christians, Jains, Muslims, neo-Buddhists, etc. These are believers of their respective faiths, and are not functioning as 'castes' and are also not quite far off from the Hindu castes. Thus, there are many interpretations of caste: (a) Dumont's typifying approach; (b) Srinivas' view on 'positional' change, with no effects on vertical order; (c) Structural or classifying approach, considering 'caste' as a phenomenon of the system of social stratification; (d) Principles of supreme human and cosmic virtue and harmony; (e) Structuralist/textual approach; and (f) Multidimensional ethno-sociology of McKim Marriott. We propose to analyse views of M. N. Srinivas and Louis Dumont separately to situate their significance in the present-day context. Besides Srinivas and Dumont, a cursory glance at other views and commentaries will be cast to have a balanced analysis of the discourses on caste.

CASTE AS AN IDENTITY

'Caste' finds its presence in one way or other in both 'public' and 'private' spheres. There is presence of 'caste' in the Constitution of India by way of reservations for the scheduled castes, and it is negated as the basis of discrimination against the 'depressed castes'. By way of granting favours and support to one's own caste members by the people holding domineering positions in politics, bureaucracy, business and industry is frequently heard of. All this exists, not because of persistence of caste as a system. It is happening as caste identity is appropriated as a means to extend favours or to deny the same to some because of a different caste label. Since caste is no more a limited phenomenon any more, it is clear or not-so-clear presence can be seen almost everywhere. We see some examples regarding caste as given below:

1. *Structure and Change in Indian Society*, edited by Milton Singer and Bernard S. Cohn (1968), Indian Reprint (1996). The topics (sections) are: Caste and Social Structure (3 Articles; The Structure of Inter-caste Relations (4 Articles); Is the Caste System Changing? (3 Articles); Caste in Politics, Economics and Law (3 Articles).
2. *Social Stratification*, edited by Dipankar Gupta (1991). The topics (sections) are: Caste (9 Articles), Caste Profiles (6 Articles); Caste, Class and Conflict (8 Articles).
3. *Social Stratification in India*, edited by K. L. Sharma. 7 Articles on caste out of a total of 16 papers.
4. *Caste in History*, edited by Ishita Banerjee-Dube (2008). The topics/sections are: Caste and Colonialism (6 Articles); Caste in Practice (5 Articles); Caste and Politics (6 Articles); and Caste in Everyday Life (5 Articles).
5. *The Problem of Caste*, edited by Satish Despande (2014). The topics/sections are: Disciplinary Perspectives (10 Articles); Caste and Class (5 Articles); Caste and Politics (8 Articles); Caste, State and Law (5 Articles); Caste and Gender (6 Articles). All the articles were published in *Economic & Political Weekly*, between 1958 and 2013.
6. *Caste in Modern India*, 2 Vols, edited by Sumit Sarkar and Tanika Sarkar (2015). The topics/sections are: Caste and Colonial Times (8 Article); Caste and the Census (3 Articles); Caste, Sect, Religion (6 Article); Caste and Forms of Labour (5 Articles); Caste, Gender and Identify (5 Articles); Caste and the Nation (3 Articles), and Caste and Resistance (3 Articles).

One can think of an end-number of themes and sub-themes on caste as it has been observed and associated with almost all aspects of social life, including religion, marriage, family, kinship, gender, village, town, occupations, entrepreneurship, business, industry, bureaucracy, politics, elections, change, development, education, etc. It is so, as argued by some scholars, that caste is a pervasive and resilient institution, and maintains its core values despite its changing nature and functions.

N. K. Bose (1975, 116–127) observes that the division of labour in the ancient Indian society existed in terms of Cultivator, Cowherd, Weaver, Blacksmith, Carpenter, Cobbler, Barber, Physician, Trader, etc. It cannot be ascertained that such occupations were hereditary or there were differences of social rank among the practitioners. Economic structure and accumulation of wealth, had taken clear roots in the society. In the middle ages, agriculture, handicrafts and commerce had become quite advanced. The Muslim rulers did not know much about the *varna* system, which had been quite developed by the time of middle ages. Some new arts and crafts were added by the Muslim rulers during their respective regimes. A sort of semblance and synthesis of the Hindu traditional economic arrangements and the new additions in the field of arts and crafts existed without any opposition and cultural confrontation. However, conversion to Islam by Hindus occurred during the second half of the middle ages. More striking feature was the emergence of the sects formed by Nanak, Kabir and Dabu, who sought to transform the Hindu social order with a view to make it more open and flexible. During the British period (Bose, 1975, 137–145), tremendous changes occurred in economy, polity, and society. Introduction of new land-tenure systems, namely, *Zamindari* and *Ryotwari*, English education, administrative system, etc., created a situation quite different from that of the medieval period. Bose (1975, 142) describes the situation as follows:

> The Tanner becomes an agriculturist, the Brahmin opens a pharmacy; *Kayasthas*, *Sadgopes* and *Ugra Kshatriyas* have at places entered services, at places started furniture factories and at places opened shoe-shops. People have lost the confidence to adhere to the occupations which were assigned to them under the *Varna* system. As a result, caste has become detached from the economic system and has become confined only to the ceremonial aspects of social life.

Bose also mentions that despite such changes, over 70 per cent of the people occupy a degraded position in society, and most of the wage-labourers belong to this category (1975, 143). We shall discuss caste in the post-Independence period based on analyses and profiles of caste based on selected empirical studies and commentaries.

COMPLEX NATURE OF CASTE

Increasingly, it is being felt that caste has a diverse and chequered path in terms of different groups and regions of India as analysed by Ishita Banerjee-Dube (2008, XV-LXIV). Based on a collection of 22 papers, Banerjee-Dube considers caste as institution, ideology, imagination and practice by way of its varied trajectories and changing contours. Caste has witnessed discrete formations and shifting boundaries, perceptions and actions. Caste alliances for sharing power and resources and intra-caste splits and factions negate the conventional definition of caste. Political and economic considerations have entered into what is known as 'caste' and the 'social' or 'essential' of caste as seen in the past has been wiped out. A new 'social' determines the new shape/form and substance of the caste as it exists today. May be that a different 'social' would emerge in the coming decades of the present century. The question is: How one experiences caste today? Why and how differently people perceive and act in terms of caste? What makes 'caste' to persist despite losing its systemic ethos? Who are the people most concerned and conscious of 'caste'? Who are the people who are indifferent or even express hatred towards caste? Who are the people who are not concerned at all about their caste identities?

An all-inclusive answer to these questions could be in Anand Teltumbde's analysis of caste (2010). Caste has survived despite capitalist production relations in agriculture in 1960s and 1970s; neoliberalism in 1980s, and in globalization of 1900s. Teltumbde (2010, 10) writes: 'Indeed, caste has showed an amazing resilience. It has survived feudalism, capitalist industrialization, a republican constitution, and today despite all denial, is well alive under neoliberal globalization'. It has been persisting as a caste-related 'hate crime'. Such a 'persistence of caste' is due to the persistence of the caste system or it is due to softness of Indian state, which has failed partly in putting a check on the transformation of the traditional power structure and partly in curbing the emergence of new power-wielders. Such a combination of powerful families and individuals, not necessarily belonging to the upper castes, has been committing atrocities on Dalits, other weaker sections and the poor people. Caste alone cannot be held responsible for suppression of Dalits and other depressed sections. It is clear that 'caste' has not disappeared, its sporadic appearance, and sometimes an ugly one, is persisting. Globalization has also not affected caste adversely; in fact, there is no evidence that, even in foreseeable future, there would be 'de-caste' of the Indian society. Intra-caste and inter-caste permutations and combinations would continue, as it has been in the past, particularly in the political domain. Since benefits of globalization have been cornered by select sections of Indian society, there is likelihood of a widened gap between the 'upper' and the 'lower' castes.

A similar view is articulated by T. G. Jacob and P. Bandhu (2009), based on their analysis of four southern states of India, namely, Tamil Nadu, Kerala, Karnataka and Andhra Pradesh. From the Dalit point of view, the phenomenon of caste discrimination and oppression has always been there in varied forms and practices. It has been so because of resilience of the caste system. Despite opposition to caste over the last many centuries from Buddhism onwards till date, conflict between the Dalits and the dominant castes has existed throughout the Indian history. Jacob and Bandhu, based on several incidences and encounters between the Dalits and the dominant castes, conclude that capitalism/imperialism by its very nature is invasive, authoritarian, centralized, hegemony-seeking and destructive of peoples and environments (2009, 269). But the fact is that 'Caste in Life' (Shaym, 2011), a volume edited by Babu and Khare, projects manifold experiences regarding caste, ranging from a non-reality to an oppressive fact of life. Autobiographical accounts by twenty-five contributors to this volume speak of both 'inclusion' of a caste for benefits as ST category, and coming together of Brahmins and Dalits under the leadership of a Dalit woman, who becomes Chief Minister of the most populated state of India. Caste conflicts and caste alliances simultaneously exist in different parts of India, and also at times within the same state.

The volume, edited by Satish Deshpande (2014), brings out succinctly caste concerns over the last six decades (1958–2013), based on 40 papers published in *Economic & Political Weekly*. After the Mandal agitation, one could see a jump in publications on 'caste'. Before the Mandal agitation, there was a relative decline in the publications on caste (Deshpande, 2014, 1–4). Deshpande, based on his analysis of the papers, included in this volume, considers caste, like many others, both as an empirical phenomenon and as a civilizational idea. Though as a civilizational phenomenon, caste has been contested by many critics. The articles included in the volume imply that the rules of heredity, endogamy and commensality are not so relevant to understand India of today. However, even being nearly extinct, these considerations are lived at times by the vested social and political interests. Mandal gave a new twist to caste as a social phenomenon. Caste can be seen in the village, in case of 'untouchability' and reservations. The volume concentrates on the following aspects of caste (Deshpande, 2014, 11–20):

1. Disciplinary Perspectives
2. Caste and Class
3. Caste and Politics
4. Caste, Law and State
5. Caste and Gender
6. Contemporary Explorations

When caste functioned as a system of social relations in terms of hierarchy, it remained adhered to particular values and norms, as analysed by Dumont, Srinivas and many others. However, with the decline of its hierarchical ethos, it entered into the realm of discretions of individuals and families, though not reaching to the vanishing point. One hears sometimes about alarming, undemocratic and inhuman decisions by Khaps under the pretext of violations of rules of marriage by young couples. Such a situation keeps alive 'caste', leaving it vague in definition. Caste as such has explored somewhat new grounds for its play, in the form of Khap, by way of participation in elections, rallies and congregations, instead of strict adherence to commensality and rules of marriage.

As mentioned earlier, *Caste in Modern India* (2 Vols.), edited by Sumit Sarkar and Tanika Sarkar (2015), includes 33 papers, exploring certain specific questions of modern caste, such as:

• How the issue of caste was variously understood in colonial times?
• How it was re-created under conditions of modernity?
• How various castes came to relate to one another and to themselves in new ways?

The editors have excluded sociological/empirical studies of the structure of castes. The emphasis in the two volumes is on ascertaining how far caste was invented, exaggerated, colluded with, and opposed by discourses of colonial social knowledge and administrative policies. 'Caste' was seen as a stigmatization of the culture of the colonized. Caste gets reframed by various factors, such as gender, class relations, nation, systems of knowledge, but it is viewed by the editors that caste as a social category does not stand alone.

Our main concern is to understand caste in terms of its ideational moorings, their applications, and the practices which are on the ground in the name of caste system. Dipankar Gupta (1991, 2) writes:

> The caste system, as it is widely understood, separates and hierarchizes Hindus. However, it is not sufficient if this separation and hierarchization are wholly internalized or intellectualized. It is only when hierarchy and differences are externalized and socially demonstrated that we can truly talk about social stratification. Rituals, dress tonsorial styles, marriage practices, and a host of other such phenomena help in socially separating one caste from another. It is these phenomena too that are appropriately valorized for the purposes of hierarchical ranking.

Caste as a system of social stratification is based on the principle of *natural superiority* (bodily purity, that is, birth). Let us say here that social differentiation between different castes has considerably vanished in public gaze. Differences based on rituals, dress and marriage practices have also minimized over the years. Certainly, *hierarchy* and *differences* are key concepts in the understanding of stratification, including caste. While accepting Dumont's concept of *hierarchy*, Gupta widens its scope and application to class, order and conflict, and also finds that both hierarchy and differences are basic features in the writings of Weber and Marx for understanding of stratification and class.

M. N. SRINIVAS ON CASTE

M. N. Srinivas could be considered till date as the one who engaged himself on understanding of caste for his entire life. His seminal work *Religion and Society Among the Coorgs of South India* (1952) is considered as a paradigm shift in the studies of Indian society, its religion, culture and social change. Rampura, a village, in the princely state of Mysore, was the locale of his study. In another work *The Remembered Village* (1976, 164–210), based on his field notes and memory, Srinivas mentions that every caste had a traditional occupation (in the year 1948) and the various castes of a region were mutually dependent. Money played a minimal role in the traditional economy of the village. A man inherited an occupation, and liked to pursue like his forefathers. Expectation of the village elders was also for adherence to the traditional occupations generation after generation. However, to supplement one's meagre income from traditional occupations, people also took up agriculture and trade. Srinivas writes: 'While occupational specialization resulted in the interdependence of castes, hierarchical ideas, especially as expressed in endogamy and in the restrictions on inter-dinning, emphasized their separation from each other' (1976, 166). Srinivas considers caste as a commensal group, and the ideas of purity and pollution were the basis of inter-caste separateness and structural distance.

Much before Louis Dumont (1970a), Srinivas, based on his study of Rampura in 1948, describes that the idea of hierarchy was present everywhere. 'Each man belonged to a caste which formed part of a system of ranked castes' (Dumont, 1970a, 167). Everything was considered higher and lower, including diet, occupation and custom and ritual, and animals, vegetables, plants, grain, timber and fuel (Dumont, 1970a, 167). Pride in one's caste was common. Besides caste hierarchy, landownership patterns were also not egalitarian. 'There was a certain amount of overlap between the hierarchies of caste and land' (Dumont, 1970a, 169). Srinivas clearly distinguished between *Varna* hierarchy and the hierarchy at the grassroots level. The first is vague, and the second is specific in terms of actual inter-caste relations (Srinivas, 1962). However, self-evaluation of caste-rank by its members and evaluation by other castes at times were at variance and even disputed. Hierarchy was *sui generis*, underlying every area of culture. Srinivas also observed that opportunities for mobility also existed, 'and the emulation of the customs, rituals and life-style of the higher and more sanskritized castes was a condition precedent for mobility. Emulation did also occur within the local section of a caste, the richer, more prestigious and sanskritized households being imitated by the others' (Srinivas, 1962, 183).

Srinivas does not draw a line of difference between 'hierarchy' and 'stratification'. For example, for Dumont hierarchy is a system of rigid and fixed social relations in terms of high and low positions. For Srinivas, no doubt based on birth-ascription, 'hierarchy' is a system of social relations, though all-pervasive, but having a scope for change and mobility, within the parameters of the caste system. Even the peasants formed a hierarchy, as stated by Srinivas. Thus, Srinivas also implies 'class' within caste, and 'status distinctions' as an aspect of hierarchy. Srinivas provides a detailed account of purity and pollution, the way the notions regarding practices relating to purity and pollution are internalized, particularly among the Brahmins.

While providing minute details, Srinivas (1987, 79) defines caste hierarchy as:

> The essence of hierarchy is the absence of equality among the limits which form the whole: in this sense, the various castes in Rampura do form a hierarchy. The caste units are separated by endogamy and commensality, and they are associated with ranked differences of diet and occupation. Yet it is difficult, if not impossible, to determine the exact, or even the approximate, place of each caste in the hierarchical system.

In this paper, Srinivas describes about 'patrons and clients' and structural unity of the villages. Patrons and clients refer to the relationships of master and servant, landowner and tenant, and creditor and debtor. The structural unity refers to the loyalty of all those who live in the village, irrespective of their castes and economic status and positions of command and compliance.

Srinivas writes about the significance of dominance for understanding of rural social life. He observes:

> When a caste enjoys all the elements of dominance, it may be said to be dominant in a decisive way. But decisive dominance is not common; more frequently the different elements of dominance are distributed among the castes in a village. Thus, a caste, which is ritually high, may

be poor and lacking strength in numbers, while a populous caste may be rich and ritually low. (1987, 97)

'Dominance' of a caste in one or other context becomes a reference for emulation. To explain change from within the caste system and change in the caste system from outside, Srinivas has used the concept of 'sanskritization' and the idea of 'westernization', respectively. For Srinivas: 'Sanskritization is the process by which a "low" Hindu caste, or tribal or other group, changes its customs, ritual, ideology, and way of life in the direction of a high, and frequently, "twice-born" caste' (1966, 6). The dominant caste(s) may not concede to the claims of the lower castes for higher status. However, 'sanskritization is generally accompanied by, and often results in upward mobility for the caste in question; but mobility may also occur without sanskritization; and even vice versa' (Srinivas, 1966, 7). Sanskritization results only in *positional changes* in the system and does not lead to any structural change (Srinivas, 1966, 7).

Thus, change occurs *in* the system and not *of* the system. 'The system itself does not change'. Ups and downs occur in an essentially stable hierarchical order. The model of sanskritization may not be necessarily Brahmanical; it could be Kshatriya, Vaishya and Shudra in terms of region and other elements of dominance. Srinivas has thus modified his initial idea of Brahmanical model of sanskritization. A caste to be dominant for imitation 'should own a sizeable amount of the arable land locally available, have strength of numbers, and occupy a high place in the local hierarchy' (1966,10). There may be multi-caste dominance in a village at the same time, and one caste may give way to another over a period of time to achieve decisive dominance.

To explain the external source of social change, Srinivas (1966, 46–88) uses the term 'westernization'. It characterizes 'the changes brought about in Indian society and culture as a result of over 150 years of British rule, and the term subsumes changes occurring at different levels—technology, institutions, ideology, values' (Srinivas, 1966, 47). Srinivas prefers the term 'westernization' instead of other terms, namely, industrialization and urbanization (1966, 46–50). The term 'westernization' is more apt because of the British impact on India through introduction of new institutions and also due to fundamental changes in the old institutions. English education, army, civil service, law courts were innovations of the British. In defence of the concept of Westernization, Srinivas observes: 'Implicate in Westernization are certain value preferences' (1966, 48). Humanitarianism is such an important value, imbibing both equalitarianism and secularization in it, irrespective of caste, economic position, religion, age and sex. Srinivas also rejects the use of the term 'modernization' as advocated by Daniel Lerner as he finds it unsuitable, being too local a label, more relevant for the Middle East (1966, 50–52). 'The term "Westernization" unlike "modernization" is ethically neutral. Its use does not carry the implication that it is good or bad, whereas modernization is normally used in the sense that it is good' (Srinivas, 1966, 52). 'Westernization is an inclusive, complex, and many-layered concept' (Srinivas, 1966, 53).

The question is: Who have/had been sanskritizing and westernizing? Sanskritization has performed a cohesive role (Srinivas, 1996, 87–101). However, Srinivas observes that 'the caste system provided an institutional basis for tolerance. Living in a caste society means living in a pluralistic cultural universe: each caste has its own occupation, customs, rituals, traditions, and ideas' (Srinivas, 1966, 75). Caste councils of the locally dominant castes are the guardians of such pluralism. Pluralism and hierarchy could coexist as mobility (positional change) or sanskritization occurs within the parameters of the caste system.

Based on dissension and conflict, new castes/sects have emerged throughout India's history. The Sikhs, *Lingayats*, and Jains and some tribal groups, such as the *Kotas*, *Todas*, *Badagas* and *Kurumbas*, have used the model of the caste system to regulate their mutual relations (Srinivas, 1966, 75–76). Tolerance, syncretism and self-criticism manifested early in the British rule brought about a westernized intelligentsia, who became the torchbearers of a new and modern India. The new elite was ambivalent due to their double association—one with their own society, and two with the West.

Dumont and Pocock (1957) have been quite critical of Srinivas' understanding of caste and village community as they observe that caste differences prevent villages from becoming communities. Dumont and Pocock erroneously assume that egalitarianism is a prerequisite of community formation. Indian village is a community as its parts are related to the whole, expressed in the unity and common concerns shared by different castes as explained by Srinivas. Srinivas asks: How in the west communities having egalitarianism could exist despite existence of social classes? Dumont (1970a, 161) characterizes the concept of 'dominant caste' as 'vague', and suggests to make it more precise. According to Dumont (1987, 1–19), ownership of land or the possession of superior rights in land could be the sole source of dominance, but Srinivas (1987, 1–19) says that the notion of dominant caste was an initial formation for him. For Dumont, the strength of numbers is not an important factor in dominance. However, Srinivas argues that a combination of numerical strength and big landholding can contribute to power of a caste or a number of castes in a hierarchical manner. Landowning and landless and brute force matter decisively in the village community. But landless castes, despite their large numbers, cannot be 'dominant'. Srinivas finds that strength of numbers plus a tradition of violence are essential elements of dominance. He writes: 'All in all, post-independent India is, certainly at the regional if not at the state level, the India of dominant castes' (Srinivas, 1987, 8). Srinivas further observes: 'The dominant castes are prominent in politics and the professions, and they have left their mark on every institution, and on the culture of each state' (1987, 8). Rejecting Dumont's criticism, Srinivas explains that 'dominant castes performed kingly functions in a very real sense at the village, and sometimes, also at slightly higher levels' (1987, 9). Maintenance of law and order by the informal council of the village elders, imparting of justice and ensuring social order were the main functions. However, Srinivas ignores the situations of the misuse of 'power' vested in the dominant castes and also at times prevailing incongruence between high power and low social status and vice versa.

'Dominance', more than governance, becomes a system of patron–client relations, that is, it encourages and reinforces inequality in the village community, in addition of the inequality built into the caste system. Srinivas also responds to the criticisms made against the concept of dominant caste by Peter Gardner (1968) and S. C. Dube (1968), particularly the one by S.C. Dube. Both Gardner and Dube consider numerical strength as *necessary* condition of dominance, but not a *sufficient* one. More numbers does not imply more land as observed by both Gardner and Dube. However, for Dube the important point is that if power is not diffused and exercised in the interest of the whole group or a sizeable part of it, it cannot be a dominant caste. There are, according to Dube, dominant individuals, who exercise dominance over their own caste members and also that of other castes. In such a situation, 'dominant caste' as a concept and as a reality suffers from cognitive limitation. If a 'dominant caste' does not bring benefits to its members, it cannot be called a dominant caste. Dube prefers the notions of 'dominant individuals'; and 'dominant faction' as more useful tools for understanding of power structure. Srinivas finds Dube's criticism as out of context. Use of power by the dominant caste after it has acquired it, is not the concern of Srinivas, as this is dependent upon the composition of the dominant caste. Patron–client syndrome is indicative of multi-caste alliances, and it expresses power relations in rural India. Srinivas vehemently holds on to his concepts, namely, sanskritization, westernization and dominant caste to explain society and its dynamics in rural India.

CASTE AS A SYSTEM OF HIERARCHY

Louis Dumont's work *Homo Hierarchicus* is an unparalleled treatise on the caste system. In view of his *typifying* approach, it has been commented by Leach (1971) as:

> By taking this approach, Dumont rejects the ethnocentrism of western sociology, which has usually viewed caste as the ultimate form of social distinctions found in egalitarian societies. He insists instead on viewing India on her own terms, as a society based on different principles for which new sociological concepts are needed.

Dumont focuses on hierarchy, ideology and observation, problem of comparison and change, ideology of caste, pure and impure, division of labour and egalitarian society (Sharma, 1994, 102–113). T. N. Madan (1971, 1–2), an ardent admirer of Dumont's view on caste, observes: '*Homo Hierarchicus* is an unusual work in its conception, design and execution'. Dumont (1970a, 7) states that caste cannot be interpreted and understood from the point of western ideas of egalitarianism, individualism and pre-eminence of politics and economics in society. Caste stands for inequality in theory and practice both, but is not just an opposite of 'equality'. The inequality of the caste system is a special type of inequality. Dumont (1970a, 7) writes:

> The ideas which they (the people) express are related to each other by more fundamental ideas even though these are unexpressed. The caste system, for example, appears as a perfectly coherent theory once one adds the necessary but implicit links to the principles that the people themselves give.

The notion of the fundamental opposition between the pure and the impure like that of Bougle (1971) seems to be the hallmark of Dumont's understanding of caste. Dumont considers the pure-impure opposition as 'a single true principle' to understand the caste system. Hierarchy is the essence of the pure–impure divide. Such a separation of the pure from the impure implies division of labour, and in fact, division in the entire society, in entirety. 'The whole is founded on the necessary and hierarchical coexistence of the two opposites' (Bougle, 1971, 43). For Dumont, hierarchy is the principle by which the elements of a whole (society) are ranked in relation to the whole (Madan, 1971a, 1971b). T. N. Madan remarks that 'such a perspective helps us to obtain a holistic view of the caste system and to overcome the dualism of opposition' (1971a, 3–4). As such, both theory and observation of actual behaviour can explain the whole of social reality of the caste system. In India, the opposite of equality is hierarchy and not inequality. Thus, inequality of the caste system is a special type of inequality.

Bougle (1971), who writes on caste much before Dumont, explains caste in terms of hierarchically arranged hereditary groups, segregation, and interdependence, and Dumont recognizes significance of these three mutually entertained 'principles', though the opposition between the pure and the impure remains the main key to Dumont's understanding of caste. Dumont calls it 'a single true principle'. The crux of the opposition between the pure and the impure is hierarchy. The pure and the impure and their layers make the *whole* caste-society.

'The whole is founded on the necessary and hierarchical coexistence of the two opposites' (Dumont, 1970a, 43). Ideological determinism is reflected quite clearly in Dumont's formulation of caste, but he also realizes that ideology is not everything, and cannot explain everything. However, observation of actual behaviour can reveal everything. Such is the anomaly between ideology and observation in Dumont's understanding of caste. There is 'dualism' in Dumont, and yet he prefers to give more significance to the 'whole' of the system. He uses historical and indological sources, but does not provide a history of the caste system.

Dumont presents analysis of the present-day caste system based on electrical indological sources, ignoring the studies and analyses of caste since India's Independence. The fact is that some of the writings of noted Indian scholars, such as M. N. Srinivas, Iravati Karve, A. R. Desai and A. K. Saran (see Surendra Sharma, 1985, 54–57) have been rejected by Dumont. There are aficionados of Dumont, particularly, T. N. Madan (1970a, XX). According to Madan, Dumont's method is of a theorist; his analysis is both deductive and dialectical, and his method is an 'experiment'. Dumont does not consider caste like many others as 'the most dangerous and blighting of all human institutions' (Sharma, 1994, 108). Dumont's preference for defence and perpetuation of caste, like India's colonial masters, such as Risley (1909) and Hutton (1948) is not a hidden fact. Madan's superlative admiration for Dumont is full of adjectives and testimonials. In fact, Dumont and Pocock, when decided not to edit the journal *Contributions to Indian Sociology* (1957–1966), decided to hand it over to T. N. Madan as its custodian and perpetuator of Dumontian legacy.

Homo Hierarchicus poses Indian society as a unique and insulated system, ignoring its social dynamics and changes in political and economic formation, as noted by Thapar (1974), Habib (1974), Panikkar (1955), Kosambi (1958), Barber (1968), Harper (1968), Rowe (1968), Stein (1968), Marriott (1968), and many others. It seems that Dumont was more inclined to contrast the Western so-called egalitarian society with the hierarchical/non-egalitarian Indian society. The study of caste provided Dumont a ground to reinforce his structuralist stance by using the pure–impure syndrome. Bailey (1959, 88–101) calls

Dumont's study as a very 'odd kind of inverted ethnocentrism', and it is 'more of an assertion than an evidence'. A. K. Saran's analysis of Indian society is criticized by Dumont as 'cultural solipsism', a Hindu sociology (Dumont, 1964, 32); and A. R. Desai's *Social Background of Indian Nationalism* as 'an over-grown political pamphlet clad in a university gown' (Dumont, 1964, 32). Dumont's *Homo Hierarchicus* too seems to be more of 'a Hindu sociology', rather than a sociology of India. Reducing India to caste alone would amount to a gross neglect of India's diversities—social, cultural, regional, religious and political and economic.

The structural aspects of caste, which remained under-rated and unexplored, due to colonial rule on the one hand and over emphasis on cultural distinctiveness on the other, have been studied at length, highlighting on analytic and empiric distinctions between caste, class and power. 'Increasingly, caste is becoming a desideratum, a state of mind, a plastic and malleable institution. No more hypersymbolization is manifest to express caste differences and typifications on a continuing basis' (Sharma, 2001, 78). The role played by family and individual has enhanced weakening of the caste system. Habib (1995, 161–179) denounces Dumontian theory of caste as *Homo Hierarchicus*. Habib comments:

> The caste system, in its classical form, could therefore function with as much ease in a natural economy as in a market-oriented one. In either case, it helped essentially to maintain not a fabric of imagined purity (if it did, this was accidental), but a system of class exploitation as rigorous as any other.

K. L. Sharma (2014a, 232) observes that in medieval India, caste system remained a means of a system of class exploitation, and the British colonized the caste system by their policy of 'divide and rule', and by propagating the norms of social distance as is evident in the Censuses of 1901 and 1931 (Hutton, 1946; Risley, 1969).

The studies and analyses of several scholars (Dumont, 1970a; Inden, 1990; Marriott, 1989; Oster, 1984) have emphasized on a renewed culturological approach to the study of caste, by way of an application of ethno-sociology and indigenous concepts and categories. Dipankar Gupta (2000, 224–264), a critic of such an approach, pleads for an inter-subjective sociology/anthropology against typification (as suggested by Dumont) to study the caste system. Gupta is of the view that castes need to be seen as discrete entities, being all abiding and durable entities. Gupta locates 'individual' in caste; and Beteille emphasizes on 'family', as K. L. Sharma did emphasize long ago on individual and family vis-à-vis caste (1969, 1974). 'Individual' and 'family' are emerging fast as units of social status and ranking, challenging caste as its basis.

In the edited book *Contextualizing Caste: Post-Dumontian Approaches*, Mary Searle-Chatterjee and Ursula Sharma (2003) bring out a couple of empirical studies which claim to go beyond Dumont's dichotomies, such as individualism v/s holism and tradition v/s modernism. Though Dumont argues that caste needs to be seen not from western-centric eye of individualism or ethnocentric perspective of the western scholarship, but he forgets that there is an element of 'general' or 'universal' ideology and reality in the culture-specific caste system, and vice versa. To name India as a premodern mode of thinking and social organization is negated by the facts of its dynamics over the past many centuries. False dichotomous ideal types as conceived by Dumont and then fitting India in one type is not a substantial way of reaching to the roots of social reality. The papers in the above volume look at caste as found in action, and not just as described in the indological texts as done by Dumont. Based on the studies included in the volume, Searle-Chatterjee and Sharma (2003, 9) observe:

> We can think therefore of caste in terms of a system of groups or as an ideological system of thought, but it is probably more useful to regard it in terms of a system of action (flexible and mutable—perhaps in reality a collection of modes of action).

Thus, caste is what people do in certain situations and the manner in which they identity themselves. The relationship between 'doing' and 'being' as a member of a particular caste can be more useful consideration. What you 'do' and what is 'done to you' are important elements in defining the caste system.

There are also many non-caste identity interactional contexts, in which Dumont's 'dualism' does not apply. The fact is that there is what Y. Singh (1973) calls *Modernization of Indian Tradition*, comprising of both culture and structure, micro and macro patterns and levels of social reality and orthogenetic and heterogenetic sources of change. Caste has been shaped and reshaped in terms of such a complex situation of Indian society. Status dissonance between caste and class, particularly at the micro level has always been there due to the lack of a perfect fit between caste cleavages and class divisions. However, caste has often been appropriated as a device through which class relations are marked and thus perpetuated (Singh, 1973, 13). Mencher (1991, 109) substantiates such a view on caste. She writes: 'The caste system has functioned to prevent the formation of social classes with commonality of interests and purpose. In other words, caste derives its viability from its partial marking of extreme socio-economic differences'. Castes are internally divided by class differences, and classes are at times unified in terms of caste identities, despite the fact that there is persistence of some caste ideology and class stratification. Thus, the space that caste occupies vis-à-vis class and power in determining status is a matter of a great significance, and also the extent of incorporation of caste into class and power and vice versa is equally important in our future studies.

While concluding, Searle-Chatterjee and Sharma (2003, 19–21) observe that caste groups are now coming to sound suspiciously like ethnic groups, within the modern polity which are largely endogamous. 'Difference'/'distance' is key to caste groups, particularly in the urban context. Two points are specifically stated by Searle-Chatterjee and Sharma (2003). (a) Caste can be seen as one among several principles of classification which can be drawn upon for particular purposes. For example, in what context notions of 'purity' and 'honour' are used, and 'who uses the language of caste to whom and when'? (b) What are the ecological and social parameters for particular types of kinship of caste systems?

CASTE, CLASS AND POWER

So far we have analysed that caste is not reducible to class and vice versa. Caste is also not an explosive class as perceived by some Marxist scholars, but it has not been simply a socio-religious and ritualistic system. Class in India functions within the context of caste, and also independent of caste. This is true of caste as well. Caste–class nexus, not correspondence, has always existed (Sharma, 2014a, 338–354). Caste and class are mutually inherent phenomena in different contexts and situations. The ideas of 'contra-priest' (Gould, 1967) and 'reverse hierarchy' (Smaje, 2000), 'hegemony of feudalism over the caste system' (Sharma, 1994, 209–224) are some of the examples of caste–class nexus, and not of correspondence between caste and class rankings. Even class basis of the caste system has been explicated in several studies (Sharma, 2014a). Castes have been functioning as classes in real life to a considerable extent, with the exceptions like poor Brahmins, well off lower castes, landless middle castes etc.

Early studies like *Caste, Class and Power* (Beteille, 1965), *Caste, Class and Politics* (Bhatt, 1975), *Caste, Religion and Power* (Aggarwal, 1971) and *The Changing Rural Stratification System* (Sharma, 1974) bring out that caste is not an encompassing system as it has been argued by Srinivas, Dumont, and many others. Studies of social mobility and structural changes, migration, conflicting claims, and feuds relating to land, property and resources clearly indicate presence of 'class' in everyday life as a stark social reality. Coexistence of caste and class as interconnected phenomena and also as independent entities has been reported in many studies. A close nexus between caste and agrarian class structure has been found in Bihar (Chakravarti, 2004, 47–88). Chakravarti writes: 'My argument is that agrarian class relations in Bihar are embedded in caste because whether a person controls land or not is conditioned by that person's caste status'. Due to caste-related factors, a substantial segment of rural Bihar continues to be subjected to extreme forms of exploitation. Chakravarti names the exploited landless agricultural labourers as the *underclass*. Caste and class are not two distinctly compartmentalized phenomena as seen by Chakravarti. While agreeing with Ashok Rudra (1978, 916), who follows Marx on class (1975, 159–160), Chakravarti observes that 'a full exploration of the interface between caste and class should highlight not only antagonistic relations of production—arising from the role of caste in determining, or denying, access to land-but also how these relations translate into class struggles' (2004, 48). Violence in rural Bihar is neither symptomatic of 'class war' between 'landlords' and the 'landless', nor of 'caste-war' between dominant castes and subordinate castes (Dalits).

In rural Bihar, dichotomy between caste and class is a false one as the contradictions of 'caste' are also that of 'class'. As such, Chakravarti rejects Dumont's interpretation of 'caste-system' as a 'structure of ideas'. Power is not subordinate to hierarchy, Chakravarti says while discarding Dumont's understanding of caste. Caste is also not 'superstructure'. Following Godelier (1978, 763), Chakravarti agrees that superstructure and infrastructure represent *functional* spheres that are found in all societies (2004, 50). Functions of caste and class are not clearly defined and earmarked. In such a situation, caste would also perform certain crucial economic functions by determining access to land, control over the labour process, and the form of exploitation (Chakravarti, 2004, 51; Habib, 1995, 176). This shows the economic/material significance of caste by way of its role in organizing 'relations of production and reproduction' (Meillassoux, 1973, 92, 100–101). Caste, thus, could be seen in terms of class. Caste becomes as such the ideology of rationalization of class relations. *Jajmani* system was used as an institutionalized means of dominance/subordination. Beneath the caste hierarchy lies the relations of class—that of patrons and clients. Chakravarti (2004, 52) suggests a framework, imbibing of the basic elements of both caste and class to understand rural India.

Such a framework is needed to expose the nexus between caste, class, power and the state as this results in the oppression of the underclass. Agrarian reforms have largely failed due to privatization of the coercive functions of the state (Das, 1983). The fact is that 'the gulf between the underclass and the dominant class has widened in those areas where agriculture has developed along capitalist lines' (Chakravarti, 2004, 61). In conclusion, Chakravarti (2004, 78) observes: 'My basic argument (....) is that caste continues to be the fundamental basis of social inequality in contemporary Bihar, (....) both the traditional and new dominant castes have privileged access to material and political resources, and constitute the dominant class'.

K. L. Sharma (2010; 2014a, 207–209) explains that the nexus between caste and class, and its continuity and change is evident in the structural and processual aspects of social stratification. Intra-caste competition for economic gains indicates 'class' in caste, and parallels between caste hierarchy and economic standing show the presence of caste in class and vice versa. Beteille (2007, 945–952) finds that identity politics, mainly in terms of caste, and economic inequalities or disparities of wealth, occupation and income coexist side by side. There are large and increasing economic inequalities among individuals, households, and communities (castes), and these are structured and projected in the political arena. Sabharwal (2006) observes that middle class plays a major role in identity politics. Educated middle class is dominated by the upper castes. Class relations are mediated by castes (Stern, 2003, 56–87). The distinction between caste and class is blurred at the ground level when we notice social climbing through sanskritization, and the failure of land reforms as described by Chakravarti (2004) and Das (1983) due to the use of political muscle.

A couple of questions (Sharma, 2014a, 209) may be raised here regarding caste–class nexus:

1. Is caste a barrier in social and occupational mobility?
2. How have the rules of caste rank or strength or political networks been evaluated in upward mobility?
3. Can a person not receive education irrespective of his/her caste rank?
4. Can someone not migrate to a town if he/she is of a lower caste?

These questions become important to know the incorporation of class into caste and vice versa, and particularly to understand the formation of a new class structure.

Deshpande (2003) mentions that caste is being challenged not by way of sanskritization, but through competition for power and scarce material and cultural resources by the Dalits and the OBCs. Caste is not, in itself, a sufficient condition to ensure entry into the privileged group.

CASTE AND SOCIAL MOBILITY

James Silverberg (1968, 7–8), in an edited volume *Social Mobility in the Caste System in India*, has specified the following points for debate by the participants:

1. Who is evaluating?
2. Whether or not ranking is a matter of local consensus?
3. Whether the ranking of castes and other aggregates reflect the social interaction between their members or their distinctive behavioural attributes, real or stereotyped?
4. To which activity contexts, these international or attributional criteria of rank refer—contexts, such as ritual prestige, power-wielding, economic influence.
5. Whether the criteria of rank are employed consistently?

The participants of the symposium, held on the above theme, were also asked to spell out the aspired but unrealized 'social mobility' and actual change in rank by way of wealth, political power or connections, educational attainment, ritual symbols, etc. Change in the caste rank and its acceptance by other castes were also the points of the debate. Thus, by the end of the 1950s and early 1960s, when Dumont talked of caste as an ideational system, James Silverberg, Bernard Barber, Edward B. Harper, William L. Rowe, Burton Stein, Y. B. Damle and Mckim Marriott, the participants in the above cited symposium (1968), were debating on social mobility in the caste system both as historical and contextual phenomenon.

Barber holds responsible the heavy reliance of many scholars on the official, orthodox, system-maintaining ideology in describing and comprehending the caste system, as immobile and anti-egalitarian. Recent researches abundantly reveal movement, conflict and change vis-à-vis the caste system. Harper, based on comprehensive data gathered from myriad sources, analyses changes in the interaction of Brahman landowners and untouchable (Holeru) labourers. Changes cover over a period of a century and a half, from a relationship of 'slavery' through contractual life indentureship, to a present-day mixture of unstable temporary indentureship, occasional part-tenancy, and part-wage labourer. The 'untouchables' gain by way of 'sanskritization', but also tend to suffer because of reduced dependence of the patrons on them on occasions of rituals and ceremonies. They accept the idea of a hierarchically ranked society, but do not accept their own low rank as they have sanskritized and have a more prestigious self-image, linking themselves to the pan-Indian *Harijan* movement or larger urban middle-class culture.

The other field study in the volume is presented by Rowe, relating to a caste mobility movement of a scheduled caste in Northern India (Agra). Over a period of half a century, the *Noniyas* used their economic power to claim and eventually to gain a partially successful entry into the higher Kshatriya *varna* rank (Chauhan Rajput).

Burton Stein discusses social mobility during the 15th century in South Indian sects. He observes: 'They became fully integrated into the functioning ritual system of the greatest South Indian temples of the time' (Silverberg, 1968, 16). Such a change was a challenge to the existing stratification system and its orthodoxy. Ultimately, more enduring was individual mobility on the part of the low-caste persons. Such mobile individuals were able to achieve status–roles, equal to that of Brahmins.

McKim Marriott's paper (1968, 103–113) provides a comprehensive theoretical framework for an empirical study of mobility in Indian caste system. Marriott distinguishes: (a) 'rural from metropolitan types of ranking systems, (b) individuals or groups from corporate units in ranking and (c) a series of successively wider zones of reference for the units in any local system, the several zones generally being characterized by distinctive values' (ibid., 103). Marriott states: 'Villagers even when acting within their villages may require us to make all of these distinctions, for each village contains several kinds of rankings and is part of larger systems of stratification which reach beyond it' (ibid., 113). 'Multiple reference' applies to both urban and rural settings, but to see 'urban' and 'rural' systems of stratification as dichotomous, negates the parameters of ranking applicable to both the settings. India's metropolises and towns and villages of the 1960s are not the same in 2017. To call rural stratification as 'interactional' and urban as 'attributional' (Man in India, 1959, 92–107) would undermine the role of 'group' in urban context, and the place of 'individual' in the rural setting. 'Individual prestige' is acknowledged by Marriott, but its determinants as perceived by him are at variance in the urban and the rural settings. Education, employment, income and standard of living are common criteria today applicable to both urban and rural situations.

Marriott refers to three zones in the context of the mobility of castes: (a) the zone of the village community and its directly connected part of the countryside, (b) the zone of the recognized cultural or linguistic region, and (c) the zone of the whole civilization (Marriott, 1965, 16–19). In understanding of caste mobility, all the references to zone, are necessary points, keeping also in mind the contrast between closed, interactional, rural systems of stratification on the one hand and open, attributional, urban systems on the other (Marriott, 1968, 114). People may refer their behaviour to either or both kinds of contrasting systems. For each caste, in relation to ranking and mobility, local, regional, sectarian, civilizational, or national hierarchies and audiences need to be taken into consideration. 'Only with these multiple worlds in our minds can we hope to comprehend that castes move not only among social positions, but also among realms of thought' (Marriott, 1968, 114). 'Ranking and mobility, then, are analytically distinguishable for the individual, for the secularly ranked household and/or extended family, for the ritually ranked corporate caste, and perhaps for aggregates of an intermediate nature' (Silverberg, 1968, 126–127).

Anomalies have always been there regarding ranks of different castes. Claims for caste ranks have often been rejected and accepted by other castes. There is not much ambiguity regarding the top ranking and lowest castes. Even then all Brahmin castes/sub-castes do not enjoy the same status/rank. Compared to the *Gaur/Adi* Gaur Brahmins, the other Brahmin castes/sub-castes are perceived as inferior, for example, in Rajasthan, Haryana and Western Uttar Pradesh. Even Banias and Jains claim themselves ritually superior than Rajputs in north-west Rajasthan, though Rajputs were a ruling caste, and were at the second rank after Brahmins. Among the intermediate castes, such anomalies are more pronounced, particularly among Jats, *Ahirs,* Gurjars, *Malis,* etc., in parts of Rajasthan. Some functionary castes and their chosen families who enjoyed patronage of the *Jagirdars* (landlords) enjoyed higher status than members of slightly higher castes and also higher status compared to the other families of their own castes. Such a situation also indicates that feudalism (*Jagirdari* system) was more powerful and decisive over that priestly order. Brahmins were even at times ridiculed by other castes when they accepted *dan* (gift and offering) on occasions like death. A lot of articulation about life-ways and practices pursued by Brahmins, Banias, Rajputs, Jats, Gurjars, *Chamars*, etc., have been prevalent and uttered to pull down each other. In other words, there has not been a clearly defined and accepted yardstick to rank castes, except in terms of ritualistic consideration. Each caste, though was linked to other castes, not necessarily in a symmetrical/reciprocal manner. A particular caste was an insulated, segregated entity, having its own set of norms and practices, including relations with other castes, higher, lower and equal ones (Sharma, 1998).

Social mobility is quite a complex phenomenon. After Independence, the lower and depressed castes had a sigh of relief from the dictates of the *Jagirdars* and *Zamindars* (Rajputs) and priests (Brahmins). To assert their existence in the new situation, they started discarding of traditional occupations performed under the jajmani system. Some of them imitated Brahmanic lifestyle and cultural practices, such as keeping fast, celebrating certain rituals and festivals, wearing of western dress, and naming themselves as done by the upper castes, particularly Rajputs. Such a process was a sort of cultural mobility (sanskritization). But soon, the emancipated castes realized that it was not enough, without corresponding economic and political empowerment. Realising the importance and value of economic and political empowerment, the castes, families and individuals aspiring for upward mobility began to climb the social ladder without ignoring sanskritization as an effective means of status-emulation.

Today, people realize that caste as a system is more or less dead as it has become ineffective in everyday life. However, individual castes have been active in certain respects to seek access to resources and benefits from given programmes in both public and private spheres. Even M. N. Srinivas (1996, 2003) talked of the passing away/an obituary of caste as a system. A. M. Shah (2007, 109–116), while endorsing Srinivas' view on caste, quotes him:

> Indian rural society is moving from status to contract. An essential characteristic of the system was hierarchy, which expressed itself in the idiom of ritual purity and impurity. This hierarchy is breaking down under the impact of new ideas of democracy, equality, and individual

self-respect. While caste as a system is dead or dying, individual castes are thriving. (Srinivas, 2003, 459)

Even G. S. Ghurye (1932, 26–28), much before Srinivas and many other scholars, had observed that caste as a community and caste patriotism were increasing at the expense of harmony of parts.

Caste has never been uniform as a functioning institution. A. M. Shah and I. P. Desai (1988) observed that it would be false to assume that the nature of caste in cities was the same as that in villages in the past. Caste in urban India has acquired increasing silence. Shah (2007, 110) notes two social facts regarding caste, namely, (a) since the people of different castes are spread both in villages and in towns, the culture of the urban section in any caste spreads easily to its rural section; and (b) the urban centres wield disproportionately greater influence in society as a whole in comparison with the size of their population, hence urban caste will overwhelm rural caste during the 21st century. However, such a divide between urban and rural caste(s) is quite debatable issue. Rigidity–flexibility of caste as D'Souza (1967) observes refers to *social status* as a common denominator of the caste and the class societies. Both are rigid and fluid in varying proportions. As such, the individual and his status (even with the caste-fold) become the basis of ranking. The question is as follows: Is class replacing caste and individual is replacing the group as the system and unit of social stratification?

Often it has been observed that caste is a characteristic system of India's agrarian way of life, and class is a product of urban industrial development. But now it is a well-accepted fact that agrarian classes, such as big landowners, rich farmers, middle peasants, poor and small cultivators/landowners and landless agrarian workers form agrarian stratification in class terms as one could see the urban industrial classes. In a recent article, Sonali Desai and Amaresh Dubey (2011, 40–49), based on a study of 41,554 households, conducted in 2005, suggest continued presence of caste disparities in education, income and social networks. Today, caste is required to be studied as a phenomenon, and not as a hierarchy. Desai and Dubey state that caste in the 21st century would transform from hierarchy to elite capture (2011, 47). They observe that: 'the results show that status hierarchies seen to be on the decline with considerable civic and political participation by marginalized groups, but economic and educational disparities between large caste groupings continue to flourish. The discourse on caste keeping the vision of social hierarchy based on purity and pollution has lost its appeal. New models of social stratification in India based on class relations would be perhaps more relevant in the present-day situation. However, Desai and Dubey find that education and skill remain closely associated with caste. They observe: 'Children from lower castes continue to be educationally disadvantaged compared to children from the upper caste' (Desai and Dubey, 2011, 47). Despite religious and ideological decline of caste and emergence of market mechanisms, material resources remain consolidated in the hands of certain groups, particularly Brahmins. Caste associations play a significant role in consolidation of economic and political domination of some castes in India.

CONTINUITY AND CHANGE IN THE CASTE SYSTEM

A. M. Shah (2007, 109–116) also observes that caste as a system is more or less dead, however, individual castes are flourishing. Every individual caste has had complex internal structure and organization. 'There was considerable economic, social and political differentiation in every caste. No caste should be viewed as a monolith, with its members having had egalitarian relationships in the past' (Shah, 2007, 114–115). Shah analyses how the dynamics of individual caste is likely to be dominant feature of caste during the 21st century. Today, we have to identify hierarchy, in terms of its changing nature, and place individual castes in the changing social and cultural environment. Caste has a peculiar tenacity for its continuity and change (Beteille, 2012, 41–48). Generally, in post-Independence India, caste has been viewed both, as antithetical to democracy and as an essential part to play in the advancement of democracy. Media has played a significant role to argue the salience of caste in Indian society. In not-so-significant situations even, media has acquired a tendency to highlight the so-called 'caste factor' and or 'caste question'. Besides the Indian media, a couple of social scientists, including Srinivas (1962, 1987, 1995), Kothari (1975) and Rudolph and Rudolph (1967, 1987) have argued that caste has not been antithetical to democracy, and at times it has functioned as an 'interest group' in electoral process and sharing of political power. Beteille (2012, 42–43) observes that three basic aspects of caste have undergone a considerable change. These are: (a) the observance of the rules relating to purity and pollution; (b) the regulation of marriage according to the rules of caste; and (c) the relation between caste and occupation. These changes have made caste weak, less stringent and more flexible. Caste survives despite such relational changes. For example, caste-based reservations and caste-based mobilization in elections have kept caste consciousness alive. Khap panchayats, taking advantage of such a consciousness, impose stringent punishments on the violators of rules of caste endogamy and clan exogamy.

Besides the presence of caste in reservations, elections and politics, it has been reported to be there in gender relations, education, public goods distribution, religion, entrepreneurship, etc. The nature of society, in terms of gendering of statues and roles, economic standings or class differences, the schools which children attend—government, ordinary private, good English/convent, etc.—would make a difference in terms of caste background. In some parts of India, segregation between higher and lower castes' children has been reported in the schools. Differential treatment given to sons and daughters at home is reflected in the schools which they attend and also in facilitating higher education and having jobs thereafter. Even the projects sponsored by the governmental agencies smell caste bias. Rishabh Khosla (2011, 63–69), based on his study of Andhra Pradesh, finds that the functioning of Panchayati Raj institutions is highly context-dependent. 'There are tremendous variations in socio-politics, caste-competition, and local institutions, all of them conspire to influence the outcome of reservations' (Khosla, 2011, 68). Political parties and caste alliances influence the operation of the Mahatma Gandhi National Rural Employment Guarantee Scheme (MNREGS). While analysing the gender-caste overlap, Ashwini Deshpande and Smriti Sharma (2013, 38–49) have reported that the SC and ST women are doubly disadvantaged on account of their gender and their low-caste status. They have been subject to greater material deprivation and oppression, while they have experienced greater egalitarian gender relations within the family, as well as fewer restrictions on mobility (Deshpande and Sharma, 45). On the contrary, upper caste women have enjoyed relative material prosperity, but have been subject to greater immurement and constraints on public visibility.

Every part of India has had rigid or somewhat flexible caste system in terms of observance of its norms and practices. Even in West Bengal, which remained under the rule of the left parties for more than three decades, caste is as much a political-economic reality as a ritual one. The domination of the modern liberal *bhadralok* remains intact even today, whereas challenge to the traditional dominance of Brahmins and other upper castes over the 20th century had been quite strong. Like elsewhere, in West Bengal, emulation, acculturation and assimilation have been accepted by the Namasudras (a lower caste) to sanskritize their social standing. The *bhadralok* have even resisted such efforts on the part of the *Namasudras*. 'West Bengal is, in any sense, an exception to wider realities of caste, it is in the continued dominance of the upper-caste *bhadralok* over the rest of the society' (Chandra and Nielsen, 2012, 60). Caste remains in West Bengal certainly a political resource in politics prominently as a category that shapes local relations of power and influence. However, it is observed that due to the relative retreat of the left in West Bengal, the possibility and scope of identity-based (caste-based) political mobilization may definitely increase (Kumar and Guha, 2014, 73–74).

Caste-class identities are quite interconnected in complex ways in Andhra Pradesh (1956–2014) as reported by N. Purendra Prasad (2015, 77–83). Disparities in agrarian structure are quite evident in terms of caste conflicts, violence and dissent. 'In coastal Andhra there were intense caste conflicts between the rich peasant class and that of landless, tenants and agricultural workers belonging to Dalits during 1985 and 1991' (Prasad, 2015, 81). However, in a north Indian state like Uttar Pradesh, there is no doubt decline of caste representation in the bigger parties like the Congress and the BJP, but the state-based parties like the SP and the BSP are exclusivist caste-oriented parties.

There are divergent views on the role of caste in occupational/social mobility. Kumar et al. (2002, 2983–2987; 2002a, 4091–4096)

observe that class origins make a substantial difference to class destinations (upward mobility), and argue that caste is not a good predictor
of mobility. However, Dalits have been benefited by getting into the
salaried class. On the other hand, Rajeshwari Deshpande and Suhas
Palshikar (2008, 61–69), though support the above view regarding
upward mobility among Dalits, they, however, have seen that some
caste groups were located in particular occupational categories one
or two generations ago, and they had a clearly differentiated occupational location, and this shows the effects at the present juncture.
'This underscores the need to take into account the relevance of
caste in plotting occupational differences across caste groups' (Kumar
et al., 2002, 68).

Caste in urban and rural contexts does not function in the same
way. Occupational trajectories in the two contexts are quite different. The urban people draw a line between their cultural-symbolic
universe and secular-material life, thus, make a balance between
'caste' and 'non-caste' factors and spheres of activities. Kumar et al.
observe that

> caste is important for upward movement in the sense that the middle
> peasant and Dalit castes are indeed making progress in real terms.
> This is due to resources, opportunities and power structure in the
> case of Maratha-Kunbis and affirmative action and urban location
> combined with the background of social awakening in the case of
> Dalits. (2002, 68)

The concepts of 'sanskritization', 'dominant caste', the idea of 'pure-
impure' and 'hierarchy' are seen quite relevant and useful by some
scholars. A. M. Shah (2005, 238–249) states that the use of the concept
of sanskritization cannot be limited to emulation of the culture of high
castes by the lower castes for upward mobility, because caste hierarchy
is gradually getting dissociated from sanskritization, and many non-caste
structures and institutions have become its powerful agents. This has
led to greater sanskritization of the society as a whole.

Beteille (2002) puts now more emphasis on inequalities of wealth
and power than that of caste. Besides caste, family and individual are

equally or even more effective limits and factors in social mobility (Sharma, 1974). There are several contradictions today relating to functioning of the caste system. For example, untouchability is declining, but incidences of violence against the lower castes have increased. Beteille is of the view that today inequality is more through the family route, rather than caste or even class (2005). K. L. Sharma has posed the question: 'Is there no caste or class vis-à-vis family?' (2014a, 204). A number of contributors to the volume edited by Mary Searle Chatterjee and Ursula Sharma (2003) claim to 'put caste in its place'. They critically question the ritualistic notions of caste and offer explanation of caste in relation to other important dimensions. Some contributors consider monarchy/kingship equating with political and ritual aspect of the dominant caste as an important dimension. The concept of 'territoriality' is also seen important in relation to local dominance and self-description. K. L. Sharma (2014a, 204) observes:

> Caste is more a resource that political actors use in order to negotiate their status, wealth, and power. Today, there are multiple references in classification of people. Political power, networks, wealth and assets, income, occupation are all used to assess people as individuals and families, which may not be true with caste hierarchy.

Even Srinivas (2003, 455–459) argues that factors that could uproot the caste system would take a long time; hence it would persist, despite the destruction of the caste-based system of production in the villages at the local level. K. L. Sharma (2014a, 205) has raised the following questions:

- Who cares for caste?
- In what matters does one think of caste?
- Can there be caste without inter-caste relations?
- What is the nature of inter-caste relations?
- Who from among different castes appropriate caste for vested political or some other interests?
- Is caste represented by such appropriators for its progress as a whole?
- How is this done?

CONCLUDING REMARKS

One needs to address such questions to know caste as a system and caste as a phenomenon. Sharma (2001) has suggested a three-pronged strategy to understand caste in a comprehensive manner: (a) caste–class nexus: its continuity and change, (b) changing character of intra-caste and inter-caste relations; and (c) nature of practice and levels of mobility in the caste system. While attempting reconceptualization of caste, K. L. Sharma (2014a, 251–252) has formulated the following questions:

1. How and to what extent ideas and values are important to know actual and observable behaviour of people?
2. In what way clichés such as tradition and modernity, continuity and change, hierarchy and stratification, organic and segmentary structures have led to unfounded dichotomies/antinomies of a resilient and harmonic society?
3. Why does one find a revival of a culturo-logical framework to look once again at Indian society through caste and religion?

We conclude the discussion on caste by saying that 'caste for itself' and caste as an everyday life phenomenon are two different aspects, generally unrelated to each other. In the first case, caste is an episodic, metaphoric and goal-oriented phenomenon; and in the second sense, it is a discrete, personalized and family-specific behavioural/interactional phenomenon. Both the interpretations are not in tune with the 'caste model' of Indian society. New status dynamics and power relations are being determined by a multiplicity of factors, and 'caste' is one of them, and that too not as a persistent one.

A couple of scholars observe that even when the institution of caste and other structures associated with it have changed, caste has not disappeared. Caste-based decisions and inequalities continue to matter and generally overlap with new disparities (Jodhka, 2015). Jodhka writes: 'The realities of caste in contemporary times are also not exhausted by analyses of electoral politics. Caste matters in multiple ways and in different spheres of social, economic and political life—sometimes visibly, sometimes not so visibly' (Jodhka, 2015, XIV). The reality of caste has been quite diverse in different parts of India. A uniform yardstick to measure the reality of caste becomes a difficult task. Jodhka asks the question: What kinds of conceptual frameworks have been used to study caste and where have they come from? In response to this question, Jodhka (2015,1–18) analyses the following points:

1. The popular view of caste (textual)
2. Conceptual trajectories of caste
   a. Caste as tradition,
   b. Caste as power and
   c. Caste as a system of humiliation and discrimination.

The last point in the conceptual trajectories, namely, caste as a system of humiliation and discrimination seems to be the main concern in Jodhka's understanding of caste. The Dalit question occupies the centre stage in the discourse on caste. Emergence of Dalit identity posed a threat to the earlier Brahmanic and colonial constructions of caste. Caste becomes, thus, a system of domination and exclusion, disparities (inequalities of resources), and discrimination and denials.

The question is: Can a system like caste survive for such a long time having humiliation and discrimination alone as its core value and practice? Our experience of a town, namely, Chanderi (Sharma, 1999) indicates that different castes and communities interact and mix up showing clearly 'pragmatism' required for day-to-day life and living. Moreover, our visits to some villages in Rajasthan are a clear pointer to mixing up of upper, middle and lower castes, without placing much emphasis on social segregation and distance. It is not because of electoral gains to be earned by the upper castes; it is a gradual realization of the fact that the old values and norms would not work anymore because of the overall change in the country and in the state of Rajasthan. Sharing of public space is a well-recognized fact, and even in private domain discrimination is consciously avoided so that message goes out for equality and dignity of all the castes and communities. Despite such a changed situation, there are certain families and individuals who are not so open to the wave of social and cultural equality, and keep themselves somewhat aloof on the occasions that demand sharing of social and cultural space by both upper and lower caste members. There are no dictates regarding observance of particular norms by the elders of different castes, nor there is presence of caste councils/panchayats to issue directions to its members. However, the fact is that at times to seek reservations or favours from the government, caste-based mobilizations could be noticed. Caste has become a mutilated institution, and has given a way to status and power of select families and individuals who do not form a 'dominant caste', or even an amalgamation of different castes as such.

Chapter 3

Caste, Inequality and Social Mobility

Caste dynamics have acquired strange contradictory dimensions since Independence. Caste has ceased to exist as a 'system', and therefore, systemic caste dominance, power, subjugation and oppression also do not persist. However, caste as a notion, as a phenomenon and as a self-created mechanism by societal 'foxes', using V. Pareto's idea (1935), can be seen in different fields of life, particularly in the political domain. At times, caste is viewed in terms of the 'powerful' and the 'powerless'. Some have associated almost everything with caste, including science and technology, distribution of goods and services, hygiene and sanitation, poverty and unemployment, language and speech acts, professional proficiency, gendering, entrepreneurship, ideology, etc. It seems that there is nothing beyond caste. Dumont (1970a), though with a different perspective, talks of the 'encompassing' and the 'encompassed'; upper caste hegemony in the case of encompassing, and the lower caste subjugation in regard to the encompassed. The pure–impure syndrome, as binary opposition, but as parts of an organic whole (caste system), can be seen in the present-day functioning of caste.

CASTE AS A PRACTICE OF DISCRIMINATION

By implication, today the big divide is between the upper caste people and Dalits. There should be no barriers, particularly political and cultural, between the two. Castes are a preserve of the upper castes, and hence there is a need to annihilate this by every possible way. Although such a view was held by Bolmurli Natrajan (2013, 16–19) and some other scholars, there are different findings as well (Iyer, Khanna and Varshney, 2013, 52–59). It is observed that the SCs, the STs and particularly the OBCs have made significant progress in the political domain. The OBCs have made far more progress in entrepreneurship than the SCs and STs. The political gains made by the SCs and STs are not reflected in their entrepreneurial status. There are some Dalit millionaires, but they are not representative of their presence in numerical context. One main reason is that the SCs and STs do not have strong networks required for entrepreneurship.

Ashwini Deshpande, in her book *The Grammar of Caste: Economic Discrimination in India* (2011), argues that economic outcomes are shaped by caste identity. Caste identity invokes economic decisions and practices. Economic preferences, choices and limitations are ingrained in the caste system. Deshpande discusses the economic outcome of the caste system in terms of caste and gender disparities in human development, as also endorsed by Thorat (2012, 32–34). Deshpande uses the term 'Caste Development Index'. Thorat writes: 'She comes out with strong evidence of persistence of caste disparity, and also indicates that the scheduled castes (SCs) continue to belong to the lowest rung of the economic ladder, calling into question any notion of substantial upward mobility' (Thorat, 2012, 33). The problem with Deshpande's view and also with the endorsement by Thorat is that they ignore the fact that caste as a system has ceased to exist, and caste as a notion, as a phenomenon, persists. Because caste as a system does not persist, there is upwards social mobility among the SCs and the OBCs, and also to a noticeable extent, there is 'downward social mobility' (K. L. Sharma, 1973) among the upper castes, who were ritually higher and also had control over land and resources.

However, Thorat and Sadana (2009, 13–16) observe that in the private sphere enterprises by the SCs and STs are much less in both rural and urban areas in proportion to their population in the country. The businesses run by the SCs and STs are mainly household enterprises organized around family labour, and they are also a lot poorer than other caste members. Once again the question is: To what extent and in what way caste as a system is penetrating into businesses and enterprises run by different castes? Can the idea of pure–impure in metropolises like Delhi, Mumbai, Kolkata, Chennai, Bengaluru and Hyderabad help the upper castes and harm the SCs and STs? Certainly, 'casteism' has surfaced as a means of political mobilization, and as a way for extending favours to one's own caste members in some cases. But there is nothing 'ascriptive' in casteism, except that a person, who indulges in such a narrow practice, has some idea of his own caste/sub-caste, different from other castes. It is a sort of false 'consciousness of kind' and a feeling of ethnocentrism. Such a feeling may be short-lived, contextual and influenced by some contingent factors, such as discrimination, disadvantage, humiliation, etc., on the part of a particular member of a given caste.

Gopal Guru and Sundar Sarukkai (2014, 27–29) claim, through an unusual sociological experiment, to know about caste, through motivated writings in the Kannad daily *Prajavani* in 2013. Their aim was to know: Do caste experiences and untouchability really exist in India, particularly in urban and middle-class India? Based on the public articulations of caste, Guru and Sarukkai mention that gated communities are now strongly becoming 'casted-communities'. Our view is that talking about caste in print or orally is different from practising caste as a system in everyday life. The mechanisms by which ethics/norms of caste system were put in practice in the past in all aspects of life are no more seen in both rural and urban India. The occasional so-called caste-related incidences are not indicative of caste as a system of social relations, rather these have deeper political and other implications of the self-appointed leaders/guardians of particular castes/sub-castes. Decisions of Khap panchayats in Haryana are an example of such a situation. Reservations, no doubt, have helped a select section of the SCs, the STs and the OBCs, but such a policy has evoked 'casteism' among the beneficiary castes/families and also among those who have remained deprived of the benefits of reservations. Reservations do not imply revival of the caste system/casteism, but its unanticipated consequences have created feelings of division between the chosen beneficiaries and the rest.

CASTE AS AN OMNIPRESENT PHENOMENON

There is a tendency to see caste in almost every field, including science, technology, communication, language, culture, media, etc. It has become a common feature to look for caste in schools, hostels, hotels and restaurants, markets, enterprises, jobs, politics, gender, etc. 'Caste' is appropriated by creating its nuance in all the possible ways. When such an 'adventure' fails, permutations and combinations of different castes/sub-castes are attempted, particularly in elections. Identity of caste is accorded undue importance when caste as a system does not help (Gupta, 2005, 409–427). 'Caste Associations' are used for political goals, and not for social and cultural dictates of the caste system (Rudolph and Rudolph, 1967, 29–36). Based on the Content Analysis of 44 magazines founded for caste-related publications in 21 cities of Uttar Pradesh, Sumit Chaturvedi (2014, 33–37) mentions that print culture plays an important role in election times by way of printing everything about a given caste to attract attention of voters. Chaturvedi (2014, 37) concludes as follows:

> Thus print capitalism serves the interest of the modern urban individuals who despite their claims for objectivity, secularism and egalitarianism can still maintain a caste identity for personal and political ends, without explicitly participating in caste activities, but by merely subscribing to a print commodity. The print culture thus becomes a cultural component of the caste subculture and also the space for its observance.

The upper castes in the big cities have more of such a print culture as they are more resourceful for political activities. In recent times, India has moved beyond the caste system, but it is still not out of 'caste'. Some castes have their social and cultural identity by remaining attached to their respective temples. Association of a religious nature also provides a political mileage to particular castes. This is particularly seen in case of lower castes in rural India.

AMBIGUITIES AND CONFUSIONS REGARDING 'CASTE'

Many scholars hold the view that caste is a new idea produced by the British through its census operations, particularly from the Census of

1901 conducted by Herbert Risley. Caste was seen prior to British as a system of social division of labour and functional gradations, without hardly any space for hierarchy and power (N. B. Dirks, 2003). Padmanabh Samarendra (2011, 51–58) mentions that the British defined and classified castes on a single pan-India list, where each caste had to be 'discrete, homogeneous and enumerable'. All types of social hierarchies and identities that existed at the time were subsumed uniformly under the term 'caste'. Samarendra, emphatically adopting a contrasting stance, writes: 'I argue that caste, as conceived in contemporary academic writings or within the policies of the state, is a new idea and that the social form imagined through this term never characterized the Indian society' (2011, 51). There is a lot of confusion regarding the terms 'caste', 'varna' and 'jati' among the scholars such as M. N. Srinivas (1962) and Mckim Marriott and Ronald Inden (1977, 227–318) as these have differing connotations and also do not reflect the real differences and statuses and their permutations and combinations among the people of India. Samarendra observes:

> Caste, I believe, cannot be equated either with *varna* or *jati*. The components of the *varna* are not indeterminate; yet, these are not empirically verifiable. The presence of jatis, on the other hand, can be observed; however, these never had a singular and uniform identity in the Indian society. Caste thus is fundamentally different from both *varna* and *jati;* yet because of its associations with both *varna*-names and *jati*-practices struck in the course of the census operations, it has been misconceived as a component of indigenous society. (2011, 57)

As a consequence of definitional confusion regarding the terms such as caste, *jati* and *varna*, different versions of racial theory of caste were given by Risley (1969), Nesfield (1885) and Sarat Chandra Roy (1927). Such views allowed 'racist ideas', implying superiority of the Europeans over the Indian people. It also accorded approval to the caste-based discrimination, hereditary supremacy and justification for caste as a rigid system of stratification. No doubt, there were strong reactions to such a colonized perspective on caste. The science of genetics was appropriated to argue that Indians were a 'single race', with its regional and cultural differences, but not comparable with Europeans.

Science influenced the racial theory of caste; and scientific practice was influenced by the social uses (Samarendra, 2011, 48). Such a view is scientifically not sound and socio-politically a fraudulent argument.

Another viewpoint is presented by Mãrzabu Jal (2014, 41–49), stressing the relevance of 'revolutionary Marxism' to understand India's caste system. The Indian left needs to see the real implications of the idea of Asiatic Mode of Production as enunciated by Karl Marx. This needs to be seen by avoiding Eurocentric reasoning and the search for a fictitious 'Indian feudalism'. Based on an elaborate discussion, Jal makes some observations on caste which we would briefly mention here. 'One thought that modernity and modern industry would destroy caste, but caste sat comfortably on the seat of this modern industry. True, caste alliances and power structures change continuously, but caste per se refuses to leave' (Jal, 2014, 46). The bourgeoisie accommodated themselves in the caste system, and became allies of the RSS and Khap panchayat leaders and made caste as the base rather than a superstructure. It was only B. R. Ambedkar (2008) who advocated 'annihilation of caste'.

Caste is a peculiar mode of social stratification and control; it is *clannish oligarchy*. 'Caste is basically inherited class status, or simply frozen classes that are reified and hyperostosised and based on segregation' (Jal, 2014, 47). Caste is a status based on the double ideas of graded inequality and division of labour. It is a structure of human alienation and a form of social exclusion. Casteism is equivalent to racism. Jal (2014, 48) observes that caste in this sense is no longer class on a primitive level of production. It is an essential part of the most modern of moderns, mimicking not only the German form of fascism, but also the Israeli form of imperialist occupation.

Jal, no doubt, makes some quite bold observations, equating Ambedkarism with revolutionary Marxism as Ambedkar alone gave a call for rooting out caste from Indian soil and Marx considered caste as class, in effect. As we have mentioned time and again that caste was never a class in a true sense, nor class was a caste in entirety. Moreover, 'caste' functioned as a 'system', and Jal nowhere in his paper mentions about 'caste system', he talks of 'caste' only. Caste as a system has been challenged and protested from time to time before Independence. Since Independence, caste system has become considerably weak and diluted. Exclusiveness of castes or boundaries between castes have become fragile due to lack of systemic support to caste. Reasons are obviously the constitutional provisions, the demands of the present-day democracy, such as elections, reservations, and education, migration and mobility. Dalit assertion and the strong OBCs presence in politics and economy are evidences of systemic changes in the caste system.

REGIONAL VARIATIONS IN CASTE

Let us now see how today caste is found in some states of India. The brief descriptions are only indicative of the functioning of caste vis-à-vis the present-day socio-political milieu. To begin with Haryana, one can say that economically the state is ahead of many other states of India, but socially and culturally it is perhaps far behind, particularly in the context of status of women (gender) and caste exclusiveness. A state like Bihar has witnessed caste-wars engineered by caste *senas* (armies). Maharashtra, a forward state, has seen atrocities on Dalits as a worrying situation for the state and society. Haryana, despite remarkable green revolution in the 1960s and 1970s, did not have corresponding social change. While comparing two villages in South India, S. Epstein (1962) found that the irrigated village witnessed economic well-being, but no social change, and the dry (unirrigated) village had no economic development but witnessed social change as a lot of people migrated out of the village for seeking employment; hence exposure to the wider world created sociocultural and political awakening.

Casteism and not communalism is a stark reality of Haryana. The numerically preponderant Jats have shown ethnocentrism, claiming their exclusiveness in regard to caste endogamy and clan exogamy. Urbanization in Haryana is not because of education, migration and mobility. It is there because Haryana surrounds Delhi, and expansion of Delhi, known as National Capital Region (NCR), has transformed erstwhile small towns of Gurgaon, Faridabad, Sonipat, etc., into industrial and software hubs. High price of land fetched by the NCR villagers has not only made them economically prosperous, but also thrusted urbanization upon them. In such a situation, Haryana has become a curious mix of rural–urban complex on the one hand, and rural caste-ridden formation on the other.

Prem Chowdhry (2011), in a well-researched volume, explains that before Independence Haryana was though a part of Punjab, it had a substantive basis on agriculture and animal husbandry. Jats enjoyed socio-economic domination as they owned fairly big landholdings. Women were excluded from activities outside the four walls of their households, except agricultural work. Women did not own land and were also forbidden to inherit land and property. To avoid division of land and property, the *Karewa* (levirate) system was enforced. The British encouraged the *Karewa* system and discouraged inter-caste mar-riages which were common before the British. Patriarchy and gendered relations have been strong elements in Haryanavi society as the caste system is the backbone of these two institutions. Caste, custom and community issues in rural or semi-urban Haryanavi society dominate social life of the people (Mehrotra, 2011, 36–37).

Now briefly about the Khap panchayat, we may say that it refers to brotherhood/*bhaichara*, *biradari*, a community of the same kind. *Khaps* were used/appreciated even by the British for their political ends. Ajay Kumar (2012, 59–64) mentions: 'Khap panchayats uphold the concept of *bhaichara* on a *gotra*, caste or territorial basis'. It is based on clan exogamy and caste endogamy. In modern times, Khap panchayats have awarded severe punishments, including indulgence in violence, to those who have violated rules of marriage, namely, clan exogamy and caste endogamy. Political leaders, for the reasons best known to them, have called *khaps* as 'social institutions', and legal action against them would have dangerous consequences for the state and society in Haryana. Some leaders have demanded an amendment in the Hindu Marriage Act of 1955 to declare same *gotra* marriages as prohibited and invalid. Kumar (2012, 63) writes: 'The power of khap panchayats exists parallel to the political power of the state government.'

Uttar Pradesh, Bihar, Rajasthan and to some extent Madhya Pradesh (known as Bimaru states) are quite low on development index compared to Tamil Nadu and Kerala. An important comparison of Uttar Pradesh with Tamil Nadu by Santosh Mehrotra (2006, 4261–4271) brings out that despite a movement to mobilize Dalits in Uttar Pradesh, the lower castes have low social indicators in health, nutrition, fertility and education after Independence. In UP, 'mobilisers of the Dalits have focused exclusively on capturing power, the gains to the lowest castes have been entirely of a symbolic nature'. In Tamil Nadu, despite the less lower caste mobilization, gains on the same indicators are of a high and egalitarian level. Mehrotra has compared the two states based on similar official data of the two states. On all counts, Mehrotra observes that the mass mobilization of neither the Dalits nor that of the OBCs in UP has contributed to the wellbeing of the poor. In Tamil Nadu, mass mobilization (in the past as well as in present) was broad-based to create space for wholesome well-being of the entire population of the state. Technical interventions in Tamil Nadu to transform health, nutrition and education of the poor have been effectively taken up by the state. The state has spent nearly 90 per cent of total government expenditure on health and education. Kerala too has the same level of advancement in these social sectors.

The state governments in UP, Bihar and Rajasthan have been unwilling to devolve transfer of functions and finance on basic health and education to the PRIs (Mahipal, 2004; World Bank, 2004). Mehrotra, while quoting his earlier writings on this issue, observes: 'Transferring these functions and finance will help make functionaries (teachers doctors, auxiliary nurses, midwives and nurses) at least partly responsive and accountable to their clients, they are meant to serve, rather than to a superior official in their ministry' (2006, 4270–2471).

It is not that there is all-round prosperity in Tamil Nadu, Kerala and other southern states. Landlessness among the SCs and other lower castes, for example, in Kerala is rampant. Land reforms of the 1970s did not result into effective redistribution of agricultural land. Many leaders, artisans, masons, carpenters and semi-skilled people moved to West Asia to seek employment. From Tamil Nadu, a lot of women moved to north India to work as nurses.

Compared to the North Indian Hindi-speaking states, West Bengal presents a different scene. Caste does not influence politics as it does in Bihar, UP, Rajasthan, Haryana, MP, etc.; it is the supremacy of politics and ideology that makes caste subservient and passive. Sukanta Bhattacharya (2003, 242–246), based on a case study of a village in Burdwan district of West Bengal, arrives at the following conclusions:

1. Each of the castes has its own hierarchy, higher–lower principles. The overlapping nature of various sub-castes is in tune with Dipankar Gupta's idea of 'continuous hierarchies and discrete classes'.
2. The lower castes and classes have a significant numerical presence at the level of panchayat, but at the leadership level, power is vested in the hands of the middle peasantry.
3. Even at the panchayat level, there is no radical restructuring of the rural power structure (Bhattacharya, 2003, 246).

The CPI(M) rule in Bengal relegated 'caste' to the background, and made 'class', in Marxian sense, a true idea to deal with politics and society. Both caste and religion, in orthodox Marxism, are treated as superstructures, and 'class' is the real 'basis for classifying, organizing and mobilizing people' (Kumar and Guha, 2014, 73–74). The question being raised today is: Will caste now replace class, and play a decisive role in the West Bengal politics? Dwaipayan Bhattacharyya (2011, 245), even before the defeat of the CPI(M), had thought of 'identitarian politics of community', with an emphasis on caste, ethnic and religious associations, in the post-CPI(M) era, or now in the Mamata Banerjee regime. Now the question is: Will caste in West Bengal overpower politics? In Bengal, caste was never absent but remained suppressed under the upper-caste doctrine of 'class'. But caste as a political phenomenon in West Bengal would be different from other north Indian states.

PERSISTENCE, CHANGE AND CASTE-BASED INEQUALITY

Caste is persisting as well as it has lost its essential character as a system in everyday life. Caste is used/misused, hence its persistence. Caste as a system is today obsolete, hence its discontinuity. It is a strange paradox of Indian social reality. Regional variations of caste manifestation are also found across India. But one common phenomenon is its appropriation by specific people, political leaders and individuals for realization of their specific goals. B. R. Ambedkar (1935) was for annihilation of caste as a system as it was the genesis of inequality, exploitation and super-ordination of the lower/'untouchable' castes who were the underdog in the caste hierarchy. D. D. Kosambi looked at caste as a category to understand socio-economic differences. He equated caste with class: He stated: 'Caste is an important reflection of the actual relations of production, particularly at the time of its formation' (see Roy, 2008, 78–84). Along with economic dimension, Kosambi also brings in the religious and ritual dimension (historical change), and its static/stagnant nature as well. Caste–class nexus is the most crucial factor that has enabled caste to survive for centuries in one or other manner. Inequality emanating from the caste–class nexus has been quite complex as incongruence between caste and class would have created imbalances and mobility in economic and political domains even if caste remained a static socio-religious system.

M. V. Nadkarni (2003, 4783–4793) demolishes the myth that caste system is intrinsic to Hinduism. Contrary to the common belief that caste system is ingrained in Hinduism, Nadkarni, based on scriptural evidence, argues that Hinduism did not support the caste system; 'it rigorously opposed it in practice and principle' (Nadkarni, 2003, 4783). Even along with the existence of the caste system, Hindu society witnessed considerable occupational and social mobility. Some Hindu legends and later on reform movements pronounced the disutility of the caste system. Despite all these factors, caste system survived as it maintained socio-economic and ecological balance and a communitarian equilibrium. Nadkarni defines caste system as follows:

1. Caste implies a division of labour determined by birth permitting no occupational/social mobility. This distinguishes caste from class.
2. Caste is a rigid system, separating one caste from other caste, by way of restrictions on communal relations and connubial ties.
3. It is a hierarchical system. The distinction between status and power is basic to understanding of the caste system (Dumont, 1999, 65–91).

4. The caste system is associated with a notion of purity/pollution.
5. The whole system (including its taboos and restrictions) is authenticated by religion or canon giving it a religious sanctity.
6. A production system is a basic foundation of the caste system, reflected through jajmani system, a system of patron–client relationships.

Nadkarni mentions that even Ambedkar was of the view that there was a division of labour, but there was no hierarchy. In fact, the features of the caste system as mentioned above in various writings on caste never existed in practice. Social and occupational mobility was quite significant and pronounced across *varnas*/castes. Intermixture of castes was also an accepted fact. Caste system was a system of checks and balances, a scheme of division of labour (easy acquisition of skills and knowledge), ecological harmony, and security of livelihood and employment, hence it survived.

Traditionally, commensality and connubiality are the essence of the caste system. Despite considerable weakening of these two basic features, 'caste' has survived till date in India. Abraham (2014, 56–65) observes that no doubt endogamy has been 'critical to caste and to the reproduction of caste, the shifting circle of endogamy is instructive of how castes and their practices are dynamic' (Abraham, 2014, 63).

'Shifts in the assertion of endogamy vary according to a caste's consciousness and its aspirations at a particular historical moment' (Abraham, 2014, 65). Honour killings imply more of reassertion of patriarchy, and control of female sexuality rather than purity of caste/clan. Abraham mentions:

> Thus, the idea of the 'purity of the caste' masks forms of power often played out in the local—in the domestic, the village, or caste. Endogamy is reproduced less as a value in itself and more as an ideal critically tied to power and forms of social status. (Abraham, 2014, 64)

However, one cannot ignore the fact that family and individual, within a caste or even without caste, are playing a decisive role in regard to marriage. *Khap*-like phenomenon is limited to a particular caste/sub-caste and an area.

Caste is losing its strength in India, though not uniformly or dramatically as observed by Andre Beteille (2012, 41–48). The weakening of the caste has been in three areas: (a) in the observance of the rules relating to purity and pollution, (b) in regard to the regulation of marriage and (c) in relation to hereditary occupations. Rules of commensality and rules of caste endogamy and clan exogamy have become quite flexible. Such a view is also held by A. M. Shah (2007, 109–116) as he argues that caste as a system is more or less dead, but individual castes are flourishing. Individual castes are flourishing in both rural and urban India, but caste as a system persists though in a modified way, in rural India by way of endogamy. Shah emphasizes on the study of individual castes and their dynamics. At the same time hierarchy may be studied in terms of its changing nature, and place of the individual castes in it in the changing social and cultural environment. In the 1970s, K. L. Sharma (1969, 1970a, 1970b, 1970c, 1974) has analysed the changing patterns of mobility while describing the family and the individual as the important units of social mobility along with caste/sub-caste.

A somewhat different view is articulated by Sonalde Desai and Amaresh Dubey (2001, 40–49), based on a study of 41,554 households selected from different parts of India. Desai and Dubey conclude from their study that there is a 'continued persistence of caste disparities in education, income and social networks'. The study considers 'caste as a status hierarchy', caste as a system of exclusion and exploitation, caste in transformation, and caste as a social construction, based on several studies and analyses. The results of the study conducted by Desai and Dubey show that though status hierarchies seem to be on the decline, but economic and educational disparities between large caste groupings continue to flourish (Desai and Dubey, 2001, 47). A new system of social stratification is emerging, but it would be simplistic to say that caste relations are superseded by class relations. Desai and Dubey mention that 'access to productive resources, particularly education and skills remain closely associated with caste. Children from lower castes continue to be educationally disadvantaged compared to children from the upper castes'. Brahmins have been positioned to consolidate material resources and have continued dominance in Indian society and economy. Using Bourdieu's idea of 'social reproduction' (1984), Desai and Dubey argue that 'in a variety of ways, castes manage to shape the access to social, political and cultural capital to their members' (Desai and Dubey, 2001, 47). In the fields of education and entrepreneurship, for example, historically wealthy castes play an interesting role in shaping opportunities (Desai and Dubey, 2001, 47).

The problem is that 'differences' within caste are being ignored. To consider caste as an 'entity', having homogeneity in terms of economic, social and political standings of the individuals and families who belong to particular castes is an erroneous assumption. The study by Desai and Dubey suffers from such a mistaken notion of internal equality among members of a given caste. Some families and individual members of a particular caste may be rich and resourceful, but a substantial number may have average and low statuses. Our recent revisit to two villages of Sikar district in Rajasthan shows that Jats, a middle caste, and formerly (before Independence) a peasant caste, an exploited lot, after being beneficiaries of land reforms, Panchayati Raj institutions and developmental programmes, have practically captured trade and commerce, government services in the district. Sikar town, being the second largest hub, after Kota, for coaching, is being dominated by Jats as they have maximum ownership and control of coaching centres. Even M. N. Srinivas (2003, 455–459), at the fag end of his life, recognized that

> a combination of wholly new technologies, institutions based on new principles and a new ideology which includes democracy, equality and the idea of human dignity and self-respect has to be in operation for a considerable time to uproot the caste system. Such a combination of forces is today bringing about the destruction of the caste-based system of production in the villages and at the local level. (Srinivas, 2003, 455)

EXPLAINING SOCIAL INEQUALITY

Inequality in general is a universal phenomenon. Even the developed western countries are infested with poverty, unemployment and inequality. Unequal distribution of resources is the main cause of inequality. Complete and full income equality is impossible. However, a reasonable system of redistribution could reduce inequality to a considerable extent (Böröcz, 2005, 886–892). Karl Polanyi (1957) suggests that along with managing economic institutions, society requires the construction of social institutions leading to political action for fighting against inequality. Polanyi talks of such a provision at the global level, but such an arrangement is far more relevant for India where nearly 40 per cent people are below poverty line.

Susan Engel and Brian Martin (2015, 42–48), based on a succinct glance at the relevant literature, observe that economic and social inequality is a major problem, implicated in poverty, ill health and exploitation. Inequality has increased and persisted since the 1980s all over the world. There have been tactics that reduce public outrage over inequality. Martin (2007) mentions the following tactics of outrage management regarding inequality: (a) to cover up the action, (b) to devalue the target, (c) to reinterpret the action by lying, minimizing consequences, blaming others or reframing, (d) to use official channels that give an appearance of justice and (e) intimidate or reward people involved. In view of such a situation, Engel and Martin (2015, 48) conclude: 'Generation of public outrage is part of the process in addressing poverty and disadvantage, and in promoting social justice; it needs to be accompanied by long-term efforts towards different ways of organizing society'.

'Caste' persists, but 'caste system' is extremely weak. Since 'caste' plays a significant political role within the village and of a supra–local level. Sumit Guha (2013, 15) considers caste as 'a societally important institution'. Along with dynamics of the state, caste has also evolved and modified itself. Caste has thus restricted and also shaped and reshaped social mobility. A study of 1500 entrants to a variety of engineering colleges, business schools, and higher services by Anirudh Krishna (2013, 38–49) finds that 'class and caste continue to make an important difference'. The main question asked in the study is: 'Are children from less well-off sections also able to rise to higher playing positions, or are these positions going mainly to the established elites?' Rural upbringing and parents' lack of education are the main obstacles. The entrants have been there as they have received support and assistance from a teacher, a relative or friend who motivated and inspired them (Krishna, 2013, 38).

Krishna observes that 'inequality is rising alongside rapid economic growth'. The reason is that high achievers in India come principally from among its established elites. Wealth inequalities have also grown. Economic liberalization has led to an increase in inequality. A new system of stratification based on quality education and skills has also come to stay. Parental background in terms of education, occupation and economic standing influence opportunities for upward social mobility. Krishna (2013, 41) reports the following results based on his study:

1. People who were brought up and educated in rural areas are at a disadvantage.
2. Higher economic status confers an advantage in terms of gaining entry. However, relative poverty has a more severely disabling effect.
3. Proportional to the population of the SCs and STs, the number of their students in engineering colleges and business schools is considerably lower.
4. Women have made a significant presence, but less than 50 per cent of the intake.
5. The parental background of the entrants is reasonably good, being a salaried class.
6. Being rural and poor, or SC/ST and rural, or the child of less-educated parents and female is a more severe handicap.
7. In urban setting, the professional elite tend to reproduce elitism by giving advantage to their sons and daughters.

Though there are 'degrees' of being rural, but after all 'rural' is not 'urban'. Krishna poses two important questions (Krishna, 2013, 42). (a) Why do rural origins impose handicaps to social mobility? (b) Why have rural individuals more often made it to lower-tier compared to higher-tier institutions? 'Education in English' (Fernandes, 2006, 69) makes a difference, from which rural entrants are deprived of. English language proficiency is more than seven times higher among urban compared to rural school children. Affordability for migration to urban areas for quality English-medium education is another factor in social mobility. 'Relative wealth', parents' occupations and education, religion, caste and gender are other factors that affect social mobility. Thus, the four main factors mentioned by Krishna (2013, 46) are: (a) rural upbringing, (b) parents employed in agriculture or as homemakers, (c) relative poverty and (d) parents' (specially mothers') education, as disabling factors in social mobility.

While conceptualizing poverty and inequality, Andre Beteille (2003, 4455–4463) mentions that in the context of Indian society, hierarchical systems (like castes and classes) and systems of stratification based on occupation, education and income coexist. The two sets of divisions act upon and influence each other. A variety of patterns have emerged from the combination of new inequalities with the pre-existing disparities. Today, internally differentiated and stratified society could be seen in the formation of middle class in India. Beteille observes in his other writing (2003, 181–203) that the Indian middle class is the most polymorphous in the world. Beteille (2003, 4462) writes: 'The divisions of education, occupation and income combine with those of language, religion and caste create a kaleidoscope of shifting social distinctions'. Old and new occupations coexist. There are large material inequalities within the middle class as a result of differential impact of technological and market forces. Such a situation of economic inequality exists despite social mobility.

'Wealth increases' and 'wealth disparities' emerge during the period of liberalization (Jayadev, Motiram and Vakulabharanam, 2007, 3853–3863). Absolute wealth levels have increased, in an uneven manner across different groups and axes. The wealthiest 20 per cent are diverging away from rest of the population. The top 1 per cent is making solid gains relative to the rest of the population. Accumulation has enhanced and financial sector has become strong. 'The story is also replicated across caste, occupational groups, rural and urban groups and so forth' (Jayadev, Motiram and Vakulabharanam, 2007, 3861). The share of wealth of the bottom 80 per cent of the population is either stagnant or has suffered wild declines. The rural–urban gap is also widening. Due to unfavourable social basis, the SCs, the STs, Muslims and the uneducated encounter economic exclusion and poverty. 'Caste and economic discrimination' is the central theme in several writings (see *EPW*, 2007, 4121–4146). Caste-based social inequality is visible in spatial distribution of caste groups, consumption, education and employment (Mohanty, 2006, 3777–3779).

PATTERNS OF SOCIAL MOBILITY

Migration from rural to urban areas is one strong evidence of social mobility. Generally, migration is of an individual member of a family who can find a job and support his family in the village. A successful migrant inspires other villagers and family members by extending a helping hand. Such a pattern of migration was quite pronounced among the Marwaris of Rajasthan (Timberg, 1978). Today, there is more of family migration, particularly from among the poor rural people. One earning member alone is unable to feed a family of five or six or even more members in the family. On construction sites, one can see all the adult family members working for their bare survival. In some cases, women and adolescent girls work as domestic helps. Besides this, educated employed people living in towns and cities do not leave their spouses in villages of their origin. Married couples prefer to settle down in towns, leaving behind their parents in villages. Thus, social mobility is a reality, forced upon by compelling circumstances and also due to ambition for a desired type of living in towns.

Subramaniam and Jayaraj (2015, 39–47) considering migration as 'spatial mobility' observes that it is seen as being induced by increased opportunities in urban India. Migration is also being induced by failure of rural India to provide employment opportunities to the people. Subramaniam and Jayaraj describe four types of migration (spatial mobility): (a) rural–rural, (b) rural–urban, (c) urban–rural and (d) urban–urban. School teachers, healthcare personnel and some other service providers coming from urban areas move to villages for employment. From small towns people move to big ones. From interior villages people move to the villages situated on highways. From rural to urban migration is a common feature all over the country. It has been observed that a complex interplay of variations in the labour market, social and political reasons, the living environment, natural disasters, and development-related factors determine the decisions to migrate.

Migration is one form of mobility (spatial) either due to coercive circumstances at the native place(s) or due to aspirations for moving up in social ladder. People normally do not move away from their ancestral places or birthplaces if they do not suffer from social inequality, subjugation and deprivation. Social mobility is not an easy ropeway. Whenever people move out from their settled abodes, they visualize anxieties and tensions at the new places. Mobility emanating from a social pathology is related to search for new job opportunities/ sources of income aiming at a better living. In course of time, such a mobility may give rise to a 'middle class', at a lower level in towns and cities (Fernandes, 2006). But then, opportunities to have access to new sources/jobs is not an easy task. Several barriers would hinder such a process of mobility. Victory over hindrances in social mobility may provide opportunities for equality in social life. Reproduction of inequalities indicate that we have failed in overcoming the barriers that have deep-seated roots in our society.

It is often reported that India has jobless economic growth. Despite economic growth, inequalities have not come down in a meaningful way. Social background, caste, gender, education and resourcefulness determine social mobility of an individual and his/her family. The measure of social mobility is a shift in the position of an individual over a period of time, which would benefit members of his/her family to a certain extent. Such a measure in concrete terms would imply enhanced income, assets, lucrative job and modern house and comfortable lifestyle. Intergeneration mobility can be an authentic yardstick in terms of the first-generation mobile people, the second-generation people and so on. Today, attainment of higher status is considered as an indicator of mobility.

Social mobility whether of an individual or a family or of a group (caste/class) needs to be seen in a particular social/structural context. Role of parents, caste, gender, rural/urban background cannot be undermined despite efforts and aspirations of individuals and families for moving up in the social ladder. Social mobility is not simply a 'market situation', determined by pure competition. In the process of competition and achievement, one can see the hidden/open presence of ascription. Even in the change induced by the Indian State and various governments from time to time, some have extracted undue benefits and the deserving and needy ones have remained deprived of their due benefits. Manipulations in cornering benefits by the entrenched individuals and select groups of people are an open secret.

R. H. Turner (1960, 855–867) observes 'sponsored and contest mobility' in the context of school education system. 'Sponsored' implies 'ascription' and 'contest' refers to an individual's ability. A similar view is expressed by P. Bourdieu and Passeron (1977; Bourdieu, 1996) regarding higher education in France.

In the western societies, the main arguments regarding social mobility, irrespective of social origin, are: (a) the 'meritocratic', (b) the 'egalitarian' and (c) the 'historical'. All the three arguments imply a rearrangement of families over the social structure in the long run. Education and occupational mobility are significant equalizers impacting reduction in social inequalities (Coxon and Jones, 1975, 9–15). In India, social mobility is through a gradual process of change. Certainly, India's Independence in 1947, and its constitution, implemented in 1950, are a mark of social transformation of Indian society.

Economists look at economic inequality in terms of income levels and poverty and gains and losses of utilities in a given society. Amartya Sen (1995, 1–11) explains that it is not just 'equality of opportunities', more important is the acquisition of capability, which can be acquired by overcoming of some specific *barriers or constraints*. Equality of *overall* freedoms would ensure 'real' equality of opportunities. While agreeing with Rawls' (1999) idea of 'justice as fairness', in terms of holding of 'primary goods' (incomes, wealth, opportunities, and the social bases of self-respect), Sen focuses on the substantial assessment of equality and also of efficiency. It is necessary to understand the means of freedom, and different freedoms depend upon inequalities related to gender, location, and class, and inheritance. Two questions are relevant as explained by Sen (1995, 12–30). These are: (a) Why equality? and (b) What sort of equality? The obvious answers to these questions in the context of rural India are: (a) There is a pervasive social inequality (in terms of caste, class and power), and (b) There is a capability deficit among a large segment of population, hence equality can be gained by making the people more and more capable to have a 'real' equality.

Andre Beteille (1969, 13) observes:

The problem of social inequality has two aspects, a distributive and a relational aspect. The first refers to the ways in which different factors such as income, wealth, occupation, education, power, skill, etc., are distributed in the population. The second refers to the ways in which individuals differentiated by these criteria are related to each other within a system of groups and categories.

Since the distributive aspect of social inequality provides only an understanding of how individuals interact with each other in socially significant ways, Beteille emphasizes more on the relational aspect of social inequality. There are different types of societies, hence different modes of social stratification. Indian society is a complex formation even today due to its colonial legacy, caste system, rural–urban and rich–poor divides. The distributive aspect is quite important today as there are some richest of the rich, and a large number of people are poorest of the poor. In between these two top and bottom strata, there is a varied and multi-layered middle class. Though the top and bottom layers are also highly differentiated and all the three components are not independent of their socially structured origins, like caste, religion, rural background, education, etc.

CASTE AND SOCIAL INEQUALITY

Caste alone is not the sole agency of social inequality, though it has often been appropriated as a system of high and low groups of people. Besides caste, and also to a certain extent, there have been both equality and inequality among the people. Such a situation has not been seriously probed historically as well as contextually. The questions thrown up by R. Dahrendorf (1969, 17) regarding the origin of inequality among men are relevant in the Indian context as well. The questions are: (a) Why is there inequality among men? (b) Where do the causes lie? (c) Can it be reduced, or abolished altogether? (d) Or do we have to accept it as a necessary element in the structure of human society? In response to the above questions, Dahrendorf (1969, 36) writes:

> To sum up, the origin of social inequality lies neither in human nature nor in a historically dubious conception of private property. It lies rather in certain features of all human societies, which are (or can be seen as) necessary to them. Although the differentiation of social positions—the

division of labor, or more generally the multiplicity of roles may be one such universal feature of all societies, it lacks the element of evaluation necessary to explain distinctions of rank. Evaluative differentiation, the ordering of social positions and their incumbent scales of prestige or income, is effected only by the sanctioning of social behavior in terms of normative expectations. Because there are norms and because sanctions are necessary to enforce conformity of human conduct, there has to be inequality of rank among men.

Thus, Dahrendorf advocates Talcott Parsons' view of stratification as 'patterning' or 'ordering' of social relations (1954, 386–439). Davis–Moore (1945, 242–249) also strongly advocate the functionalist approach to social stratification. A review of approaches to social stratification is there in K. L. Sharma (1974, 1–22). The functionists see social stratification as a very real element of everyday lives as a system of distributive status, a system of differential distribution of desired and scarce things. Honour and wealth (prestige and income) are the most accepted means of differentiation of rank (Dahrendorf, 1969). But such a view of inevitability of social inequality has been questioned (Tumin, 1953; 1955, 417–423; 1957, 32–37). Tumin questions justification for social inequality as provided by Davis and Moore. His emphasis is more on distribution of rewards according to assignments and performances rather than positions of power and prestige.

In the Indian context, caste has persisted as a system of institutionalized inequality, labelling caste as a functional system (Hutton, 1963; Risley, 1909). But such a view has been contested from time to time by way of protests, reforms and legislations to weaken rigidities of the caste system. Since, caste rank is preordained by birth, a member of a caste is supposed to abide by the norms and sanctions of the caste system and of his/her caste rank. The prevailing patterns of occupational mobility indicate that a large number of people do not follow their hereditary occupations as ordained by the caste system and its allied institution of *Jajmani*. In our study of six villages in Rajasthan (Sharma, 1974), out of 1900 working people, 377 were engaged in secular (non-caste) occupations. The situation is much different today. Even non-farm income is more than 30 per cent in rural India. Thus, if a person is genuinely independent of his caste with regard to occupation, education, marriage, etc., he/she has acquired 'freedom' from bonding to the caste system. In case, women are also free to have access to education and employment ignoring patriarchal hegemony, they are enjoying equality of opportunity with men.

The question is as follows: Is caste significant in influencing social mobility? If yes, in what way, it affects/checks social mobility and supports status quo in Indian society? If caste system is, in effect, a system of an 'encompassing' nature as Dumont (1970a) opines, how does caste-based mobility occur among the lower and deprived castes/sub-castes? In case, caste does not impact social mobility of the deprived sections of our society, caste-based reservations cannot be accepted. Views on caste are clearly indicative of polarity, explaining persisting play of caste in social mobility on the one hand, and weakening of caste by way of caste-free areas on the other. Caste and gender discrimination in human development is a stark reality today. Ashwini Deshpande (2011) talks of 'caste development index', based on a persistence of caste disparity. There is caste-based discrimination in labour markets. Affirmative action is only partially successful. There is a need for restructured affirmative action policy. Such a view is corroborated by Rama Baru et al. (2010, 49–58) as they point out that caste-based inequalities are observable even in healthcare sector. Three forms of inequalities are in health sector: (a) Colonial policies and practices persisting even today having differential discriminatory effects on various castes and communities; (b) socio-economic inequalities manifest in caste, class and gender differentials; and (c) inequities in the availability, utilization and affordability of health services.

The SCs, STs and OBCs have been benefited politically by way of reservations and other policies of the state, but proportionate to their population, they are far behind in the domain of business and entrepreneurship (Iyer, Khanna and Varshney, 2013, 52–60; Jodhka, 2010, 11; Thorat and Sadana, 2009, 13–16; Weiner, 2001). Society in Haryana revolves around land, caste and gender, reflecting caste-based patriarchal social organization (Chowdhry, 2011). Haryana is a state where diktats of castes (Khap panchayats) have been granted political legitimacy. Leaders of the stature of Chief Ministers and Member(s) of Parliament have extended support to Khap panchayats (Ajay Kumar,

2012, 59–64). Casteism has been encouraged by way of reservations and electoral vote-bank politics (Bhambhri, 2005, 806–808). Many castes encourage casteism and caste/sub-caste culture by bringing out booklets, magazines, articles and other forms of published material, including addresses, telephone diaries, etc.; to create a social and cultural space for particularistic ends (Chaturvedi, 2014, 33–37).

MARXIST VIEW ON CASTE

An extreme view of caste is seen in the nexus between 'Asiatic mode of production, caste and the Indian Left' by Murzban Jal (2014, 41–49). Jal borrows the ideas of 'regressive thinking' from Theodor Adorno and the 'divided self' from David Lang to explain the caste system. He writes:

> Because caste is essentially based on this idea of the 'divided self', which itself is based on the 'regression of thinking', we claim that this form of caste-cretinism in India enforced the order that even though wars and famines raged over it, the caste-inflected Indian forgot them and was obsessed only with this miserable caste identity. That is why 'caste is both a neurosis as well as a cretinism'. (Jal, 2014, 43)

The question is also: Can there be a 'casteless society' (Ambedkar, 2008) and a 'Classless society' (Marx, 1964). Indian society has demonstrated amazing resilience in persistence and change of both caste and class, and of the nexus of the two as two sides of the same social formation.

Murzban Jal (2014, 46) writes: 'One thought that modernity and modern industry would destroy caste, but caste sat comfortably on the seat of this modern industry. True, caste alliances and power structures change continuously, but caste per see refuses to leave'. Jal labels caste as an awful schizophrenic system that needs to be 'annihilated'. Caste is understood as the base, having its double roots in Brahminical counter-revolution and colonialism. Caste is a *clannish* oligarchy, basically an inherited class status. It entails graded inequality and division of labourers. Jal (2014, 47) writes: 'One could understand caste as a structure of human alienation and a form of social exclusion'. Further, Jal considers caste as a peculiar system of class based on the ontology of segregation. 'Varna' means 'colour', hence caste-based stratification implying class relations, consists of race-inspired markers. Casteism is equivalent to racism. Thus, accordingly to Jal, caste incorporates both class and race. Jal (2014, 48) observes: 'Caste in this sense is no longer class on a primitive level of production. It is an essential part of the most modern of moderns, mimicking not only the German form of fascism, but also the Israeli form of imperialist occupation'. While relating caste with modern classes (global capitalism), Jal says that modern classes have emerged from the caste system. 'Caste is not something that is outside the ambit of class struggle' (2014, 48).

Such an unquestioned application of the Marxist thought on the caste system ignores India's ground reality, which is constantly changing since India's Independence in 1947. The emergence of 'middle peasantry', abolition of British land-tenure systems, introduction of adult franchise, elections, Panchayati Raj institutions, reservations for the weaker sections, expansion of education and healthcare, development programmes, etc., have transformed society, polity and economy. Social division of labour/labourers based on caste does not exist. *Jajmani* as the bedrock of inter-caste relations and pure-impure syndrome are no more in practice. Pursuing equality has become the needed creed and also a practice to a certain extent. To compare caste with class (capitalism) and race seems to be an untenable stand. Differences among the people are certainly based on certain attributes, such as income, occupation, education, etc.; but these are found in all human societies though in varying combinations and proportions.

Today, caste has a reduced role and significance in relation to social and economic inequalities. Based on a comparative study of slums in four major cities, namely, Jaipur, Ludhiana, Mathura and Ujjain (in 2006–2007), despite intercity substantive variations, it is observed that networks (social capital) play a significant role in accessing an entry to the urban job market (Kumar, Kumar and Mitra, 2009, 55–63). More than 90 per cent of the 2000 workers have used networks to get an urban employment. Networks could be caste based as well. The networks provide accessibility to livelihood, but also inhibit the process of social assimilation and lead to segmentation and possibilities of conflict (Kumar, Kumar and Mitra, 2009, 59). Within the slums, there are variations across social groups in terms of certain important indicators like education, occupation and income. Religion-based distinction seems to be more prominent than a caste-based one. However, there is a somewhat higher incidence of deprivation among the socially deprived groups. The socially backward classes do not enjoy/experience well-being beyond a threshold limit. The higher castes experience more well-being than the backward ones (Kumar, Kumar and Mitra, 2009, 62).

Kumar, Heath and Heath (2002a, 2983–2987; 2002b, 4091–4096), while analysing 'determinants of social mobility in India', argue that class origins make a substantial difference to class destinations. Caste is not a good predictor of mobility. Dalits have become a salaried class, particularly due to reservations in education and jobs. However, a study of Pune City by Deshpande and Palshikar (2008, 61–70) indicates that different caste groups had a clearly differentiated occupational location a few generations ago, hence the effects of that historical differentiation at the present juncture. While disagreeing with Kumar et al. (2002), Deshpande and Palshikar observe: 'This underscores the need to take into account the relevance of caste in plotting occupational differences across caste groups' (2008, 68). Caste may be less tangible in urban India. But its effect on upward mobility is quite strong. Caste is not disappearing. In the case of upward mobility, caste still matters (Deshpande and Palshikar, 2008, 68). Deshpande and Palshikar makes three points while concluding their study: (a) It is simply not possible to plot the class map of India without integrating the caste dimension. (b) Each caste is sharply stratified and possibly 'multi-class'. 'Caste will apparently continue to be organizing principle of collective action'. (c) There is a limited entry of the lower castes Dalits and OBCs into the core of the middle class. They have concentration in lower occupations and lower-class environs, hence their collective action as lower classes (Deshpande and Palshikar, 2008, 69).

Chapter 4

Individual and Family

HOLISM, INDIVIDUALISM AND CASTE

Western social science has shown that Indian society, being a holistic and corporate entity, incorporates both individual and family. In its pursuit of 'methodological individualism', western social science has propagated the idea of 'methodological holism' in the context of India. In Indian society, group (caste), family and individual have co-existed, not as opposite poles, but, in fact, as interacting units, with their distinct presence and functioning. In Indian society, 'group' is not an abstraction or a constructed phenomenon, in relation to individual and family. Indian society has both wholes (castes, ethnic and religious groups), families and individuals. All three, namely, caste, family and individual, are real. Hence, holism and individualism are co-existent. In phenomenological sense, the relationship between subjectivity and objectivity or individual and society provides a basis for understanding of the apparent antinomies/dichotomies, such as holism–individualism, objectivity–subjectivity or macro–micro, as man is at the centre of such a discourse (Smart, 1975, 88–89). Family is also as real as man (individual) along with group/collectivity (caste). Inferences drawn from such an ill-conceived notion of 'individual' or 'individualism' as a way of thinking and practice did not take roots, and it has/had a 'composite'/'holistic'/totalistic society, leading to rigid inequality and unfreedom.

The basic premise is that individualism entails equality (Dumont, 2006, 225–230). Dumont contrasts between holism and individualism and hierarchy and equalitarianism. Heuristically, holism entails hierarchy while individualism entails equality. But all holistic societies do not stress on hierarchy to the same degree nor do all individualistic societies stress on equality to the same degree (Dumont, 2006, 226). Dumont explains that individualism entails not only equality but also liberty; equality and liberty are not always convergent; hence, there is a varying range of individualism in terms of these elements. India, as observed by Dumont, is a unique society, where distinction between hierarchy and power is non-existent as hierarchy is there in its pure form, exclusively and undiluted. France, for example, at the time of French Revolution, could be characterized by an extreme stress on equality at the expense of liberty.

Dumont (2006, 226) states: 'What I have in view here are wholesale, all embracing, or encompassing social valuations, not the mere occurrence of a feature or an idea at one level or another of the society or of the ideology'. Further, Dumont (2006, 226) says that 'equality and hierarchy must combine in some manner in any social system, as the ranking of social groups entails equality within each of them'. Caste, for Dumont, is a system of 'values' and 'norms'. Let us say that caste, being a system of inter-caste relations and interdependence, entailed (in the past) both inequality and equality. In most studies, including the one by Dumont, inequality, in a rigid form, has been analysed, ignoring the implicit and embedded equality in terms of reciprocal arrangements under the jajmani system. Jajmani was the bedrock of inter-caste relations, characterized by economic, social and cultural power relations between the patrons and service providers (functionaries).

A CRITIQUE OF DUMONT'S VIEW ON HOLISM

The concept of 'contra-priest' (Gould, 1967, 25–55) explains to a considerable extent equality in concrete situations and symbolically as well between the higher and the lower castes. Each caste had its own identity and individuality, and within this bounded space, families and individuals had their distinct and diverse statuses/standings. We have discussed three levels of social mobility (Sharma, 1969), namely, group (caste/sub-caste), family and individual, and these are distinct as well as interrelated, but not reducible to each other.

Individualism is a comprehensive idea and so is the idea of hierarchy. Both are universal and found in some measures in all human societies (Bose, 2006b). Bose refers to Dumont as the champion of 'Indo-Hierarchy Theory', by considering the uniqueness of the Indian caste system, distinct from Muslim culture and western individualism. The notion of 'unchangeable' and 'unchanging India' obstructs emergence of an egalitarian–libertarian society. While disagreeing quite vehemently, Andre Beteille (2006, 110–119) denies the hierarchy of values as pointed out by Dumont through the principle of pure and impure. Beteille (2006, 112) says: 'I do not believe that there is any society in which all values are of *equal* significance, and I doubt if any sociologist believes in such nonsense'. All values cannot be arranged in a *single* hierarchy. Dumont wrongly looks for what he calls 'paramount values' and a symmetry in hierarchy. Beteille mentions that hierarchy is a theological rather than a sociological concept, and Dumont's idea of value is close to the theological concept of hierarchy. Even the concept of equality has various meanings and connotations. As we mentioned earlier that in a particular context, an 'untouchable' or a low caste functionary becomes ritually equal to a 'priest', indicating an element of equality within inequality.

In Dumont's view, Indian caste system is not simply a system of patronage and clientele, because there is a purely cultural view of caste. Dumont characterizes caste by the *typifying* in opposition to the *classifying* approach (Dumont, 1967, 28–38; 1987). Dumont's structuralist view is evident as he says: 'I believe this is the real, or deeper, comparative approach. The main thing is to understand, and therefore ideas and values cannot be separated from "structure"' (Dumont, 1967, 31). Caste is a gradation of statuses in society, an extreme form of stratification. According to Dumont, since caste is a hierarchical system, a hierarchical relation is a relation between larger and smaller, or more precisely between that which *encompasses* and that which is *encompassed*. Division of labour in caste (jajmani) does not imply a theory of social stratification (Dumont, 1967, 33).

Dumont asserts that the orientation to the whole (holism) is in opposition to the element (individualism). Liberty and equality are values corresponding to the individualistic orientation, while the caste society ('closed society') represents the holistic orientation (Dumont, 1967, 33–34). Max Weber (1957) refers to caste-based division of labour as a 'demiurgic liturgy' as it answers the needs of all households in the village. Jajmani is not, strictly speaking, an economic fact, it is a 'holistic' fact. Further, Dumont says that in practice the king is both the high priest and the ruler in one person. But in theory, the two are absolutely distinguished. In principle, even a poor Brahmin is superior to the ruler. Priest and King are not persons as such, they represent the institutions of 'priesthood' and 'kingship'.

INDIVIDUAL IN INDIAN SOCIETY

It is Max Weber who, in opposition to Marx, considers the individual and his action as the basic unit, as an 'atom' in his interpretative sociology (1970, 55–61). Weber (1970, 56) writes: 'Man can "understand" or attempt to "understand" his own intentions through introspection, and he may interpret the motives of other men's conduct in terms of their professed or ascribed intentions'). Weber worked out an amalgamation of 'ideas and interests' in his interpretative sociology. While comparing Marx and Weber in terms of their respective perspectives, H. H. Gerth and C. Wright Mills (1970, 64) observe as follows:

> He (Max Weber) tries to establish an intimate relation between the nature of a predominant psychological state, the structure of an act of perception, and the meaning of an object. All three aspects, in turn, are facilitated by and have an affinity to the socio-historical situation of the intellectuals within the social structure. This historical structure, by itself, does not determine the direction in which the strata of intellectuals may elaborate their conceptions; rather it permits or blocks the attempt, characteristic of intellectuals, to tackle the senselessness of suffering of the world. In the occident, intellectuals also experimented in the direction of mystic contemplation; but such endeavors, according to Weber, were repeatedly frustrated. A more volitional and active search for meaning became predominant in the occident.

Some misgivings have been created about the occident and the oriental, as the former has 'individual', hence freedom, equality and mobility predominate social life; and the latter has group (caste) as the foremost entity, hence bondage, inequality and immobility. These are misperceptions. 'Holism' of the oriental and 'individualism' of the occident are not absolute phenomena, as no society can survive meaningfully without a semblance of the ideological and practical strands. Excessive individualism had to be curbed by creation of social solidarity for good of the society in France in the 19th century. In the same way, for equality and freedom, the excessive social control had to be mitigated for human dignity and freedom. Dipankar Gupta (2005, 7) comments that Dumont committed a critical error by equating equality with individualism and treating the two as near synonyms. This is evident in Dumont's two books—*Homo Hierarchicus* (holism) for India, and *Homo Aequalis* (individualism/equality) for the West. The 'typifying' implies absolute inequality/hierarchy and the 'classifying' refers to stratification, having individual, freedom, equality and mobility as the core features. To say that there is only caste, kinship, clan and community in India, and in contrast to this, in the West individual, competition, equality and mobility characterize its social fabric. This is real misconception in Dumont's understanding of Indian society, and also that of French society.

COEXISTENCE OF INDIVIDUAL AND SOCIETY

Individualism stresses on achievement, and since individuals do not have the same level of capability, it results into differential rewards and inequality. The functional approach to stratification (Davis and Moore, 1945, 242–250) emphasizes on the value of achievement in terms of unequal skills and consequent rewards. This approach has, however, been criticized as a contrived mechanism of structured social inequality. Formal equality and individualism are also core of the functional approach to social stratification. As per the Constitution of India, both 'individual' and 'group' are treated as legal and formal entities. An individual is a voter, competitor, contestant and a citizen. A caste/community based on its social and educational backwardness is given benefits in terms of opportunities for education, employment and representation in the bodies, such as panchayats, municipal councils, assemblies and Lok Sabha (parliament). Some such categories have also been created and provided means of employment, namely, below poverty line (BPL) families. Such a reckoning of both 'individual' and 'group' is based on both formal and substantive reality. Family has always been a key unit along with individual and group. Recognition of 'family' as a unit for assessment of poverty in regard to employment and education is also a significant dimension along with individual and group.

Beteille (1998, 435–446) draws a distinction between individuals and groups as the claims made for benefits and burdens for the two are not identical. The questions are: (a) Is individual subordinate to his/her group? (b) Is an individual incorporated in his/her group? (c) In what way, a group is present in an individual? There are situations that may not be related to economic domain, in which, an individual accepts willingly or unwillingly the gestalt of his/her group, particularly in social and cultural matters. However, this does not imply that an individual becomes subordinate to his/her group. Secondly, an individual always belongs to a group, namely, caste, tribe, community, etc., but this does not mean that he/she ceases to be an 'individual' in his/her own right. In an individual's sociocultural consciousness, his/her 'group' (caste, village, town) is always existent, but it is not that his/her group dictates all his/her actions and activities.

The spirit of individualism is becoming stronger among the upper castes and urban middle classes due to modern education, employment, migration and mobility. Nuclearization of family on a faster rate is a clear evidence of change from collectivism to individualism. Decision of assets owned by a joint household leads to nuclearization of families. This implies a process of 'limited individualism' in the sense that normally an individual separates from his joint family, along with his wife and children, if any. A. M. Shah (2014, 181) observes that whether the Indian family fosters individualism has always been a topic of discussion since the middle of the 19th century. 'The preponderance of elementary family households is itself considered a sign of the emergence of individualism' (Shah, 2014, 181). Indian family has been encountering change, for example, what Maitrayee Chaudhuri refers as 'from ideology to market research' (2010, 363–389).

FAMILY AND INDIVIDUAL

The professional class in large cities is encountering exogenous change, and such a situation results into the nuclear family and the ideology of individualism, both of which are thought to have been diffused from the West (Shah, 2014, 240–241). But Shah questions such a view quite critically. He writes: 'First of all, the association of individualism with the nuclear family is problematic in the context of the joint family. A nuclear household by its mere existence cannot be considered as signifying the assertion of the ideology of individualism' (Shah, 2014, 275). Individualism cannot be inferred from numerical proportions of family; it is a way of thinking, a mindset about life. Moreover, nuclearization from joint families and vice versa is an ongoing process depending upon both structural and cultural factors. Individualism is not a monolith. It has different forms, shades and practices. In some way, it is found among the lowest strata as well as among the top ones. Such a complex nature of individualism is often coexistent with the concerns of extended/joint family, community/caste and larger society. The question is as follows: Is there or not an 'individual' in a nuclear family? If yes, then what is the nature of relationship among the members, namely, husband, wife, son and daughter? How they remain as 'individuals' in such a unit? What is the nature of corporateness in a nuclear family?

Shah (2014, 473–474) pleads for a desirable process of adjustment for the well-being of the elderly in India through a new socialization. He writes:

> This is a matter of society and culture, of ideas and attitudes, not of law and force. While individual freedom should be valued, individualism as a cult does not seem to have a place in the ideas and aspirations of the vast majority of people in Indian society. Mindless, uncontrolled, rabid individualism, ideas about which are often spread by the media among the younger generation these days, is not likely to be conductive to the well-being of the elderly and the creation of a healthy society. (Shah, 2014, 473–474)

A. M. Shah's loaded view, with its moral concern, undervalues the intra-family dominance—subjugation, suppression, discrimination, discords and undue advantage by some members at the cost of other members. Indignities are imposed on some members in the name of 'unity' and 'jointness' of the family. Equality among the members of a family becomes as such more of a 'drama' than genuine egalitarian relations. The conceptions of joint assets, resources, cooperation, mutual aid, emotional bonding, etc., have acquired new connotations and contexts in which they are practised.

For our own sake, we do not draw a line between 'man' and 'individual' as done by D. P. Mukerji (1958, 228–241). Mukerji says that if the group is still the unit of action, aspiration and orientation, normative, affective and cognitive alike, then the Indian social life is the life of bees and beavers, regimented, totalitarian, in fact, almost communistic. But the fact is that the majority of us do not feel regimented. Mukerji (1958, 235) writes: 'Our conception of freedom is different, because our conception of man is *purusha* and not the individual, or *vyakti*'. We are not a 'free' society of individuals, but of *purushas*, performing *purusharthas* or duties assigned by our tradition and its continuity, *sampradaya parampara*, based on collective experience, *anubhava*, as the principle of change. Thus, there is a man in tradition and a tradition in a man. Such a relation between man and tradition is the basis of continuity and change in Indian society. Mukerji talks of three principles of change, namely, *sruti*, *smriti* and *anubhava*. *Anubhava* or personal experience is the revolutionary principle, but it soon flowers into collective experience. This does not mean that today, 'voluntarist' individual action is non-existent or not an effective means of an individual's fulfilment of aspirations.

In an essay on 'Man and Plan in India', Mukerji (1958, 30–76) talks of the new society and the new man as a consequence of the Five-Year Plan (s) in India. Commenting on India's social change, just after Independence, Mukerji (1958, 31) says:

India's social change, which is both a fact and an act, has not had the benefit of a clear or a systematic theory or design of new society behind it. Nor was the outline of the new man which could be filled in by the movement towards the new society ever firmly sketched.

Gandhi, Tagore, Dayanand Saraswati, etc., projected their own conceptions of man. There was no 'ideal type' of man in Weberian sense. No projection of a man in terms of real life praxis and rationality has been envisioned in Five-Year Plans and other legal and statutory enactments. Mukerji blames for such a situation Indian intellectuals to a considerable extent.

According to Yogendra Singh (1984, 23–75), 'man' (individual) is present invariably in sociological theory. Positivism and emphasis on empiricism have brought in mainstream sociology man as a concrete entity. Marxism and functionalism both subordinated 'man' to the grandeur of 'society' Homans (1964), an ardent advocate of micro-functional approach, emphasized on the urgency of 'bringing man back in' at the centre of the disciplines of sociology and social anthropology. Concept of man is inherently present in positivism, functionalism, dia-lectical and interpretive sociology, phenomenology and critical theory, etc. The notions of rationality, existential conditions, interaction, basic needs, motivational orientations, action, actor, etc., lead ultimately to a substantive reality, which is related to man in relation to his society and culture. This does not mean that all men have a uniform pattern of existential conditions, capabilities and aspirations. This only means that a man (individual) is not reducible to his family and group in absolute terms.

Individual is in family and family is in individual, and both are in caste or caste is in both. Such a matrix between individual and caste has, however, changed considerably since Independence. Intra-family relations can explain the place and role of individual members. Shaping of a child as an adolescent and then as an adult depends upon the family and caste to a great extent. More than a caste, family plays a decisive role in the process of socialization of its children, both male and female. When a joint or extended lineal or lateral family finds it difficult to live with all the members, members become restive and acrimonious. Strains in the family lead to quarrels and accusations (Mandelbaum, 1996, 29–50).

CASTE, FAMILY AND INDIVIDUAL

The more property there is to divide, the more protracted is the throes of parting, the more touchy is each brother's honour (whether by *jati*'s tradition or by personal bent), and the more bitter is the aftermath.

Those whose education or job sends them forth from the household are often spared this fraternal fracas; so too is an only son spared. And among the poorer families of lower rank, the decisive quarrel tends to come earlier, usually between father and son. The son and his wife leave quickly, and whatever rancor flares then, generally dissipates before long (Mandelbaum, 1996, 32).

Among the higher and middle castes in the village, the division not usually takes place at all once, in a clean, decisive break. There is a sort of resilience, despite continuing strains. However, among the lower castes, the separation, perhaps due to economic hardships and scare resources, takes place quicker than the upper and middle rungs of rural society. Individual and individualism are thus inherent in the family, but remain unexpressed and unarticulated due to family gestalt and *jati* consciousness. Individual's space and significance have been viewed as subsumed by his family and caste. The family 'as Module and as Model' is the crux of Mandelbaum's thinking. Mandelbaum (1996, 34) writes: 'Relations within a family are in certain important ways similar to relations within a *jati* and in community'. He further observes:

> What a villager does in his role as family member underlies his behavior as *jati* member. His family serves both as module and as model for his *jati* relations. It provides the matrix for the beginnings of his conduct and contains the ends, the purposes, of his social striving. It is his fundamental corporate group, the locale of much of his social action, and is also a main unit of attribution, by which expectations of his behavior are projected and judgments of his activities are made. (Mandelbaum, 1996, 34)

A man cannot readily put out of either family or *jati*. A man is born in a *jati*, and his family is a structure of his roles. A man's emotions, motivations, conflicts, achievements are in the family domain.

Let us say here that caste is seen as *sui generis*, and family and its members are viewed under the supremacy of caste on family and of family on its members. In this perspective, 'differentiation' is undermined at all the three levels, namely, caste, family and individual. Differentiation is not just physical or material, though material differences matter a lot among individuals, families and castes. Different sub-castes, sub-sub-castes, and lineages differ at the ground level in sociocultural and material terms. Families belonging to the varied caste groups differ in terms of economic, cultural and occupational standings. Members of different families of the same caste/sub-caste are quite different from each other in terms of education, income, employment, assets, etc. Members within a given family (both undivided and divided) differ in terms of prestige and social honour. We can safely say that weakening of the hold of caste on family, and that of family on its members has strengthened 'individual' as a basic unit of role-playing and status-determination.

Andre Beteille (2005, 313–327) observes that in a society there would always be some continuity and reproduction of social and cultural aspects. He writes:

> It is my central argument that the family plays a crucial if not decisive role in the reproduction of social structure, including the structure of inequality. To be sure, the family as an institution is not equally effective everywhere, and it does not act in isolation from other institutions anywhere. But all things considered, it will be safe to say that the family plays a far more active role than caste in reproducing the inequalities associated with the new occupational system. The retreat of caste as an active agent for the reproduction of inequality at the upper levels, and the continuing, if not increasing, importance of the family constitute two of the most striking features of contemporary Indian society. (Beteille, 2005, 313)

The role of family in shaping fortunes of its members has greatly changed due to the benefits drawn by the middle and lower castes since Independence. On the contrary, erstwhile priestly, mercantile and ruling castes, due to loss of their privileged ascriptive positions, are no more effective in continuity and reproduction of inequality of the yesteryears. Inroads made by the intermediate and lower castes into politics, education and government jobs have not only made them more equal, but have also placed them in commanding positions. This, however, does not mean that all the families belonging to the beneficiary castes/sub-castes have been benefited or equally benefited.

Some have remained even today at the lowest rung due to the nature of distributive shares in the process of social and economic development. A new pattern of inequality and stratification has emerged among the intermediate and the lower castes.

FAMILY, INDIVIDUAL AND MOBILITY

K. L. Sharma (1969, 34–43; 1974, 125–168) analyses three levels of mobility: (a) mobility of one or a minority of families; (b) mobility of a group or a majority of families to a higher or lower position; and (c) mobility of individual members within a family. These levels of mobility are obviously within a caste as all those who aspire to move up belong to a particular caste. What role caste plays in their social/occupational mobility cannot be easily ascertained. These levels indicate that an individual and a family can move up socially and occupationally even independent of their caste. A given family or an individual may or may not be in congruence with norms of caste in relation to social mobility. Mobility of families and individuals have implications for enhanced class distinctions within a given caste or also between different castes. Sharma has cited several examples of the three levels of mobility in his study of six villages in Rajasthan (1974). Three patterns could be seen in terms of consequences of social mobility: (a) some families and individuals raise their status marginally or considerably; (b) some families and individuals go down as they remain incapable to cope up with macro and micro structural and cultural changes; and (c) some families, individuals and groups (castes/sub-castes) have made efforts to regain their lost status or they have adjusted themselves in the face of adverse circumstances.

In a paper on 'Changing Aspects of Merchants, Markets, Moneylending and Migration', based on insights from a village in Rajasthan, K. L. Sharma (1997, 174–194) explains that four factors, namely, the *jagirdari* system, mercantile activities, village exogamy, and literary and priestly endeavours, ensured a distinctive pattern of interaction in the past between the rural masses and the outside world. Today, with drastic changes in these traditional mechanisms of social relationships, rural–urban connections and social networks have not only acquired a new form and character, but have also become more widespread and intense (Sharma, 1997, 174). All the people who have moved out of the village have done so individually, certainly appropriating their contacts and linkages. Movement from the village has been in phases and to different places in Uttar Pradesh, West Bengal, Bihar, Jharkhand, Chhattisgarh, and also within Rajasthan. Sharma observes: 'Today the situation has changed drastically, due to the collapse of the traditional patterns of merchanthood, markets, moneylending and migration' (Sharma, 1997, 185). There are today petty shops, quite different from the bazaar that existed nearly half a century ago. The pattern of moneylending–borrowing has also disappeared. Besides the merchants, several people have moved out for government jobs, jobs in private and corporate sector, and for entrepreneurial activities. Such a change is certainly differentiated in terms of education, skills networks, income, but it is there across all castes in the village.

Multiple references and indicators of social inequality are evidence of challenges to the established or pre-ordained or taken for granted inequality. Inequality as seen in terms of attributes of individuals or of families more than their respective castes/communities implies the role of education, income, occupation, assets, lifestyle, etc., in status determination. Quality of education, skills, nature of jobs, and income are the criteria for success in the present competitive situation. Natural inequality is being undone by social inequality. All over the world, gendering of roles, patriarchal norms, ascriptive/primordial entities are being questioned and negated. Social implications of biological, racial, ethnic differences are refuted and qualities/virtues are accorded premium as they are indicative of fair justice and equality. Different values attached to men and women and division of labour are artificial, a cunning device of those who are stronger for some reasons. Variations and differences or diversities cannot be equated with inequalities (social).

But there is a fact that inequality is reproduced even in a democratic society, where values of fair competition, opportunity and justice are prevalent. For example, education is appropriated as a means of stability/status quo as higher educational institutions stand out at the top of hierarchy, and common people do not have enough resources to acquire ability to compete for seeking access to prestigious colleges/universities. On the other hand, education is also a liberating and equalitarian force for the first/second generation learners. Some people acquire skills to seek coveted jobs, to get entry into market and professions.

The Indian family, having professionals, civil servants and even politicians, plays a significant role by providing resources and ambience to their children in regard to education and shaping of careers. In the West, families are the source of means and motivations for the children. The problem of reproduction of inequality has been explained in France (Bourdieu, 1984; Bourdieu and Patterson, 1977) through the concept of cultural and social capital along with economic capital. Who get admissions in the best schools/institutes of France? In the same way, in India, who are those who succeed in seeking admissions in AIIMS, top-ranking IITs, IIMs, JNU, Delhi University and other reputed universities and institutions? Andre Beteille talked of *Caste, Class and Power* (1965) nearly half a century ago, but after four decades, there is a paradigm shift in what he says in *Family, Class and Caste* (2005).

At the global level, particularly in the industrially advanced societies, in the 21st century, distribution of wealth at the individual level would determine inequality. Institutional and political differences would play a key role in restructuring of inequality across the globe. Some role would also be of inherited wealth and income from labour. In a way, labour, inheritance, competence and birth are the main considerations in regard to inequality (Piketty, 2014, 237–270). The structure of inequality is today really different globally and also in the Indian extent.

Recognition of individual as an entity is an important feature of Indian Constitution and several other legal enactments. Recognition of family comes next to individual, and recognition of caste/tribe/ethnic group comes at the third place for specific purposes. Such a formal ordered reckoning of individual, family and group has implications for freedom, equality and democracy. Freedom to individual's efforts and achievements, family's binding for its members in terms of certain benefits, and space carved out for 'backward' castes and tribes (SCs, STs, OBCs) to encourage towards equality are the coordinal points. No more 'caste alone' is there as an encompassing institution. Beyond a point, individual members do not remain with their extended or joint families. And even within nuclear families, individuals assert their own identities, which are their own and not of the entire family.

Individuals or nuclear families in India are separated from their joint families, not due to industrialization as it is the case in the West (Goode, 1963). Separation from families of origin occurs in India due to education, migration and mobility, in other words, as a result of urbanization, which is not necessarily concomitant with industrialization. However, separation does not necessarily imply 'individualism' in absolute sense. A nuclear or 'conjugal family' remains 'functionally' attached to the family from which it has emerged out as a new entity. Patricia Uberoi (2003, 1061–1103) based on a comprehensive review of the studies on Indian family and kinship rightly suggests that one needs to see family in India beyond the debate on nuclear versus joint family. Not only the compositions, functions and obligations, intra-family relations, and social, cultural and emotional aspects of family have undergone a sea-change.

In an essay on 'The Person Beyond the Family', Margaret Trawick (2003, 1158–1178) raises a very serious question: Is There Such a Thing as South Asian Personhood and is Family Essential to It?' (Trawick, 2003, 1174). The Western scholars, from Morgan (1975), Maine (1861/1972) to Goode (1963, 1964), and the Indian scholars, from P. V. Kane (1930–1962) to Karve (1953), Kapadia (1955), A. M. Shah (2014), etc., have looked at the Indian family from the lenses of 'individual' and 'industrialization', and from the angle of joint family as an ideal inviolable institution, respectively. In the first instance, one finds a 'person', but not the same as it is there in the West. In the second case, there is no 'person' as such, and even if it is there, it is not independent of family and caste/community. Trawick (2003) says that there is the longing for individuation sometimes in the Indian context, like the West. The longing for autonomy and freedom from family is caused by the very strength of the family bonds. There is a peculiar 'Indianness'—characterized by familism and religiosity. There is a 'person' in Indian family, but this person is not 'individual', he is a 'purush' (man) as D. P. Mukerji (1958) explains: 'individualism of the western type is yet to emerge in Indian society, family and culture'.

However, the following questions raised by Trawick (2003, 1174–1175) are suggestive of further serious studies and research:

1. Will the power of the West eventually erode Indian society as it is presently constructed?
2. Will 'family' be reduced to its minimal limit?
3. What effects such processes might have on actual individual?
4. Can one be raised with a strong kinship orientation and live happily as an adult with one's orientation towards extra-familial matters?
5. Can a person be both non-religious and independent of family and still be an 'Indian'?
6. Can a society endure in which the needs of the individual take precedence over the needs of the whole (family)?
7. Is the family-embedded 'Indian' person somehow more natural than the individualistic 'American' person?
8. Is high valuation of the individual person the mark of advanced sociocultural evolution?

CONCLUDING REMARKS

Trawick raises these questions for further exploration, and observes that there are no timeless structures, hence change is the main *mantra*. Short-term change is more crucial. Role of economic conditions, media and communication systems, and experience or as Mukerji (1958) mentions *anubhav* would determine the nature of change in both person and family and in the nexus between the two. We may point out that the sociocultural and economic diversities have been shaping and reshaping family and its role vis-à-vis individuals (persons) in Indian society, and these diversities have also been changing and adjusting with the new situations that have emerged due to both internal contradictions and external exigencies.

A. M. Shah (1964, 1–36; 1973; 2005, 19–23) observes that our understanding of the Indian family is insufficient due to lack of rigour in the field studies. Dimensions of family relationships include a whole range of non-legal and non-ritual aspects. It is necessary to see how the old/traditional norms are eroding. Even the notion of 'jointness' is not just 'spatial' or a living together having members of three or more generations in the family (Desai, 1964). There are 'degrees' of jointness. Patricia Uberoi (2003) explains that today the family in India is beyond just being either nuclear or joint. Shah (2005) points out we have to see whether change is in the household or in the wider family. He argues that change is often the normal shift from one phase to another in the developmental process. Moreover, directions of change could be divergent due to heterogeneous nature of Indian society.

Mobility by way of migration is a most pronounced phenomenon as indicated by increasing urbanization and decreasing rural population. Reduction in dependence on agriculture and enhancement of nonfarm income in rural India also indicate the emerging patterns of social mobility. D. Jayaraj (2013, 44–52) examines a family migration in terms of 'push' or 'pull' or both 'factors' in India. His analysis suggests that there are four types of migration: (a) rural–rural, (b) rural–urban, (c) urban–rural and (d) urban–urban. Migration as such implies spatial mobility, but is guided by a complex of factors, including expending opportunities, failure of the rural labour market, social and political reasons, living environment, natural disasters (droughts, floods, earthquakes, etc.), and development-related factors. Jayaraj thus explains that both push and pull factors and social and political reasons determine social mobility by way of migration.

PART II

Glimpses of Village Economy

Chapter 5

Peasants
A Declining Backbone of Rural Economy

Village studies have focused more on caste, inter-caste relations, religion and rituals, undermining the key role of peasantry in rural India. While describing village studies, M N. Srinivas (1987; 1998, 181–197) highlights on caste, gender and participant observation (as the sole) method of study. In another writing, Srinivas (1978, 102–136), under broad caption 'The Universe of Agriculture', describes 'land as a value'. He observes that a great emphasis was on acquisitiveness in village society, and land was the most important object of acquisition irrespective of any caste or religion. Srinivas further observes: 'Landownership meant not only wealth and status but power over people' (1978, 110).

EXPLAINING PEASANTRY

There is no mention of the word 'peasant' as an economic entity in the village community. The volume *The Village in India*, edited by Vandana Madan (2004), has as many as twenty papers, written by well-known scholars, which focus on Indian village as a sociocultural and political entity rather than a significant economic reality in terms of structure and mode of agriculture and allied activities, explaining class character vis-à-vis peasantry and labour. Even in a recent volume *Changing Village India*, edited by Brij Raj Chauhan and A. Satyanarayana (2012), except for one article, and that too just mentions 'peasants and workers', nothing is analysed about peasantry in India. It is a group of economists who, with their Marxist method and framework, have made quite emphatic analysis of mode of production in agriculture, differentiation of peasantry and also its social genesis (particularly caste). Besides this fact, it was also realized that the Indian village was ridden with class cleavages and factions, and it was not a 'republic'; it did not have 'self-sufficiency' and 'autonomy' as romanticized from Munro (1806) to Dumont (1966a). Country–town nexus was a real historical and conceptual phenomenon (Sharma and Gupta, 1991). Was village ever a community? The village polity and agriculture have been organically linked. There was a complex system of land tenures and relations. Different forms of land tenure, administration and exploitation represented a nexus between village and town.

Teodor Shanin, in a comprehensive edited volume *Peasants and Peasant Societies* (1971), analyses the existence of peasantry as a realistic concept for both empirical and conceptual reasons. Realizing 'peasant society' as a quite distinct entity, Robert Redfield (1955) observes that there is something generic about peasantry. Peasantry can be seen in varied historical experience. Conceptually, it does not imply a claim of homogeneity, or an attempt at uniformity. Shanin (1971) refers to four traditions regarding study of peasantry as follows:

1. The Marxist class theory,
2. The 'specific' economy typology,
3. The ethnographic cultural tradition and
4. The Durkheimian tradition as developed by A. L. Kroeber (functional theory of change).

In the Marxist Tradition, peasantry is seen in terms of power relationship, that is, as the suppressed and exploited producers of pre-capitalist society—a leftover of an earlier social formation—at the bottom of the social power structure. The Specific Economy Typology view refers to the way a family farm operates. The debate in India regarding 'middle peasants' also centres around this approach. The Ethnographic Cultural Tradition looks at peasants as the representatives of an earlier national tradition, preserved as a 'cultural lag' by the inertia, typical of peasant societies. Finally, the Durkheimian Tradition implies 'dualism', that peasant societies are 'part societies with part cultures', partly open segments in a town-centred society. Such a view needs to be critically examined in the Indian context as India continues to be a village-centred social formation, despite access of the peasants to urban markets, participation in power politics, and non-farm income by the peasants and farmers. Based on such a complex conceptual and empirical bearing of peasantry, Shanin arrives at a general definition of peasant societies as follows:

1. The peasant family farm is the basic unit of multi-dimensional social organization.
2. Land husbandry is the main means of livelihood directly providing the major part of the consumption needs.
3. There is a specific traditional culture related to the way of life of small communities.
4. The peasantry has the underdog position as there is domination of peasantry by outsiders.

There are also analytically marginal groups, which share with the 'hardcore' of peasants most of their characteristics, such as agricultural labourers, rural craftsmen, armed peasants, pastoralists, peasant-workers in industries, etc.

We must note that peasant exists only as a process as structural changes have always been there in peasant society as a consequence of policies of the state, urbanization, market relations and acculturation. Peasants are definitely rural, yet live in relation to market towns. They form a class segment of a larger population. They lack the isolation, the political autonomy and self-sufficiency. However, peasants retain much of their old identity. integration and attachment to soil and cults (Potter, Diaz and Foster, 1967). Such a culturological approach has lost vitality due to multiple structural factors, including migration, education, social movements and state policies.

In the context of Europe, generally the word 'peasant' connotes a historical, social and economic aspect of life in the Middle Ages, when agricultural serfs clustered around great manors, or marginal farmers in small villages lived in juxtaposition to towns and cities, to which they came to sell their produce and buy the items they could not themselves provide. Today, peasants are seen in a wider perspective, as a major societal type, not just in terms of time and place. We look upon peasants as peoples whose lifestyles show certain structural, economic, social and perhaps personality similarities. Multiple economic roles are also associated with peasantry. Fishermen and rural craftsmen are also of the same social class as the agriculturalists and of the same families (Firth, 1956, 1964). Firth sees a wider utility of the concept of 'peasant', referring to the Malay fishermen. But Firth says that the concept of 'peasant' has a somewhat different meaning when applied to oriental people, then when applied to European communities. The similarities between the European and the oriental peasant communities are based on the fact that both are communities of producers on a small scale, with simple equipment and market organization, and both produce for their subsistence. According to John F. Embree (1969), peasants are a distinctive societal type in a Japanese village, having the following characteristics:

1. An intimate local group.
2. Strong kinship ties.
3. Periodic gatherings.
4. A part of a larger nation.
5. Education in national schools.

In fact, Robert Redfield (1941, 1955) is the one who first equated 'folks' with 'peasants' and later on considered peasants different from folks, and treated folks as tribes or primitive people. In this way, Redfield referred to 'Folk-Urban Continuum'. For Redfield, the peasant was like the primitive tribesman, 'indigenous', but unlike the tribesman, as he is for long used to the existence of the city. Peasants are rural people who look to and are influenced by gentry or townspeople. Relationship between village and city is a structural relationship, including social, economic, political, religious and temporal dimensions.

Eric Wolf (1969, 1971) holds quite a different view as he says that peasants are agricultural producers, and they do not include fishermen and rural craftsmen. Peasants have a structural relationship to some larger integral whole. It is the state and not the city. Foster (1965, 1967) also agrees with Wolf's view as he considers peasants primarily agriculturists in structural and relational terms rather than occupational.

In peasant societies, a substantial segment of people earn their living from non-agricultural occupations. This is not only true about the European Peasantry. Today, a large number of Indian peasants too earn from non-farm sources Foster (1965, 1967) is of the view that it is not what peasants produce that is significant, it is how and to whom they dispose of what they produce that counts.

Farmers are not peasants. They are semi-peasants. Peasants are not a part of any city, but of a particular kind of city, that is, a 'pre-industrial city'. A modern city does not produce peasants, but peasants survive into the modern world because of the phenomenon of 'cultural lag'; they are becoming post-peasants. Today, modern world demands 'secondary peasantry', urban workers or a rural proletarian than peasants in a complete sense.

Peasants have very little control over the conditions that govern their lives. They are poor and powerless, hence peasant revolutions. But we may see that peasants are not a monolithic lot. 'Peasant power' has been witnessed in post-independent India in terms of political leadership and movements. Mode of production in agriculture and direction of peasant movements largely determine nature and all over the world, the classical conception of the development of capitalism in agriculture, as in industry, has not crystalized. Petty commodity producer in agriculture persists. There are no agrarian bourgeoisie and rural proletariat. There are, however, some big farms, managed by capitalist farmers, employing landless labourers. The number of big estates (farms) has decreased all over the world. Family farm is the typical unit today. Rural labour force has become a stark reality, including agricultural labourers. To what extent landless and poor people are tied to big farmers/peasants? In India, regional variations are quite sharp; hence there is no common answer to this question.

PEASANTS IN INDIAN HISTORY

Barrington Moore (1966) characterizes the post-independent India in terms of its two cultures, namely, (a) pre-industrial age and (b) largely successful political democracy. The first speaks of the continuity of peasantry as a very substantial societal segment, whereas the second implies the continuity of political institutions along with newly created administrative and electoral structures and processes. The British, however, depended upon landed upper classes. Gandhi provided a link between village community, peasantry and the nationalist movement.

In medieval India, three broad segments constituted the state and society: (b) sovereign (ruler), (b) army (support to the throne) and (c) peasantry (paid taxes for the first and the second). Caste could also be added as a fourth component as it was the basis of division of labour. Under feudal system in medieval India, the society had two sets of people: (a) rich and poor, and (b) ruler and praja (common men). There was hardly any middle class. The mercantile order did not threaten the agrarian system. The Mughals retained the system of payment of a share of produce to the kind by the peasants. Akbar established direct relationship between the peasantry and the state. For assessment and collection of the royal share assignees were appointed. To rule and tax through native authorities, intermediaries were appointed, known as *zamindars*, who varied in size and authority.

Land was available in abundance. The problem was to make peasants to cultivate it. Such a problem also persisted in parts of India during the British period. A share was to be paid as revenue. Private rights of ownership were definitely subordinate to and derived from the public duty of cultivator. Moore (1966) observes that this fact has affected social relationships on the land even under completely altered conditions down to the present day.

Agrarian instability was always a worrisome issue before the rulers. Assignees had a tendency to extract as much as possible from the peasants. Peasants were heavily assessed and were kept under strict discipline. They were also decreasing in number, fleeing away to other areas. There was an increased pressure on the peasantry put by the assignees. Peasants were a little better off under the independent *zamindars*. Such a situation gave impetus to peasant rebellions. Peasants refused to pay revenue, took to arms, and plundered under the leadership of their chieftains.

Frykenberg (1969) makes an interesting observation. He says: 'What we see is a spectral view of socially structured land control relationships with gradations between two theoretically absolute polarities'. These are (a) lord over land and labour, and (b) the labourer on land, absolute in servility, so long as beneath him there is no lower level of subjection. Between the two are innumerable strata of lesser lords and larger labourers. Frykenberg makes another observation indicating complex nature of land relations. The relationships between land control and social structure are so complex that at points in the spectrum some lords may be forced to labour and some labourers may have the opportunity to 'lord'. Someone could be both landlord and tenant to another person.

All kinds of holding and rights were intricately linked to definite socio-ceremonial and communal as well as economic and political roles. Hence, the tenant and landholder and *Zamindar* and *Ryot* (proprietary peasant) look very much the same. However, there are innumerable superior, intermediate and subordinate categories and the innumerable designations for rank and role (Hasan, 1979, 18). Irfan Habib (1974, 264–316) pleads for a simple Marxist definition of peasantry. He writes: 'I take the peasant to mean a person who undertakes agriculture on his own, working with his own implements and using the labour of his family'. This definition is close to what is known today as 'middle peasants'. There is no reference to hired labour and control over land in Habib's conceptualization. Based on property relations, the Marxist scholars distinguish peasantry as (a) the rich peasant, (b) the middle peasant and (c) the poor peasant. In addition to these categories, there are also the peasant proprietor, and the seasonal share-cropper. These categories do not fit in with the above threefold classification, as it is by 'wealth' alone. Agricultural landless labourers, though do not possess wealth, remain a part of peasant history. Another question is: How peasants who pay rent, or surrender their surplus, are placed as the exploited and the exploiters in the peasant history?

Prior to India's Independence, three distinct groups shared the product of the land, namely, (a) cultivators, (b) controllers of cultivators and (c) the state (Cohn, 1979). The three were in constant conflict and negotiation. The British destroyed the pre-British system of land control by making land a saleable commodity. Cohn observes that under the British, men who had been tax farmers, petty revenue collectors, bankers, moneylenders and traders obtained control of the land, first at the auctions of the rights of delinquent revenue payers and later through moneylending activities. Thus, a new class of landlords emerged, and it reduced the importance of the cultivators and smaller intermediaries economically and politically. Many cultivators lost their heritable rights, the number of tenants-at-will increased. In such a situation, craftsmen like weavers, potters, blacksmiths, and carpenters became impoverished because of the increased supply of British manufactured goods. Village servants (*Kamins*) too lost their clientele. Thus, village became headless, disorganized body, having poor, degraded and helpless people.

There was a wide variety of individuals and groups with widely different claims of legitimacy regarding control of land. Each of them had differing legal, political, social and economic rights to the land and obligations to the rulers. Their ties to the agricultural producers also differed. Cohn describes caste-based ranked land ownership, land-tenure systems, purchase and sale of land, payment of land revenue and administrative setup in the 18th and 19th centuries Banaras region. The British created a new class structure of agriculturists through its land-tenure systems like *Zamindari* and *Ryotwari*. During the 20th century, a 'class analysis' (Marxist) of peasantry and peasant movements as initiated by Lenin and Mao attracted many scholars to analyse the capitalist mode of production in agriculture and differentiation of peasantry. Jacqes Pouchepadass (1980), based on the Marxist perspective, refers to landlords, rich peasants, middle peasants, poor peasants and the rural proletariat as the main categories in India's agrarian structure. In such a classification, landownership and the relations of production are the main considerations. The degree of support to a peasant movement is dependent upon a class position. Higher the class less is the support. Rural proletariat is backbone of the agrarian revolution.

Such a view may not always be there in reality. Some of the peasant leaders and the issues taken up by them served the interests of the rich peasants (*kulaks*). To name some of them, such as Charan Singh, Devi Lal and Mahendra Singh Tikait, would show that their supporters were mainly rich peasants and farmers. Even Mahatma Gandhi depended upon rich and well-to-do peasants of high-ranking castes during the Champaran movement. The Kheda movement in Gujarat had also similar character. In the United Provinces (1920 to 1922), the *Kisan*

Sabhas, peasant associations set up by the young nationalist intelligentsia and rich peasants under the auspices of the Congress Party led the peasant movements. Bardoli movement (1928) also had the same class character. The *Patidars*, who were rich and well-to-do, were in the forefront of the movement. Under the leadership of N. G. Ranga, in Andhra Pradesh, entire peasantry participated in the peasant movement, including the local powerful middle and rich Kamma and Reddy peasants. Under the influence of the Communist Party in Andhra Pradesh in the 1930s, class character of the peasant struggle hardly changed.

Eric Wolf (1966, 1971) is, however, of the view that the middle peasants possess the necessary material security to revolt against the exploiters. Hamza Alavi (1975, 1235–1262) too supports this view saying that the rural proletariat are incapable despite having the potential. The arguments against the view expressed by Wolf and Alavi are as follows:

1. The very nature of the middle peasantry as a class does not inspire its members to participate in any peasant movement.
2. The traditional structure of the Indian rural society places middle peasantry in-between the upper and the lower strata of society, hence no enthusiasm for involvement in peasant struggles.
3. The ideological inspirations of the Indian peasant movements do not influence the middle peasantry.

In the course of time, divergent situations could be observed as well. There are instances of tenant-farmers against landlords. Poor and middle peasants were drawn from all castes. The Kisan Sabhas were also dominated by the poor peasants in due course of time. There are instances of looting of landlords and rich peasants by the lower peasantry. One could also notice class collaboration in some peasant struggles. Initiative was from the upper strata of the peasantry, that is, rich and middle peasantry. Driving force was from the lower strata of the peasantry. However, Tebhaga and Telangana movements showed some antagonism between the rich and the poor peasants. Telangana had peasants of high castes. The Tebhaga of 1946 had urban middle class origin (Kisan Sabhas). Even the Great Depression of 1930s affected more the better off peasants (Dhanagare, 1983). In fact, Dhanagare's study of *Peasant Movements in India* (1983.) brings out a critique of Marxist thesis on peasantry, commentary on the views of Lenin and Mao, Barrington Moore, Shanin, etc.

MODE OF PRODUCTION IN INDIAN AGRICULTURE

The main points discussed by Alice Thorner (1982, 1961–1968, 1993–1999, 2061–2066) relating to the debate on the capitalist mode of production in agriculture are as follows:

1. Modes, forces and relations of production.
2. Modes of exploitation.
3. Agrarian classes.
4. Social formations, contradictions and articulation.
5. Movements and dominant tendencies.
6. Effects of imperialism and of centre–periphery links.

In the debate, there are ample references to classics by Marx, Engels, Kautsky, Lenin and Mao. There are also references regarding the views of Althusser, Balibar, Bettelheim, Amin, Cardoso, Gunder Frank, Kalecki, Herbert Marcuse, Martinez-Allier, Mandel Poulantzas, Pierre-Philippe Rey, Claude Meillassoux, Rudolfo Stavenhagen, etc.

The main question is: How Marxist methodology should be applied to the Indian case? Marxist historical methods exist, but there is no consensus as to the nature of these models. The other questions are:

1. Is there capitalism in Indian agriculture?
2. Is the dominant form of production relations in agriculture not capitalist but pre-capitalist or semi-feudal?
3. Can India today be characterized with one or another of Marx's well-known modes of production?
4. What was the mode of production at the time of Independence in India in 1947?
5. What are the principal rural classes?
6. What are the main lines of conflict, and contradictions in rural India?
7. What is the role of political parties and the State in India in relation to these questions?

Based on a couple of studies, the following points may be noted down:

1. Hired labour existed along with family labour.
2. Hired labour was indicative of capitalistic tendency in agriculture.
3. Gentlemen farmers were a new phenomenon, and could be termed as 'agricultural capitalists'.
4. Inroad of capitalism in agriculture created differentiation of peasants in terms of big, middle and small peasants.
5. 'Capitalist' farmers were distinguished from 'big' farmers.
6. No pure socio-economic type of peasant exists as there is a limited degree of capital in agriculture.
7. There is a small but growing class of capitalists within the non-capitalist economy of India.
8. Colonialism and imperialism had the elements of capitalism.
9. The pre-capitalist formation is characterized with 'semi-feudalism' in agriculture.

To conclude the debate on the mode of production John Harriss (1982) quotes Karl Kautsky as follows:

> To study the agrarian question according to Marx's method, we should look for all the changes which agriculture experiences under the domination of capitalist production. We should ask: Is capital, and in what ways is capital taking hold of agriculture, revolutionising it, smashing the old forms of production and poverty and establishing the new forms which must succeed?

> Even Lenin realized that 'infinitely diverse combinations of elements of this or that type of capitalist evolution are possible'.

The mode of production in agriculture is dependent upon the direction and pace of change in today's India. Utsa Patnaik (1972) observes that the trend since Independence is towards capitalist production, but this tendency is narrowly based since landlordism has not been abolished and there has been no substantial redistribution of land. Nirmal Sengupta (1982) states that the feudal model is still prevalent along with continued deterministic role of imperialism even in the post-independent India. Earlier it was colonial, semi-feudal, today it is semi-colonial and semi-feudal mode. Sharat G. Lin (1980) refers to such a complex situation as a dual mode of production. Dipankar Gupta (2005) mentions this as an uneven penetration of capitalism, hence feudalism. A large number of studies and analyses imply that there are pre-capitalist modes of production in which both caste and feudalism play a significant role (Banaji, 1977; Omvedt, 1981; Sengupta, 1982). Actual relations must be considered as the basis of the mode of production. However, Ashok Rudra (1978) vehemently argues that there is capitalist mode of production in Indian agriculture. Let us say here that since 1991–1992, with the initiation of liberalization and globalization, Indian economy has taken a new turn, and mode of production in agriculture has also been affected to a considerable extent. Distress among the peasants has caused suicides in the states like Maharashtra, Karnataka, Andhra Pradesh, Punjab, etc.

DIFFERENTIATION OF PEASANTRY

The British interjected land-tenure systems in 1793, with 'permanent settlement of Bengal', by creating intermediaries called as *zamindars*. Moore (1966, 346) calls such a situation as 'parasitic landlord'. Exploitation of the peasantry was intensified due to colonial land policy. During the British period, agrarian hierarchy, for example, in Bihar (Jonnuzi, 1974, 11; Sharma, 2005, 960–972) consisted of:

1. The state (the 'super landlord')
2. The *zamindar* and tenure-holder (the intermediary)
3. The occupancy *raiyat*
4. The non-occupancy *raiyat*
5. The under-*raiyat*
6. *Mazdoor*

Such a situation was characterized by exploitative, stagnant and pauperization of peasantry in most parts of British India. Guha (1983, 8) observes that the peasantry was under the subjugation of the institutions of *sarkari* (state), *sahukari* (moneylending) and *zamindari* (landlordism). After India's Independence in 1947, despite limitations and lacunae, land reforms have quite visibly changed the patterns of landholdings (see Joshi, 1975; Lal, 1982; Sharma, 1974, 1982). Despite uneven consequences (benefits) of the land reforms, there has been a 'redistribution' of landholdings and a visible change in the nature of ownership of land. Green revolution in the late 1960s and 1970s has though benefited more the substantial and big peasants and farmers, in some areas, it has benefited even the small and middle peasants (Bhalla and Chadha, 1983).

The traditional agrarian hierarchy has ceased to exist due to the abolition of feudalism, land reforms, the green revolution, improved means of transport and communication and planned development, including Panchayati Raj institutions, cooperatives, and rural development schemes (Sharma, 2013, 201–219). Today, there is an increased differentiation of peasantry which indicates economic distinctions, on the one hand, and exploitation, modes of livelihood, the spread of capitalism, the persistence of indigenous capital, peasant movements and mobilizations, etc., on the other. In the 1950s, just after Independence, Daniel Thorner (1956) referred to three main categories of peasants: (a) *maliks* (the landlords or proprietors), (b) *kisans* (the working peasants) and (c) *mazdoors* (the labourers).

While referring to inequalities in the new agrarian system (after Independence), Andre Beteille (1974, 91) observes: 'When agriculture becomes capitalized a new basis of inequality is introduced'. He further writes: 'structurally the problem of inequality can be viewed in terms of three pairs of categories: landlord/tenant, big farmer/small peasant and landowner/agricultural labourer'. Owner of the land remains a constant phenomenon in all situations, and so is an agricultural worker, and in some situation as a sharecropper. Even a small peasant can be at times a sharecropper and an agricultural labourer. Such a situation persists even today. However, three points in Beteille's analysis are quite significant: (a) Tendencies towards change from cumulative to dispersed inequalities, (b) Emergence of a new class of landlords and farmers, with a multifunctional character and (c) the diverse social origins of the new class of farmers (Beteille, 1974, 92–93). Along with agriculture as a means of livelihood and earning, the better off peasants are seeking increasing non-farm income from entrepreneurial ventures. Jodhka (2003, 2013) also observes that Indian farmer is becoming outward looking and getting oriented to the demands of the market. The farmer is no more confined to subsistence cultivation.

Differentiation of Indian peasantry is no more an attractive issue of academic discourse. In the heydays of the Marxist frame of reference in the 1970s and 1980s, the mode of production and the differentiation of peasantry (Gough, 1980, 337–364; Patnaik, 1972, A-145–A-151; 1976, A-82–A-101; Rudra, 1978, 916–923; Sau, 1973, A-27–A-30) were the intensely debated themes. Penetration of capitalism into India's agriculture was seen with a serious concern and somewhat disdain (Sharma, 1983). It may be mentioned here that even today penetration of capitalism in agriculture is quite eclectic and discrete. K. L. Sharma (2013, 204) observes:

> The use of electricity, chemical manure and fertilizers, hybrid crops, tractors, thrashers, sprinklers, etc., does not justify the presence of the capitalist mode of production in agriculture. Rich and well-off farmers make use of the new mechanical devices with a view to make more benefits, but all this is not sufficient to make agriculture a capitalistic phenomenon.

MARXIST DISCOURSE ON PEASANTRY

Agriculture cannot be equated with industry, at least in the Indian context. Capitalism is based on a system of relations between the owners and the workers, following a set of rules and regulations. Moreover, peasants are not a homogenous entity. They are internally differentiated and have differentiated ranks in the hierarchy of society. Internal differentiation has generally been viewed from an economistic–Marxist perspective. The position of the peasants in relation to other categories outside agriculture has not received due attention of social scientists. Let us see how the Marxist perspective is reflected in the differentiation of peasantry.

Using the Labour Exploitation Index (E-Criterion), Patnaik (1976) classifies peasant households into six economic classes. 'The E-criterion has been used for each household considering both direct labour exploitation through hiring-in and hiring-out as well as the indirect exploitation of labour through the leasing-out and leasing-in of land' (Sharma, 2013, op. cit., 200). The six-fold classification consists of

(a) rural labour, (b) poor peasant, (c) small peasant, (d) middle peasant, (e) rich peasant and (f) landlord. Nirmal Chandra (1988) also considers 'exploitation' as the main criterion as he talks of the exploiting classes—the landlord and rich peasants—and the exploited classes—poor peasants and agricultural workers. Chandra indicates that there are also implications of the class structure for political action. Ashok Rudra (1978) describes that classes are defined by class contradictions (like Marx). The relations between classes are relations of production, but 'not all relations of production define classes'. They define various 'social groups', but only some social groups are classes. Thus, according to Rudra, there are only two classes in Indian agriculture. The other classes, other than the Big and the Small, have classlessness—no contradictions or insignificant ones. Close to this view is the analysis done by John Harriss (1982). According to Harriss, there are two criteria of the differentiation of peasantry: (a) the size of production resources and (b) the labour relations. Four classes are formed, namely, (a) capitalist farmers, (b) rich peasants, (c) independent middle peasants and (d) poor peasants.

Another view is that the specificity of the colonial system should be taken note of for the mode of production in Indian agriculture (Bagchi, 1982; Banaji, 1975, 1887–1892; 1977, 1375–1404; Gough, 1980, 337–364; Omvedt, 1982; Rudra, 1978, 916–923; op. cit.). Hamza Alavi (1975, 1235–1262) observes that neither 'feudalism' in colonial India nor contemporary rural 'capitalism' can be theoretically grasped except in the context of the worldwide structure of imperialism into which India was, and is, articulated. This conception should lead us toward a conception of a colonial mode of production. If 'feudal' and 'capitalist' modes coexist in India, Marxist theory requires that they must be in contradiction: one emergent and the other disintegrating. Each stage is characterized by a mode and its principal contradictions. It is therefore necessary to explain conflict between the new rural capitalist class and feudal landlords, to distinguish them structurally. Alavi further states that 'colonial feudalism' is supported by 'metropolitan capitalism'. He agrees with Paresh Chattopadhyay (1972, A39–A46) and Jairus Banaji (1973, 679–683). Banaji observes that 'a colonial mode of production is neither feudal nor capitalist, though resembling with both at different levels'.

'Feudal' mode refers to localism. 'Colonial' mode refers to imperialism. In colonial mode, no contradictions were found as such between uneven segments. Colonial period is also characterized by de-industrialization and de-commercialization of Indian agriculture. Bagchi considers such a situation as 'stagnation'. Bagchi asks: How to label the amalgam of usury, bondage, wage-labour, and tenancy prevailing in the Indian countryside. He lists semi-feudalism, 'semi-capitalism' as neither feudalism nor capitalism, but both feudalism and capitalism as possibilities. Bagchi does not talk of a colonial mode of production. Banaji pleads that there was capitalist mode of production in the 19th century western India as the peasants in the villages used to borrow from moneylenders and small artisans in the towns. Alavi refers to this as 'peripheral capitalism'.

EMPIRICAL STUDIES ON PEASANTRY

Let us now mention a few empirical studies to know the ground reality of peasants, peasant organizations and mobilizations/movements. In Tamil Nadu, in Tanjore and Chingleput, and in Kuttanand in Kerala, the landless labourers unconstrained by possible ties to the land have been the main agitators and strikers (Mencher, 1974, 309–323). Mencher thus does not agree with Eric Wolf's hypothesis that it is the middle peasants who constitute the pivotal groups for peasant uprisings. In Tamil Nadu and Kerala, the landless labourers have successful organizations characterized by sharp agrarian conflicts as 50/50 basis of share-cropping exists in the two states. Caste allegiances are used by people in the system, to mark class differences. For example, share-cropping with one's poor caste members hides class distinctions. Mencher studied 10 villages in Chingleput district in 1967–1968 and 1970–1971, and found 'a very rough socio-economic classification of the rural population'. Caste loyalties tend to blur class boundaries. Pradhan H. Prasad (1979, 1980) makes a similar observation about Bihar. There are three broad categories of people in rural Bihar: (a) Top peasants, who are from the upper castes, but they engage themselves even in family labour; (b) middle and poor-middle peasantry who hire labour but do not work for others, and belong to middle castes (Backward Castes); and (c) agricultural labourers who have small operational holdings, and come from the SCs (earlier also STs).

In Bihar, there are rising middle castes and traditionally dominant upper castes at the top of agrarian hierarchy. Contradiction between landlords, cultivators and big peasants on the one side and the poor peasantry on the other emerged, and Prasad defines such a situation as 'semi-feudal', which was also analysed by Bhaduri (1973). Further, disintegration of semi-feudalism would result into contradiction between the Kulaks and the poor peasantry.

In a study of rural Bihar, Gaurang R. Sahay (2002, 195–206) substantiates Prasad's analysis of caste–class nexus. Based on his study of four villages in Bihar, Sahay mentions that land, tractors, threshers, pump sets, harvesters, are unequally owned in terms of caste. Castes also differ as regards the use of the forces of production in agriculture. Both the 'backward castes' and the 'forward castes' are heterogeneous in economic terms. Brahmins own nearly one-third of the total land. Koeris, Yadavs, Rajputs and Banias, along with Brahmins own 87.7 per cent of the total land. The lower castes, namely, Bind, Gond, Bari, Paneri and Dom, do not own land at all.

We have two quite illuminating studies of peasantry, (a) in Tamil Nadu and (b) in Gujarat. John Harriss (1982), in his study of capitalism and peasant farming in northern Tamil Nadu, states that analysis of economic, ideological and political condition to understand the development of capitalism and the present agriculture, structural–historical method is quite useful. But the dilemma erupts when capitalist development is taken as 'progress', and the persistence of peasants (small ones) is identified with social and economic 'backwardness'. It poses a theoretical problem. The practical problem is of changing them or incorporating them into the modern, more progressive political economy. Harriss thus explains that why it is that small-scale household producers persist, hence the persistence of the phenomena of 'underdevelopment' and poverty. Harriss discusses the 'peasant problem' and the conception of 'development'.

Harriss suggests three main views on the agrarian question: (a) greatest priority to large-scale production (industrialization), (b) emphasis on subsistence economy (small-scale production) and (c) collective ownership of land and the direct socialization of agricultural production.

These are also possible paths of development of capitalism from simple commodity production.

In north Arcot district, 90 per cent of the operational holdings are of only 3 hectares, and less than 1 per cent of holdings are more than 20 hectares. 90 per cent of holdings are in the hands of the owner-cultivators (1970–1971). Since ownership is with cultivators, conditions for the development of capitalism are more favourable in this district. Availability of electricity, electric pumps, and other means of green revolution (in 1972) were far more than the national average. Small producers have become involved in the market. Harriss finds the following agrarian classes:

1. Landowner-merchant capitalists.
2. Rich peasants (middle peasantry).
3. The mass of rural households, with substance cultivation.

The other two states, which have attracted attention of scholars are Uttar Pradesh and Maharashtra. Both Uttar Pradesh (Western UP) and Maharashtra have peasant culture, have no Brahminical pretences and have prejudices against zamindari innovative. Both the states have small-to-middle landholders. Economic disparities persist despite cultural similarities. There have been strong farmers' movements in both the areas. But there are differences between the two. In regard to mobilization of their members and their sympathizers on the agrarian front, in 1989, at the Boat Club, in New Delhi, differences surfaced between M. S. Tikait, a Jat (the leader of Bhartiya Kisan Union (BKU in UP), and Sharad Joshi, the leader of Shetkari Sangathan in Maharashtra. In UP, the BKU is concerned with the farmers. In Maharashtra, the Shetkari Sangathan (SS), whose leader Sharad Joshi, a Brahmin, presents a different scene. He has an urban background and intellectualist's disposition. His supporters are urban intellectuals. The BKU and Mahendra Singh Tikait (a rural Jat) do not approve of this. The cooperative movement (sugar) is another important factor in Maharashtra. The BKU is an organization of owner-cultivators. The SS includes within its ambit agricultural labourers and other landless workers (Dipankar Gupta, 1992).

Jan Breman's study (1979, 1985, 2003) of the rural economy of South Gujarat highlights on the exploitation and alienation of labour due to the accumulation of capital within and outside agriculture. Labour mobility or immobility revolves around the triangular relationship between migrants, local landless, and dominant landowners, who are the principal employers. Breman finds that caste–class nexus plays a predominant role in this configuration. Class oppositions are along caste lines. A net set of contractual relations has replaced the old patron–client relationship. Exploitation does not take place only through market forces. Jobbers and other middlemen have come to the fore as new manipulators in labour transactions. There is no more a framework of integration and cohesion. A growing divergence exists at both the top and the bottom of rural society. This sets clear limits to the caste-for-itself type of social mobilization.

A new ideology bearing the unity of farmers and labourers against the State has emerged. Michael Lipton (1977) asks: Why poor people stay poor? He says that there is Urban Bias in World Development. The book *Sons of the Soil*, by Weiner, (1978) also depicts anti-government or anti-outsider stance in rural India. A shift from caste to class has taken over the 'caste alone' syndrome. Caste as an ideological frame in appearance is one thing, and in it, in essence, the reality of a hidden class structure is another thing. Both caste and class refer to inequality and existence of two patterns of stratification, which were interlocked in the past, but now have begun to diverge. Leach (1960, 1–10) also recognizes economic differentiation in each separate caste. K. L. Sharma (1974) analyses social mobility within a given caste in terms of sub-groups, families and individuals. Jats in Rajasthan have organized themselves as *Kisans* (Sharma, 1998), and so it has been the case of Jats under the banner of BKU in western UP Today, *Patidars* of Gujarat are seeking the status of a 'backward class' (2015). The Marathas (2016) have also started a movement for reservation as a 'backward class'.

RURAL DEVELOPMENT

Dynamics of rural development and change can be seen historically in terms of the land-tenure systems introduced by the British rule and after

Independence by way of land reforms, green revolution and non-farm sources of income. Mobility of poor peasants and agricultural labourers is also indicative of change in rural landscape. Even the big peasants have acquired new sources of income within the village and outside as well. The middle peasants have been relatively more attached to land. Neat categories, such as *maliks, kisans* and *mazdoors*, as stated by Daniel Thorner (1956) cannot be found today. A considerable change in the structure of land relations and mode of production and birth of non-farm sector in rural India have led to reconceptualization of both 'rural' and 'development'. What is rural? It is no more as observed by Wiser (1936), Wiser and Wiser (1964), Srinivas (1952), Dube (1955), Majumdar (1958), etc. The conception of the Indian village in Bailey (1957), Mukherjee (1957), Beteille (1966), Espstein (1962) and K. L. Sharma (1974) is quite different compared to the one in the earlier studies. Caste and economic life, economic and social change, caste, class and power, family and individual along with caste, caste, class and power nexus indicate new dynamics of rural society. Clearly, these studies conducted in the 1970s and 1980s explain that the Indian village is no more a little community, and no more 'isolable'. More important are the 'networks' (Mayer, 1960; Sharma, 1963, 1969) and 'country-town nexus' (Sharma and Gupta, 1991). This is not to say that divide between village and town has ceased to exist. One has to see the nature of nexus and the divide in terms of the dynamics of change and development.

Development discourse has changed from the standpoint of integration and cohesion to competition and self-identity. For example, Kolenda (1989, 1831–1838) analyses how dignity (*izzat*) discourse has taken over in a Western UP village as a result of an overall development, including land reforms, green revolution, transport, education, telecommunications and employment, which have benefited the lower castes. Poverty alleviation, empowerment and social justice through various programmes and schemes have emboldened to some extent the people at the bottom of social hierarchy.

Who holds land? What does he produce? What are the means of production? Such questions are still relevant, hence debates on mode of production and differentiation of peasantry remain relevant. This does not mean that poverty has been eliminated. Djurfeldt and Lindberg's studies (1975) of ill-health and poverty remain quite relevant even today. The point is that instead of 'sanskritization', or 'caste alone' or adherence to Brahminic religious and ritual practices, 'empowerment' of the OBCs, SCs, STs, women and poor people has become the focal point of discourse on change and development. Independence of caste/ sub-caste, family and individual, instead of interdependence as characterized under the *jajmani* system, has taken up the centre-stage in the studies related to Panchayati Raj institutions, environment, girl child, mother care, prices of agricultural produces, employment, politics, etc.

The rural poor is the key entity in the study of rural development as policy and as process. There are no landlords anymore, but there are poor, underemployed people. The categories, such as rich farmers, kulaks and capitalist landlords are as such non-existent (Gupta, 2005, 751–758), but there is a range of owner-cultivators. Our visits to the six villages in Rajasthan (Sharma, 1974, 2006) show that the middle peasants and some above them are economically well off because they have also considerable non-farm incomes. Some also earn from agribusiness crops as well. According to Gupta, today, the issues are: larger state subsidies, higher prices, more favourable terms of trade with the urban world as seen by him in his study of the Bhartiya Kisan Union (BKU) in Western UP.

CONCLUDING REMARKS

K. L. Sharma (2013, 207) observes: 'The relations of production and modes of surplus extraction in agriculture remain central foci for our understanding and analysis of change in rural India'. Basole and Basu (2011, 41–58, 63–79) raise some pertinent questions about the peasant as a class, a constructed stratum, caste and peasantry, differentiation within the peasantry, etc., and they say that the peasantry exists as a structure in process, due to several regional, contextual and historical differences. Above all, the recent distress among peasants, as culminated in suicides, due to the changing nature of agriculture and policies of the State, refers to another dimension of change. Suri (2006, 1546–1552) lists the reasons of farmers' suicides as: cultivation as an unrewarding occupation, the growing disparities of wealth between the rural and the urban areas, the lack of unity among farmers to bring pressure on the state governments, and a disjunction between the interests of the farmers and those of the political representatives.

In four states, namely, Andhra Pradesh, Karnataka, Kerala and Maharashtra, between 2001 and 2006, there were 8,900 suicides by farmers. These are the 'developed' states of India. The main reasons are structural and social. The farmers who have committed suicides were well-off, but being ambitious, undertook risks to become wealthier, without realizing the negative factors in their ventures. Along with these four states, Punjab is also prone to farmers' suicides (*EPW*, 2006, Vol. XLI, No. 6). K. L. Sharma (2013, 201–219) has analysed differentiation of peasantry, social change and agrarian distress in succinct manner. At the end, we would say that the peasant (agrarian) question is not dead. Since agriculture and its allied economic activities persist, the question remains relevant.

Chapter 6

Artisans
Proto-industrial Workers

Artisans were not independent entities in India because they were associated with society as a whole. Secondly, they were also not a result of industrialization and urbanization. In the first case, artisans, such as carpenters, potters, tailors, barbers, blacksmiths and shoemakers, served other people who needed their services in lieu of customary system of payment at the harvest time and on occasions like birth, marriage and death and on festivals, such as Dussehra, Diwali, Holi, etc. The artisans of yesteryears thus cannot be equated with proletarians connected with manufacture for market. Patron–client relationship determined the nature of activities of artisans. The British rule adversely affected the artisans as the goods and services rendered by them were substituted by the finished goods manufactured in England. English created a market for their goods in India.

EXPLAINING ARTISANSHIP

Artisans in India, prior to the British rule and to a considerable extent even during the British period, were a part of agriculture in particular, and of the State in general. They were not linked to the 'market' in terms of their goods and artefacts. The whole family of a potter or a carpenter was engaged in pot-making or carpentry. There was no system of getting wages on a regular basis. In the early 19th century in England, the wages of the skilled craftsmen were often determined less by 'supply and demand' in the labour market than by notions of social prestige or 'custom' (Thompson, 1984, 260). Services were rendered from farm to farm and fair to fair in the countryside. In the large villages, there were stone makers, thatchers, carpenters, wheelrights, shoemakers, blacksmiths, etc. In the small market towns, there were saddlers and tanners, tailors, shoemakers, weavers, etc. Thompson (1984, 260) observes: 'Many of these rural craftsmen were better educated and more versatile and felt themselves to be a "cut above" the urban workers—weavers, stockingers or miners—with whom they came into contact when they came to the towns'. Thompson further mentions: 'Custom, rather than costing, governed prices in many village industries, especially where local materials—timber and stone—were used' (1984, 260). Customary traditions of craftsmanship normally went together with vestigial notions of a 'fair' and a 'just' wage (1984, 261). Social and moral criteria—subsistence, self-respect, pride in certain standards of craftsmanship and customary rewards for different grades of skill—were prominent along with economic considerations. The phenomenon of a 'labour aristocracy' was coincident with the skilled trade unionism. Along with the old elite (master-artisans), a new elite arose with new skills in the iron, engineering and manufacturing industries.

Thompson's analysis of artisans and other associated skilled workers highlights on the trajectory of artisanship and its transformation related with the state's policy and interventions on the one hand, and linking with industrialization in the early 19th century on the other, particularly in London. The artisanship, as described by Thompson in the early 19th century, exists in India in the second decade of the 21st century. One can see a lagging behind situation of 200 years in India, compared to England. Soumhya Venkatesan (2009, 7) writes: 'Artisans are imagined to share a deep and meaningful relationship with their work, which is embedded in their social relations not only within the community but also in "traditional" networks'. Venkatesan argues that the problems emanating from industrialization and urbanization such as unease and disquiet of industries, alienated labour and unenjoyable lifestyles are not there with regard to traditional 'craft producers'. Traditional craft producers are deeply integrated in their natural environment. Artisans adhere to important values of the crafts and their society/community.

Anand Coomaraswamy (1905, 1909, 1912, 1956) has written extensively on the art and crafts of India. Romantic image of Indian craftsman has always existed, particularly in rural India. Colonial industrialization has broken the romantic stereotype and dehumanized the Indian craftsmanship, by making it commercial and also by displacing and deforming its reality and essence. The ideas of work, ritual and the nature of objects acquired new contexts and meanings from the colonial encounter (Bayly, 1992). Coomaraswamy (1909) has placed a great deal of emphasis on the central role of the Indian craft producer in the socio-religious order. He characterizes craft as a sacred mystery, a sacrament, and not as a secular trade (Coomaraswamy, 1909, 72–73). Though colonialism adversely affected the Indian arts and crafts, national movement for freedom, particularly under Mahatma Gandhi, created national identity for indigenous goods and crafts, including Khadi clothes.

THE STATE OF ARTISANS IN INDIA

The Government of India has made all-out efforts to recreate some crafts and to encourage and promote some languishing crafts which have/had been lifelines of lakhs of people. Haats, craft melas, festivals of India (abroad), etc., have encouraged craftsmen within the country and abroad as well. Venkatesan (2009, 43–44) sums up the Indian artisans and their work as follows:

1. The craft producer is a creator of traditional aesthetics.
2. Craft is a national resource.
3. Craft production (artisanship) symbolizes village life.
4. The craft producer is isolated, anachronistic and tradition-bound.
5. Craft is an economic and political phenomenon.
6. The craft producer, who is unsuccessful, tries to pursue some other occupation.
7. There is a 'crafty' artisan who desires to make disproportionate profit from his work.
8. The craft objects symbolize the collective/national heritage, hence promote unity among the people of India.
9. The craft objects link the past with the present, associate people of different social origins.

Venkatesan (2009, 266) says that craft is both an idea and a thing (produce). It is a wholesome engagement as it implies networks between artisans, development agents, the state, and philanthropists, patrons, consumers and other concerned individuals and institutions (2009, 266). Such a broad generalization could be made based on a study of mat-making (weaving) in a small town in Tamil Nadu. Also important is the point that craftsmanship is a utopian phenomenon; it is a reality (practice of utopia) at the ground level. Borrowing from Michel Foucault and Jay Miskowiec (1986), Soumhya Venkatesan uses the word 'heterotopia', an effectively enacted utopia. The study brings out all the positive dimensions of the craft of mat-weaving as a social, cultural and national activity.

The Society for Rural, Urban and Tribal Initiative (SRUTI) published *India's Artisans: A Status Report* (1995), with a serious concern and empirical evidence. The Report provides a reliable picture of the artisans of India, who are broadly categorized as *Boonkar* (Handloom Textile Workers), *Mochee* (Leather Workers), *Lohar* (Metal Workers), *Tarkhan* (Wood Workers), *Bansphor* (Cane and Bamboo Workers), *Sonar* (Jewellers), *Darjee* (Tailors) and *Koomhar* (Potters).

These are broad categories of artisans. Long ago, Wiser (1936) provided a list of castes of artisans who worked under the *jajmani* system. Up to 1947, the year of India's Independence, patron–client system was the guiding factor for the artisans, with some exceptions such as *Sonars* and *Bunkers*. The condition of the artisans was no good as they had to work as per the needs and command of the patrons (upper castes, landlords, moneylenders, etc.). The Report by the SRUTI also expresses that 'the current state of India's artisans is a matter of grave concern', as most of them are struggling for survival. This also came out clearly in a study of the textile weavers of Chanderi (Sharma, 1999). As per the SRUTI, many artisans have given up, and moved away from their traditional occupations. Some do not have a way out, hence they cling to their occupations despite unwillingness. The modern market mechanisms are also unfriendly with the traditional artisans. The SRUTI (1995, 11) states as follows:

> The new economic and industrial order that is emerging concedes no space to the artisan sector. The powerful marketing machinery

that is a concomitant of such an order progressively expands markets for 'modern' goods and services at the cost of the artisans' markets. The research and development efforts in the new order are oriented towards developing capital-intensive processes and technologies which replace age-old, human friendly processes, rather than adapting them. Government schemes and programmes are hijacked away from the poor artisan to the rich industrialist.

The major reasons for the current state of artisans in India (SRUTI, 1995, ii–iii) are:

1. Disappearing markets,
2. Technological obsolescence and
3. Poor government planning.

The SRUTI (1995, VI) mentions that an artisan can be defined in terms of (a) essential and (b) incidental characteristics: The essential characteristics are (a) goods and/or services provided to others, (b) use of skills and labour for the product and (c) traditional goods and services. The incidental characteristics are (a) self-employment, with a sense of fulfilment of making a product(s), and (b) performance, individually or at the family level. Classification of artisans suggests division of labour, and enhanced use of technology indicates further differentiation of artisans, implying diversity and improvement in skills. In modern India (pre-Independence period), *jajmani* system not only reflected social differentiation of castes and communities, it also implied patron–client relations (power of the patrons), and arts and crafts of the skilled, semi-skilled and unskilled people, who were artisans and manual workers.

A HISTORICAL GLANCE AT ARTISANS

There were associations of artisans, known as *srenis* (guilds) in ancient India. And there were professional groups, who evolved into *varnas/jatis* in course of time (Raychaudhuri 1984). Today, there are guilds of artisans in India. However, there are also trade unions, associations of professionals, such as doctors, engineers, teachers, industrial and agricultural workers and peasants. The Government of India and the provincial governments have encouraged in a lacklustre manner cooperative societies for the good of the artisans and weavers, which have not been quite effective, barring some exceptions. Artisans have been at the bottom of socio-economic hierarchy (see K. L. Sharma, 1999). Sharma's study shows how the weavers in Chanderi town (Madhya Pradesh) have remained under the strict hegemony of the master-weavers (traders) for a very long time. Efforts of the government through cooperative societies, loans and subsidies have not provided them an enduring respite from the strong clutches of the traders, who trap them by providing advance money and raw materials, to make an absolute claim on their finished products (Saris). During the slackening periods, at times, the weavers in Chanderi took up odd-jobs and manual labour for survival within the town and also outside.

Tapan Raychaudhuri (1984, 277–295) mentions that the bulk of artisanal production in India, until the colonial period, was for the immediate rural market and small production units used very little capital. Artisanship was generally hereditary and family was the work unit. The master craftsman provided necessary training in skills. However, the coming of foreign rulers and also the indigenous rulers linked/ integrated the artisanal economy with the wider economic system, in their own interest. L. Alaev (1984, 315–317), based on the *Arthashastra* of Kautilya, refers to two types of artisans: (a) the master craftsperson who employed a number of artisans on a wage, and (b) the artisans who were self-dependent, and worked in their own workshops. The production was also of two kinds: natural and commodity production. In the first case, it was for immediate consumption, and in the second instance, it was essentially market-oriented. Caste-based crafts, at the level of family, community, and workshops, were in existence throughout the country. Centralized production through *karkhanas* was introduced during the colonial period for both market and to cater the needs of the imperial court or army.

From the late 18th century, there were three levels and forms of production organization in the artisanal sector (Bhattacharya, 1983). The SRUTI (1995, 12–13) mentions that these levels continue to be representative of the sector even today. These are (a) family-based production, and sale/supply was without intermediaries. These are common artisans, the rural potter, the blacksmith, the carpenter, and also the 'low artisans' like the basket and mat-maker. (b) In the second category, production is through the middleman. The middleman regulates production, resources and disposal of finished goods. (c) At the third level, there is expansion of the workgroup and inclusion of artisans other than family members, though from within a given caste/community. There is differentiation in the functions and rewards of labour within the workgroup. And there is more mediation by middlemen and advanced integration with the market.

The SRUTI expresses its concern over the present pathetic state of the artisanal sector. The main broad artisan activities are (a) cane and bamboo work, (b) jewellery work, (c) leather work, (d) metal work, (e) pottery, (f) tailoring, (g) textile work and (h) wood work. In all these work-domains, there was considerable decline between 1961 and 1981. As a consequence of this, there was a decrease in the number of workers, and a considerable increase of workers in non-household sector. Decline was in number of women workers from 25 per cent to 81 per cent in these artisanal activities (SRUTI, 1995, 15).

In India, craft is a cultural and creative manifestation; it is also a mainstream commercial product. This duality is a source of strength and a means of livelihood for more than 10 million people. The duality is also in the crafts as both men and women are engaged in making of particular goods and commodities as observed by us in Chanderi. Working together creates a balance of power and authority in the family. But women, children and even older members often work harder than the young ones. When women become earning members, this shows a social transformation and a change in gender relations. As women find new strengths and freedoms, men too find their minds and horizons expanding. The process is not without conflict, but it is invariably catalytic.

Today, one out of every 160 Indians is an artisan. In the wake of industrialization and globalization, handicraft is confronted with a big challenge. Despite such a situation and onslaught of branded goods, Indian craft has survived with 14 million people as actively engaged in the traditional arts and crafts. The State and the NGOs have also taken up the cause of the Indian craft. Craftspeople need to be involved in the development process. Crafts' organizations must open their doors for the craftspeople in decision-making and production process. They may not be seen as a cog in the machine. To have a coordinated approach, the main actors in the artisan sector, namely, the artisans, the government, the business people, mediating organizations, and the market must work in harmony (Kak, 2003, 42–48).

Based on her study of crafts from a historical perspective, Vijaya Ramaswamy (2003, 48–49) states that 'crafts were a part of the everyday vocabulary of the Indian people'. She further states: 'In India, crafts were the specialized work of certain caste groups or communities'. Depending on the economic importance of the craft work, a particular group or community would go up or down in social status. The *shilpis* moved up the social ladder compared to the *rathakaras*, who continued to build temples with wood. *Shilpis* made temples with stone. Temple as an institution harboured craftsmen, weavers, musicians and dancing girls. Carpenters, blacksmiths, goldsmiths and jewel-stitchers were also a part of the temple complex. Since all the craftsmen functioned within their respective communities, they rarely revealed their individual identities. Since community and within that family were the arena of craftsmen's activities, their special skills were transmitted from generation to generation or from father to son. Ramaswamy (2003, 52) also mentions: 'crafting techniques constituted an oral tradition based on traditional knowledge systems'. Tools of crafts were worshipped, and it is so even today. Vishwakarma Day is celebrated on a pan-India basis, as a day in honour of the creator of crafts. Craft guilds or *sanga* or craft *Panchayats* played significant role in protection and promotion of crafts in medieval India. Guilds or even the rulers issued instructions regarding the functioning of the *Karkhanas* (workshops). Today, the State and its agencies and in some cases NGOs are engaged in this task.

SOME RECENT STUDIES

A recent study of artisans in early modern Rajasthan by Nandita Prasad Sahai (2006) highlights on the role of the state and society in extending patronage to the artisans. Sahai looks at artisanal caste dialectics to unravel how caste structures animated artisanal life, both in the rural and the urban environments. Caste defines the relationship of its members with others, especially dominant castes and the state. 'That a low position in the ritual hierarchy of caste regulated various aspects of the artisans' lives and resulted in myriad forms of exploitation is indeed well-known' (Sahai, 2006, 7). Caste had political and civic overtones, oppressed and also empowered and enabled its members. Caste offered possibilities for association and action to the underlines. Sahai focuses on the multiple dimensions of caste politics. She writes: 'Rather than a homogeneous class, artisans represented a distinct caste following different occupational trades, enjoying differential ranking, social status, and economic resources' (Sahai, 2006, 12).

Women from the artisanal castes suffered a lot due to upper-caste exploitation, and also within their own households. There was a tacit understanding between the state, society and male head of the family to control women as per the patriarchal ethos of the society in Rajasthan. Despite such a rigid hierarchical society, autocratic state and patriarchal family structure, Sahai observes that 'artisans negotiated with the administration and state authorities, tackled local hierarchies, and dealt with their caste fellows' (2006, 234). There were frictions, conflicts, contradictions as omnipresent phenomena. Artisans protested against the hegemony of the state and society, but the resistance and protest were never absolute. The fact is: 'Artisans accepted the larger structures of power, caste hierarchy, and the state' (Sahai, 2006, 234).

Production of rural handicrafts in Eastern India (1757–1857) was dispersed, family/household was the workplace. Work was done with the aid of family members, with minimal division of labour, marketing was done without intermediaries. These were the 'common artisans', such as potters, blacksmiths, carpenters, etc. There were also 'low artisans', such as basket and mat-makers. But for marketing with outsiders, local middlemen were engaged (Bhattacharya, 1983, 284–285). Middlemen regularly purchased artisanal products for resale, and for this they made an advance of cash (*dadan*) to the artisans. This led to expansion of the workgroup and inclusion of artisans other than family members, though within the caste as a rule. Such a situation enhanced connectivity with the market. In some castes, there was an emergence of an entrepreneur-proprietor, that is, growth of a proto-capitalist enterprise. We have noted such a situation regarding manufacturing of silk sarees and its marketing in Chanderi (Sharma, 1999).

Banaras is one of the most known city for artisanal crafts. Weavers, metalworkers and woodworkers are the main artisans in Banaras (Kumar, 1995, 12–39), and the weavers of Banaras are famous for manufacturing of sarees like some of the towns in southern India, Odisha, West Bengal and Madhya Pradesh. Though Kumar is more interested in understanding of artisans' popular culture and identity than their existential condition, and participation in wider society and economy. The following passage is, however, significant to have a glimpse of the artisans in general (Kumar, 1995, 12):

> The fundamental fact of life for artisans is their poverty. Economic stringency and insecurity seem to be an essential part of the nature of their work and artisan occupations are uniformly classifiable as 'lower class' ones. Among these are the three main craft industries of Banaras described below: silk weaving, metalwork, and woodwork; as well as other less important ones not described here: manufacture of gold and silver thread; pottery; iron and stone products; theatre masks and curtains; decorative articles and cosmetic articles, such as beads, bangles, forehead spangles, and flower garlands. The basic features of these industries—their low capital investment, the control of the market by middlemen, the uncertain supply of raw material, and the low level of demand—keep their manufacturers at a barely viable state of existence.

The artisans, besides having poverty, have illiteracy, the spatial arrangements of the home and the workplace; the position of women; family size; and a subordinate position with regard to others in the marketplace (Kumar, 1995, 12). But Nita Kumar's emphasis is on the *identity* of the artisans which sets them apart from other poor, lower class and dominated people. They consider it their *pride* in being masters of themselves. They enjoy actual Independence and control of their work and their time, and the consequent ideology of freedom (Kumar, 1995, 12–13). The nature of handicraft production and the urban roots of the artisans and their understanding of being citizen of Banaras have created a deep sense of unique culture and identity.

After a fairly long spell of decline in weaving, by 1900 the period of hard days was over. Weavers were on their way to improve their production and earnings (Kumar, 1995, 20–21). The special nature of the products and the versatility of the producers kept silk weaving in Banaras surviving despite the presence of colonial products in the Indian market. The traditional skill of the weavers, the suitable climate of the place, and the virtues of Banaras as a market, and as a pilgrim centre and a favourite of the gentry contributed to the survival of silk weaving. Both 'cloth of gold' and 'cloth for specific religious purposes' were manufactured. By 1930s, besides the nobility, even the middle-class people started to use the Banarasi silk products.

Metalworkers are mainly engaged in brass and copper industry. The main products are: domestic utensils, articles of idols and worship, and decorative pieces. The visibility of metalworkers is much less compared to the weavers. 'Metalworkers today, in contrast to weavers, have a clear sense of loss' (Kumar, 1995, 31). Many have left and taken up other jobs. The industry has died out within living memory. Some have taken up furniture work or shop keeping, or service or some other skilled work (Kumar, 1995, 31). Some have migrated, particularly to Delhi.

Woodworkers have been a rare group, not more than 1000 in Banaras between 1880 and 1950. They were engaged earlier in the making of toys and artistic articles for nobility. Today, they are restricted to lathe work, making boxes for *sindur* (vermilion powder), vases and decorative pieces of the simplest kinds, model tea sets and cooking sets, tops, and other fashioned toys. This has been a hereditary craft as it is in the case of weavers and metalworkers. Woodworkers are not a united 'community' like the weavers and the metal workers.

A report on Economic Status of Handicraft Artisans by National Council of Applied Economic Research (1993) throws light on the present conditions of artisans. The report makes a reference to sixteen export-oriented crafts, based on socio-economic condition of 1,035 artisanal households. The study shows that self-employed artisans were more numerous among Hindus than Muslims. Hardly 15 per cent of the artisans belonged to the SCs/STs. Nearly 37 per cent of the households were gainfully employed, and it was the primary activity for 28.9 per cent of the households. Handicraft, with some exceptions, is dominated by male artisans. Both children and aged people were also engaged in crafts. Adolescent children were engaged in large numbers. Nearly 50 per cent of the artisans were illiterate. Educated artisans had primary and secondary level education. The self-employed artisans were better off than the wage-earners in terms of both education and income. Nearly 95 per cent of the artisans had received some basic training in their concerned crafts. Indebtedness was more among the wage-earners. Knowledge regarding labour laws was lacking among the artisans. Entrepreneurial skills were also not found. Nearly 80 per cent of the artisans had inherited their handicraft skills from their forefathers, and they were also not satisfied with their crafts. Some of them were looking for alternate employment.

A comparative study of carpenters and blacksmiths in Haryana and Rajasthan (Solanki, 2002, 3579–3580) shows that despite the plan outlays and institutional initiatives, rural artisans have not been substantially benefited. There has been a wide gap between policy and the actual support received by the artisans. The study by Solanki was conducted in four clusters, two of Haryana and two of Rajasthan. Solanki states: 'It has been found that these artisans hardly manage a square meal and a majority of them has studied only up to primary level and illiteracy still exists in this unorganized sector' (2002, 47). They do not have any formal training and learn their respective crafts in their own workshops (*Karkhanas*). The artisans do not own any technical infrastructure for value addition. There are no linkages with marketing agencies, training and technical institutes and district level centres. The artisans do not participate in any rural upliftment programme.

RURAL INDUSTRY

How do we look at the Indian artisans as a segment of our economy and society? In Europe, on the eve of industrialization, a clear distinction was drawn between the capitalist factory, 'domestic' or 'cottage' industry, and 'rural export industries'. Karl Marx (see Bottomore and Rubel, 1973, 137–154) draws a dividing line between 'modern' and 'old-fashioned' domestic industry, but he gave importance to rural domestic industry and town handicrafts, not ignoring them in the wake of capitalist-manufacturer. The idea of 'industrialization before industrialization' or 'proto-industrialization', as given by Peter Kriedte, Hans Medick and Jurgen Schlumbohm (1981), explains the condition of rural industry in the genesis of industrialization in Europe. Proto-industrialization as a concept is useful in locating Indian handicrafts, particularly in the context of half-baked industrialization and capitalistic mode of production.

In European context, 'domestic industry' and rural handicrafts were interpreted as a transitional stage between handicrafts and the factory (Kriedte, Medick and Schlumbohm, 1981, 2–3). With the expansion of trade, the household/domestic industry transformed itself as a rural export industry.

> The origins and diffusion of domestic industry as a handicraft export or rural export industry were explained primarily by the expansion of trade during the early modern period and the resulting bottlenecks of supply which could no longer be overcome within the framework of the guild system. (Kriedte, Medick and Schlumbohm, 1981, 3)

However, such a theory was subsequently modified as the emphasis was laid upon the specific forms of social organization, which characterized domestic industry as a historically new 'system of production'. 'As a "unique mode of production", it differed from the handicraft mode of production as much as from the factory system' (Kriedte, Medick and Schlumbohm, 1981, 3). Such a conception of domestic industry aptly applies to K. L. Sharma's study (1999) of weavers in Chanderi, a town in Central India. Chanderi has two classes, (a) weavers, though internally a differentiated lot, and (b) entrepreneurs/merchants/master-weavers. A large number of weavers work for their master-weavers who have patronized them by way of supply of raw materials, giving loans and money in advance. 'Interaction' between the two classes is a decisive factor. 'A primarily domestic production process was dominated and organized by "entrepreneurs" who were traders or putters-out' (Kriedte, Medick and Schlumbohm, 1981, 3). As it was at the beginning of industrialization in Europe, today it is in India that 'the artisans are the body and the merchants are its head' (Kriedte, Medick and Schlumbohm, 1981, 3). Marx's theory of 'class' seems not to be out of context, then in Europe, and now in India.

Domestic industry produces for market. For example, sarees woven by the weavers of Chanderi are not in demand for its inhabitants. In fact, earlier Chanderi turbans and *duppatas* were manufactured for the royal families, and today sarees and also salwar-kurta suit-length clothes are women for outside urban middle class women (see Sharma, 1999). To understand the persistence of domestic industry with a small *karkhana/* family as a unit of production, (Kriedte, Medick and Schlumbohm, 1981, 1–11) have coined the term 'proto-industrialization' as a framework. This framework 'made it possible to analyse areas of rural industry, that emerged during the formative period of capitalism, within the context of socio-economic development in general and to determine their regional as well as supra-regional importance' (Kriedte, Medick and Schlumbohm, 1981, 6). 'Proto-industrialization is here conceptualized as "industrialization before industrialization", which can be defined as the development of rural regions in which a large part of the population lived entirely or to a considerable extent away from industrial mass production for inter-regional and international markets' (Kriedte, Medick and Schlumbohm, 1981, 6). During the colonial period and also in the princely states of India, domestic industry was a lifeline in several parts of India, but it was not independent of the colonial and the native rulers. In India, proto-industrialization co-existed with feudalism (and also colonialism), and in Europe, it marked the disintegration of feudalism and the advent of merchant capitalism, and a sharp divide between town and countryside. Countryside encountered differentiation and polarization with the inroad of proto-industrialization. Today, in India, a sharp divide between 'urban' and 'rural' cannot be drawn because of multi-layered nexus between the two, historically, socially and contextually (see Sharma and Gupta, 1991). In India, colonialism created a situation of 'de-industrialization' (Thorner, 1962), but even along with such a situation pro-industrialization continued, though in limping manner. Between rural industries and agriculture, there was a complex but unavoidable relationship. Uncertain monsoons, droughts and famines, excessive taxes on agricultural produces, etc., provided a space for domestic handicrafts as a supplement to the rural people.

FAMILY AS A UNIT OF ARTISANAL PRODUCTION

In both agrarian societies and in the proto-industrial system, the locale of production is household/family. The production, consumption and generative reproduction have been the characteristic features of the peasant household and family as the basis of socio-economic and political order. This is also the character of the proto-industrialization system. Proto-industrialization implies cottage industry, such as manufacturing of sarees in Banaras, Kanchipuram, Chanderi, etc., and metal works in several other towns. Proto-industrialization, for example, refers to social mode of the weavers, namely, *Ansaris* (Muslims) and *Kolis* (Hindus). Both Muslim and Hindu weavers are at the bottom of their respective communities. Medick (1981, 38–73) observes that despite a wholesome change in regard to relations between peasants and their landlords, family continues to be an effective unit under the proto-industrial production system. Peasant also lost his land; hence peasant–craftsman tie-up also disintegrated. The family labour without land, concentrated more on domestic industry. Such a situation brought about a noticeable change in the family structure and in relations among the family members. The weavers in Chanderi, for example, have access to the market, either through their master-weavers, or on their own also, in case they are not dependent on the merchants. As such, proto-industrialization manifests itself as a transitional phase between pre-capitalist agrarian societies and industrial capitalism (Medick, 1981, 41). Under the proto-industrial production system, there are clear tendencies of capitalist exploitation, and capitalist attitudes for profit, but all this has caused somewhat slowly and incompletely as compared to the fully developed capitalist system of production. Medick observes: 'A decisive structural element of pre-capitalist social formations, the family economy was a condition of historical progress as well as of the contradiction which was inherent to the system of proto-industrial capitalism with its specific mode of production and its characteristic relations of production' (Medick, 1981, 41).

Family-based production is not geared to maximizing profit and achieving a monetary surplus. 'The maximization of the gross produce rather than the net profit is the goal of family labour' (Medick, 1981, 41). Individual members' labour or input or share in income are not counted. 'Use value' rather than 'exchange value' is the motto of the family-based production and consumption. Family acts as a socio-economic formation, as one-whole, not as a fragmented entity in terms of its members. Artisans (weavers) in Chanderi have amply shown such familial unity of production, consumption and access to market. 'Unity' and 'survival' are the key *mantras* of the proto-industrial production system. But what happened in Europe in the 19th century, is happening today in India with regard to artisans. In Europe, there was a configuration of the rural industrial family economy and merchant or putting-out capital, and it was seen as a transitional mode of production. However, the domestic producer exercised a considerable control over the production process as the raw materials and finished products and everything else were controlled by the merchant. Such is the situation of the relations between the weavers and master-weavers in Chanderi (Sharma, 1999).

The proto-industrial household invests its 'emotional capital' into its sociocultural reproduction (Thompson, 1974, 382–405), and also monetary income. Rural artisans have a 'plebeian culture', and live in the 'plebeian public realm'. This leads to a process of 'self-exploitation'. Capitalistically structured market and exchange economy govern artisans' proto-industrial production, but they continue to live as the traditional artisan family, satisfying their basic subsistence needs. Thus, we do not see much difference between the proto-industrial production system of Europe (before industrialization), and the present-day production of artisanal crafts in India.

Chapter 7

Weavers
Under the Dominance of Master-Weavers

Weaving, besides being a handicraft, also involves rudimentary machinery, that is, handloom, either manually handled or with electric power. Cloth is one of the three basic needs, the other two being food and shelter. In traditional India, although weavers were not linked with *jajmani* system, yet caste/community was its bearing. Weavers were/are employed by master weavers/traders. Thompson (1984, 298–299) distinguishes between four kinds of weaver–employer relationship to be found in the 18th-century England: (a) the customer-weaver–master-weaver; (b) supervisor, self-employed, autonomous weaver, (c) the journeyman weaver, working for a single master, and (d) the farmer or small holder weaver, working only part-time in the loom. This is an overlapping classification, but is needed for a heuristic purpose. Weaving often has been affected by the policies of the state, industrialization, wars and calamities, such as famines, earthquakes, etc. Weavers are also stratified based on their skills, commitment to work and relationship with the master-weavers. The weavers who have/had other sources of income, including agriculture, have/had been better off compared to those who survived on weaving only as ordinary weavers.

DYNAMICS OF WEAVING

It is not so simple to systematize facts and analyses about weaving and weavers in a chronological and understandable manner. Based on some selected writings and sources, and some studies, an effort has been made to see weaving and weavers as an important aspect of Indian society and economy. Tapan Raychaudhuri (1983, 3–35) mentions that with the decline of the Mughal Empire, large groups of craftsmen moved to other towns in quest of more secure livelihoods. However, manufacturing organization was stable in the mid-18th century. 'The rural consumer was still dependent for the bulk of manufactured goods on local produce, much of it distributed through the *"Jajmani* system", rather than secured through any form of exchange' (Raychaudhuri, 1983, 20). Peasants manufactured for themselves as well as for the market. 'Many traditional crafts were practiced by hereditary artisan castes living in villages (except for textile manufacturer) and receiving customary shares of the village produce, often supplemented by rent-free land and cash payments' (Raychaudhuri, 1983, 21). The fact is that the traditional system of rural manufacturing was not on decline, it coexisted with a commercialized sector of artisan industries—both rural and urban. There was, however, the merchants' growing control over the producers and production (Raychaudhuri, 1983, 22). The artisans received raw materials and cash advances from the traders. There was a direct control and supervision by the traders; in fact, the employer–wage-worker relationship was fully installed (Raychaudhuri, 1983, 23). Along with this, traditional caste basis of the entire system continued. A particular 'sub-caste' manufactured a specific variety of cloth. The artisans' guild was in fact the local caste guild of manufacturers of particular commodities, the head of the caste ensuring the maintenance of traditional methods and standards (Raychaudhuri, 1983, 24). Even the merchants were guided by their own castes in relation to the artisans.

'With the exception of the weavers, the rest of the workforce was composed of small members of artisans and suppliers of services in the *"Jajmani* system" just sufficient to supply the needs of the agriculturists' (Kessinger, 1983, 249). The weavers produced cotton cloth on order for the villagers and for the nearby villages and the *qasbah* (town) in North India. In South India too, cloth was woven practically in every village. Cloth was sold or exchanged in lieu of raw cotton and food. Finer varieties of cloth were woven in towns and large weaving villages.

Ordinary weavers did not employ labour outside the village, during the late 18th to the early 19th century. A majority of the weavers were in debt. The East India Company opened up foreign markets, finding the native merchants incapable of meeting its needs. The company imported skilled artisans from England to train weavers The company compelled the weavers to work for it even at a loss.

C. A. Bayly (1992, 144–150) based on several sources states that there was between 20 and 30 per cent of the total artisan population of towns and villages in the textile industry, during 1770–1870, in North India. Banaras, Awadh, Rohilkhand and the lower Doab were the main regions inhabited by artisans. mainly weavers. There were three grades of weaving: (a) the highest quality, meant for royal and aristocratic consumption and for the East India Company; (b) the medium level of production, for the local military, gentry and small royal courts; and (c) coarse clothes, produced for the common people, and also sold at the peasant markets or *haats*. Weaving and spinning in the villages were linked with peasant economy. The weavers who produced high quality and fine clothes for elites and aristocracies remained in a strong position. Several towns became famous because of weaving of clothes for royal families and elites. The company's export of India's raw materials and import of finished goods in the Indian market caused 'de-industrialization' of the traditional arts and crafts, including weaving, and dislocation of the craftsmen and weavers.

WEAVERS IN MODERN INDIA

In a different context, Gyanendra Pandey (1990, 66–108) observes that there were marked distinctions of status and privilege among both Muslim and Hindu weavers. Such a distinction was based on ancestry and caste. The *julahas* (Muslim weavers) were 'separate' and had lower status. They had their separate mosques. The *julahas* had lower status than other Muslims. 'The weavers, in their turn, recognized the considerable gap that existed between those with wealth. education and social standing, and those without' (Pandey, 1990, 140). The people made a clear distinction between the 'big people' and the 'small people'. However, in situations of crises, Muslim weavers turned to their own community for seeking resolution and relief. *Julaha Panchayat* remained on the side of the distressed *julahas*. Pandey observes that at the end of the 19th century the noted Muslim weavers of eastern UP and Bihar had an organized system of caste government on par with that operating among lower and intermediate Hindu castes (Pandey 1990, 144). The weaver identity and solidarity was not exclusive of the solidarity with other Muslims or with other inhabitants of the weavers' villages and *qasbas* (Pandey, 1990, 145).

Tirthankar Roy (1993) depicts vividly the state of weaving in the 20th century India in the wake of 'industrialization'; perhaps such a situation was in Europe in the late 18th and early 19th centuries. Roy makes three observations in the 'introduction' of his book: (a) cloth production in handlooms has been growing in the 20th century, regardless of what happened earlier; (b) any account of weaving must admit that this is a very heterogeneous industry; and (c) craftsmen respond to increasing competition, innovations in products and methods (Roy, 1993, 1–2). An important point that Roy makes is that the state in India is sympathetic to handlooms, but does not explicitly talk about inequalities among weavers (1993, 2). The persisting inequalities render that collectivization is unrealistic as it hides the complexity of the weaving. Despite 'deindustrialization', some institutional change has occurred in weaving.

Both stagnation and change have been there in handloom production. Rural and low-skill weaving has stagnated, whereas weaving with new products, new techniques and strict control on work processes have progressed (Roy, 1993, 3). As a result of such a situation modern and old technologies have co-existed in textiles. Our study of Chanderi (Sharma, 1999) shows weaving in Chanderi has been for the upper and middle-class people (for women particularly), and it has survived for a long time with simple technology, without using any electric gadget. Such a segment of weavers has survived, being dependent exclusively on family's labour, and also because of binding with the master-weaver for credit (cash advances) and raw materials.

Based on a national handloom census in 1987–1988, Roy (1993, 188–224) throws some light on recent situation of weaving in

India. The 1987–1988 census reported 3–9 million looms, of which 2.20 million were full-time commercial looms and 1.7 million were domestic looms in the north–eastern states. There were also some idle looms. Looms have increased since Independence. Of all the looms, one-third were pit looms and the remaining were frame looms. Twenty per cent of pit looms and 7 per cent of the frame looms have dobby and jacquard attachments. Sixteen per cent of all looms are in towns and cities. Some looms are in suburbs, and are classified as rural (Roy, 1993, 188–189). The four southern states of Tamil Nadu, Karnataka, Kerala and Andhra Pradesh (including the new state of Telangana) had 42 per cent of all looms in India as per the 1987–1988 census of handlooms. Bihar, Uttar Pradesh, West Bengal and Odisha have nearly 30 per cent of the looms. Western UP and Rajasthan make household textiles, using coarser yarn, durries, bedspreads and blankets. Punjab, Maharashtra and Gujarat are relatively less significant in weaving. But Assam and the rest of the north-east have weaving for domestic needs, and Jammu and Kashmir is famous for carpet and woollen looms.

DIFFERENTIATION AMONG THE WEAVERS IN INDIA

Weavers are a differentiated lot. Like the peasants, they can also be distinguished as high, middle and low-income weavers. Weavers are also differentiated in terms of rural–urban locale of weaving. Urban weavers earn more than their rural counterparts. The 1987–1988 census also mentions that of all the full-time weavers, 54 per cent are 'independent', 20 per cent are in cooperatives, 15 per cent are in putting-out with master-weavers, and 11 per cent are working in factories, both private and government (Roy, 1993, 193). Both government and market have been playing a decisive role in weaving by a way of cooperatives, loans, subsidies and marketing of finished products. Roy (1993, 222–224) concludes that weaving today remains a segmented industry, despite the efforts made to reduce inequalities and private power. Some new divisions among the weavers have also surfaced. The nature of weaving, consumers of the products, contracts and employment practices are main factors relating to inequalities among the weavers across India.

Nita Kumar (1995), in her book *The Artisans of Banaras: Popular Culture and Identity*, 1880–1986, discusses the nature of work done by weavers, metalworkers and woodworkers. Here we will briefly describe about the weavers of Banaras as reported by Nita Kumar. Artisans constitute 'lower classes'. She describes 'certain aspects of lower-class life' as popular culture of the artisans of Banaras, particularly the weavers, more than the metalworkers and woodworkers. Kumar treats artisans' leisure activities as 'popular' and 'urban', their culture as a 'system' and the lifestyle of Banaras as 'Banarasi'. She says that the term 'popular culture' is used to characterize a post-industrial, capitalist-controlled reality. But Kumar uses culture of the artisans of Banaras as 'popular' and 'urban' rather than as 'popular culture' to characterize specific character of Banaras or 'Banarasipan'. Under the rubric of popular culture in Banaras are some specific activities and ways of doing things: outdoor trips, wrestling, fairs, festivals, and music 'sittings' (Kumar, 1995, 5–6). All these activities are actual as physical objects and also as symbols. Kumar claims to uncover the 'structure' in 'history' and 'history' in 'structure' as done by Marshall Sahlins (Kumar, 1995, 6).

As a group, artisans are often referred to as *mazdoor, garib log, garib tapke* or *neechi qaum*, that is, as labourer, poor people, poor classes or lower classes, castes, respectively (Kumar, 1995, 13). In the context of weavers, Nita Kumar asks: (a) 'What kind of man is weaver?' and (b) 'How does his product determine his being?' (1995, 14). The census data from 1872 to 1981, as reported by Kumar (1995, 19) shows that the following categories of people have been associated with weaving:

1. Kincob (brocade) maker.
2. Silk weavers.
3. Weavers.
4. Gold cloth weaver, seller.
5. Silk dealer.
6. Cotton weaver.
7. Silk spinners and weavers.
8. Workers in textile industries.

9. Manufacturers of wearing apparel and made-up textile goods.
10. People engaged in the silk industry.

Based on her anthropological–historical study and analysis, Nita Kumar (1995, 229–236) concludes that the artisans of Banaras are poor, due to the nature of their product, the means of its production, and the structure of relations. This itself explains the essential character of popular culture in Banaras, which implies 'the premium put on free time, the high evaluation of leisure, and the elaborations of the festival calendar' (Kumar, 1995, 29). The artisans of Banaras can be characterized as 'pre-industrial'. They are real subaltern classes of people. Nita Kumar's observation is quite relevant:

> Artisans are not factory workers, and their ideology of freedom and leisure is clearly dependent on their actual control over their time and production. Yet their cultural system is important in itself as a complex structure of meanings whereby they relate to their natural and social world. It is not the only one possible, it is not known in advance, and it has its own logical and aesthetic rules. (Kumar, 1995, 229–230)

Kumar sees a synthesis of material and cultural aspects with regard to weavers in Banaras. She brings out an objective reality of poverty, time and freedom (that is, both material and sociocultural aspects) in the life of weavers of Banaras. With social mobility, culture also changes. When a weaver becomes an independent artisan to master-artisan, his notions and actions become that of a superior class of people.

The study by Nita Kumar is based more on observations of the families of Muslim weavers in Banaras, and so is the study of Banaras Muslim weavers by Vasanthi Raman (2010). Raman focuses on Hindu–Muslim relations in Banaras through her study of the Banarasi sari industry and the social reality of weaving. She claims to envelop the relations between men and women, and children, and both in the 'outside' and public domain and in the domestic 'inside' one. A weaver has multiple identities and is located at a particular level in the social hierarchy. He encounters conflicting pressures of religion, caste, class and gender. Momin Ansaris are weavers, and Hindus are master-weavers and traders in the sari industry. A situation of conflict, interdependence and composite culture characterizes the weaving community of Banaras. Weavers of Banaras are also differentiated as we have seen elsewhere, in four southern states and in the case of Chanderi (Sharma, 1999).

WEAVERS AND MASTER-WEAVERS

A study of weaving, weavers and master-weavers in Chanderi (Sharma, 1999, 71–88) shows that in 1995, there were about 3500 handlooms in the town, including the adjacent village Pranpur. It was estimated that more than half of its population, that is more than 10,000 inhabitants, were dependent on weaving of sarees and some other clothes (Sharma, 1995, fn. 1,71). Today, after a turbulent period, both before and after Independence, the weaving of silk, fine cotton, and silk and cotton mixed sarees has become the backbone of Chanderi's economy. Nearly all the *Kolis* and three-fourths of *Momins/Ansaris* (Muslims) survive on manufacturing of sarees in Chanderi. More than one hundred fifty families of Jains, Maheshwaris (Banias), Brahmans, Muslims and Kolis are dependent on the saree trade. Since Chanderi products, worth rupees 15 crores a year, are exported to other parts of India, we can say that the very art of weaving in Chanderi is germane to its economy. At the same time, employment, control and domination by the master-weavers and the middle and upper middle-class women (who wear the Chanderi sarees) determine the nature of weaving itself. As such, the cultural perspective in weaving is important, weaving is a way of life, irrespective of its economic viability and as a means of livelihood.

Today, the weavers of Chanderi enjoy more autonomy than ever before, particularly due to intervention by the state and also because of an increased demand for the Chanderi products. Till 1979–1980, weavers in Chanderi had a pitiable life. Vijaya Ramaswamy's study of weavers in medieval South India (op. cit.) reveals what a weaver says: 'It is the grave pit, not the loom pit'. Weavers were 'poor and emaciated'. Looms were primitive and the weavers were dependent on the market for yarn and dyes. So is the situation even today in Chanderi, though there have been cooperatives of the weavers for quite some time and there are also the recently established self-help groups. In the past, calamities and epidemics and the 1857 revolt created a setback to handloom weaving in Chanderi. In such adverse circumstances, weavers fled away to other places in search of security and survival. Some of them were brought back to Chanderi by the rulers with assurance of a secured source of livelihood. The intervention, from the Gwalior State in 1910 and subsequently up to the P. K. Lahiri Report (1979), has kept the weaving in Chanderi alive (see Sharma, 1999). In all, in 1979, only 523 families with 929 looms were engaged in weaving, and of these, 756 looms were owned by the master-weavers and traders. 229 looms were active for 200 days and 100 looms could get work for 100 days or less. The technical level was low. Local weavers were simply trained to use *fly-shuttle* looms operated by one person, not the more effective *throw-shuttle* looms. The designs provided by the Textile Institute (at Chanderi) were few and old-fashioned. The total annual production was around 300,000 metres, valued at ₹4,500,000.00 only (see Sharma, 1999, 77). K. L. Sharma (1999, 88) concludes his study of Chanderi in relation to weaving and weavers as follows:

> We may conclude by saying that Chanderi has a unique formation and class structure. It has capital but no capitalism. It has entrepreneurs but no directly employed workers. It has industry but no industrialization. It has workers, but without fixed salaries and wages. A sort of proto-industrialization characterizes the town.

At the same time, the economic weight of sari weaving makes this activity a kind of mono-industry: other activities (*biri* manufacturing, stone-quarrying, pottery and basket-making) become pale in comparison. Nevertheless, the two main bazaars remain all the time bubbling with a variety of economic activities and transactions. The white-collar workers add to the differentiation of the class structure of the town without bringing in any perceptible class antagonism and cleavages.

Master-weavers/traders in Chanderi have undergone some noticeable change. Earlier Muslims had a monopoly of the sari trade. But from the middle of the 19th century, Jains and Maheshwaris (both Banias in common parlance) entered into the sari trade. Only Kolis are newcomers, particularly those who have not been dependent upon the Jain and Maheshwari traders for advance money and raw materials. Some

Brahmins have also been in the saree trade. Now they are disinclined to take up this enterprise. In 1993, there were about 120 master-weavers, big and small, of which 5 were Brahmins, 60 were *Ansaris* (Muslims), 11 were Kolis, and the remaining 46 were Jains and Maheshwaris. The Jain and Maheshwari traders were at the top of the saree trade, and controlled a large number of looms. A Maheshwari controlled more than 300 looms and advanced ₹1,000,000 at any given point of time to the weavers. A Muslim master-weaver controlled more than 100 looms. It may be mentioned here that the Jain–Maheshwari traders have weavers associated with them from both among the Ansaris and Kolis, whereas Muslim traders had only Muslim weavers working under their control. Maheshwaris are a very small community (caste), but they are at the top of the traders' hierarchy (Sharma, 1999). However, Muslim and Hindu weavers, master-weavers, particularly Jains and Maheshwaris (upper castes), Brahmins and other castes live in clearly demarcated parts of Chanderi (Sharma, 2003, 405–427).

CASTE/COMMUNITY, STATE AND WEAVERS

Mobility among the weavers has been there in both the communities, namely, Kolis and Muslims. Some weavers have moved up as independent weavers. Some have moved up further as master-weavers. In fact, all the Muslim and the Koli weavers have moved up over a period of time through such a process. The Muslim and Koli weavers feel more secure and confident, while the remaining are attached to the master-weavers of their own caste/community. There is also a feeling that they are not as much exploited as it is in the case of Jain and Maheshwari traders. The cooperative sector (cooperative societies) has not been effective in weakening the bond/binding of the weavers to the master-weavers. Because of a weak cooperative sector, nearly 75 per cent of the textile production is controlled by the master-weavers. Some of the top-ranking traders have their outlets and trade links in cities, like Kolkata, Delhi, Chennai, Mumbai, Pune, Jaipur, Bhopal, Bengaluru, Indore, etc.

While explaining the structure of handloom industry in India, Niranjana et al. (2006, 3361–3366) list the main characteristics as follows: (a) dispersed production base, (b) diversity, (c) organization of production and (d) state policies vis-à-vis handlooms. The handloom industry has a dispersed base as the producers are spread across numerous villages and towns. It is largely home-based, with labour inputs from the entire family, men, women, children, young and old members. Diversity of products ranges from coarse cloth to medium and fine fabrics. The modes and relations of production are also diverse as there are independent weavers, weavers associated with cooperatives and those working under master-weavers. Lastly, the government policies supporting the handloom industry has also contributed to its survival.

Handloom production uses simple, low cost tools and equipment. It has survived for centuries due to relations of the weavers with the market and the master-weavers. The local market, and the weavers' cooperatives have made it possible for the weavers to work generation after generation. The question of marketing of handlooms cloth has been a main point for the weavers, the cooperatives and the merchants. Case studies of FABINA, DESI, ANOKHI, URMIL show organized marketing of the handloom products. As we have mentioned earlier that master-weavers dominate, and cooperatives in Chanderi are practically non-existent. So is the case in Andhra Pradesh (*EPW*, 2006, 3377–3379). Some organizations/cooperatives have been doing well as 'profit' is not their sole motive (*EPW*, 2006, 3367–3398).

Handloom in itself is sustainable, simple 'socio-technology' (Mamidipudi, Syamasundari and Bijker, 2012, 41–51). Weaving communities show a more strategic mobility and flexibility. As also observed by K. L. Sharma (1999), weavers in stressful conditions switch to other sources of livelihood, including masonry, carpentry, manual work, agricultural work, etc., and on improvement in the condition of weaving also return to restart weaving. Considering weaving as premodern, unproductive and unsustainable due to its low-level of technology, poor condition of weavers and lack of marketing is a distort of the fact that weaving is a 'socio-technology', an ensemble of knowledge, skills, technology and social relations (Namidipudi, Syamasundari and Bijker, 2006). The following observation is quite apt as made by the authors Namidipudi, Syamasundari and Bijker (2006, 50):

Weavers do realize that their technical expertise is closely linked to their ability to build and leverage social networks, and they understand the nature of interpersonal relations as being crucial to support their place in the complex systems of pre and post-loom processes and the market. They understand that cyclical practices of technology and the transactions over time build and transfer not just skills, but also knowledge. This complex mix of human and machine, embedded in social and transactional networks, works together—they understand—towards a goal of sustainable existence.

Thus, the Indian weaver is not 'an embarrassing anachronism', because handloom products and skills are in demand (Chatterjee, 2015, 34–38).

CONCLUDING OBSERVATIONS

Two broad conclusions can be drawn from the studies of textile industry and weavers: (a) weaving is an ancient art and craft, it enjoyed a place of honour, and became a part of both temple and palace; and (b) with the coming of the East India Company, it lost its glorious heritage and cultural aroma. Indebtedness, alienation from products, middlemen, unemployment and dehumanization unsettled the weavers' community of trained skilled workers. To a considerable extent, such a situation is perceptible in relations between master-weavers and weavers. Weavers are, however, not a monolith. They are divided as superior and lower categories, based on their ability, income and recognition by the master-weavers. In recent times, the handloom weavers have made adjustments to the changing larger economy and to the available access to markets, cooperatives and administrative and financial agencies. These adjustments have been due to their own constraints of making a livelihood and lack of ability to manipulate the market for cloth. The master-weavers have been far faster in the process of adaptability to the weavers, technology and market. The share of cotton cloth for home market is about 27 per cent, and in silk, it is two-thirds of the yarn (Roy, 1993, 24). A multi-loom house is becoming a common feature. In Chanderi, such a situation prevails, overwhelmingly. The decline of the handloom weaving of the 18th and 19th centuries is no more a feature in the 20th and 21st centuries.

The weavers have, perhaps, a strong cultural aspect associated with weaving as stated by Nita Kumar for the weavers of Banaras (Kumar, 1995) and Deepak Mehta for weavers of Barabani (1992, 77–113). According to the cultural perspective, weaving is a way of life and just not an occupation or source of livelihood. But a pertinent question is asked by Mattison Mines (1984), who says: 'What do we know about Indian society by studying weaving?' Mines mentions that Kaikkoolar weavers of Tamil Nadu have been organized for centuries into supra-local organizations and have been engaged in commercial trade beyond Tamil Nadu and even in international trade. The Kaikkoolars have also organized themselves as a strong group in the past to protect against the threat posed to them by other sections of society. They have also formed a regional association/territorial council to maintain their distinct ritual and social identity. Nita Kumar talks of popular culture and identity of the artisans of Banaras, particularly of the weavers, as the main consideration. Economic and political ends override the cultural and social aspects in Mines' analysis of the weavers of Tamil Nadu. Deepak Mehta sees a middle path in his study of the weavers of the Barabanki villages. Work and worship are interchangeable phenomena in the lives of the *julahas* (Ansari weavers).

Today, in all the regions of India, the entire family of a weaver is engaged in weaving, including women and children. Women and children are not generally counted as 'weavers', they are treated more as 'helping hands'. There is no initiation ceremony for joining weaving among Hindus, as it is, for example, among the weavers of Barabanki, as mentioned by Mehta. No doubt, the cultural dimension of economy is a very important aspect, but it cannot be over and above the basic conditions of the existence of weavers, wages, relations of production and the role of the state.

As weaving is family-centred, so is the textile trade. Business class has a certain sociocultural background, a work culture. The Banias of the 18th and 19th centuries underwent a change in the 20th century by way of differentiation of socio-cultural background and management strategies. Supra-local contacts for trade and commerce, for example, have become the main mechanism of saree trade in Chanderi. Merchants in Chanderi, without ownership of looms, control the looms and weavers. 'Binding', not 'bondage', is the spirit of weaver–master-weaver relations. 'Patronage' is a proper word to explain the control of the master-weavers on the weavers. The fact is that with the exception of a few 'independent' weavers, the entire weaving could be seen in terms of the complex of 'binding' of weavers with master-weavers; and this is an open-secret. A sort of patron–client relationship characterizes the complex of weaving in Chanderi.

PART III

Rural Power Structure

Chapter 8

Reflections on Indian Polity vis-à-vis Indian Village

There is social origin of power; hence it is vested in institutions, groups, families and individuals. Before we discuss these arenas of political power, let us have a glance at Indian society as a socially and culturally diverse entity with innumerable regions and sub-regions, languages and dialects, castes and sub-castes, religious and ethnic communities, natives and settlers (migrants), insiders and outsiders, etc. These entities also tend to be cleavages along with unequal economic resources and assets. Distinctions in terms of social status and cultural symbols or traits also influence power and authority as do the divisions based on caste, religion and language. From the viewpoint of political economy, Barringon Moore's (1966, 314) following statement reveals the true character of Indian polity (political economy):

> That India belongs to Two Worlds is a familiar platitude that happens to be true. Economically, it remains in the preindustrial age. It has not had an industrial revolution in either of the two capitalist variants discussed so far, nor according to the communist one. There has been no bourgeois revolution, no conservative revolution from above, no peasant revolution. But as a political species it does belong to the modern world.

DYNAMICS OF INDIAN POLITY

Indian political democracy has survived without substantial industrial revolution. However, since India's Independence, market has acquired a new form and functioning, particularly during the post-globalization period (1991–1992 till date). However, the presence of caste, ethnicity, religion and region clearly shows the role of 'tradition' or primordiality in modern Indian polity and economy. Moore (1966, 317), while referring to Mooreland (1920, 1929), observes: 'According to a well-known description, the fundamental features of the traditional Indian polity were a sovereign who ruled, an army that supported the throne, and a peasantry that paid for both'. Moore adds to this the notion of caste as a system of social organization, which Mooreland undermined, perhaps for political/administrative reasons.

In a comprehensive description of India's journey of political economy from medieval India to Nehruvian era, Moore (1966, 314–410) describes that Mughal India was an obstacle to democracy, and village society was an obstacle to rebellion. The Mughal system was too predatory as it put the ruler and his subjects in a situation where greedy behaviour was often the only kind that made sense. The establishment of peace and order was such that it did not create a conducive situation for the rise of mercantile influences vis-à-vis agrarian system. Prior to Mughal rulers, there were more direct and functional relations between the peasantry and Hindu rulers.

There was no economic and political movement in India like Europe, from the 16th to the 18th centuries (Moore, 1966, 330). There were two reasons for this: (a) widespread poor cultivation and (b) the apparent political docility of the Indian peasants. Moore mentions that 'peasant rebellions never assumed remotely the same significance in India that they did in China' (Moore, 1966). After providing a vivid account of the place of peasantry in Indian society, Moore (1966, 341) observes: 'I would suggest that, as an organization of labour, caste in the countryside was cause of poor cultivation, though certainly not the only one'. Caste inhibited political unity. But flexibility of Indian society also rendered fundamental change very difficult. The British, in the initial period, brought out significant changes in regard to land-tenure systems of the Mughal period.

UNITY AND DIVERSITY IN INDIAN SOCIETY

Indian society is characterized by its diversity, sometimes as a boon for nationalism, unity and secularism, and at other times as an obstacle in seeing India as a strong country due to its divisionary character. In a perceptive essay, M. S. Gore (2002, 223–242) describes 'India's Unity in Diversity', in terms of its 'diversity, differentiation and stratification'. Gore says that diversity poses two problems: (a) differences imply different styles of living, value frameworks and preferences; and (b) diversity gives rise to disparities, disparate access to opportunities and an unequal power share in the power structure of society. Political institutions need to deal with these problems, in terms of their acceptance or substitution by new ones. Questions relating to equality/inequality also become pertinent in view of diversities, which take the form of inequalities. Can there be 'differences' without hierarchization?

Indian society has been resilient as it has survived with the Vedic *dharma*, and has adjusted with Buddhism, Jainism, Islam, *Bhakti* movements, Christianity, and with many castes and sub-castes. Embree (2013, 23–39) explains that Indian civilization has survived along with regional cultures. As such, Indian civilization implies the concept of 'India' as an enduring political and social entity in the form of a modern nation. The 'regional cultures' imply the opposite, as there is existence of 'the perennial nuclear regions', having their respective geographical boundaries, and political and social history (Spate, 1960, 148). No uniform pattern and practice of Indian civilization is found all over India. However, Embree (2013, 24) says that 'a supremely important feature of Indian civilization is that the linkages are stratified, and it is these linkages of religious and philosophical ideas, literary culture, political theories, and historical memories that provide the unity for the modern political society' (Embree, 2013, 24).

Embree identifies two such broad categories of linkages: (a) in ideological, the Brahmanical tradition, and (b) in the historical experience, resulting from the Islamic and the Western civilizations. The Brahmanical implies a set of values, ideas, concepts, practices and myths that are identifiable in the literary tradition and social institutions

(Embree, 2013, 24). While proposing a paradigm for an integrated approach to the study of social change in India, Yogendra Singh (1973, 1–27) analyses sources of change in terms of heterogenetic and orthogenetic changes, impacting both cultural structure and social structure, focusing upon little and great traditions and micro and macro structures. India as a civilization, as a conglomerate of diverse social and cultural entities, is evident in both Embree's and Singh's analytical constructs. Historian Vincent Smith (1923) was amazed to see the bewildering diversity as a history of India rather than as histories of ephemeral regional principalities. His answer was: 'India offers unity in diversity'. Jawaharlal Nehru (1981) saw the principle of unity as a form of high-minded secularism. But Nehru was dead against 'India primarily as a Hindu country. Reconciliation between regional identification and an overarching Indian civilization is the essence of the idea of "unity in diversity"'.

INDIA AS A PLURAL SOCIETY VIS-À-VIS A PLURAL POLITY

A couple of writers have equated 'caste system' with 'Indian society', and have looked at it as a 'plural' society. M. G. Smith (1965) emphasizes on the structural condition of the plural society, namely, the caste society. Caste system is based on intense cleavages and discontinuity between differentiated segments. Various groups have differing systems of value, action and social relations. Berreman (1967, 53) observes: 'The plural society is held together by power rather than consensus'. Institutional distinctiveness and Independence (the economic and administrative ones) are also key features of pluralism. However, Furnivall (1948) talks of 'cultural pluralism' in the context of the caste system, emphasizing on considerable consensus and institutional sharing. The question is: Is India a plural society? Furnivall is of the view that the culturally diverse and institutionally separated constituted sections of plural societies are held together by dominant and often exploitative economic institutions. Berreman says that India's caste system has 'plural features', and it does not meet the criteria of an ideal type of a plural society. Berreman holds the view that caste systems combine the principles of stratification and pluralism. Berreman (1967) states: 'A caste system resembles a plural society whose all discrete sections are ranked vertically. A plural society resembles a caste system wherein the groups (except the dominant one) are unranked relative to one another.'

A 'plural society' or a society with 'plural features' can be characterized by a 'plural polity' as its social base lies in diversities of all sorts and logically also in social inequalities emanating from its diversities. Indian society has shown resilience to the core as it has absorbed or adapted itself to the past cultural stock of ideas and practices and also to the new and present ideals and praxis, including the philosophies of Tagore, Gandhi and Nehru. Mukerji (1958, 76) observes in this context:

> Gandhiji's creativity has been transformed into a tradition. This is the real Indian technique, which is more powerful than non-violence and satyagraha. India made of the Buddha, a God in her popular pantheon and broke the back of Buddhism. Her capacity for absorbing anything, including poison, is superb. India's genius lies in her lever.

While commenting on the First Five-Year Plan, Mukerji states that it is a combination of two sets of values: (a) Western and (b) indigenous. In the first instance, the values of experimentalism, rationalism, social accounting, bureaucratization, industrialization, technology and urbanization are included. In the second case, Indian traditions, its forces of conservation and powers of assimilation are important elements. To connect past with present is basic to Indian sociocultural and political ethos. Mukerji says: 'Adjustment is the end-product of the dialectical connection between the two' (past and present) (1958, 76).

However, Moore (1966) differs considerably from the viewpoint of Mukerji as he argues that the Indian aristocracy and bourgeois were not able to challenge the Mughal rule. Peasants were also not a force strong enough as cultivation was lackadaisical and inefficient. Caste system overshadowed agriculture and peasantry. The British discouraged any kind of reaction to its policies and programmes. Certainly, Gandhi tried to bring in the village community and peasantry in the forefront through his doctrine of non-violence, trusteeship, etc. The outcome of Gandhi and such other forces was a political democracy on the eve of India's Independence, but without much modernizing India's social structure. Caste, religion, region, etc., continue to influence Indian polity and economy even in the post 1991–1992 globalizing India (Moore, 1966, 315–316).

Wendy Doniger and Martha C. Nussbaum in the 'introduction' of their recently edited volume (2015, 1–17) raise quite pertinent questions regarding the present-day Indian polity (democracy). These are:

1. 'How does a decent constitution become a working political reality?
2. What mechanisms did the founders put in place to effect the transition between ideal and reality, how have these mechanisms evolved over time, and what are their strong and weak points?
3. How governmental institutions such as public education, political parties and movements, and national economic policy function in transmitting (or blunting) national ideals?
4. How do a variety of other institutions, from poetry and religion to the media culture, play their part, when protected by constitutional guarantees?
5. What role do gender norms play, as they interact with explicitly political and legal aspects of society?' (Doniger and Nussbaum, 2015, 4).

We have left out two questions from the set of questions posited by Doniger and Nussbaum as not seeing them relevant for the present study. However, we also feel like the two editors that 'pluralisms' as 'toleration' are key to Indian polity (democracy) as they govern our people's real lives. Doniger and Nussbaum are also of the view that India has a rich tradition of critical argument and it has also a rich humanistic tradition, and the two play a significant role in democratic public culture. Amartya Sen's idea of an 'Argumentative Indian' (2005) is an apt example of connection between man, society and polity.

Moore (1966, 413) talks of four routes to the modern world: (a) capitalism and democracy (bourgeois revolution); (b) capitalism, without a strong revolutionary surge (fascism); (c) the communist route (origins among the peasants); and (d) a modern industrial society route (none of the above revolutions). India, according to Moore, had such a route during the Nehruvian era. India has not taken the routes of capitalism, fascism and communism. It has a route of its own, eclectically worked out, in view of the colonial legacy, freedom movement and aspirations of the people in general and of the backward sections of society in particular. India may claim the route of an industrial society, but without an industrial revolution. It may claim itself a democratic and secular country, but not without communal strife, caste wars, oppression of women, children and poor people. Rural–urban divide persists, implying vast and stark inequalities between the rural and urban people.

What Moore said in the mid-1960s (1966) about India is not untrue about the India of 2017 (after half a century). Moore (1966, 431) writes: 'India indeed constitutes an important instance where at least the formal structure of democracy and a significant portion of its substance such as the existence of legal opposition and channels for protest and criticism, have arisen without a phase of revolutionary violence'. India's prolonged backwardness and the extraordinary difficulties are due to the absence of a revolutionary break with the past and of any strong movement in this direction. Yogendra Singh (in personal conversations) often says that India has/had no revolutions, it has/had only revolts, which are momentary and short-lived, without enduring effects.

INDIA AS A 'TROUBLED DEMOCRACY'

On the eve of Independence, India's foremost task was to establish its new identity as a strong country, by preserving, consolidating and strengthening its unity in diversity, in other words, its plural character in a new form, as a smooth and consensual formation to be renewed and reinvented. The Indian nation-state needed to recreate itself as a mechanism of development and change as per the expectations of the newly independent India. Its complex diversities and multiple identities had to be acknowledged and given due space in the socio-economic and political fabric of India. B. Chandra, Mridula Mukherjee and Aditya Mukherjee (2000, 1–19) look at India at this point of time (in 1947 and thereafter for some years) as 'a troubled democracy'. Selig S. Harrison (1960, 3–11) characterizes the situation as 'The Politics of National Survival'. Harrison writes: 'India', warns one of her leaders, 'stands the risk of being split up into a number of totalitarian small nationalities' (Harrison, 1960, 3). Such an observation was made by Suniti Kumar

Chatterji, a famous national icon. C. Rajgopalachari feared a period of political anarchy and the risk of fascism, due to disorder and misrule (quoted from Harrison, 1960, 3). The main challenge at the time of Independence was to curb the threats and demands for balkanization of India, after formation of Pakistan. India's 'unity in diversity' became the most crucial appeal to the people of India.

Recently, some of the leaders of the ruling Bharatiya Janata Party (BJP) gave a call to chant *Bharat Mata Ki Jai*, as a gesture of devotion and commitment to the Indian nation. Some people objected such a call as it implied the message for a *Hindu Rashtra*, which amounted to ignore a space for other nationalities (cultural identities), such as Muslims, Jains, Christians, Sikhs, etc. Citing Frank Moraes (1956), a biographer of Jawaharlal Nehru, mentions that once, Nehru recalls, when a crowd of villagers shouted the inevitable *Bharat Mata Ki Jai*— Victory to Mother India—he conducted an unpremeditated experiment in the semantics of nationalism. 'Who', he asked, 'is this Mata you salute? *Dharti*—the earth'—responded the villagers. 'Whose earth? Your village earth? Your province? India? The world?' (Harrison, 1960, 319). The villagers realized too symbolic of India as a whole to discover a coherent nationalism in *Bharat Mata Ki Jai*. Harrison observes: '"Bharat Mata" is the standard of a nationalism that is subcontinental in its horizons' (Harrison, 1960, 319). It can't be reduced as such to a slogan of a caste unit or a linguistic region. Harrison further writes: 'It is the responsiveness of the new nationalism to contradictory political invitations which above all guarantees that the decades ahead will be turbulent ones for India' (1960, 319). This was used, perhaps, for a political foundation of national unity. But then unity depends on rapid and egalitarian development and the latter presupposes unity. Today, in 2017, when one hears *Bharat Mata Ki Jai*, one can see the underlying claim and conviction of a select section of society, and this tends to irritate other people, who also claim themselves as true and more 'nationalists' than the advocates of *Bharat Mata Ki Jai*. But the fact is that more than six decades ago, Jawaharlal Nehru, an ardent champion of democracy, secularism and socialism saw in this slogan a great nationalist ethos, perhaps much more than the present-day enthusiasts of *Bharat Mata Ki Jai*.

India got its Independence with multiple longstanding problems, such as violent communal events, unification of the princely states, agrarian unrest, etc. But the colonial legacy also provided, for example, a highly centralized state system (bureaucracy and military); an advanced judiciary; flourishing universities; and scientific establishments; and partly industrialized economy (Stein, 2012, 368). There were some other favourable factors, including sympathetic assistance from America. Jawaharlal Nehru, keeping distance from the rightist ideology and free-trade advocacy, adopted a policy of 'the left of the centre', which did not annoy obviously both Gandhians and the left ideologues. The elections of 1952 and 1957, and even of 1962, could be viewed as recognition of Nehruvian model of planning and development. Consolidation of India as a nation-state by way of accommodating interests and aspirations of different regions, religious, linguistic and ethnic communities, rural and urban people, backward sections, women, etc., was the main goal of Nehru. At the world fora, Nehru made efforts to create a respectable space for India as well.

But India's economic and social situation was quite pathetic and alarming, say, during 1947–1951. National income per person per year was ₹246.9, and it was the lowest, compared to most of other countries. India was, in effect, poor and underdeveloped country. There was a serious contradiction between population size and development (Bettelheim, 1968, 1–7). Rural India was clearly hierarchized in terms of what Thorner (1956) calls *Mazdoors*, *Kisans* and *Maliks* (that is, agricultural labourers, peasants and landlords—owners of land and money). Caste was overwhelmingly entrenched into rural economy and political domain. Urban India was seen more in terms of population size rather than as a centre of 'urbanity', formal organization structure, impersonal–legal–rational ethos of social relations. Even today, the enhanced urbanization is mainly due to out-migration from rural India for the reasons such as underemployment, scarcity, droughts, etc.

CONCEPTUALIZING INDIAN STATE

Conceptualizing 'state' is quite problematic as it is often confused with 'nation', 'democracy' and with many types of governance.

However, there is no country which does not proclaim formally its goals and means for good of the people. The Constitution of India, in the 'Preamble' itself mentions that India is a sovereign, secular, democratic and socialist country. There can be a hiatus between the proclamation and the ground reality. The nature of the state influences socio-economic and political relations among the people in a particular country. But let us confess that no society is absolutely of one or other type. Dichotomies such as sacred and secular, traditional and modern, and inscriptive and achievement-oriented are only heuristic and simplistic classifications. The classification suggested by A. R. Desai (1975, 40–47), in terms of 'capitalist' and 'socialist' types, is also too broad and far away from ground reality. Desai does not agree with the idea of the 'Welfare State' as it is neither a 'socialist state' nor a laissez faire one. It is, in effect, a capitalist state. One needs to draw a line between the welfare state and other types of states, such as 'Night Watchman State', Laissez Faire State, Police State, Social Services State, Totalitarian State, Nazi State, Socialist State, Negative State, Democratic State, etc. Let us make it clear here that a given type of State is a nominalistic, abstract notion, and it is not a single trait notion/idea.

A. R. Desai (1975, 54) refers to Dorothy Wedderburn's definition of the welfare state (1965, 128) in which by regulating the play of market forces, a minimum real income is assured for all. The state guarantees solutions of the problems arising out of sickness, old age and unemployment. Another view, quoted by Desai, is given by Venkatarangaiya (1962, 11–12), where he states that a State does not merely perform 'police functions', but works for removal of social evils and promotes welfare of the people. As such, a welfare state is: (a) positive, (b) democratic and (c) encourages 'mixed economy' (Desai, 1975, 55–59). In Desai's view, the Indian State has not been able to realize these stated goals; hence it can't be seen as a 'welfare state'. About twenty capitalists/CEOs control India's capital (Seth, 2015). Though Seth, with his Associate Sunny Sen, has all the praise for these 'capitalists' as they have mantras to chant for success. Desai felt long ago, before Seth, that the Indian Welfare State was a state with 'monopoly capital'. R. K. Hazari (1966) mentioned in his famous report that the Marwari big businessmen alone owned 13 per cent of India's capital in the 1960s.

In his seminal work *Asian Drama* (Vol. I), Gunnar Myrdal (1968, 26) talks of India as a 'soft state'. Myrdal writes: 'These countries (South Asian) are all "soft states", both in that policies decided on are often not enforced, if they are enacted at all, and in that the authorities, even when framing policies, are reluctant to place obligations on people'. The so-called 'democratic planning' is made a pretext for weak implementation of economic, social and political policies and decisions. Nicholas Dirks (1992, 175–208) observes that when the Indian state appears, it is as a weak form of oriental despotism, destined to disappear as suddenly, and as casually, as it emerged. The Indian state does not possess mechanisms that could enable it to sustain itself for long. Dirks observes: 'It (Indian state) depends mostly on ruthless short-sighted taxation of the countryside, which eventually leads to such chaos that it dissolves on its own or is conquered by some new entrant on the political scene' (1992, 3). However, Dirk considers the pre-colonial Indian state as a system dependent on relations of power that were culturally constructed. Even caste was shaped by political struggles and processes. Thus, Dirks observes that ritual and political forms were fundamentally the same. Based on his study of a small region of southern India, Dirks says that the Indian state (a small kingdom) revealed the complex and integral interrelations of political processes which ultimately culminated in larger kingdoms that are held to be autonomous and non-political. Thus, the state in India was constructed of 'the cultural, political, social, economic and ritual basis of the little kingdom' (Dirks, 1992, 56)

Such a state system was changed by the colonial state, though it retained some elements of the pre-colonial state. Political transformation of the caste system was the main concern of the colonial rule. The colonial rule did not aim at the creation of an Indian state as such, but its interest was in having deep roots of colonial administration in India. European/British institutions were imposed such as taxation, education, census, etc. All these institutions were not germane to Indian society. Such new institutions aimed at the subordination of Indian political formations and indigenous institutions. The colonial rule created and imposed institutions which helped its domination of the Indian people.

India, coming out from the colonial yoke, after a fight for freedom for more than 150 years, longed for a 'true' democratic functioning of the state and society. The notion of 'compulsion' lacked, which, in turn, frustrated several initiatives for India's economic, social and political modernization. Though, India has often spoken of 'socialism', but it has never advanced the idea of the Marxist approach to the study of Indian society. Desai (1981, 1–20), a staunch votary of Marxism, writes: 'Marxist approach considers property relations as crucial because they shape the purpose, nature, control, direction, and objectives underlying the production. And further property relations determine the norms about who shall get how much and on what grounds'. Further, Desai (1981) observes:

> The Marxist approach also will help to understand why institutions generating higher knowledge-products, sponsored, financed and basically shaped by the State, pursuing a path of capitalist development will not basically allow the paradigms and approaches to study, which may expose the myth spread about State as welfare neutral state and reveal it as basically capitalist state.

After Independence, from 1952 to 1962, India held three general elections, that is, in 1952, 1957 and 1962, under the Congress Party rule and Jawaharlal Nehru was premier of India during this period. Generally, it is believed that under the stewardship of Nehru, roots of a democratic Indian state were made strong enough during this period cutting across divides of region, religion, caste and community. India's was not a phony democracy. It was a democracy with true sovereignty, without fear of its colonial past. There was no more alien oppression. An era of 'conscientization' and 'critical consciousness' (Freire, 1973) had emerged in India in the first one and half decades after Independence.

The state in India, has curious antithetical, ambivalent and egalitarian features. Both inequality and equality coexist. For example, wealth and power of some people have increased enormously. Many people in high positions, in public domain, have accumulated wealth and assets through fraudulent activities. Some of them have been caught in their nefarious endeavours and punished. But such a malady does not stop. At the same time, a large section of people continue to remain extremely poor, and suffer from malnutrition and other maladies. Myrdal (1968) makes 'a plea for an institutional emphasis' for accelerating economic development of India, which needs to be an 'official creed', a 'new nationalism', and a 'radical' one both in policy and action. Myrdal calls such a framework as the 'Modernization Ideals', which are 'mainly the ideology of the politically alert, articulate, and active part of the population—particularly the intellectual elite' (Myrdal, 1968, 55).

CONSTITUTION, GOVERNMENT AND THE STATE

A common perception in India is of the *Samviahan* (Constitution) and of *Sarkar* (government). Strictly speaking, these are two aspects, though no doubt important ones, of the State, but even put gather do not make equal to the idea of State. The notion of state implies completeness regarding man and society, order and disorder, continuity and change, ideal and actual and 'management' of relations between different aspects, such as social, cultural, political, economic, etc. Generally, the state was supposed to solve the problems and to bring about progress and peace. Today, the state, if it is a democratic one can't be absolute in nature, and factors such as globalization and terrorism have also challenged its sovereignty in more than one way. The story of state-formation is quite intriguing. In the 19th century Europe, it was characterized by 'absolutism', and later on, it was followed by revolution and reformation. Absolutism was replaced by sovereignty of the nation. 'The modern state became a nation-state' (Rudolph and Jacobson, 2016, IX). It was an era of high stateness, which did not allow civil society. Monopolistic sovereignty discouraged institutions such as estates, parliaments, the church, guilds and autonomous towns.

Despite chequered and fluctuating character and functioning of the State, people look for the State for security and for protection from market forces. Karl Polanyi (2001) spoke of two points regarding the State: (a) the relentless and ubiquitous drive by market forces to commodify human beings and nature as wages and rent, and (b) the efforts by organized societal forces such as political parties and trade unions acting through the state to save forms of life and the biosphere from the dehumanizing and destructive effects of market forces (Rudolph and Jacobson, 2016, X–XI).

In common parlance, as mentioned earlier, people perceive *Sarkar* as State, as often it is narrated that *Sarkar* has power and authority and can go to any extent to exercise its supremacy over the people. But then there is a counter-perception that *Sarkar* is not over and above the people, and it needs to seek mandate after every five years. Rudolph and Jacobson are of the view that the state is not as a thing, a bureaucracy, an army, a police force, and also not as an idea, and an obstruction. 'Experiencing the State', through historical process, is the main concern of the contributors to the volume edited by Rudolph and Jacobson (2014). There are patterns of 'stateness' and 'statehood'. According to Paul Brass (2014, 110–139), the State in India can be gauged through: (a) political development and organized demands, (b) democratic development and (c) governance and governability. A discourse on the Indian state would thus be on the nature of political cultures, political idioms and political debates in terms of time, place and circumstances (Rudolph and Jacobson, 2014).

We can historicize the nature and functioning of the Indian state in terms of politics, development and change. The main phases are:

1. 1947–1964 (National development, Nehruvian era).
2. 1964–1966 (a brief period under the leadership of Lal Bahadur Shastri).
3. 1966–1975 (Left of the Centre era, under the leadership of Indira Gandhi).
4. 1975–1978 (Emergency, authoritarianism).
5. 1978–1980 Janata Party (a loose coalition and weak state).
6. 1980–1984 (Strong State, Re-emergence of Indira Gandhi).
7. 1984–1989 (Opening up of the Indian State and vision for the 21st century, Rajiv Gandhi era).
8. 1989–2004 (Globalization era, P. V. Narasimha Rao as Prime Minister).
9. 2004–2009 (Accelerated pace of LPG, Manmohan Singh as PM, also coalition era).

10. 2009–2014 (As above, but with more political turmoil).
11. 2014 (State and Sarkar under Narendra Modi's leadership, BJP rule).

For brief spells, Lal Bahadur Shastri, Gulzarilal Nanda, Charan Singh, Chandrasekhar, V. P. Singh, H. D. Deve Gowda and I. K. Gujral were Prime Minister of India. Shastri died of heart attack in Tashkent, where he had gone to have a dialogue with Pakistan after the latter's defeat in the 1965 war. Nanda was twice an interim Prime Minister, once after demise of Jawaharlal Nehru and again after sudden passing away of Lal Bahadur Shastri. Most of the short-lived Prime Ministers of India did not make noticeable impact on Indian state and society, with the exceptions of Shastri and V. P. Singh. Shastri gave a crushing defeat to Pakistan in the 1965 war, and also created a great goodwill for the government and politics with sincerity and integrity. V. P. Singh became a votary of reservation for the OBCs in educational institutions and government jobs, based on the B. P. Mandal Commission Report, which was not considered by the earlier regimes.

Chapter 9

Dynamics of Elections and Its Reflections on Rural India

Elections in post-independent India are seen as a festivity at all levels from village to state to centre. Indian democracy has survived quite successfully based on regular and timely elections for all the bodies, including panchayats, municipalities, legislative assemblies and Lok Sabha. India is viewed as the world's largest and effective democracy. Despite electoral democracy, the state's policies and actions and uneven development of people and regions have distorted the constitutional provisions proclaimed for the downtrodden. Inappropriate linkages between society, democracy and development have been characterized by L. I. Rudolph and Rudolph (1987, 1–5) as a result of 'the weak-strong state and the rich-poor economy' as a political and economic paradox. In such a situation, 'class politics' is marginal, and social formations and cultural identities become pronounced. One could see this in elections every five years, and also during the interim periods, as the elected people often act as votaries and spokespersons of those who have voted for them on primordial basis.

ELECTORAL POLITICS AND DEMOCRACY

'Non-class' factors such as caste, religion, and language even shape Indian economy, industrialization and democracy. L. I. Rudolph and Rudolph (1987, 396) observe:

> Of the many cleavages that animate Indian politics, class usually matters less than other social formations, such as caste, religious and language

communities, and religious nationalisms. Other cleavages rival or surpass class in political silence because the consciousness and commitment focused on them are usually more transparent and accessible than those focused on class.

Role of caste, religion, region and specific groups such as peasants, students, etc., has led to the emergence of 'demand groups'. These are articulate and alert sections of society, and therefore try to corner the major share of the state's resources at the neglect of more needy and deprived sections. As such 'demand politics'—that is, pluralistic character of democracy—gets subdued and 'command politics'—that is, centralization of authority and power—reflects the nature and functioning of the Indian state. L. I. Rudolph and Rudolph (1987) thus talk of disjunction between society, development and politics. Since L. I. Rudolph and Rudolph (1987) have expressed this view before the advent of liberalization, the nature of class politics since 1991–1992 has been undergoing a sea change. Even then, two points are important, as Brass (2004, 1–28) says: (a) a massive contradiction between the rhetoric of Indian public discourse and the reality of political practice, and (b) a dysfunction between the language of planning, equality, socialism and social justice and the practices of day-to-day politics.

Elections in India have raised several new questions as stated by K. L. Sharma (2011, 254–255):

1. Who controls land, resources and people (caste and communities)?
2. Who gets elected to local bodies and legislatures?
3. Who are caste leaders or leaders in villages or of factions thereof?
4. Who makes the mafia in politics?
5. Who decides about the public spending?
6. What are the priorities for resource allocation and public spending?
7. Who are benefited by the development programmes?
8. What is the structure and hierarchy of political leadership?
9. What is the modus operandi of political mobilization and raising of funds?

Answers to these questions make it quite obvious that politics is used and abused for personal and partisan goals. A 'true politician' is rare to be found in today's politics. Pierre Bourdieu (1996), while referring to Marx and Engels, mentions that there are no painters but at most people who engage in painting among other things.

Based on this, Bourdieu says that there are no politicians but at most people who engage in politics among other things. A true politician needs to extract good from bad, truth from false. A true politician is required to recognize a political question politically, and not ethnically. This is 'political competence' and 'political culture'. Bourdieu thus draws a clear line between 'electoral democracy' and 'technocratic democracy' (Bourdieu, 1996, 405). Bourdieu considers politics as a practice in relation to socio–economic conditions. Most politicians in India, barring the first-generation politicians such as Gandhi, Nehru, Patel, Bose, Azad, etc., have not been above the partisan politics. Today, for a large number of elected politicians, politics is, in effect, a source of amassing wealth. Rural politicians are also in this game of amassing wealth by hook or by crook. Transformation of 'political capital' into 'economic capital' has become a common practice.

In her book *Why India Votes?* Mukulika Banerjee (2014) answers the questions which we have posed earlier regarding elections in India. Voting serves two purposes: (a) it is helpful to understand Indian democracy, and (b) it is a vital indicator of how India may survive and evolve in the future (Banerjee, 2014, 2). It is true that elections alone do not make a true democracy, but even then, common people in India take elections quite seriously as a national activity. In fact, political parties and leaders make the ordinary people, first, to realize the importance of elections and then voting as their duty for an altruistic purpose. No doubt, the motive behind such a prompting may be an ulterior one, and a good number of people have such a realization also that political parties and their leaders and some other campaigners have their own ends in view. Some people are lured to vote, and some vote for those whom they consider worth voting on the basis of their own chosen considerations.

Banerjee (2014, 4) observes that 'the Indian electorate behaves in unexpected, indeed baffling, ways'. Despite illiteracy and poverty, voter turnout has been rising over the past seven decades. In the recent elections in West Bengal (2016), voting was as high as 84 per cent.

The poorest and the most disadvantaged are prepared to vote for the betterment of their lives during the next five years, if a particular party is voted to power.

Banerjee (2014, 9–10) mentions that the voters talk about their material needs and a better future by way of voting. However, they show a hiatus between the pragmatic and the normative thinking at the level of discussion. The following points have been mentioned by Banerjee:

1. 'The importance of voting for generating a feeling of citizenship, and for signalling the values of that citizenship.
2. Voting as an expression of their identity as Indians
3. The duty they felt to exercise what they saw as the most precious of rights.
4. The sense of gratitude and obligation they felt towards the Election Commission of India for organizing free and fair elections.
5. The importance they attached to the fact that "each and every vote", was important to any election.'

DYNAMICS OF ELECTIONS

We can say that in recent years, hijacking and rising of elections is no more there as it was in the past. Electoral reforms have been quite effective in curbing malpractices in the elections. Significance of a single vote is realized by everyone. In Rajasthan, in the 2009 Assembly elections, Dr C. P. Joshi, a well-known Congress party leader, lost just by *one* vote. The people who live in towns and cities are persuaded to participate in elections to vote for the candidates of different parties. Elections are like 'carnivals', rightly as said by Banerjee (2014, 10). It is an occasion on which even the most ordinary voter is approached by the candidates. Elections create an atmosphere of apparent concern, anxiety and gaiety and importance for the voters in rural India. Pamphlets, posters, slogans, flags, etc., adorn houses, markets and common places. Every election has a language of its own. One could see the divides and unities among the people across the political parties, candidates, castes and communities.

New slogans are coined to attract the voters in terms of promises and hopes for the people. It is a quite common practice to arrange meals, transport facility, money and clothes for the flexible/indecisive voters in particular. A lot of rural women collectively come singing to the polling booths to caste vote.

Banerjee has also raised the question: 'Are elections a key indicator of democracy?' (2014, 16). She answers this question in her earlier study of elections in a West Bengal village (2007, 1156–1162) by locating the ordinary act of voting in terms of expression of power. Elections are a yardstick of democratic politics and its popular imagination. Elections at the same time also reflect social inequalities and asymmetries of power (Banerjee, 2014). In elections, one can see social differentiation at all the three levels, namely, individuals, families and castes/factions. In fact, elections clearly indicate the complexion of a given village in all the elections from panchayat to Lok Sabha. Everything seems to be a political phenomenon on face of it, but in the background is the social character of the village where elections are conducted.

A. M. Shah (2007) has put together 18 ethnographic studies of elections conducted during the 1960s and 1970s. These are 'in-depth' studies regarding selection of candidates, the campaign, factionalism, the electoral process and choice/preference of voters for particular candidates. But the nature of electoral process has considerably changed since the 1990s. The Election Commission of India has taken some effective steps to curb malpractices, including rigging, booth capturing and strict supervision on the actual conduct of elections, including the use of voting machines.

The main trends relating to elections from 1952 to 1995 have been described by Butler, Lahiri and Roy (1997, 125–176). They ask two questions: (a) Who is the Indian voter? (b) How do the various demographic groupings get divided among the parties? There are no clear answers to these questions. Some exit surveys/polls provide vague answers. Indian elections are an elaborate and complex activity. Sometimes, corruption, intimidation and violence have also occurred. Despite this, the principle of equality of suffrage (18 years) is practised in letter and spirit. But the size of constituency (both Assembly and Lok Sabha) has never been the same. Reservation of seats for the SCs and the STs has always been there. India has followed the model of constituencies of Westminster democracy.

POLITICAL PARTIES AND ELECTIONS

Political parties play a key role in elections in India, both formally and informally, through caste lobbies, influential families and individuals. Fortunes of political parties and their influential leaders are always in flux. Continued one-party domination has become an exception rather than a persistent fact of Indian polity. Some political parties come to power alternatively. This has been the case in Rajasthan, where BJP and Congress have been replacing each other after every five-year rule. DMK and AIDMK in Tamil Nadu, Congress and PDF (Marxist coalition) in Kerala; BJP and Congress-led coalition in Maharashtra are some of the examples. In some states, BJP has been ruling even for three terms, such as Madhya Pradesh, Chhattisgarh, Gujarat, etc., and in some the Congress has ruled, such as Haryana, Delhi, Uttarakhand, Assam and some other north-eastern states. In some other states, such as J&K, Punjab, Bihar, coalitions have been at the centre-stage. Odisha is an exception, where, based on his father's legacy, Navin Patnaik has been ruling the state for the last two decades. In Delhi, the Congress party ruled for three consecutive terms under the leadership of Sheela Dixit. In the Modified (Narendra Modi) situation, the Congress party was reduced to 44 seats only in Lok Sabha. From Uttar Pradesh, only Sonia Gandhi and Rahul Gandhi were elected for Lok Sabha. In Rajasthan, all the 25 Lok Sabha seats went to BJP. The Congress lost all the 7 seats in Delhi. The BJP came to power in 2014 at the Centre with a clear majority. One could sense that BJP had reached to the rural India and it was no more a party of the Brahmin–Kshatriya–Bania as it was perceived in the past, in general.

Splits, amalgamations and coalitions have always been there in both 'national' and 'state' level political parties. The Indian National Congress had its major split in 1969. One group was led by the supporters of Indira Gandhi, and the other was of those who opposed her leadership (Butler, 1997, 144–155). Only in 1977, after the Emergency was lifted, there was a clear two-party situation. (a) the Congress led by Indira Gandhi, and (b) the newly formed Janata Party, led by leaders of several parties and splinter groups. Janata Party, a motley crowd, did survive just for two and half years in power, just after the Emergency was lifted. Congress emerged as a stronger party after the defeat of Janata Party in 1980, and the groups which had formed it, fell down soon after its crushing defeat. After the assassination of Indira Gandhi in 1984, the Congress party won more than three-fourths of the Lok Sabha seats under the leadership of Rajiv Gandhi.

There have been 'swings' in election. For example, in the first three elections, that is, 1952, 1957 and 1962, there was a 'swing' in favour of the Congress party as the euphoria of freedom struggle and inde-pendence and charisma of the Congress with Jawaharlal Nehru as its undisputed leader earned victory for the Congress party. In 1971, after the formation of Bangladesh and humiliating defeat of Pakistan, there was a swing in favour of the Congress. However, in 1978 elections, swing was in favour of the Janata Party in the aftermath of the emer-gency imposed by Indira Gandhi. In 1980, the failure of the Janata Party (motley formation), there was a resurgence of the Congress party. In 1984, Indira Gandhi's assassination created a big swing for the Congress party. After 1989, till the 2014 elections, 'swings' have disappeared and only coalitions have come to power. Only in 2014, there was a swing in favour of the BJP, under the leadership of Narendra Modi.

Political-fronts and counter-fronts by the ruling as well as opposition parties have been a common feature in Indian political system. The unity of the opposition parties has often weakened the ruling parties, particularly the Congress party at the Centre. Both 'swing' and 'split' have been a quit common feature. Whenever, the non-Congress parties have united against the Congress party, there has been a split in the Congress and also an attitude of distance from it. In elections, the margin of victory goes up in case of a swing in favour of a given party. Margin of victory is considered as an indicator of the swing and acceptance of a particular party.

ELECTIONS AS A REAL-LIFE ENACTMENT

Elections in India are no more held in one-go. Yadav and Palshikar (2009a, 33–46; 2009b, 55–62) rightly observe that there was (in one decade) one major round of the state assembly elections every year; putting the central government under continuous assessment. Despite such a situation, Indian people have shown keen interest for participation in elections. State level elections or even the national ones show mature choices of the village people. People in villages often discuss pros and cons of elections for themselves and for their district and state. Generally, their perceptions and choices for the elections of Gram Panchayat, Vidhan Sabha and Lok Sabha are shaped based on ideologies of political parties, the nature of competition, election manifestos, election campaign and social cleavages (caste and class boundaries). One may vote for different parties and candidates depending upon different factors at the three levels. Multiple levels of elections, the contests, continuity, change, development (*vikas*), reconfiguration and coalition, etc., shape opinions of the voters.

There are no uniform patterns of voters and parties as reflected in the state elections in 2007–2008 in Rajasthan, Delhi, Jammu and Kashmir, Madhya Pradesh and Chhattisgarh. In Rajasthan, BJP was defeated by its conventional rival Congress party. Meenas opposed the BJP, and Jats and Gujjars were divided between the two parties. The fact is that the traditional supporters of the Congress, namely, the Dalits, Adivasis and the Muslims, once again were on the side of the Congress party (Lodha, 2009, 23–26). Moreover, Rajasthan has not witnessed consecutive two terms of rule for either BJP or for Congress for quite some time. And it was due for the Congress in 2008.

The story of Delhi was very different once again for the third time. There was a time when Jan Sangh won all the seven Lok Sabha seats in Delhi, in 1967. In fact, Delhi is considered as a Jan Sangh (now BJP) fort. The winning of elections under the leadership of Sheila Dixit for the consecutive third time was a really hat trick. A large number of Dalit and OBC voters, who are mainly poor or belong to the lower income groups voted for Congress party, as its natural allies (Kumar, 2009, 27–30). In Madhya Pradesh, apparently like Rajasthan, Congress was expected to replace BJP. But BJP's rise, weak anti-incumbency, and factionalism in the Congress party helped BJP to come again to power (Shankar and Sisodia, 2009, 35–38). BJP in Chhattisgarh also was not affected by anti-incumbency factor (Joshi and Rai, 2009, 38–41).

The story of Karnataka surprised the election fortune-tellers by the victory of BJP, for the first time, coming to power in south India (Shastri and Padmavathi, 2009, 42–45). Squabbling in the Congress and erosion in the support base of the Janta Dal (Secular) were the main factors of the defeat of the Congress. The OBCs, Dalits and Muslims voted more for the Congress, but the Janta Dal(S) shifted its loyalty more for the BJP. In the case of Himachal Pradesh (Chauhan and Ghosh, 2009, 46–47), there was a shifting of the electorate beyond region, caste and religion, and this helped the BJP in displacing the Congress from power. The situation in Jammu and Kashmir was very different from the present one, in which the PDF and the BJP are sharing power. In 2008, in J&K, there was a huge voter turnout, indicating reduction in political alienation of the people and a decline in sympathy for separatist politics in the valley (Puri, 2009, 31–34). The government formed by the National Conference (NC) and the Congress kept out the PDF and the BJP from power. But today, the latter combine came to power defeating the NC–Congress duo.

COALITIONS AND ALLIANCES FOR POWER-SHARING

For six years, the National Democratic Alliance (NDA), a motley group of more than two dozen parties, was in power at the Centre under the leadership of Late Shri Atal Bihari Vajpayee as Prime Minister and Advani as Deputy Prime Minister. Another coalition was headed by the Congress party under the leadership of Sonia Gandhi. Since NDA had less elected MPs than that of the United Progressive Alliance (UPA), the NDA had to quit. Yogendra Yadav calls it, 'the elusive mandate of 2004' (2004, 5383–5398). Yadav writes: 'Neither the political establishment nor the knowledge industry has been able to forge anything like a shared consensus regarding the message of this general election' (Yadav, 2004, 5383).

After the decline of the Congress system, particularly after the P. V. Narasimha Rao's regime, there was a greater mobilization and active participation of the lower orders of society in electoral politics (Yadav, 2000, 120–145). The BJP developed a 'new social bloc' of the upper strata. Yadav writes: 'The Congress is no longer the rainbow party that it used to be. Its profile has changed into a party that depends exclusively on support from women, poor and the marginal communities, including the Dalits, Adivasis and Muslims' (2003, 64–70). Suhas Palshikar and Sanjay Kumar (2004, 5412–5417) observe that the pattern of participation in 2004 was in line with the pattern noted in the 1990s. Social composition being the same, it was a question of more mobilization of some groups by the Congress, and that gave an edge to it over the NDA. Rural–urban base of votes was more or less equally distributed. However, the NDA had more support of the upper castes than the UPA. Even the OBCs were more in favour of the NDA. However, the Dalits, Adivasis, Muslims and Christians provided a decisive lead to the UPA. In terms of class, the underprivileged people voted for the Congress, and for its allies, the Left, the BSP and other regional parties.

The elections of 2014 clearly show that there is an enhanced voter turnout compared to the elections for the 1990s. There is also more interest and participation in elections than before indicating a democratic upsurge. However, this has not resulted into corresponding campaign-related activity. Palshikar and Kumar (2004, 5417) observe:

> Thus, we have a paradox here. Diversification of voters is not matched by a broadening of the social base of participants and the active citizens. Active participants are still from the more privileged sections of society. Education and class are the determinants of who will be the participants in politics and who will be the more involved citizens.

There is a difference between active participation/leadership and the support and vote to a particular party. Dalits, Adivasis, poor and women support the Congress, but they are not in leadership role. The OBCs (the upper layer) have made some entry into active political arenas.

The elections for the Lok Sabha in 2009 were an improved repetition for the UPA. The main reason was the depolarization of the social bloc which the NDA had created earlier. The UPA was also benefited from its somewhat positive image and welfare measures that it had during its five-year rule. As reported by Yadav and Palshikar (2009, 33–46), gender, age, locality and class were all tilted more towards the UPA than the NDA, compared to the 2004 elections. Economic concerns, basic services, welfare policies and citizens' security influenced the voters as voiced by the UPA than the issues such as the Indo-US nuclear deal and the Ram Sethu controversy (Rai, 2009, 80–82). Leadership of the NDA and the UPA at the state-level mattered a lot in voter-mobilization and campaigning.

The results of the 2014 national elections have been a turning point in Indian politics. These elections had a lot of dramaturgy, a new social engineering, claims and assurances for inclusive development and change. The role of the NDA (BJP) leader Narendra Modi in managing the elections and announcement for him as the next Prime Minister has been a decisive factor in campaigning and in keeping together the rank and file of the BJP. Modi kept away tactfully the old guard of BJP, namely, L. K. Advani, Murli Manohar Joshi, Shanta Kumar and Yashwant Sinha, from the electoral process. However, Advani and Joshi were allowed to contest, but without any role in the post-election period. The BJP has demonstrated its presence all-over India, beyond Hindi heartland, Gujarat and Maharashtra. Its presence in Karnataka, Jammu & Kashmir has surprised many psephologists. To have a clear majority (with 284 seats) in Lok Sabha, with a vote-share of 31 per cent (more than its earlier share) is also a new landmark. Though the lowest vote-share of the Congress was 41 per cent in 1967 when it came to power (Palshikar and Suri, 2014, 39–41).

A TURN TO THE 'RIGHT' OF THE CENTRE

The elections of 2014 are seen as 'an ideological consolidation of the right', a 'Modi Wave' (Chhiber and Verma, 2014, 50–56). The BJP claimed itself as a 'national party' in a true sense after the 2014 elections. Some of the promises made by the BJP and its leader Narendra Modi have created ambiguities, confusions, controversies and misgivings during the past two years. Statements made by several leaders of the BJP regarding Hinduism, dress code, food choice, cow-worship, etc., have been seen as counter-productive and retrograde and unsecular. The most important point is that even villages got 'Modified'. BJP created a viable rural base for itself. The Congress was left with only

44 seats in Lok Sabha. Even the regional leaders of the Congress party could not bail it out from such a terrible decline. Another characteristic feature of these elections was the role played by India's middle classes, as they came out openly against the Congress, particularly to expose it on account of corruption and scams, during UPA's second term. Role of media and systematics of elections have played a notable role in the victory of the BJP. Verma and Sardesai (2014, 82–88) explain the elections in terms of 'Modi, Media and the Message'. Someone has referred the situation as 'Modi Mythology'. Modi's rhetoric of development and governance was seen by the people as a possible reality, and this minimized the role of caste, religion and region in the 2014 elections to a considerable extent.

All the elections in India have created anxieties, curiosities and engagement among the voters, though not uniformly across the rural and urban people, poor and rich, weaker sections and women. More important fact is that the Indian voter realizes the meaning and substance of coming to power through ballot box. The voter knows his/her value and significance at all the levels of elections. This is how India's political democracy has become strong and vibrant. Enormity of elections in India is the biggest in the world (Jaffrelot, 2010, 583–603). It is so despite low level of literacy and education, poverty, unemployment and sociocultural backwardness, particularly in rural India. A large number of voters identify parties and candidates by the symbols allotted to them by the Election Commission of India. Certainly, the voters are repeatedly advised to remember and recollect the symbols at the time of voting. Voting machines and certain steps taken by the Election Commission have minimized impersonification and rigging in elections. Even then, casteism and communalism are appropriated by some parties and candidates in their favour. At times, violence and booth-capturing have also marred the elections. Jaffrelot (2010, 596) observes: 'Indians tend not to vote as individual citizens but as members of religious minorities or caste groups, be they come from the upper or from the lower castes'. Let us not ignore the fact in some cases, even two brothers have fought elections for Lok Sabha belonging to two different parties, for example, in Rajasthan, in the 2014 elections.

Indifference to elections has come down. The apathy of the urban middle class is not as much as it used to be in the past. The urban rich and the middle class now see their stakes more in the particular political party's victory. Liberalization and privatization have motivated these sections for getting interested in power–politics. Criminalization of politics needs to be seen carefully. It has become less pronounced due to greater participation of the people in the elections.

Chapter 10

Panchayati Raj Institutions and Empowerment

Panchayati Raj implies self-governance in rural India. Before Independence, gram panchayat (a council of elderly people) dealt with common problems, and jati panchayat (*biradari*) was concerned with affairs of its members in the village. Both the bodies were autonomous to deal with in their respective domains. However, inter-*biradari* disputes were generally dealt by the gram panchayat. In some cases, there were also inter-village caste panchayats. B. R. Chauhan (1967) calls the inter-village panchayat as *Chaukhala* (a cluster of villages having a common panchayat). Such a system of decision-making at the village or caste level has almost ceased to exist. Villages are no more self-sufficient and isolated. Intra-caste homogeneity has nearly disappeared and intra-village social differences have become pronounced based on income, occupation, assets and political power. The Indian village, in fact, was never 'static' and 'isolated' as depicted in several 19th-century writings. Inter-village and intra-village differences, inequalities and conflicts were quite pronounced. At the same time, different castes both cooperated and competed. Today, the nature of cooperation and competition has taken a new form.

THE GENESIS OF PANCHAYATI RAJ

Immediately after the implementation of the Constitution of India, statutory panchayats were formed. With a view to make gram panchayats as more effective institutions at the village, block and district levels, the Government of India constituted a committee under the Chairmanship of Balwant Rai Mehta, the Chief Minister of Gujarat. The Mehta Committee (1957) recommended democratic decentralization of power to encourage participation of the people at the village level. On 2 October 1959, Jawaharlal Nehru, the Prime Minister of India, inaugurated the Panchayati Raj in its new avatar at Nagaur in Rajasthan. The main objective was to ensure democratic decentralization of power and authority in the planning and its execution. Devolution of power to the village people has not been taken kindly by the top-level bureaucracy and even by the state level leadership (Brass, 1990, 138–147).

In 1977, the Janata Government appointed a Committee under the Chairmanship of Ashok Mehta (1978) to suggest measures for solving the problems of Panchayati Raj Institutions. Zila parishads (district level bodies) were entrusted with all the development activities. Besides the zila parishads, panchayat samities (block level bodies) functioned as a medium between the parishads and the panchayats. Powers of taxation were also given, but so far it has remained on paper. Karnataka and Andhra Pradesh adopted most of the Mehta Committee recommendations. But a large number of other states have not been enthusiastic to follow the guidelines of the Mehta Committee report (Mehta, 1978, 138–141).

Since Panchayati Raj Institutions were having divergent patterns of functioning, funding and development activities, the Government of India enacted a constitutional amendment, namely, the 73rd amendment, which came into force in 1993. The aim of the amendment was to grant uniform statutory status to the Panchayati Raj Institutions throughout the country, such as the state legislatures and Lok Sabha, in terms of timely elections, finances and development activities. Under the amendment, gram sabha has been given wide-ranging powers and functions (Mathur, 2013). Mathur argues that the rising tide of unrest at the grass roots forced the government at the centre to enact such a change in the Panchayati Raj institutions. Democratization of politics at the grass roots is evident today. Panchayat has become a centre of power-politics because it has all the authority in today's village in India. All other institutions relating to health, education, drinking water, roads, cooperative society, etc., are under the general guidance of the gram panchayat.

As a result of the 73rd amendment, the OBCs, Dalits, Adivasis and women have more opportunities, as a result of reservations, for participation in the PRIs. Reservation for women up to 50 per cent in some states, and 33 per cent all over India, has created a new sociocultural awakening regarding gender equality, at least in a formal way. In fact, the 73rd amendment aims at to grant real political strength to the PRIs. To a considerable extent, the 73rd amendment has curbed discrepancies in allocation of functions, finances and functionaries, and has established organic links between the three tiers of the PRIs (Pal, 2004, 137–142). The question is: Have PRIs become effective self-governing institutions? Mahi Pal observes that pressure for greater autonomy for the panchayats is not generated from the grass roots. The reasons are: (a) the villagers do not consider panchayats as their problem-solving institutions, and (b) elected representatives of the panchayat consider themselves helpless in solving people's problems due to lack of control with them on the issues affecting the villagers (Pal, 2004, 142).

EMPOWERING RURAL PEOPLE

Why is there no empowerment of the village community despite the 73rd amendment? The aim of the PRIs in the post–73rd amendment period is to ensure egalitarian, participatory and inclusive solution of the needs of the people. But it has not happened so far. PRIs are generally controlled by a select section of people in a given village. Such a select group is drawn from the general category. SCs, STs, OBCs and women. Contest and competition is often among the individuals and families drawn from such a group. Such a situation jeopardizes the idea of 'decentralized democracy' at grass roots as envisaged in the 73rd amendment. Rahul Banerjee (2013, 173–176) argues that the three Fs, namely, functions, functionaries and funds, in the 73rd amendment have not changed the PRIs as they still operate as poor adjuncts to the bureaucracy and higher-level governments.

The 73rd amendment has comprehensive provisions of powers and funds to PRIs, but the mismatch (conflict) between a centralized system and a new local government system has not been adequately dealt with. The leadership at the grass roots has not been strong enough to weaken the hold of the higher echelons of power and authority on the functionaries and funds. The system continues to be top-heavy despite the so-called devolution of power to the PRIs. The PRIs have not been made capable of preparing and implementing the plans and projects at their own level. Banerjee (2013, 176) observes: 'The crucial clash of political interests between state governments and PRIs remains unaddressed, and the reality is that awareness and mobilization of politicians and people at the PRI level is much less than that of state-level politicians'. Today, in the villages, one can see three different political/administrative functionaries: (a) the PRIs function-aries, from village to block to district levels, (b) the state government functionaries and politicians, including the MLA, MP and block and district level officials, and (c) the functionaries overseeing the central government schemes and MP. These functionaries change along with the change of the government at the state and central levels. The fact is that the political functionaries in the PRIs remain aligned to one or other political party. A particular party in power at the Centre, if, it is opposed to the party in power at the state level, it affects the three Fs at the level of the PRIs. It also happens that if the leadership of a particular PRI is politically at variance with the ruling party at the state/central level such an incongruence may obstruct smooth functioning of particular PRIs.

FUNCTIONING OF THE PRIS

During the CPI (M) rule in West Bengal, the practice of patronizing its own support base by use of public funds through PRIs, created violence during panchayat elections. Party-based division in the rural polity has become a stark reality. PRIs, in fact, have become fiefdoms of the rural power elite of different political colours and orientations. However, there are some states in which PRIs have made a considerable impact on socio-economic life of the village people. A study of 500 villages in the state of Andhra Pradesh, Karnataka, Kerala and Tamil Nadu shows that the functioning of the PRIs after the 73rd amendment has made an impact on the economic status of villages and on the families therein

(Besley, Pande and Rao, 2007, 661–666). The democratic decentralization at the grass roots has improved the delivery of public services. The target groups/beneficiaries/families have been benefited by the welfare schemes of the PRIs. The PRIs have also delivered positive outcomes. Political participation has enhanced through the gram sabha whose members are all the adults in the jurisdiction of the gram panchayat. Reservation in the PRIs has enhanced inclusive social development and change. In fact, today, there is more pragmatism among the villagers and they also romanticize the village life.

A study of three villages in Nagpur district of Maharashtra (Kumar, 2004, 228–233) also corroborates the findings of the 500 villages of four southern states of India. Village politics is no more caste-ridden as it used to be in the 1960s. By the 1990s, institutional politics with a broader base exists and caste is also there as one of the factors. Political parties have given a new twist involving a cross-section of village people. Village factions are no more confined to castes as used be earlier (Carras, 1972). Village politics has evolved over the years over and above caste consideration. A conjunction of leadership, caste and land is sensed by the people. Ajit Kumar observes: 'The social base of the leadership outlines the direction and limits of the political process' (2004, 231). Caste alone is not the social base. Long ago, Edmund Leach (1960, 1–10) talked of competition among the upper caste patrons to seek support of the common people. But such a rivalry characterizes a class situation, as members of the same caste cooperate and do not compete. Ajit Kumar based on the elections held in 1998 in the three villages states: 'Cutting across family and caste barriers the changes reflect institutional politics finding roots within the village community' (2004, 233). Such a view is also corroborated by George Mathew (2003, 155–162) as he says that PRIs have enhanced momentum to the decentralization process having deeper positive implications for the human rights in rural India. Weakening of the caste-based restrictions help to the poor and the BPL families, Dalits, tribals, women, etc., and have created a new social situation in rural India. Mathew writes: 'The new Panchayat system, with all its current weaknesses, has helped to weave the village into the broader social fabric' (Matthew, 2003, 161). Despite the role played by muscle, money and caste, decentralization process is moving forward. Elections for the rural people are like an agency of political socialization. A sense of identity, dignity, social justice and value of vote as a citizen are seen as new parameters in rural India.

PRIs and particularly the gram panchayats are not functionally uniformly despite the 73rd amendment being a common law for the entire country. G. K. Lieten (2003) provides a comparative analysis of the functioning of the gram panchayats in West Bengal and Uttar Pradesh. Lieten's study is based on around 50 villages from both the states, with profiles of nearly 1,000 elected panchayat members. The following points may be noted about the two studies:

1. In Bengal, the panchayats have become a household name, but in Uttar Pradesh a panchayat office does not exist, and people generally know the *pradhan* of the panchayat.
2. In Uttar Pradesh, the *pradhan* is usually from a landed family, and in some cases, a poor villager elected as *pradhan* remains as the rubber stamp of the dominant landlord. In West Bengal, the majority of the members of the panchayats belong to families of rich peasants, landlords and professional classes, such as school teachers. Even women are quite active members in West Bengal.
3. In West Bengal, members are normally qualified to function in the panchayats and in the village community. In Uttar Pradesh, there is no transparency in the functioning of the panchayats, and female members are there for namesake.
4. In West Bengal, the elected members take care for devolving the state finances and the political responsibility to the panchayat. In Uttar Pradesh, the government administration keeps the control on finances and activities undertaken by the panchayats.
5. In West Bengal, there is transparency and accountability regarding utility of finances. In Uttar Pradesh, leakage and bribery are commonly reported in regard to targeted poverty alleviation programmes (Lieten, 2003, 27–31).

Finally, regarding the panchayats in West Bengal, Lieten (2003, 54) writes: 'Enfranchisement involves a continuing economic, political, and social process in favour of hitherto marginalized and/or suppressed groups. The antiquated hold of landlords and rich peasants on rural politics and economics has been breached and a reasonably democratic institution has been put in place'. On the contrary, the situation in Uttar Pradesh is quite opposite to that of the West Bengal. Panchayats exist in name only; it is more of a formality. The dominance of the *pradhan* has acquired such a magnitude that the deployment of the state resources and initiatives depends on him. The officials from the higher echelons work in tune with the *pradhan*. The members of the panchayats have no or passive involvement in the village affairs. As such, dominant members of a particular caste(s) dictate terms to the extent the traditional hold of caste/class and suppression of women is maintained (Lieten, 2003, 76–77).

CONCLUDING REMARKS

An interesting and quite complex situation has been found in Punjab regarding the limits imposed on the SCs by the rural elites, particularly in the PRIs (Martin, 2015, 37–44). In general, though there is decline of caste-based territorial dominance, and the SCs have more autonomy, space and political assertion. But still they do not wield meaningful power in the village panchayats. The wealthy farmers engaged in urban business use their political networks, money and coercion to capture power. They promote their business interests and appropriate village common lands through political connections. The SCs are so far not in a position to challenge such a dominance of the rural rich who have an urban base and political ties. The SCs have been, however, managing their own affairs and livelihoods.

The rural elite reproduce their power, through state-connected networks of influence, and participate effectively in provincial politics. Jan Breman (2007) has also found such a political situation in Gujarat. The SCs are not yet able to question the manipulation of political power by the dominant people. The basic issues relating to education, health, wages, exploitation, dominance in panchayats, etc., remain beyond the SCs domain at this juncture.

PART IV

Emerging Patterns of Stratification and Change

Chapter 11

Formation of Middle Class in Rural India

There is no unstratified human society, and there is also no uniclass/caste/ethnic society. Polar opposite groups/classes, such as upper and lower, are also a rarity. Even Marx and Engels used the term 'middle classes' in various ways (Bottomore, 1983, 333–334). Engels equated middle classes with bourgeoisie, differentiating it from the 'aristocracy'. Even in the feudal system, there were middle classes (bourgeoisie). Marx, however, used the term middle classes to designate the classes or strata between the bourgeoisie and the working class, and as such Marx referred to 'middle classes' as 'petty bourgeoisie'. Marx also realized the expansion of the middle classes along with the development of capitalism. But differentiation within the middle class was not taken up by Marx and Engles. They did not make a distinction between the 'old middle class' of small producers, artisans, independent professional people, farmers and peasants, and the 'new middle class' of clerical, supervisory and technical workers, teachers, government officials, etc. (Bottomore, 1983, 333). Ultimately, for Marx middle class was non-existent as it would merge either with the bourgeoisie or with the proletariat. Only two classes, namely, the pro-bourgeoisie and the proletariat, would be there based on the means and relations in the production system.

EXPLAINING THE MIDDLE CLASS

D. P. Mukerji (1942) was seriously concerned to identify the Indian middle class as the key to an understanding of the modern culture. The

Indian middle class played a significant role, supporting the British. For Mukerji, educated Indians constituted the middle class. It was not anchored in Indian tradition and culture (Chakrabarti, 2010, 235–255). The landlords and literati formed the new middle class during the Raj, and they were alienated from the language and culture of the people of India. Mukerji (1948, 25) mentions this as 'the emergence of a spurious middle class'. But D. P. Mukerji mentioned about the differentiation of the middle class: (a) the upper level of the Indian middle class was dominated primarily by educated upper caste landed gentry, and (b) the lower middle class had higher education and worked under the colonial rule (Chakrabarti, 2010, 252). Mukerji, however, realized the dynamism of the Indian middle class in shaping/reshaping the Indian society. He hoped that the Indian middle class could act as an agent of social change for good of the society.

Archana Singh (2014, 307–339), in a comprehensive review of literature on 'middle class in India', traces its evolution in terms of colonial legacy, Indian state and constitutional provisions, the policies and programmes of development and change, post-liberalization, privatization and globalization. After churning the major writings, perspectives and views on middle class in India, Singh relates it with social structure and mobility, economic power, culture and consumption, politics and state, caste identities, family and kinship and marriage. Archana Singh observes: 'By changing and adjusting to outside changes, they (middle classes) have transformed the Indian society' (2014, 333). The middle classes have been torch-bearers, have provided leadership, and contributed to the nation-building and economic reforms in the recent past. However, middle classes are highly heterogeneous and stratified in terms of income, education, occupation, consumption and assets, and they are always in a flux.

Middle class has always existed in India despite hierarchical dominance of the caste system. 'Middle class' is not a monolithic entity; it is quite differentiated; and it has been changing vis-à-vis economy, polity and technology. It is also not simply an urban/industrial phenomenon. Peasants, artisans, weavers, craftsmen, etc., are highly differentiated in terms of their skills, and not necessarily based on their caste ranks. B. B. Misra (1961/1983, 11–13) states that the Indian middle class is an offshoot of the British rule in India. New occupations such as law and bureaucracy created new layers in terms of upper, middle and lower positions/statuses. Industrialization also brought about role-differentiation with several incumbents at the middle level. Land tenure systems such as Ryotwari and zamindari created intermediaries between the rulers and the tillers of land. With the expansion of the Raj, differentiation became an inevitable consequence. Despite 150 years of British rule, hardly 10 per cent of the people at the time of India's Independence formed the middle classes (Varma, 1998, 26).

Sanjay Joshi (2010) looks at the middle class in colonial India far more carefully. He asks the question: Was there a 'middle class' in India during the colonial rule or did it exist even before? Misra and some other historians are of the view that the conditions created by the British led to the birth of the middle class. But then the next question is: What was its nature? As mentioned earlier, the term middle class referred to the industrial bourgeoisie, petty-bourgeoisie, and later on as a result of modernity and capitalism, writers, novelists, intellectuals and romantics were also included in the category of the middle class (Rajagopal, 2011, 39–41). In the Indian context, the 'new middle class' included a group of officials, graduates and traders, but they comprised a 'microscopic minority' and did not represent the people of India. In the review of Sanjay Joshi's book (2010), Rajagopal (2011) mentions that 'middle class' is employed as a catch-all category for a number of groups with a variety of dimensions of social experience and standing. It is not a class in the Marxian sense nor one only in an economic sense (Rajagopal, 2011).

DIMENSIONS OF THE INDIA'S MIDDLE CLASS

Religion, caste, gender, education and power are important dimensions of middle class in the Indian context. As such, 'middle class' is also found in rural India. Those who have some regular source of reasonable income, and a moderate house to live and some assets say that they belong to *madhyam* (middle) class. This is true for both urban and rural settings. Those who are at the middle level (with their ramifications) are often seen as knowledgeable people, educated, well-mannered, upwardly mobile, politically articulate and ambitious, and such a lot is quite pronounced in rural India. The middle classes are white-collar workers. In the countryside, gram sevaks, Patwaris, school teachers, compounders, nurses, shopkeepers, moneylenders, members of the panchayats and cooperative societies, petty contractors, etc., would constitute the middle class. Of these groups of people, some are more educated than others and some have more income and also come from different castes, but they make a distinct group compared to the agricultural workers, small cultivators, masons, artisans, etc. 'Reservations' for the SCs, STs, OBCs and women have created a 'middle class' in rural India. Although the beneficiaries come from different castes, they form a distinct entity in terms of their education, salaried jobs and status (particularly in the case of elected members to the PRIs). Such a situation characterizes a 'new mix' of social, political and economic dimensions in the formation of what we here call as middle class.

An in-depth study of three lower castes from Punjab (Saberwal, 1976) brings out how occupational change has occurred over a period of time during the late 19th and early 20th centuries. 'Mobile men' of Saberwal are, in fact, 'mobile castes in making'. Saberwal says that one's experience of mobility is a function, in part, of one's castes' (1976, 220). Stigmatized hereditary occupation and availability of new opportunities have brought about social mobility. Saberwal (1976, 234) explores the process underlying the transformation of Indian society from one with hierarchically organized corporate caste groups to a relatively open society stressing individual attributes. Such a change has emanated from the structural formation of Indian society.

A couple of observations made by Andre Beteille (2007, 945–952) regarding distinction between classes and communities in general and about caste and class and middle class in particular in the Indian context may be pointed out. First, classes and communities are no doubt distinct, but not unrelated. Economic disparities are bound to be there within a community and between different communities. Identity politics creates such disparities in modern India. Second, 'identity politics succeeds where it underscores disparities between communities and obscures those within each one of them' (Beteille, 2007, 951). Today politics is all about distribution of benefits and resources among regions, groups, families and individuals. Different political parties compete for channelizing the process of distributive shares. Beteille observes: 'Those who articulate the interests of the community do not come from all social classes but predominantly from the middle class' (2007, 951). In India, approximately 30 per cent of the population comprises the middle classes, which at the time of Independence (nearly seven decades ago) was nearly 10 per cent. Of the 30 per cent of the middle classes, urban India has bulk of it, whereas rural India comprises 70 per cent. Beteille also observes:

> In India the policies typically advocated through identity politics, whether for education or for employment, have benefited the middle classes far more than other social classes, and one may go so far as to say that it is in the nature of identity politics for this to happen. (2007, 951)

Reservations have enhanced acutely the identity politics, and it is not without 'class character'. The educated and salaried people have grown numerically as a result of reservations, and there has been a notable increment in the size of the middle class. A good number of this new middle class is of rural origin. This fact is not being observed. B. B. Misra's approach to middle class (1964) is still followed as reflected in Beteille's analysis of India's middle class. Leela Fernandes (2007) also sees the middle class as the subject and agent of nationalism like Misra, and observes its place in the contemporary politics of Hindu nationalism. She writes: 'The new middle class is marked by its social and cultural visibility, yet its political role is often invisible. Meanwhile its claims tend to be coded in terms of representative citizenship yet in practice are often defined by exclusionary social and political boundaries' (Fernandes, 2007, XXIII). Fernandes limits the middle class to state, politics, urban India and liberalization. In rural India, there is a 'new consumer', a new resourceful person, a beneficiary of the policies of the state, and a new political activist. All these persons, in one or more sets of people, make the middle class in rural India. They are in a way replica of urban middle classes and also link (middle men) the rural masses and the national/state leadership, political parties and administrative agencies. At the same, the rural middle classes have their own sociocultural background, rooted in localism, caste and community. However, they are a distinct entity compared to the rest of the people. A car, a two-wheeler, a pucca house, electronic gadgets such as television, refrigerator, modern furniture, etc., are quite common assets. A mobile phone is found even among the poorest of the poor.

There is no doubt a caste-bias in the shaping or reshaping of the middle class. If upper castes are also the upper classes and so is the case with the middle and lower castes, we can describe such a situation of congruence between caste and class. And in this way, caste also amounts to class and power as well. But more important are the permutations and combinations of caste and class. For example, there may be an upper caste man with a middle or a lower class position. A middle caste family may have an upper or a lower class rank. A lower caste family may have an upper or middle-class position. All the castes and classes are not monolithic because they are internally differentiated. Inter- and intra-caste distinctions and similarly intra-class variations and a sum total of status–estimation based on such a complexity needs be worked out.

Anirudh Krishna and Devendra Bajpai (2015, 69–77) attempt to define economic classes in relation to different transport assets. Those who have motorcycles or motor-scooters are the lower middle class, and those who own automobiles (four-wheelers, such as cars, jeeps) constitute the upper middle class. It is difficult to define or identify a middle class. The term middle class is 'relational, context-dependent, and inchoate' (Krishna and Bajpai, 2015, 69). Income and assets are important considerations, and those who have substantial economic standing, have higher access to education, health, media exposure, and social capital may constitute a middle class. Let me state here that by this yardstick, there is a substantial lower middle and middle class in rural India. A large number of people have motorcycles, and some have four-wheelers as well. Besides pucca houses, people have a lot of assets such as land, control over sources of nonfarm income, salaried jobs, moneylending. Such a situation has got momentum during the last three decades. A concise description of the Indian middle class is given in Jodhka and Prakash (2016).

GLOBALIZATION AND THE MIDDLE CLASS

Globalization has given a boost to the Indian middle class as it has been the main beneficiary of the post-liberalization market-driven economy. Disposable income and consequent consumption are the main features of the Indian middle class. Household income and expenditure become the objective criteria to find out the degrees of differentiation within the middle class. A salaried class IV employee, a petty shopkeeper, a doctor, lecturer, engineer, all can be clubbed as members of the middle class, but they differ in terms of income, social status, skills, education, etc., and also in regard to their upward mobility. Assets, perceptions of ones standing, and liking for assets as status symbols are thus main considerations. Krishna and Bajpai (2015, 70) while mentioning several studies and analyses of the middle class observes: 'The new middle class in India is seen thus as "the site of commodity consumption", whose lifestyles and buying habits, valorized in TV and print advertise-ments, give rise to processes of status emulation that guide the conduct and channel the ambitions of others'. A restudy of the six villages in Rajasthan (Sharma, 1974) in 2015–2016 shows that rural India has today a substantial middle class. The upper castes had the characteristics of a middle class even before Independence.

There is a distinct decline among the upper castes in the villages, particularly among those who continue to live there. Those who have migrated to towns and cities certainly have been absorbed by the urban middle class. More conspicuous presence is of the intermediate castes as a middle class, who have been benefited from land reforms, Panchayati Raj and development programmes. Income, assets, expenditure and consumption and perceptions of prestige are main features of the rural upper and middle classes. The most striking example is spending on marriage and occasions such as birth and death. It has become quite common to give dowry by way of gold jewellery, car, television, furniture, household goods and cash and a lavish lunch/dinner for hundreds of people. Even everyday life is quite different today, and it is comparable with the urban middle class. An acute search for a match who has a respectable government job is a standard pattern, and this would imply a substantial dowry. Education, government/corporate job and networks are often seen as the main yardsticks of the rural middle class. With India's extremely rich and extremely poor people, the Indian middle class has emerged as a significant stratum, almost one-third of its total population. The myth of the middle class as an urban phenomenon has been exploded by the recent changes in rural India.

SIZE, ROLE AND FUNCTIONS OF THE MIDDLE CLASSES

In the post-independent India, size, role and functions of the middle classes have changed considerably mainly due to the Indian State and its policies and programmes. In the context of Gujarat, Ghanshyam Shah (1986, 149–183) mentions that the middle class has grown in size disproportionately with economic growth. In the new middle classes, the members are from among the upper and the middle castes on the one hand, and the lower castes on the other. Shah observes that since the middle classes are a product of both the capitalist development and the state, there would be a conflict situation between the entrenched middle classes and the lower classes aspiring for the status of the middle class by having access to lucrative white-collar jobs. A similar view is evident when Deshpande (1997, 294–318) observes that the Nehruvian era of the developmental state resulted into swelling the ranks of the middle classes. 'Globalization' marks a new phase in the size and shape of the middle classes. In both the views, emergence of new middle classes in rural India is quite evident as caste, class, development and state are the focal points in the emergence of the middle classes.

In another article, Deshpande (2003, 125–150) makes three points regarding conceptualization of the middle class. (a) The middle class is the class of the people that articulates the hegemony of the ruling bloc by way of the language of legitimation and mediation between the ruling bloc and other classes. (b) The middle class is most dependent on 'cultural capital' and on the mechanisms for its reproduction. (c) The middle class specializes the production and dissemination of ideologies. Such a characterization of the Indian middle class puts it on a high philosophical and hegemonic platform as if it is at the top of class stratification. The classification given by Pavan K. Varma (1998, 170–214), based on a survey by the National Council of Applied Economic

Research (NCAER), looks to be somewhat closer to ground reality. The three middle classes mentioned by Varma are: (a) the consuming class (150 million people); (b) the climbers (275 million); and (c) the Aspirants (275 million). These figures have changed as the NCAER survey was conducted in 1994. We will mention about the changed scenario later on. Besides these middle classes, at the top are very rich (6 million people). However, Varma does not endorse the consumerist view of the new middle class in the India context. For Varma, the middle class is a socio-economic and political phenomenon because more economic standing does not make a class a middle class. It is a systemic construction and an action entity (Sharma, 2007a, 246–251).

An ardent observer of the emergence of India's middle class is Gurcharan Das (2000, 279–290), comparable with B. B. Misra (1983) and Pavan K. Varma (1998). Das writes:

> The new middle class is displacing the old bourgeoisie—people like my grandfather and father—which first emerged in the nineteenth century with the spread of English education. It had produced the professionals who had stepped into the shoes of the departing English in 1947, and had since monopolized the rewards of the society. The chief virtue of the old middle class was that it was based on education and merit with relatively free entry, but it was a class alienated from the mass of people and unsure of its identity. The new middle class, on the other hand, is based on money, drive, and an ability to get things done. Whereas the old class was liberal, idealistic, and inhibited, the new order is refreshingly free from colonial hang-ups. (2000, 281)

Thus, the old middle class was characterized by free entry, education, and capability, whereas the new middle class is based on money alone without social responsibility. Das perceives that by 2010 (already gone), half of India's population would be the middle class, and will have a major impact on its politics, markets and society. The quintessential feature of the new middle class is competition as its core value in economy, polity and society. The present middle class is in both private and public sectors, and at times, there is an easy relationship between these classes. Political leadership is generally over and above the middle classes. Some of the observations made by Das are quite simplistic and sweeping. However, his observation on the rural middle class is quite relevant for us. He writes:

> In the 1980s the middle class doubled as the economic growth rate rose to 5.6 percent. Marketing professionals were amazed by the extent of rural prosperity. As the rural family's expenditure on food dropped from roughly 68 percent to 55 percent of its income, rural demand for consumer products multiplied. Soaps and detergents in villages grew 20 percent a year through the eighties while the urban market grew only 5 percent. By 1990, the rural market for washing products, for example, had become 55 percent of the total, compared to 30 percent in 1980. With rural prosperity, India became the world's largest consumer and producer of tractors. The spread of TV was a cause as well as an effect. In the end, millions of rural families joined up with the national middle class. (Das, 2000, 286–287)

For Das, the Indian middle class is a class of new consumers, with ample disposable income. Such a view is at variance with what Dipankar Gupta (2009) considers the middle class in India. Das also does not draw a line between the urban and the rural middle classes. Even in terms of consumption items, there is a great deal of difference in the urban and the rural settings. Costs of consumer items, nature of jobs and quality of education, for example, are at variance in the two contexts, consumerist values and lifestyles alone cannot determine the size and nature of middle class.

A couple of analyses indicate that the upper castes constitute the middle class in India (Jayaram, 1977; Lal, 1988; Navlakha, 1989; Rudra, 1989, 142–150; Sharma, 1997c, 124–129). Generally, in most of the studies, a marked lack of homogeneity among different middle classes has not been given due attention. Urban bias is also evident as often mentioned about white-collar workers, office workers, teachers, writers, journalists, artists, skilled workers, professionals, journalists, politicians, trade union leaders, etc., as the middle classes. A major chunk of these people live in big cities and towns. We would like to state here that widespread political consciousness and democratization of politics and land reforms and massive irrigation schemes, education and migration have resulted in the attack on the age-old hold of the upper castes and on their high-status positions. Tensions, contradictions and conflicts characterize the rural India at present (Sharma, 2007b, 1998a, 159). For example, the peasant castes, particularly Jats in Rajasthan, being beneficiaries of land reforms, adult franchise and democratic decentralization of power in the PRIs, education, non-farm sources of income, and also reservations, have surpassed most other castes in public domain. The advantage has gone to them as they are numerically a preponderant group in several districts of Rajasthan (Sharma, 1998). In Bihar, the middle castes have legitimized their meteoric rise in the class and power hierarchies (Prasad, 1978). Capitalist transformation in agriculture in Tamil Nadu has created a middle class.

Beteille (1969a) mentioned nearly five decades ago that 'new status groups' or 'new castes' had emerged due to role-differentiation and occupational diversification, implying the new middle classes in rural India. Such 'status groups'/'individuals' are articulate, active and quite influential in rural India. Their networks with leaders of political parties, MLAs, MPs, ministers and bureaucrats are a source of their strength in the village, and most people talk about such a fact. Some of them have more of all this than others. They have their followers as they are followers of people at the higher levels.

Differentiation in terms of occupation, education, income and networks in rural India is not a new phenomenon. In our study of six villages in Rajasthan (1974; 1970, 1537–1543; 2012, 82–92), we have discussed that 20 per cent people were engaged (in the early 1960s) in secular or non-caste occupations. At that point of time, the upper castes were ahead of the intermediate and lower castes in regard to the adoption of the new occupations. Diverse, selective, pragmatic-orientation and circumstantial situation signified such a structural change, which was a step towards modernization. In such a process, one could see the emergence of 'middle strata', or even 'middle classes'. Most of the new occupations were white-collar salaried jobs, ranging from high ranking government officers to peon, industrial worker, bus conductor, motor driver, shop-assistant, etc. A sort of class and class consciousness could be seen in this change. The main points discussed in this study are: occupation, education, power and lifestyles.

MODERNIZATION AND FORMATION OF THE MIDDLE CLASS IN RURAL INDIA

Today, most striking characteristic feature of modernization and formation of the middle class in rural India is non-farm employment and income. We are concerned here with the non-farm sources of income and livelihood within the village due to decline in agriculture or because of availability of more remunerative and status-enhancing opportunities in the village itself. Dipankar Gupta (2009, 91–94) says that a villager is not always a farmer. Nearly half the village economy is non-farm today. Even in the 1960s, as we mentioned earlier, nearly 20 per cent workers were engaged in non-traditional, non-caste occupations in the six villages of Rajasthan (Sharma, 1974; op. cit.). According to Gupta, such a situation has arisen due to decline in agriculture as a viable means of livelihood, migration and an increase in rural non-farm employment. In states such as Punjab, Haryana and Rajasthan, non-farm employment is about 40 per cent. Government service has become a craze, obviously due to regular salary, security, retirement benefits and perks relating to education of children, leave and health.

The fact is that non-farm income has always existed both within the village and in regard to the villagers who move out of the village. The Marwaris of Rajasthan (Bania and Jain traders) even used to move out to far off places in Assam, West Bengal, southern states for seeking employment (Sharma, 1997c, 176–194). As a result of such a migration, the traditional patterns of merchanthood, markets, and moneylending have been destroyed. The younger generation of the migrant-families did not find the traditional system rewarding any more. Being educated and ambitious, they looked for greener pastures in these far-off lands. Dipankar Gupta questions the conventional meaning of the Indian village as he refers to as The Hollowed Village: How Rural Is Rural India? Like us, Gupta also realizes the need for reconceptualization of the Indian village. He is not for the 'Imagined Village'. Gupta compares data on the rural non-farm employment drawn from villages of Haryana, Punjab, Uttar Pradesh and Rajasthan. Haryana and Punjab have nearly 45 per cent rural non-farm employment.

Non-farm employment in rural India is greatly differentiated in terms of its nature, intensity, income and status. Those who have access to highly rewarding non-farm jobs are resourceful, educated and enterprising people. The poor do not have access mainly to arduous manual and masonry activities. A study of 32,000 households in 1,765 villages across India, based on data, collected by the NCAER in 1993–1994 (Lanjouw and Shariff, 2004, 4429–4446) shows that education, wealth, caste, agricultural conditions, population densities and other regional effects influence access to non-farm incomes. Lanjouw and Shariff also observe: 'The direct contribution of the non-farm sector to poverty reduction is possibly quitted muted as the poor lacks assets, but it has been found that the growth of certain non-farm sub-sectors is strongly associated with higher agricultural wage rates' (2004, 4429). The question is: Does the non-farm income in rural India reduces poverty? Non-farm income/employment has implications for both continuity and change in the stratification system.

The study by Lanjouw and Shariff has focused on some important points. These are:

1. Non-farm income shares vary considerably across states of India, and also across population quintiles. A three-way classification of non-farm activities as suggested by Lanjouw and Shariff includes: (a) casual non-farm wage labour, (b) own-enterprise activities and (c) regular, salaried non-farm employment. This is the pattern of stratification arising out of non-farm income.
2. In Himachal Pradesh, Tamil Nadu, West Bengal and the Northeast, non-farm income shares are high; in contrast, in Gujarat, Madhya Pradesh, Andhra Pradesh, Maharashtra and Karnataka, non-farm income shares tend to fall with per capita quintiles.
3. Education plays a significant role in non-farm incomes in terms of access to non-farm occupations.
4. The non-farm sector offers relatively few real opportunities for women in rural India.
5. Wealth also influences access to non-farm occupations.
6. Non-farm employment is not uniformly related to communities/ casts and districts across the country.

7. Non-farm incomes vary as per the village population density.
8. The poor are not well placed to benefit from the expansion of the non-farm activities.

Let us add here that during our revisit to two villages in 2016, one in Sikar district and other in Jaipur district, we have observed that the dominant families and individuals have nominal dependence on agriculture, whereas four decades ago their sole source of employment was agriculture and animal husbandry. Now they are engaged in multiple income-generating activities, such as contractorship for local government sponsored projects, trade and commerce, construction work, and on top of all this there is involvement in village and panchayat samiti politics.

Vijay (2012, 37–45) characterizes, though a somewhat different situation, but it refers to the rise of what he calls the 'new landlords in Indian agriculture'. As discussed by Dipankar Gupta the decline of agriculture, Vijay also observes a reduction in the share of households' dependent on the farm sector. As a result of such a situation, the number of non-cultivating 'peasant' households are increasing in importance and its stakes in land are also on the rise (Vijay, 2012, 37). The beneficiaries of the non-farm income have also hold on land and benefits accruing from it either by a way of self-managed cultivation or by leasing-out on fixed terms and conditions or on the basis of share-cropping.

R. Vijay's analysis of 'new landlords' implies that, the 'new landlords' are really owners of marginal small holdings of land. Classes may be distinguished on the basis of surplus and insufficient means of subsistence. Non-cultivating landed households have existed always, but today their number has enhanced due to multiple reasons. One of the villages in Rajasthan, as observed by us, shows that most people have sold out their agricultural land as it is in the proximity of the State Capital and situated on a national highway, and also close to a huge industrial complex. Some of these people have become substantially rich as they are today successful entrepreneurs, traders, brokers, etc.

The high beneficiaries of the non-farm income, also having substantial assets, including farm land, constitute the rural upper, upper middle and middle classes. One can see them through their income, lifestyles and ambitions to be in PRIs and cooperative societies. Jonathan Parry (2013, 40–78) talks of the 'embourgeoisement of a proletarian vanguard' in the context of the Bhilai Steel Plant (BSP). Besides, income, aspirations for occupational mobility and situation at work, lifestyles and values are equally important factors. Self-perception and perception of others also determine a 'middle class' realization. What applies to 'labour aristocracy', also applies to the upwardly mobile families and individuals. Who gets what? Who is who? These questions indicate that 'class matters', despite caste, ethnic and religious considerations.

Christiane Brosius (2010) analyses India's middle class in urban context in terms of leisure, consumption and prosperity. As a consequence of globalization, a dramatic rise of new lifestyles and new forms of work and leisure with disposable incomes have emerged in urban India. Such an urban middle class has global cultural connectivity. A new culture coming out of globalization has become a part of everyday life in cities such as Delhi, Mumbai, Bengaluru and Ahmedabad.

Sahana Udupa (2013, 29) comments that Brosius:

shows how the new middle class relies heavily on the discourse of aspirational India, and is also, in a profound sense, constituted by it. Such a middle class is distinct from the 'old' middle class of the developmentalist era, the heterogeneous middle class of globalizing India is marked by self-definitions of belonging to the world class.

Brosius talks of a 'New India', a 'global India'. The notion of 'distinction' as given by Pierre Bourdieu (1994) has inspired her analysis of cultural consumption as an act of asserting class identity in a changing city (Delhi). She also looks at new cultural spaces to understand distinction through consumption of 'fetishes'. We would like to point out that long ago Thorstein Veblen (1984) talked of the theory of leisure class, wherein he discussed how conspicuous consumption, conspicuous expenditure and conspicuous waste were taken as cultural means of high status and prestige in a technology savvy society.

There is no replica of such a middle class in rural India. But it has certain implications and symptoms in India's villages. For example, even in medium-size villages, some resourceful families spend on weddings on the pattern of urban middle class. Beauty salons have become quite common. Event management at the ceremonies and functions is also gaining ground. As observed by Brosius, 'culture of celebration' is becoming a routine activity. Birthdays and marriage anniversaries are often celebrated by the rural elite. The rural middle class, which has been imitating the urban lifestyle and cultural practices, is certainly an offspring of the development ethos, but its culture is leaned towards the new urban Indian middle class. Besides this, there are villages, which have grown into towns, but are acknowledged legally as villages (Pradhan, 2013, 43–51), and a good number of them are in the proximity of large towns and cities. Such villages have a substantial middle class as a result of their transformation as towns, in a substantial way. Our experience shows that several villages situated on national highways have practically grown as towns and have increased manifold in regard to size, density of population, entrepreneurship, trade and commerce, banking, service agencies, privatization of education, etc.

Dipankar Gupta (2005, 751–758) reflects on significant change occurring in agriculture and culture in rural India. He suspects that the Indian village may vanish if the present situation persists for a considerable time. Traditional jobs are disappearing. The caste system has become weak, but caste pride and caste identity persist and are 'appropriated by the vested interests'. Prosperous landowners have their eyes set on non-farm enterprises or something outside the village. The rich look for political power. Many of them desire to have an affluent urban ambience in their rural environs. Gupta's observations imply that many well-off families and individuals have a longing for a lifestyle, urban in nature, and distinct from the poor and common village people. In our view, such a set of people constitutes a 'rural middle class', emanating from the development programmes in the post-Independence era. A 'Creamy Layer', for example, from among the OBCs, SCs and STs, has emerged, particularly as a result of the reservation policy.

THE MIDDLE-CLASS MYTH

Dipankar Gupta (2009, 68–83) questions the very idea of the Indian middle class, particularly in the context of liberalization and high-consumption. He calls it 'The Middle-Class Myth'. He puts it: What kind of middle classes are we really talking about? What exactly are the defining features of this middle class, which is quite large? Even going by consumption standard, Indian households stand nowhere compared to the US, Canada, West Europe and other developed or even developing countries much faster than India. Gupta examines these questions on a factual basis in terms of assets, technology, consumer items, standard of living, etc. After a good deal of comparison of India with other countries, Gupta asks: 'Who are the members of this prosperous middle-class?' He answers this question by saying: 'Nowhere in the world is in the middle actually in the middle' (Gupta, 2009, 79). In Britain, in the mid-19th century, the middle was a very commodious class but excluded landowners, members of the liberal professions, and weekly wage earners. 'All those in between, from the humblest clerk to the wealthiest money magnet, were middle class' (Gupta, 2009, 79). Gupta says that middle class was an attitude to life and did not necessarily connote wealth and convenience. In the Western world, except a small number of very rich and that of the very poor, the entire population constitutes the middle class. 'It signifies a way of life and not the possession of consumer items, which is taken for granted' (Gupta, 2009, 79).

Gupta also observes that 'the constituents of the Indian middle-class actually belong to elite sections of the country' (2009, 80). In Europe, formation of the middle class was a consciously formulated project by the state in the mid-19th century. In India, the top-ranking elite have never thought of such a scheme of uplifting the poor from bottom to middle or top levels. Gupta writes with a lot of annoyance: 'Clearly, the term "middle-class" does not fit well in India; it finds barely any standing space' (2009, 82). The Indian middle class in terms of lifestyle is generally viewed equal with the common person in the West. Thus, in the US, for example, almost the entire society is middle class. In India, such a situation does not exist. The middle class as a project can bridge the gap between the elite (rich) and the masses (poor). Social mobility from bottom to upward is the only way to create a society in India with predominance of middle class.

Gupta's view on middle class can be questioned in terms of the historicity of Indian society and polity. (a) The British rule created middle strata, though for their own sake. (b) Independent India created a situation which has helped people to move up, by way of education, migration and participation in power-politics. (c) The post-liberalization India has widened scope for occupational and social mobility. These points may be seen as motivators in the formation of India's middle classes.

In political realm too, the 'middle class', in both rural and urban settings play a significant role. Anna Hazare's movement against corruption and for Lokayukta was backed up mainly by the urban middle class, though some members of this class have/had their social origins in India's villages, including Anna Hazare. Ravinder Kaur (2014, 15–19) observes that there was an 'emerging middle class', in the 2014 General Elections. This class is 'NRMBs—Not Rich, Not Middle Class, Not Below the Poverty Line'. Such a middle class was eager to seek change for a secure future. This was a 'striving class', nearly one-third to one-half of India's population. Such segment is India's rural middle class, with some education and aspiring for a non-rural, non-agricultural future. Kaur writes: 'The key character of this class is that it is middle class by "self-ascription"—they are middle class because they imagine a middle class life and identity for themselves' (2014, 17). The slogans delivered by Narendra Modi and the BJP lured them for a 'good future' of a middle class standard. Pavan K Varma (2013), before the 2014 General Elections, opined that India's middle class will be a significant factor in national politics in 2014 polls. Varma includes in the middle all persons with a monthly income ranging from ₹20,000/-to 1,00,000/-, and today it is more than 160 million. Again Varma (2014) wrote that the middle class would prove itself largely constructive and pro-reform in the 2014 elections.

Middle Class was acknowledged as an 'intermediate' or a 'transitional' class (Bukharin, 1969, 282–284). 'Intelligentsia' were treated as a stratum, and not as a class in the Soviet Union (Beteille, 2013, 79–98). Beteille observes: 'The middle class, though called as a class, fits more readily into a scheme of stratification than into one of polarization' (2013, 80). Today, middle class is highly differentiated and quite large. Only non-manual and white-collar workers would not constitute the middle class. Highly skilled black-coated workers could have education, income and status equal to or even more than white-collar workers. Goldthorpe (1987) prefers to call 'intermediate classes' (IC) rather than 'middle classes'. The boundaries between classes are not static, and it is so particularly in the case of the middle classes. Beteille writes:

> When the middle class expands to the extent that it becomes coterminous, or almost coterminous, with society, the concept itself becomes redundant. This is what is happening in the US and some other Western countries. It is not happening or likely to happen in India in the foreseeable future. (2013, 81)

Barbara Harriss-White (2004, 43–71) observes that the idea of 'IC' as given by Michal Kalecki (1973) is more apt to understand development and class structure in India. A grouping of the self-employed and small farmers forms a distinct 'class force', as argued by Kalecki, 'They are "intermediate classes" (IC) and their predominance gives rise to an "intermediate regime"' (IR) (Harriss-White, 2004, 44). There is no contradiction between labour and capital or between labour and management. They are midway between the large-scale, professionally managed capitalist enterprises of the private sector, and the working classes (Jha, 1980, 95).

In our opinion, this is a narrow view of India's growing middle classes. As we know, nearly one-third population is urban, and two-thirds people live in villages. Approximately, the Indian middle classes are also equal to the urban population. All those who live in urban India are not the middle classes. A substantial section of the people is poor, and there are also rich and very rich people. By this logic, all the rural people are not excluded from the middle class, and there are some quite well off rich people. As such there are middle classes in rural India, which include shopkeepers, self-employed persons, small contractors, government functionaries, such as teachers, nurses, compounders, doctors, Patwaris, and substantial landowners. All of them constitute the rural middle classes.

MIDDLE CLASS AND SOCIAL MOBILITY

Beteille says that 'the middle class was the main driving force behind the modernization of Indian society' (2013, 182). Today, the Indian middle class is much larger and more differentiated than it was over 60 years ago. They are from 100 million to 300 million persons (Beteille). In India, there is a 'mix' of both 'old' and 'new' middle classes. In rural India, there are more of the old middle classes, which have emanated from the developmental policies and programmes, during the Raj and also after Independence. Nature of occupation, income, education, place and conditions of work, and perceptions of the self and that of others determine the 'middle class' status of a person. Despite definitional ambiguities and fuzziness, Beteille acknowledges the striking presence of the middle classes in India and its changing nature in the post-Independence era. However, he looks at the India's middle classes from the European and American perspective (2013, op. cit.). Gupta (2005c) also evaluates the Indian middle class from the American perspective. Beteille observes that the middle class in India is growing slowly as the pace of development is quite slow. 'The middle class is still in the process of formation and expansion in India' (Beteille, 2013, 92). Lack of education and scarcity of resources are the main bottlenecks for those who aspire to join the ranks of the middle class. Besides the polymorphous character, as Beteille says, there is also differentiation of the middle class by language, religion and caste. Satish Saberwal (1976) observed this in the case of his study of mobility among three lower castes in Punjab.

As mentioned earlier, some families and individuals across all castes and communities, though in varying proportions, have moved up in social ladder within the village, based on education, occupation, income and assets, and these put together constitute 'middle class' in rural India. Such a lot is no doubt differentiated in terms of the criteria as they do not have the same levels of education, occupation, income, lifestyle, etc. A good number of rural people have moved out of the village, and based on the aforementioned attributes, they have joined the ranks of middle and lower middle classes in towns and cities, sometimes quite far off from their native places. Such a two-way formation has added to an increase in the size and magnitude of the middle class in both rural and urban India. Independent India has accelerated the process of the formation of the middle class.

DALITS AND MIDDLE CLASS

A couple of studies on Dalit middle-class (Kulke, 1983; Mendelsohn, 1986; Ram, 1988; Saavala, 2001; Sachidananda, 1974) show that despite low caste status, lower castes (ex-untouchables) have moved up, and this has weakened considerably social and ritual distance between the caste Hindus and the lower castes. The Dalits who have been benefited by the reservation policy have acquired a distinct identity and status. It may be mentioned that the higher caste members maintain some distance with them in shuttle informal ways, inhibiting their assimilation with them. Gurram Srinivas (2016, 209–218) has highlighted on this point that the Dalit middle class faces 'opposition' from their counterparts in general and at their workplaces in particular. Indifference in having social networks with the Dalit members is obvious in day-to-day life. The Dalit middle class comes mainly from among the top-ranking Dalit castes in different regions of India. It has been reported that benefits of reservation and other policies and programmes have been cornered by select individuals and families of the upper strata of the Dalits.

Besides having a notable space for Dalits in public spheres, there are also some studies indicating a creation of space in the private domain. A comparative study of the Dalits engaged in business in Haryana and Uttar Pradesh by Jodhka (2010, 41–48) seeks answers to the following questions:

1. What are the experiences of Dalits who have ventured to set up their own businesses and enterprises?
2. What are the ways in which Dalits in the urban labour market negotiate with prejudice and discrimination?

The study of 321 entrepreneurs, 126 from Panipat in Haryana and 195 from Saharanpur in Uttar Pradesh shows that the Dalits are engaged in as petty shopkeeper, hotel workshop, dealer/agency/contract, factory, institute, skill-based service providers, doctors/medical clinic operators and independent workers. Seventy-one per cent of the Dalits worked alone. Only seven had engaged/hired more than 10 persons. In most cases, fathers of the Dalit entrepreneurs were labourers, traditional/ Jajmani-based workers, and some were having petty service. Jodhka (2010, 48) observes: 'Nearly all of them faced hardships because of lack of resources and the prevalent caste prejudice, but they all seemed proud of the fact that they were in business and were entrepreneurs'. Not only were they doing well economically but also felt that they had a dignified existence than before or in comparison with other Dalits. However, the Dalit situation in Haryana was more vulnerable than in UP.

A very useful study of two blocks of Uttar Pradesh, one in Azamgarh and other in Bulandshahar districts, in the context of Dalits in the market reform era, shows that material well-being, consumption and expenditure are not enough to uplift Dalits. Important changes in socially structured inequalities are equally required (Kapur et al., 2010, 39–49). The authors of the study (Kapur et al., 2010, 48) observe as follows:

> The results of this unique survey reveal very substantial shifts in dalits' lives, consistent with a growing sense of empowerment and opportunity and declining ability of others to impose social inequalities. Changes in grooming and eating are both consistent with a deliberate attempt to shed consumption patterns that reflect and reproduce social exclusion and inferiority, through rapid adoption of 'elite' consumption patterns—much faster than can be explained by economic variables alone. Traditional stratifications in social life within the village have also rapidly eroded.

Kapur and his colleagues also say that Dalits have not achieved equality with the non-Dalits. But Dalits do not perform the traditional defiling activities, and in 'public' they are not treated as 'untouchables'. Caste-based humiliation, as Gopal Guru (2009) observes, persists, despite economic well-being and legal equality enjoyed by Dalits. Anand Teltumbde (2011, 10–11) is of the view that neoliberalism has helped a lot more to the entrenched upper castes than Dalits of India. Based on stray examples of the riches of Dalit individuals, it would be erroneous to assume an emergence of Dalit middle or upper middle class in India. Gopal Guru (2012, 41–49) also like Teltumbde feels that some 'Dalit millionaires' imply a 'spectacle' within the context of caste, the corporate sector and the state. Such a phenomenon is neither a 'class collectivity' nor a 'caste entity' in terms of business and entrepreneurship as is the case of traditional trading castes in India. Guru argues that 'Caste in India tends to produce different levels of the spectacle with high and low intensities' (2012, 48). The Dalits can come out of their paths depending upon the patronage controlled by the corporate class and the Indian government. Coming out of caste has also not been an easy process. Concessions extended to Dalits are used by high castes, corporate class and the government for their legitimations. Thus, Dalit millionaires represent 'low intensity spectacle' as viewed by Gopal Guru. Sharon Fernandes (2016) observes: 'If a Dalit gets a government job, via reservation, and does his work well he is still treated as an outcaste'. Discrimination with Dalits is a common practice, sometimes in the open, and sometimes in a covert way.

CONCLUDING REMARKS

However, it is generally true that the SCs, STs and OBCs have made significant advancement in political realm, but they are lacking behind in having a corresponding change in economic arena. Among these three categories, the OBCs have manifested themselves in greater entrepreneurial process. The rise of the SC and ST millionaires do not represent their respective communities (Iyer, Khanna and Varshney, 2013, 52–63). Deshpande and Sharma (2013, 38–49) based on recent data (2001–2002 and 2006–2007) find that caste and gender disparities persist in the manufacturing sector and business. The SCs and STs are under-represented except in the north-eastern states. However, there is evidence of homophily in the OBCs and upper-castes-owned firms. As the SCs suffer from the stigma of being 'ex-untouchables', become the victims of discrimination at the hands of the upper castes. The SCs lack knowledge, know-how and strong business networks. The upper castes are privileged to possess some of these inherited skills and advantages (Damodaran, 2008). Even a minute magnitude of 'Dalit capitalism' is thus a positive sign of equality of the Dalits with the non-Dalit castes (Prasad and Kamble, 2013).

In a recent study (Harriss-White et al., 2014), a scathing attack is made on neo-liberalization that the ideology of the market 'has done little to break down India's caste based social order, and in some ways even reinforces it' (p. 7). The upper class is able to manipulate the new situation in its own interests. The annihilation of caste, as advocated by Ambedkar (1946) seems improbable. Congruence between caste and class makes the system of social stratification rigid and strong. In 2006, as per the data available, 30 per cent of Dalits were in occupations, traditionally associated them; 40 per cent of firms had involvement of a wide range of castes; and only 11 per cent had come out of tabooed activities and had entered into education, food, rice trading, etc. (Ambedkar, 1946, 12; Purakayastha and Das, 2015, 33–37). Thus, Dalits are mainly working as wage labourers. There is a sectoral unevenness and discriminations against Dalits and Adivasis. There is a clear exclusion under the state's apparent umbrella of inclusive participation and development.

Chapter 12

Education and Social Stratification in Village India

Education can be a liberating, creative and ethically sound system to create a powerful and reflective citizenry. Education can create a civil society. As a change agent, education is an emancipatory vehicle of empowerment. However, education has also created status quo, stability and reproduction of inequality. As society is stratified, so there is stratification of educational system and institutions. 'Nobilty' is reproduced by the elite educational institutions. Such a dilemma has persisted for long despite waves of egalitarianism, socialism and modernization. Thus, education in a given society, with regard to particular sections of people, may be a means of social change and transformation. But at the same time, at some other levels with regard to other sections of people, education does not make a significant breakthrough in the entrenched hierarchical social arrangements. Rather education is used as a means for enhanced consolidation of inequality and hierarchy. Along with this, education as a human resource, as a reproduction of inequality and status quo, marketization of education and export–import of education provide paradoxical focal points for discussion.

EXPLAINING EDUCATION AS A MEANS OF EMPOWERMENT

Education is universally considered as an agent of social transformation to create a desired type of society, characterized by opportunities for less privileged people to move up in social ladder. Such an aim of education invokes many questions: What is education? Education for what? Education for whom? What is quality education? Human society is diversified and non-egalitarian, and corresponding to the non-egalitarian nature of society are unequal opportunities for access to higher quality education. Ranked people and unequal opportunities create stratified schools, colleges and universities. There is a stratified society, but it is not so merely based on higher education. There is ranking of educated people, and it is not only based on the labels, such as graduates, postgraduates and PhDs, but also on the basis of the name and fame of a given educational institution/university. Thus, higher education empowers the underprivileged people, being its beneficiaries, but non-percolation of quality education to the masses results into hegemony of a select few who are privileged to take advantage of institutions and universities of high quality and accreditation.

Education can't be there without a definite pathway and direction. A definite policy and ethics are central to the system of education at all levels. As such education implies philosophy, ideology and knowledge, aiming at the good of individual and society, and a smooth interaction between them. Social stock of knowledge in a given society, incorporating philosophical and ideological tenets, would indicate quality and relevance of education for mankind. In this way, education attacks on inequality and creates hope for equality.

Education may reduce the role of community and family in social reproduction by giving due recognition to education and related achievements of individual members in the society. Quality education is a means of equalizing the 'unequal'. Education and society are interlinked and shape and reshape each other. Both education and society are hierarchical systems; hence society is in education, and education is in society. It is not at all difficult to draw parallels between the structure and process of the two. In fact, education, social inequalities and opportunities are interwoven. It is both a means of social change as well as of the status quo.

Thus, education is not a simple phenomenon. It does different things in different ways for different individuals and groups, and it is influenced by a variety of factors and forces. Education may enhance status, knowledge and skills, but what is taught and how teaching is done matter a lot. For example, education can weaken the rigidities of caste, class and gender-based segregation and inequalities, if boys and girls of higher and lower ranks study together in a school/college/university. But the problem is that students come from different backgrounds; hence they have unequal outcomes. They do not receive the same schooling and higher education. The fact is that students remain advantaged/disadvantaged even in the same school/college/university, and in the same classroom.

PERSPECTIVES ON EDUCATION

In every society, structured social inequalities influence opportunities and choices in education. Equal footing must be the goal of the State to make education uniformly available and accessible to all. Karl Marx (1964) advocates the idea of school education as a radical praxis, being free, compulsory, uniform and unfocused for all children. Marx is for the abolition of cultural or knowledge monopolies of the privileged forms of school education. Gramsci is of the view that education can weaken the role of family in social reproduction, by bringing up children under less unequal conditions and by utilizing the socializing force of the community (Entwistle, 1979). Marx considers education as a radical means by advocating for closing up the gap between manual and mental work, between conception and execution, and by providing a full understanding of the productive process. Marx is for a more open relation between school and society, and for a dialogical relation between teacher and taught. Education can ensure auto-creation, and through this, transformation of the social division of labour can occur (Entwistle, 1979).

For Marx, change and equity are main points of educational system. Marxist Educational Praxis (MEP) is essentially a theory of practice for creating an egalitarian society (Entwistle, 1979). Education has to assure an all-round development of the personality. The aim of education is to activate the individual in all spheres of social life, including consumption, pleasure, creation and enjoyment of culture, participation in social life, interaction with others and self-fulfilment (auto-creation).

An amendment in the Marxian view on education is provided by Gramsci (Entwistle, 1979), who considers the school as hegemonic. Gramsci talks of the radical rhetoric of much contemporary neo-Marxist educational theory. He examines, within the context of his radical political theory, the modern radical education, in terms of the sociology of the curriculum, the apparent continuity between the culture of the school and that of daily life, problems of language and literacy in education, and the role of the state in the provision of education. Gramsci's main concern is the counter-hegemonic educational activity. For Gramsci, school is an instrument of political hegemony; hence a radical reform of the school system, especially its curriculum and pedagogical process is needed (Entwistle, 1979).

Largely, Gramsci's neo-Marxist perspective on education seems to be relevant to understand the nexus between education and society in India. Several studies (Chitnis, 1972; Gore, 1994) have shown that there is a clear relationship between family, political culture, system of stratification and occupational system on the one hand, and the educational system on the other. Education in India is tied up with family, caste/community, social inequality, economy, politics, etc. Colonial hangover persists even after more than six decades since Independence. Disparities between educational institutions, from primary to the highest level, have created a mismatch with regard to education and employment. Education, inequality and social change could be seen with regard to rural–urban disparities, caste hierarchy, poor quality of education, policies of the state, managerialism and commodification in education, reservation and meritocracy.

Emile Durkheim presents a quite different perspective compared to the views of Marx and Gramsci. Durkheim (1956) advocates a sociological approach to the study of education with an emphasis on the interest in the educational process and the relation of formal education to social structure and to the channels of socialization in the society. Durkheim considers education as eminently social thing in its origins as in its functions. Education is intimately related to society's structure, as it reflects and maintains the society and can only partially change it. For Durkheim, education can, at best, instil the inclination for collective life and transmit emergent social ideals and cultural levels (1956). Obviously, Durkheim considers education as a means of social solidarity and stability. In Durkheim, there is no single ideal or a perfect type of education for all men and women, which is contrary to the idea of MEP. For Durkheim, the differences in sociocultural milieu and needs matter a lot.

Keeping in view the Durkheimian perspective, we can say that education is not a static phenomenon in India, although it is also not a radical means of social change. It is an ever-changing social process. Transformations in education are always the result and symptom of the social transformations. Open Schools, Community Colleges, Adult Education, Literacy Mission, etc., need to be understood in terms of the state and society in India.

While looking at the Durkheimian view, we may like to see the role of education in the preservation and development of culture in Indian society. Education may also be viewed as a process of social control and the power system. To us, Durkheim's view seems to be clearly status quoist, promoting sponsored mobility, not leaving much space for contest mobility.

John Dewey (2011) takes a generalist view of education in terms of its necessity of life, as a social function, a direction and as growth. Education supports and strengthens democracy. Education enables a democratic society to stand firmly on its own strength. In this way, as Dewey believes, education is a national and social phenomenon. Education is the process by which man becomes man. Dewey asks the question: 'Who, then, shall conduct education so that humanity may improve?' He answers the question: 'We must depend upon the efforts of enlightened men in their private capacity'. He also says: 'Rulers are simply interested in making subjects as tools of their empires' (Dewey, 2011, 102).

Dewey, however, reiterates his view as: 'The conception of education as a social process and function has no definite meaning until we define our kind of society we have in mind' (Dewey, 2011, 104). Dewey admits that both economic factors and national interests play significant role in shaping of education.

A CRITIQUE OF EDUCATION AS A MEANS OF REPRODUCTION

'Reproduction' in education, society and culture, as observed by Bourdieu and Passeron (1977) in France, indicates that education is status quoist rather than a change agent. 'The mode of inculcation and mode of imposition characteristic of a determinate educational system can never be entirely dissociated from the specific characteristics which the culture is mandated to reproduce owes to its social functions in a determinate type of structure of class relations' (Bourdieu and Passeron, 1977, 139, fn 34). The 'grand bourgeoisie' are the guardians of the cultural ideal of the aristocracy that has given its specific form to the dominant culture and to the institutions mandated to reproduce it. In the US, contrary to the French situation, the petty bourgeoisie are there for 'reproduction' in education, society and culture.

The State in France gives the means to enforce the overt supremacy of its specific hierarchies; the mandarin system constitutes a privileged case. Bourdieu and Passeron observe:

> Even the function of scholastic legitimation of hereditary cultural privileges took in this case a judicial form; this system, which claimed to accord the right to office solely on the basis of personal merit, attested by examination, explicitly reserved a privileged right of candidature for the sons of high-ranking officials. (1977, 169)

Academic performance and entry in the first year of secondary school high-ranking academic institutions are determined by social class/origin and social inequality of the students. Thus, the educational system is subordinate to the demands of the economy and the dominant social classes. Bourdieu (1996) in a later work seems to adhere to the Marxian view that education is the superstructure determined by the dominant class (base). Bourdieu argues how the education titles have become a prerequisite for assent to the apex of private corporations and public bureaucracies, and as a new mode of domination. The ruling class has devised strategies to maintain and mask itself, at the cost of swift and continual self-metamorphosis (Bourdieu, 1996, x–xi). This is a sort of a transformed feudalism in modern times reflected in educational institutions. The elite schools (institutions) are for the socially and culturally privileged people, and the universities are for the lesser ones. Bourdieu analyses the structure and functioning of the uppermost tier of France's system of higher education and its linkages to the bourgeoisie and top corporations. Bourdieu works out a model of the social division of the labour of domination, where a diversity of forms of power coexists and vie for supremacy. There is a clear nexus between social structures and mental structures (Bourdieu, 1996, 1–16).

EXPLAINING EDUCATION AS A SOCIAL SYSTEM

Education has been viewed as an all-encompassing means of social change and development. From simple literacy to higher and professional levels, education indicates not only its structure and organization, it also speaks of social ramifications and layers in general and also in a specific society. Education is thus seen as an agent of development of the people as it uplifts them from their low status. It evokes aspirations for occupational and status mobility by inculcating a desire for equality of opportunity. The most important role of education is to create the ideology and practice of liberalism and humanism and emancipation from the rigid strings of inequality.

The nature and type of education influences the process of social change in terms of education as a resource, a means of power and control, and as an agency of socialization. But an easy access to meaningful education is quite difficult for the deprived sections of society. Bottlenecks caused by sponsorship, ascription and inequality make education quite paradoxical. Contest, achievement and equality remain largely as dreams to be realized. Such a paradox obstructs inculcation of an egalitarian value system.

Though, apparently education is an agent of social change and equality, yet prevalence of unequal social opportunities makes education a scarce entity. As such, education ranks society, implying incorporation of 'society in education' and 'education in society'. Both society and education are thus structured and exist with hierarchies. However, we can't deny the fact education has created a new middle class, a select upper stratum, and a new power elite.

Education has brought about heightened consciousness and conscientization, which has led to emergence of civil liberties, civic society, public interest, judicial activism, etc. And this has strengthened democracy on the one hand and put a limit on narrow parochial and primordial considerations on the other. As such education is a radical praxis. MEP insists on education for all at the uniform plane. In such a system, there is no place for cultural or knowledge monopolies. Knowledge does not become wealth/commodity/cash. But such a situation is not yet in existence. Even the State has allowed reproduction of knowledge as wealth and a source of status and power. 'Nobility' is being produced by the state-sponsored elite educational institutions in France and in other parts of the world.

A common man-friendly system of education would not allow role of family as it promotes social reproduction. Auto-creation, transformation of the social division of labour, and in fact, all-round development of personality must be a net outcome of public educational system. If education is allowed to remain as a means of status quo, inequality and power, it becomes injurious to change, development and equality.

Irving Louis Horowitz (1967, 358–383) while explaining structure and organization of higher education and research institutes, broadly mentions two categories of people, namely, 'mainliners' and 'marginals'. Mainliners are differentiated as 'professionals' and 'occupationalists'; and marginals are followers of the mainliners and referred as 'unprofessionals' and 'anti-occupationalists'. Key considerations in this explanation are: (a) ethos and (b) organization (of the academic establishments). Unprofessionals are associated with the professionals and anti-occupationalists are followers of the occupationalists. Professionals are men of establishment and maintain liaison with the powers that be for getting funds, projects, etc. Occupationalists are generally anti-establishment people, but they are creative scholars, having humanistic orientation. Such a portrayal of the American academic situation also applies largely to the Indian academic and research organizations.

Education is stratified in many ways, based on excellence, power, ideology, patronage, etc., of the academic functionaries. Education is thus structured in terms of its organization on the one hand, and by the stratified society on the other. Bourdieu (1996, 50–51) calls it 'a double structured homology'. Bourdieu elaborates this by a correspondence between social structures and mental structures, based on differences in schools (in France), based on a cumulative index of social and academic prestige. He draws a clear distinction and a definitive social boundary between the grand pole (gate) and the small pole—between the people. It is in this way mobility is created by the educational institutions in connivance of the State. Even 'language' (medium of instruction) is seen as 'social power'. The cost of elite education implies the role of 'capital', along with the state support.

EDUCATION AS A MEANS OF SOCIAL CHANGE

We may infer from the earlier brief description that education is for both individual and society and it implies clearly a given philosophy, ideology, and knowledge. As such education is for entire society and it is holistic in terms of its contents and relevance. Education is a human resource development; it is a sum total of intellectual kit, carried out by the concerned people. However, we need to take up the questions of 'quality' and 'accreditation' of education. Can the altruistic humanism be achieved through privatization and marketization of education? We may ask: Is education a consumer service? Privatization is seen as an example of 'trade in social services'. What happens to education as a creative enterprise when it becomes an industry? Crude managerialism is taking over the critical and self-reflective curriculum. Private interest surpasses public good in the name of public–private partnership (PPP). Powerful and reflective citizenry become a rare phenomenon.

Thus, education is not a simple phenomenon. It does different things in different ways for different groups, and it is influenced by a diversity of forces. Caste, class and gender can be decisive factors, singularly or in combinations. But education can also weaken caste, class and gender based inequalities as boys and girls of higher and lower castes and classes study together in a school/college. Despite such an equalitarian conse-quence of education, it is undeniable that structured social inequalities influence opportunities and choices in education. Lack of equal foot-ing remain, a main hurdle in achieving equality through education.

Education, being a stratified system, produces differentiated men and women in terms of skills and knowledge. Bourdieu (1996, 1–16) talks of legitimation of 'unequal gifts', 'elite perpetuation' and 'status retention' by the school system. Such a situation demands a relook at education in terms of its policy, ethics and relevance. The role of the state as an institution and of the government as an agency of a ruling political party needs to be critically examined. Bourdieu opines against materiality of economic and political power in education. He rejects aristocracy of intelligence and exclusion in the name of competition, excellence and cultural capital. But the fact is that ascription is being transformed into achievement, just for further strengthening the place of ascription.

The question is: How to make education as a means of social reconstruction and egalitarian social order? India has made efforts by way of reservations in educational institutions for the Scheduled Castes, the Scheduled Tribes and the Other Backward Classes, Women and Marginal groups. But this has helped them to a limited extent and to some select segments from among these weaker sections. A 'creamy layer' has emerged from the weaker sections, and this new stratum has become a votary of status quo, hindering percolation of the benefits to those who need them most.

HIGHER EDUCATION IN MODERN INDIA

Higher education in contemporary India is not dissociated from the colonial legacy in two ways: (a) English-educated manpower having its colonial origin continues to dominate, and (b) Higher education institutions, such as colleges and universities, follow the structures, institutions, norms and procedures of the colonial era. Two social consequences have emanated from the British system of education: (a) Uneven spread of higher education; and (b) A hierarchy between the English-educated in England and the English-educated in India.

Higher education in India during the British rule was more of education in English language than disciplinary development and scientific study and research. Pavan K. Varma (2010, 64) quotes Jawaharlal Nehru (1936) for his observation in 1912 at the Congress Session:

It was very much an English-knowing upper-class affair where morning coats and well-pressed trousers were greatly in evidence. Essentially, it was a social gathering with no political excitement or tension. Invitation of the English superiors and their mannerism by the Indians in the elevated echelons had become a creed.

'But the British administrators had their own, very different, reasons for imposing their language on the people of India. Their basic purpose was not to nurture Indian Einsteins of the future but to create a bank of English-knowing clerks for the immediate present' (Verma, 2012, 59).

Macaulay was the architect of such a policy which implied that Indians who learned English were dissociated with their native languages on the one hand and also did not reach to the level of English administrators on the other (Verma, 2012, 61–63). Verma writes: 'Language, thus, became a strategic tool to achieve a variety of ends, none of which had anything to do with making the natives speak English of a literary standard'. The British created 'colonial' modernity in India, and the Indian princely states also supported the alien culture. Frenz and Berkemer (2006; 1261–1268) state that initially there was no distinction between British and 'native' patterns of education, as both were concerned with altruistic goals. However, later on, the rulers made investments in education as measures to enhance their own status in the eyes of their subjects and neighbours.

The first three universities were established in 1857 in Calcutta, Bombay and Madras. After 30 years, the fourth was established at Allahabad. And after 30 years of Allahabad University, the University of Mysore and Banaras Hindu University were opened. In 1947, at the dawn of Independence, there were only 8 universities and 600 colleges, having less than 200,000 students. B. G. Tilak (2013, 1) observes: 'The British Indian educational policy was clearly subservient to imperial economic policy, which treated the country as a source of raw materials and market for British manufactured goods. This wrecked the indigenous educational system with its great chronological depth'. Tilak further writes that the new universities (compared to the indigenous ones) were alien transplants and they could not be and were not intended to be true copies of the 'original', quoting Basu (1991, 31).

INDIAN HIGHER EDUCATION: POLICY AND EXECUTION

Besides the universities established by the colonial government, some universities were opened by the national leaders during the second and third decades of 20th century. Immediately after Independence, the Government of India appointed the University Education Commission in 1948 under the Chairmanship of Dr S. Radhakrishnan. After one and half decades from this Commission, in 1964, the University Grants Commission (UGC) appointed another Commission in 1964 under the Chairmanship of Dr D. S. Kothari. The following Committees and Commissions have been appointed till date after the Kothari Commission:

- The National Commission on Teachers (1983).
- The UGC Committee on Mobilization of Resources in Central Services (1993).
- The AICTE Committee on Technical Education (1994).
- The Prime Minister's Council on Trade and Industry (2000).
- The National Knowledge Commission (NKC; 1999).

The important policies and decisions on education are:

- The first National Policy on Education (1968).
- The second National Policy on Education (1986).
- The Discussion Paper on Government Subsidies in India (1997).
- The Supreme Court judgement in Mohini Jain Versus Government of Karnataka (1992).
- Unnikrishnan Versus State of Andhra Pradesh (1993).

Tilak (2013, 2) notes the aforementioned efforts on the part of the Government of India. He also states that the World Conference on Education for all at Jontein (1994), the World Bank paper on higher education (1994), and the inclusion of education services under the General Agreement and Trade in Services (GATS) in 1995 have made an impact on higher education in India. However, Chaudhuri (2013) observes that today the number of memorandum of understandings (MOUs) with foreign universities are being taken as criteria of success of a University. Chaudhuri (2013, 3–22) says that it is the dominant public discourse. We may ask: What is a University? Chaudhuri refers to the report of the Committee to Advise on Renovation and Rejuvenation of Higher Education (CARRHE) to say that an idea of the university is not so different from the idea of freedom. It is a place where creative minds converge, interact with each other and construct visions of new realities. Established notions of truth are challenged in the pursuit of knowledge (CARRHE, 2009, 9). The University is also regarded as the trustee of the humanist traditions of the world. Chaudhuri expresses her serious concern regarding the university of today becoming a means of the job market and a money-making mechanism.

The university can't be a place for 'sponsored' teaching and research or it can't be guided by the so-called demands of the national and the global economic conditions. A similar view has been voiced by N. Jayaram (2013, 23–40) that there is a 'decline of the university as a public institution in India'. Regulatory mechanism, such as the UGC (Sharma, 2013), focuses mainly on growth of number of universities, enrolment of students and creation of faculty positions. The UGC is merely a funding agency and really not an institution ensuring high quality of teaching and research in higher education.

Expansion of higher education has been quite phenomenal. There are 634 universities, 33,000 colleges, and 817,000 teachers, 40 Central Universities (17 of which were established during the 11th Five-Year Plan), 30 specialized science and technology institutions, 200 laboratories, 15 Indian Institutes of Technology (IITs), 13 Indian Institutes of Management (IIMs), 30 National Institutes of Technology (NITs) and 24 Indian Institutes of Information Technology (IIITs). Besides these national institutions, there are more than 3,000 colleges of engineering, technology and architecture, 210 medical colleges, 3,400 teacher training colleges, and nearly 3,000 other professional and technical institutions in areas, such as agriculture, law, management, computer applications and information (2009–2010; Tilak, 2013, 2–3). During the past 10 years, the number of institutions might have increased considerably.

Besides these facts, collated by Tilak, some observations, such as expansion of higher education, achieving the manpower needs of building a new society, and export of higher education are also relevant for analysing higher education. No serious concern is shown about quality of higher education in general. Leaving out IITs, IIMs, and a few universities, quality in higher education seems to be a big casualty. The recent expansion of higher education is largely due to the recommendations of the NKC for opening of new IITs, IIMs, Central Universities, etc. As per the NKC, India needs about 1,500 universities more to have a 30 per cent gross enrolment ratio in higher education by 2020. Universities in private sector and foreign universities may also be encouraged to contribute to achievement of this target.

Two main points, namely, inequality between different social groups vis-à-vis higher education, and quality of higher education, though very briefly stated, have not received due attention. The main emphasis has been on quantity and expansion of higher education since Independence. While analysing the crisis of Indian education, Amartya Sen (2013, 129–162) observes that governmental neglect is not one of the characteristics of the crisis of Indian education. Sen writes: 'The allocation of public funds to education has been substantial and the share of education in the total government budget has been growing steadily. Furthermore, expenditures have been incurred not in a thoughtless manner but after a great deal of deliberation and discussion' (Sen, 2013, 130). Sen applauds the D. S. Kothari Education Commission (1964–1966), and states that it has dealt with every conceivable question of the development of education in India, and its recommendations are full of insight and wisdom. Sen states that administrative neglect or thoughtless action are not the factors of the crisis in higher education. He writes: 'We have to go more deeply into the nature of the Indian society and to evaluate the impact of our social structure on educational policy making' (Sen, 2013, 130–131). The economic and social forces operative in India and the response of public policy to the forces are responsible for grave failures in policy making in the field of education. The rapidly deteriorating standards of higher education are one of the aspects of this crisis. Acute shortage of well-qualified teachers is one of the reasons. The market mechanism is also not able to tackle the crisis. Performance of the educational system is under question mainly because of the failure of public policy.

EDUCATION AND EMPOWERMENT

In a recent edited volume by Avinash Kumar Singh (2016), contributors discuss education and empowerment, education of the disadvantaged, educational policies and programmes, school education and empowerment, and higher education and empowerment. The focal theme of the volume is to evaluate educational policies and programmes in regard to empowerment of the people in India. Structures of equality (status), and not just equality of education (degrees and diplomas) can ensure empowerment. Opportunities for quality education have been limited and unequal, hence unequal empowerment through education. Now the main question is: How do we ensure empowerment through education? Can a pedagogy keeping in view the disadvantaged help the weaker sections' empowerment? Which are the ideas, policies and programmes that can lead to empowerment of the deprived people? Are there ways to deconstruct the social and educational hierarchies? How can we mitigate the nexus between the state, society and education? Is Right To Education (RTE, 2009) an effective legal instrument to demand education for a dignified life?

Education implies, as we have analysed, both 'reproduction' and 'enlightenment'; hence it is paradoxical. 'Reproduction' further empowers the entrenched sections, and 'enlightenment' is beneficial for the first-generation learners in particular. In the second case, to some extent, education becomes emancipatory, a means of new awareness of the self, a sense of dignity, a new hope, conscientization, critical awareness and radicalism (Sharma, 2011). But such a benefit is frustrated for the reasons mentioned earlier also due to marketization, neo-imperialism and lack of reflection and enlightenment in the present-day educational system.

Marketization of education brings in the element of class, and in this process 'mobility' is produced and reproduced. How do we check profit-making in education? Education is not an automobile or information technology industry. Some individuals and families who are in the private domain of education, unhesitatingly call themselves as 'educational entrepreneurs'. For them, education is an 'industry', an 'enterprise', a profit-making managerial endeavour. The state in

India has encouraged such a tendency in education. Education is thus becoming a commodity, a matter of calculus and politics.

According to Barnett (1992), higher education must perform four functions: (a) a provider of quality personnel, (b) training for a research career, (c) management of teaching and (d) better life-chances. Barnett considers as such education as a means of empowerment in terms of human development among the people. A consideration of commercial viability in higher education can't bring about empowerment and citizenship. 'Class situation' of families would determine access to high ranking educational institutions. The institutions of the first order would remain a dream for the poor aspirants. In fact, privatization in higher education has added to perpetuation of a new hierarchy with mediocrity.

EDUCATION AND SOCIAL CHANGE

We have several studies explaining education as a means of social change and modernization (Bhatnagar, 1972; Gore, 1982; Singhi, 1979), but not a clear nexus between education and social change, in terms of causal relationship, has been demonstrated. Training of teachers and assessment and accreditation of colleges and universities (Agarwal, 2009; Rao and Palsane, 1994) do not indicate specific positive outcomes in higher education. Sociology of education (Gore, 1994; B. V. Shah and Shah, 2006) is a relevant theme for an insightful connection between education and society. However, two points need to be emphasized here: (a) What is the path of access to higher education in general and to high-ranking institutions in particular? (b) How some become capable to seek admissions in elite institutions and what prevents others from such a capability-building?

We have also shown our concern for restructuring and expansion of higher education. At the dawn of Independence, we had just 8 universities, and today we have more than 800 universities. Expansion of education (Agarwal, 2009; Singh, 1998), concern for quality of education and research (Beteille, 2010; Shah, 2013; Tilak, 2013), financing of higher education (Bhushan, 2009), 'politics' in education (Rudolph and Rudolph, 1972), nexus between state, society and education

(Basant and Sen, 2013; Deshpande, 2013; Sharma, 2011), challenges and issues in higher education by way of globalization, privatization and marketization (Altbach, 2013; Chanana, 2013; S. Chattopadhyay, 2013; Nayyar, 2013; Tilak, 2013) have been raised from time to time. Who is concerned for creation of citizenship through education? The harm done by spurious and commodified education has become a serious problem for India. We have statistics for higher education, but not concern for quality of education.

In India, equality, quality and quantity, all three are necessary elements of higher education. Rapid expansion of higher education does not necessarily bring about equality and quality. But at the same time, expansion is needed in a country like ours, where a large population is deprived of access to higher education. Despite expansion and quality of education, some people would remain deprived of, and all may not have quality education. The main point is that in general, higher education is a means to reduce inequality among people. There are also other factors affecting inequality/equality independent of quantity and quality of education.

What is the root cause of unequal access to higher and quality education? We would probe this question in the light of the perspectives on higher education as stated earlier. Universities and institutions in India are as follows:

1. Central Universities
2. IITs, IIMs, AIIMS, National Institutes of Technology and Science
3. State Universities
4. Deemed Universities
5. Professional and Technical Universities
6. Special Institutions and Universities
7. Open Universities
8. State Private (self-financing) Universities

Hierarchy of the aforementioned institutions is an established fact. Inter-category and intra-category distinctions are clearly visible in higher education. At the same time, one can say that all the central universities, for example, do not have the same levels of teaching, research and publications. This also applies to the State universities and other institutions. Some private universities have created a niche for themselves by their sheer quality education, and some others have been indulging in vulgarization of education as a commodity. Some universities are 'residential', some are 'affiliating', and some are 'residential-cum-affiliating'.

Likewise, there is a hierarchy of colleges all over India. For example, in Delhi, Delhi University's Campus Colleges are perceived far better than most of the colleges outside the campus. All the campus colleges do not enjoy equal rating, but they are different from the non-campus colleges. It is also a fact that some colleges outside the campus are equally good or even better than some campus colleges. A broad classification of colleges is given in the following:

1. Campus/Constituent Colleges.
2. Government Colleges.
3. Trust-run Colleges.
4. Autonomous Colleges.
5. Private Colleges (generally managed by individuals and families).

Nearly 10 per cent of our people participate in higher education, despite the fact that we are next to the United States in the absolute spread of higher education. However, India is far behind compared to other countries stated in the following:

United States	89 per cent
United Kingdom	60 per cent
France	60 per cent
Thailand	51 per cent
Indonesia	32 per cent
Mexico	30 per cent

(Source: Collated from UNESCO Institute of Statistics GER Tertiary–both sexes, http://data.uis.unesco.org/Inden.aspx/queryId=120)

Our 10 per cent participation is greatly differentiated in terms of quality and location of the institutions and performance of the students. Despite this, the Indian students, in the USA, in 2002–2003, were 74,603, whereas Chinese were 64,757, Korean 51,519, Japanese 45,960, etc. This has been possible because of some excellent institutions, which include, for example, IITs, Birla Institute of Technology and Science (BITS, Pilani), IIMs, AIIMS/Medical Colleges, and universities, such as Delhi University, Jawaharlal Nehru University, Poona University, University of Hyderabad, etc. Earlier the universities of Bombay, Madras, Calcutta, Allahabad, Patna, Rajasthan, Banaras Hindu University, Aligarh Muslim University, etc., were the leading institutions.

NEXUS BETWEEN EDUCATION AND SOCIETY

Unequivocally, education is viewed as a means of social change and equality. But there are unequal social opportunities to have access to higher education. Impediments, such as poverty, ignorance, low caste status, religion, gender, rural–urban divide, and hierarchy of educational institutions, determine unequal access to higher education. The main issues in the discourse on higher education are as follows:

1. There is society in education and education in society. This is pointed out in a classical sense by Durkheim, while emphasizing on the role of education in social integration and stability.
2. Spread and quality of education are uneven. Bourdieu talks of elite institutions in Paris. For example, Delhi is an epicentre of high quality education. Universities, IIT/AIIMS, Colleges and Schools of Delhi are immensely sought-after institutions, where students from all parts of India aspire to study.
3. Education has a paradoxical nature. On the one hand, education plays a noticeable role in the emergence of a new middle class and a new power elite (as in the colonial period), and on the other, education perpetuates the old middle class by facilitating its access to quality education. Thus, education functions both as a means of social change and stability.
4. Right from the elementary level to the level of higher education, family plays a significant role in access to quality education.

5. There is a reproduction of society through education to a considerable extent because of the nexus between social class, elite education and status-retention.
6. Role of the State in India in shaping education has been lopsided. Political considerations prevail in expansion as well as in ensuring quality of education. There is no clear egalitarian policy, equally benefiting all the people in every possible way.
7. PPP in higher education may transform education as a commodity, a trade, and a market-oriented endeavour. Mushrooming of universities and colleges for profit-making in the private sector is giving a new twist to education. Marketization of education speaks of a 'class situation', of buyers and sellers, competition and publicity, as if products are sold out. Managerialism is becoming a creed in education.
8. The State in India is not coming out clearly on this new development of higher education in the private sector.
9. Uneven spread and deficit in quality of education persist, in both public and private domains of higher education.

A couple of questions can be pointed out as follows:

1. Can higher education in its present stratified form contribute to the strengthening of democracy, equality and development?
2. Is 'quality' education not a resource—material in a few hands?
3. Is quality education not a power, a means of control in relation to those who are deprived of it?
4. How privatization and globalization of higher education can be good for India?

EDUCATION AND STRATIFICATION

Since both education and society are stratified, K. L. Sharma (2013, 549) observes: 'The hierarchy of educational institutions obstructs equal access even to the highly motivated and capable aspirants, because being poor, they are not in a position to afford the high cost of education at the school and higher levels'. However, for the first or the second-generation learners, education is an agency of social change and equality. Education becomes a radical praxis for the deprived sections who are benefited from higher education.

Educational inequality in India is quite acute. Access to education is determined by factors such as caste, gender, religion, economic standing and rural–urban differences. Hierarchy, based on these factors, is quite evident in the educational system. We may draw the following inferences:

- In rural India, backward and weaker people do not have access to quality education.
- Women, though have moved up in education, they remain far behind than men.
- The upper castes are still ahead of the SCs, STs and OBCs in education.
- Urban people have a lot of advantage compared to the rural counterparts.
- However, education is generally a highly desired means of social mobility.

Besides the stratified educational system and the stratified society, there is an uneven spread and development of education across India. Privatization of higher education has enhanced the difficulty in having access, due to unaffordability of the poor and rural families. Non-egalitarian access to education has given a boost to private profit over public good. A new cultural and intellectual imperialism has surfaced. Tilak (2005, 4029–4036) observes that higher education is hanging between state and market. Concern has also been expressed for devaluation of merit due to caste quotes in education.

Based on several reports, we can say today that there has been a decline in inequality of educational opportunities, but inter-state disparities persist to a considerable extent. Kerala stands out as the least unequal. Rajasthan, Gujarat, Uttar Pradesh and Bihar have also witnessed a fall in the inequality of opportunities for higher education. We can say that still there are uneven spread of higher education and regional disparities in India to a great extent. Due to colonial legacy and present-day hierarchy, based on educational attainments, quality higher education remains a privilege for a select section of Indian society.

CONCLUSION

Hierarchy of schools, colleges, universities, research institutes, and also of IITs, IIMs, National Law Universities is a stark reality of Indian educational system. Rankings made by NAAC and other agencies, both Indian and foreign too, have made public the educational hierarchy. Today, the public is demanding equality, but at the same time, it does not protest against persistent inequality perpetuated by the elite institutions.

K. L. Sharma (2013, 549–568) opines that social stratification in education implies inclusion of some and exclusion of others, seeking admissions, particularly in the top-ranking universities and institutions. The so-called 'order of excellence' is legitimized by the family. Infrastructure, saleability, and placements, in particular, are important factors in marketization by the private institutions. We have raised a number of questions regarding the present-day stratified educational system. Our view is that stratified educational institutions are also a cause of inequality in academic and learning performance. Nexus between education and stratification has resulted into status stabilization, making entry quite difficult even for the talented aspirants from among the rural poor sections of society. Rural–urban differences in education are a stark reality.

Chapter 13

Understanding Rural Development in India

DEFINING RURAL DEVELOPMENT

Clearly, there are two perspectives on the concept of development, one is the official view, and the second is the social science view. The first implies state-sponsored programmes and planning, particularly for the scheduled castes, scheduled tribes, women, children, poor, unemployed and illiterate people living in rural India. The second perspective is about the ethos of development in terms of its nature and direction, referring to 'socialist', 'capitalist' and 'middle path', keeping in view the contents and beneficiaries of the development agenda. The two perspectives are not unrelated, but they are also not the same quintessentially. In fact, the second view is more of a critique of the first based on the ground-level social reality of the people living in India's six lakh villages.

Development could be through external sources in rural India, as it is implicit in the official view, that is, by the government and non-governmental organizations. Development from within is an outcome of conscious efforts made by individuals, families and groups of people with a view to improve their existential conditions and realize their cherished goals. The main questions are: What is development? Whose development? Who are capable of availing benefits from outside development? Who are capable of having self-realization of their goals? How have they acquired skills and capabilities to extract benefits from the state and society?

Since the process of urbanization has accelerated after India's Independence, rural development has taken a backseat. Agriculture alone is no more a source of livelihood in the countryside. Several non-agricultural sources of income have emerged. An element of 'urbanity' in the countryside could be seen because of the non-farm income. But then the question is: Who have access to non-farm income? With increasing urbanization, there would be a debate on the nature and direction of development. Questions relating to rural vs urban development, inclusive development, impediments in develop-ment, rural–urban divide and/or nexus, and in fact the very definition of 'rural' would be raised.

Development is linked with democracy at least in two ways: (a) there is a sustained economic growth, with consequential benefits, reasonably, equitably spread among all the citizens, and (b) a com-prehensive, institutionalized state-directed system of social welfare is in place (Jeffrey, 2015, 106). If development is for most people, and particularly for the poor ones, democracy can survive in India. Poor in India are more in villages than towns and cities; hence reasonable rural development becomes an essential feature of India's democratic fabric. The main goal of development needs to be to achieve a considerable reduction in socio-economic inequalities.

John Harriss (1982, 15–34) refers to 'Rural Development' as policy and as process. It has emerged as a strategy for social change, for the reduction of inequalities in income and employment, to access public goods and services, and for the alleviation of poverty (Harriss, 1982, 14). Distributional issues are central to rural development. The World Bank has defined rural development as 'a strategy designed to improve the economic and social life of a specific group of people—the rural poor' (Harriss, 1982, 14).

Rural development is a positive intervention in rural life, particu-larly in regard to poverty and inequality. Rural development can be a state-sponsored activity as well as an action programme initiated by NGOs. In the Indian context, even today rural development mainly implies agrarian change, namely, green revolution, electrification, irrigation, fertilizers, etc. Harriss (1982, 17–22) talks of three sets of approaches to the study of agrarian problems: (a) systems approaches,

(b) decision-making models and (c) structural/historical approaches. The systems approach emphasizes on the systemic quality of the local community, regulated by values. There is stress on the 'external' forces in regard to change and development. 'Internal' forces remain unattended. In fact, both external and internal factors (Epstein, 1962) work in rural India. In one village studied by Epstein, there is 'development' as irrigation (wet village) was made available, but without corresponding social change. In another village, where dry cultivation was there, people moved out for employment; hence there was more social change. In the decision-making approaches, emphasis is laid upon allocation of resources on the farm and the farmers' responses to markets and to innovations. Entrepreneurship is also an important aspect of this approach as it involves choices and decision-making. In the case of the structural/historical approaches, emphasis is on the process of production over a period of time. In this, besides production process, role of technology, means and relations of production, capitalism, conflict of interests and conflict resolution are the main issues.

DISCOURSE ON DEVELOPMENT

Rural India has changed a lot as rural–urban divide has considerably transformed into a new nexus. Cognitive and ontological bases of village life are today quite different from the pre-Independence colonial situation. Since Independence, one could see new village networks, emergence of a new middle class, differentiated structures and social mobility, indicating paradigm shifts in rural society (Sharma, 2014b, XXV). Today, rural India has acquired a new face, having ever-changing 'networks', 'bridge-action', non-farm income, 'caste-free' domains, transformed country–town nexus, dignity and honour as a cardinal issues, individual and family as status units, a new middle caste assertion and pragmatic peasantry.

In such a changed rural situation, we may like to ask the following questions?

- What is development?
- Where is development?
- Whose development?

- Who are the beneficiaries of the initiatives taken by the government?
- Who corner the non-farm income?

Discourse on development centred around the issues such as education, poverty, unemployment, etc., in the 1950s and 1960s, and even in the 1970s. Today, the 'rural' of the first three decades after Independence is not the same as it was in the 1980s and thereafter. Structural changes have weakened the grip of the upper castes and classes on the lower castes and classes. Those lower castes who used to ask for employment and education, they now have raised the question of honour and dignity of their womenfolk against the evil-eye of the dominant and powerful upper castes. Their women can't be looked upon as an 'object' of the gaze of the bullies of the upper castes. Oppressive acts of the landowning castes are no longer silently tolerated by the lower castes. Retaliation against injustice done to them has become a routine matter. On the contrary, the upper castes have softened their counter-reactions to the rebellious behaviour of the lower castes.

As such, caste is no more an everyday life phenomenon. Caste as an 'encompassing' system has become a matter of the past history. K. L. Sharma states that social justice, empowerment and employment are the main concerns, leaving behind the questions of land reforms, green revolution, mode of production, etc. (Sharma, 2014b, XXVIII). 'Construction of roads, opening of senior grade schools and colleges, education of girls, fair prices of agricultural produces, healthcare facilities and viable employment have attracted the attention of the rural people' (Sharma, 2014b, XXVIII). People even complain against 'urban bias' in development policies and programmes (Lipton, 1993, 641–657). New rural activism, led by owner-cultivators, characterized by income from agriculture, and earnings from non-farm activities, has changed the socio-economic and political map of the Indian village. According to Dipankar Gupta, today, the main issues are: larger state subsidies, higher prices and more favourable terms of trade with urban world. Gupta (2005) argues that caste and agriculture no longer exercise their vigorous hold in rural India.

DYNAMICS OF RURAL LIFE

We have observed recently that today there is a need to reconceptualize the Indian village. 'Fluidity in occupational choices, migration to towns and cities, and vote-bank politics overshadow the issues related to agriculture, *Jajmani* system, inter- and intra-caste relations. Country–town nexus, rural non-farm income and control over rural institutions, such as cooperatives and panchayats, are the main considerations' (Sharma, 2014b, op. cit., XXVIII). Yogendra Singh (2009, 178–195) also observes that the notion of an ideal typical village has become outdated and redundant today. He mentions that there are two levels of 'social praxis' in a village in eastern Uttar Pradesh: (a) the state policies of development, and (b) a new resurgence in entrepreneurial ventures. Singh writes: 'The inter-caste relationships have ceased to be village-centric. Increasingly, as the policies of positive discrimination in favour of the Dalits, the backward classes, and other weaker sections have gained momentum, the inter-caste relationships have been politicized' (Singh, 2009, 178–195). In fact, Singh argues that the notion of the Indian village, and its allied institutions, such as community, caste and class need to be reconceptualized in view of the present-day rural situation. In the same vein, K. L. Sharma observes: 'Caste in everyday life is no more a source of anxiety or happiness. The way it is used/ misused or not used has made caste a very different phenomenon' (Sharma, 2014b, op. cit., XXIV).

B. R. Chauhan (2009, 147–165), while studying 'rural life' in Uttar Pradesh, devotes one chapter on 'rural development'. He refers to government plans, sociological/anthropological studies on rural change, programmes sponsored by some international agencies, etc. The concept of felt needs of the people as a part of the planning process, and a respect for existing values of the people are perhaps the key concerns in rural development. In a descriptive manner, Chauhan brings in local and regional leaders, bureaucracy and village-level workers in the process of decision-making and change. Conceptual and ideological focus locks in the entangled narration by Chauhan.

G. K. Lieton (2003), while analysing decentralization in panchayats, examines the process of development in Bengal, Uttar Pradesh and

Kerala, focusing on the issues specific to these states. The issues range from the role of caste, class and gender, natural disasters (floods), land reforms, human development, expectations and aspirations of the people, religion, communalism, weaker sections, child labour and education. Freedom in Kerala, interference by dominant caste(s) in Western UP and concern for the poor and downtrodden in West Bengal are the essential points in Lieton's vivid descriptions of the three states of India.

Thus, in view of the changing Indian village, a corresponding model of development needs to be evolved. For example, a decreased dependence on agriculture, agricultural labour, traditional occupations, *Jajmani* system, etc., on the one hand, and expansion of non-farm income, means of transport and communication, irrigation and cash crops, emergence of institutions, such as schools, primary health centres, Panchayati Raj institutions, and presence of governmental programmes on the other, would necessitate a paradigm shift in the development discourse. In the late 1960s, the development discourse centred around the issues, like nature of planning, poverty, agriculture, green revolution, transport and communication, employment, Panchayati Raj, etc. Land reforms, semi-feudalism, adult franchise and country–town divide were key concerns. During the 1960s, impediments in development process were attributed to sociocultural institutions in particular by Gunnar Myrdal (1968, Vol. I), while explaining 'modernisation ideals' in his monumental work *Asian Drama*. In a modified form, Myrdal's institutional approach has been carried forward by Amartya Sen (2000), as he says that development needs to be seen as 'freedom'. Sen talks of 'freedoms' as 'capabilities' and social opportunities, and 'unfreedoms' as impediments in the process of development.

In the background of such a changed rural scene, Indian village cannot be treated simply as caste-centric, interwoven by family and kinship ties, religious beliefs and community ethos (Dube, 1955; Majumdar, 1958; Marriott, 1955; Srinivas, 1966; Wiser and Wiser, 1963, 1971). In the first instance, we can confidently say that all villages are not internally homogenous as they are differentiated not only in terms of caste hierarchy, but also in regard to economic standing, assets and power and dominance of different castes/sub-castes, families and individuals. In the second instance, inter-village variations are also quite pronounced within the same districts, regions and between the states in India (Bailey, 1957; Epstein, 1962; Mukherjee, 1957; Sahay, 1998; Sharma, 1974). It is quite certain that Indian village is no more of a 'little community' (Redfield, 1956), and not even an 'isolable entity'. There are multidimensional 'networks' of the Indian village with outside world, and these have been changing, depending upon internal contradictions and external forces of change and development. Both 'divide' and 'nexus' between village and town have been changing, depending upon the nature of the contradictions and exteriority of the factors of change.

MODES OF CHANGE IN RURAL INDIA

In the 1970s, the development debate was on the consequences of land reforms, green revolution, white revolution, transport, telecommunications and employment, in terms of increased inequality and differentiation of peasantry (Sharma, 1983). Mode of production in agriculture and differentiation of peasantry attracted a lot of attention as capitalism made inroads into agriculture, and a clear differentiation between rich, middle and poor peasants emerged. The poor have become poorer and the rich have become richer became a popular dictum, particularly in the analyses of the Marxist scholarship (Sharma, 2001, 17–43). Such a view created a new space for a dialogue on poverty alleviation, empowerment of the weak and social justice for the deprived sections, such as the SCs, STs, women and the poor. The idea of Below the Poverty Line (BPL) people caught attention of the policy-makers and the government. The studies, such as 'Pills Against Poverty' (Goran and Lindberg, 1976) caught attention in understanding of the nature and diagnosis of poverty as a problem and not as a disease. Programmes and schemes like Mahatma Gandhi National Rural Employment Guarantee Act (MNREGA, Government of India) were enacted to provide limited employment to the poor people in the countryside. The MNREGA has received mix reactions in general from both the beneficiaries and the public, in terms of its positive effect on employment and poverty alleviation and its negative aspect regarding corruption, bureaucratic impediments and apathy towards the rural poor. Based on the NSS data for

2009–2010, Puja Dutta et al. (2012, 55–64) observes: 'We confirm expectations that the demand for work on MGNREGS tends to be higher in poor states. This appears to reflect the scheme's built in "self-targeting" mechanism, whereby non-poor people find work on the scheme less attractive than poor people' (Dutta et al., 2012, 63). The scheme has benefited the weaker sections, and particularly the poorest of the power. Rationing of workdays is certainly a limiting factor. Non-BPL families have also availed of the scheme. But, the well-off families are not looking for the scheme. It is more popular among women. Let us make it clear the scheme does not implying sort rural development. It is only for some employment for the rural poor.

It would be pertinent to raise the following questions regarding Dumont's view (1970a) on Caste:

1. Do people bother about cultural mobility in the manner as implied in the concept of sanskritization?
2. Is there visible interaction between the Little Traditions and the Great Tradition?
3. Can we say that the principle of 'pure and impure', in terms of the encompassing and the encompassed, is in practice in everyday life?

During the last four decades, clearly issues and demands for structural change have been focal theme of studies in sociology and other social sciences. In the 1960s, one could see a decline of *Jajmani* system or in other words of the traditional caste-based division of labour. Land reforms gave a bit of jolt to the *Jajmani* system. Hence, caste as a system of social relations, having a hierarchical structure and interdependence of different castes, witnessed a beginning of its systemic decline. In the wake of such an institutional breakdown, issues such as functioning of the Panchayati Raj institutions, mode of production in agriculture, empowerment of the deprived, environment degradation, watershed, electricity, girl child, mother care, reservation in jobs and institutions, prices of agricultural produces, caste and politics, caste and employment have become the matters of concern in the realm of sociology and other social sciences.

RURAL DEVELOPMENT AS A POLICY AND PROCESS

Since the second half of the 20th century, agencies such as World Bank, United Nations Agencies, Government of India, NGOs, etc., have been engaged in the process of development in rural India. Harriss (1982) rightly refers to rural development as policy and as process. The World Bank considers that rural development is a strategy defined to improve the economic and social life of a specific group of people—the rural poor (The Report of the World Commission, 2004). As such, rural development implies interventions in the life of the rural people; hence it requires an interdisciplinary approach, not limited to agriculture or economic activities alone. Theory of development is nothing but a policy to provide hints for channelization of the practice of actual interventions, for example, regarding health, education, employment, etc. A holistic approach, taking into consideration technological and environmental factors and social and cultural relationships, needs to be adopted for entire gamut of rural development. Demographic factors, role of markets and social structures of producers are also unavoidable considerations in both policy and process of rural development.

In this context, the approaches to rural development as mentioned earlier by Harriss (1982).

These approaches imply the nature of the present rural society, policies and programmes of rural development, and a basic change in village India over a period of time. Implications of the policies and programmes of rural development could be seen in the argument that there is 'urban basis' in the programmes, hence 'poor people stay poor'. Michael Lipton (1977) talks of urban-biased nature of development policy. A counter-viewpoint is held by T. J. Byers (1977) as he mentions that there is 'rural bias' in India's policies and programmes of development, because a tendency could be seen more in favour of rural capitalist/landlord, and in favour of the urban poor. Examples of Bhartiya Kisan Union (BKU) and Shetkari Sangathan are often cited as movements of the rich farmers (Gupta, 1988, 2688–2696). In view of these contradictory standpoints, it becomes imperative to examine the nature of urban bias, rural bias, and industrialization in the present-day India.

According to Dipankar Gupta (2005c, op. cit.), Indian village is changing fast in terms of its culture and agriculture. A transformed village exists with a new nexus with the wider world. Tradition is under severe stress in rural India. No more one finds landlordism and bonded labour as it used to be in the past. Agriculture is no more *uttam* (best) pursuit. Government job is considered most honourable, whereas earlier *chakari* (service) was low in the occupational rank-order. Business is preferred by most people as a second choice. In the present context, categories like rich farmers, kulaks, capitalist landlords do not bring out the real face of rural India. In fact, there is a range of owner-cultivators. The category of the rural poor agricultural labour also needs to be changed. Kolenda (1989, 1831–1838) describes how in a West Uttar Pradesh Village over a period of three decades, discourse on development has changed from unemployment, poverty, ignorance and illiteracy to honour and dignity.

The share of rural income declined from 66.8 per cent in 1975–1976 to 55.6 per cent in 1996, and it has further declined as a result of migration, mobility and education. Industry is favoured. Urban white-collar jobs ensure regular cash income, which is not secure in agrarian sector. Farmers are ignored, hence the unrest among them. Suicides among farmers are due to financial stress as they are unable to repay bank loans and meet their other obligations.

It is widely recognized that land reforms have not failed. Subsequent to land reforms and green revolution, other reforms have been ineffective. Today, a mismatch between nature, man, and state has caused a stressful situation for the aspiring and upwardly mobile farmers. Along with such a situation, a new rural activism led by owner-cultivators has occurred. These are the people who have income from agriculture, and they are also non-farm income earners. Gupta (2005c, op. cit.), therefore, says that today the issues are: (a) larger state subsidies, (b) higher prices and (c) more favourable terms of trade with the urban world. As a consequence of such a scenario, caste and agriculture have become weak mechanisms to hold tightly the Indian village as a community. Occupational diversification has given more than one choice to make a living. Decline in agriculture has enthused migration to towns and cities. Today, rural development has witnessed a paradigm shift in the face of a transforming country–town nexus, changing conceptions of village India, farmers' movements, marginalized world of the owner-cultivators, rural non-farm employment, etc. (Sharma and Gupta, 1991).

Today, the question is How to measure development? Can one measure development in terms of poverty estimates, literacy, health-care, etc.? There is 'growth' without development (Gupta, 2009). This raises the question of social justice and distributive shares in India in general and with reference to the poor and deprived people in particular. Shankar Acharya asks a pertinent question regarding the process of development vis-à-vis Indian society. The question is: Can India Grow Without Bharat? (Acharya, 2007). In his monumental work *India: After Gandhi*, Ramchandra Guha (2008, 605–719) emphasizes on the understanding of Rights, Riots, Rulers and Riches, which he calls as the Four R's. These R's bring out the sharp divides between the beneficiaries and the deprived ones, based on caste, class, rich, poor, gender, rural and urban people, etc.

EXCLUSION AND INCLUSION VIS-À-VIS RURAL DEVELOPMENT

In view of the lopsided, ad hoc and incoherent nature and dynamics of development, recently the idea of 'inclusive development' has received a considerable attention in social and political realms. Let us reflect on this new addition to the discourse on development. 'Inclusion' and 'exclusion' are though apparently opposite notions, but in reality, the two refer to the two sides of Indian society. For example, the principle of 'inclusion' and 'exclusion' is a pronounced feature of the caste system. Inclusion of one's caste members, and exclusion of the members of other castes from caste-specific domains, as a principle, is adhered in practice. Pure–impure hierarchy is simply inclusion–exclusion syndrome (Dumont, 1970a). It is a different matter that such a hierarchical inclusion–exclusion has been under attack from time to time.

The idea of 'inclusive growth/development' is being used as a policy measure to extend benefits of development to the 'excluded', 'deprived' and 'neglected' sections of society. The idea of 'inclusive development', therefore, has been initiated to include the poor, the

SCs, the STs, the OBCs, women, minorities, etc., in the process of development by way of constitutional provisions, legislations and programmes by the Indian State. We have to know also as: How people have been excluded? What are the exclusionary devices? How the inclusive measures ensure benefits to the deprived ones? What is the nature of consumer expenditure distribution?

Inclusion is both intra-group and inter-group phenomenon in a plural society, like ours, having segregation in terms of caste, gender, rural–urban divide, etc. Who are the people to whom we may call as the mainstream of Indian society? From an economic viewpoint, inclusive growth refers to estimates of production, income, and consumption distribution. It implies the included/excluded people, hence appropriate policy design/strategy for the inclusion of the excluded in the mainstream growth process.

In India's Eleventh Five-Year Plan, it is stated that a new vision based on faster, more broad-based and inclusive growth would reduce poverty and bridge the various divides fragmenting Indian society. The following points may be noted regarding inclusive growth:

1. Expanding access to assets and thriving markets and expanding equity in the opportunities to the next generation of Indian citizens.
2. No widening of disparity in per worker income between agriculture and non-agriculture.
3. Growth elasticity of poverty as measures to access inclusiveness of the poor in the development process.
4. Focus on health, education and agriculture.
5. Opportunities, empowerment and security for the deprived.
6. A balance between the organizational structure and benefits.

Inclusive development thus focuses on inclusion of people based on their socio-economic standing, gender and marginalization. Emphasis is laid upon both horizontal and vertical changes vis-à-vis the constituents of social structure. Despite inclusive policies, hierarchies remain sustained. Domination and access to resources are reflected in the society. It seems that there is a structured inclusiveness; hence there is structured dominance. (Generally, one finds that inclusion and exclusion are concomitant phenomena. Inclusion of some implies exclusion of others. The included ones are bestowed with benefits and gains drawn from the state, whereas the excluded ones remain deprived of the same. Hence, structured inclusiveness results into structured dominance of the select beneficiaries.)

Amartya Sen (2005) talks of Three R's of Reform, namely, (a) Reach, (b) Range and (c) Reason. The Reach 'implies' the Reach of the results to be achieved. The Range means the Range of the ways and means to be used. The Reason refers to choosing the priorities pursued. Thorat and Umakant (2009) argue that it is not just economic explanation of exclusion/inclusion, it is equally important, what he calls 'The Grammar of Caste'. Economic outcomes are shaped by caste hierarchy. Thorat observes that discrimination based on caste is the root cause of exclusion from sharing of resources. Caste, being a resilient system, enables people to corner the new opportunities and freedom of choice. Discrimination enforces inequalities in regard to jobs, education, healthcare and social relations.

As there are policies implying discrimination and inequalities, there is also 'politics of inclusion' as explained by Zoya Hasan (2009). Certain castes and minorities are included through affirmative action in the distributive shares for seeking their support and favour. On the contrary, there is social exclusion in the private domain, particularly in the informal sector.

Ignacy Sachs states that inclusive development can be defined by opposition to the pattern of perverse growth. It implies 'exclusion' from the consumer market, to keep people confined to informal activities, condemned to eke out precarious livelihood, without any access to social protection. The excluded people have no or feeble participation in political life, and they are poorly educated, under-organized and struggle for mere survival. Gender discrimination is one such example (Deshpande, 2011). Inclusive development calls for the exercise of civil, civic and political rights. Democracy with transparency and accountability can ensure inclusive development process. Disabled, mothers and children, the aged must be benefited by inclusive development. Redistribution of income and employment opportunities on an equal basis are basic to inclusive development. Inclusion thus implies exclusion due to scare resources and also due to easy accessibility of some people than most others.

DEVELOPMENT AS A HUMAN RESOURCE

Several aspects, such as human rights, civil society, state, market, etc., are associated with development. In a society where there is no space for alienation, commodification, exploitation and dehumanization, there would be a reign of civil society and human rights. (The victory of the proletariat over the bourgeoisie would ensure coming up of a civil society with human rights as it would provide no space for alienation of labour, commodification, exploitation and dehumanization. Such is the view of the traditional Marxists.) In a developed society, rulers are in small numbers and have greater resources. The rulers are in an advantageous position compared to the ruled in their capacity or collective action and counter-action (Anderson, 2012). This is what Perry Anderson observes about India. He further says that their (rulers) internal lines of communication are more compact, their wealth offers an all-purpose medium of power; convertible into any number of forms of domination. Their intelligence systems scan the political landscape from a greater height. The subalterns do not anywhere materially and culturally compare to their rulers.

While attacking on 'social arrangements', which prove bottlenecks in development, Amartya Sen (2000, 2005b) argues that there are a couple of 'unfreedoms', and development can prove as freedoms, provided it aims at capability-building to create choice(s) for the subaltern classes and the deprived ones. In other words, development and social opportunity are interlinked phenomena, and the two are not independent of each other. A lack of link between the two speaks of discontent and crisis of governance. Governance, in social context, refers to the well-being of individual, family, and community. There could be cultural dilemma in social governance, such as caste, religion, inheritance, etc. (Amartya Sen, 2000, 2005). 'Demand groups' (Rudolph and Rudolph, 2008, 234–246), as new middle classes, ask for bigger shares in state's resources. Ultimately, the real measure of development is 'social justice', a 'fair justice' (Rawls, 1971). 'Justice' implies a creation of such institutions which can ensure a 'just society', a 'desired type of society', with accompanying public sense of justice and civic friendship. There are varied practices of social justice, implying political, social and cultural connotations. Let us say here that in a just society, the liberties of equal citizenship are taken as settled. Justice is natural and not a matter of political bargaining. However, some political parties and outfits try to take credit for seeking justice for its members. The public's sense of justice is far more important than that of a political party.

India Rural Development Report 2012–13 (2013) describes rural social change, livelihood and inclusion, infrastructure, sustainability, local governance and MGNREGA as the dimensions of development in rural India. According to the Report, 'a new rural India' is on the anvil. The ground reality of rural India is complex and diverse. Villages differ in size, social composition, infrastructure, socio-political awakening and economic resources (both land and non-farm income). They also differ in terms of country–town nexus. Generally, agriculture is on decline. It is about 15 per cent of India's national income, whereas nearly 60 per cent of people depend upon it. A significant change is taking place in regard to youth, gender relations and caste and inter-caste relations. Girls are going for higher education even among the lower caste, and they aspire for government jobs in particular. Our revisit to the six villages has shown this trend amply across castes and communities. Surinder S. Jodhka and Tanvi Sirari (2014) mention about the marginalization of agriculture in the national economy, a majority of rural workers are engaged in agriculture. Non-farm activities and other multiple economic engagements also provide employment and supplement poor cultivators and agricultural labourers. Many rural people work outside the village. Generation change has also affected traditional village economy, arts and crafts and ties binding caste and family.

The marginalized have a voice and make assertions too. But inequality has not reduced to a considerable extent. There is marginal and superficial inclusion of the 'excluded', and new practices of exclusion have emerged in regard to education, employment and social networks.

PART V

Theoretical and Empirical Concerns in Village Studies

Chapter 14

Subaltern Studies in the Wake of Globalization

WHY SUBALTERN STUDIES?

A romantic and somewhat glorified communitarian depiction of the Indian village has created serious misgivings about its highly non-egalitarian and hierarchical character both in theory and practice. Characterization of the Indian village as a self-sufficient and homogeneous community hides the agonies and oppression of the lowest and poorest of rural India. A 'field view' or 'view from below' could reveal the nature and functioning of structural social inequality. It was quite unrealistic to describe Indian Collage Community as a land of a 'republic'. Those who were at the bottom of socio-economic hierarchy were not allowed to participate in village affairs. Decisions taken by the rulers and priests coming from high castes were unquestionable and absolute in nature. *Jajmani* system, in fact, was an arrangement of patronhood, dominance and subjugation. It was not a system of respectable mutual relations between different castes. However, it was often eulogized as a functional system for the society as a whole. The reality was that it was appropriated socially and culturally to perpetuate economic and political dominance of the upper caste patrons. Since the people at the lower level did not have freedom to take decisions about their own affairs, their existence was totally dependent on the powerful patrons under the garb of the caste system. According to B. R. Ambedkar (1948) village was a site of oppression where the institution of caste presented itself in its most brutal and inhuman form.

A large number of village studies conducted in the 1950s and 1960s (Beteille, 1965; Dube, 1955; Epstein 1962; Lewis, 1958; Majumdar, 1958; Srinivas, 1955) have viewed village as a 'system' revolving around caste, religion, family and community. None of these studies depicts the miserable life of the oppressed. The colonial idealization of the Indian village persisted to a considerable extent in the studies of the 1950s and the 1960s. However, in some studies, the pathos of the poor and oppressed have been taken up (Breman, 1974; Djurfeldt and Lindberg, 1976). Even a simple fact that hierarchy and interdependence of different castes were untenable was not seen as an antagonistic reality of village life. Even in the pre-colonial era, land was not communally controlled; right over land was quite differentiated. People never had equal rights over village resources (Habib, 1963). There were tensions and conflicts as one could see from the peasant struggles and uprisings.

After Independence, land reforms were effective to some extent as the privileged landowners lost their landholdings, and the tenants-at-will, who were deprived of ownership rights, were beneficiaries of the reforms by way of confirmation of rights on land. Land reforms and several development schemes, including Panchayati Raj, have brought about some levelling in social relations. However, even today, a large section of rural society is without access to benefits, as the dominant families and individuals have cornered a big chunk of the fruits of rural development. Globalization has adversely affected most of the deprived sections of rural society. Both the landless and the cultivators have suffered, though for different reasons. The landless people are resource deprived; and the farmers, though innovative and enterprising, do not get due return from agricultural produce. Hence, farmers' suicides have become a chronic phenomenon.

Economic and political disparities have also led to emergence of new social and cultural inequalities. Dalit studies indicate that Dalits suffer alienation, indignities and humiliation because of the oppressive and domineering behaviour of the power elite, in particular. Poor and marginalized, women, bonded labourers and weavers need to be studied from 'below'. The subaltern approach would remain relevant so long as there are poor and deprived people. Caste-class divides, poverty and unemployment would necessitate the perspective from below ('from below' here implies the perspective of the people at the bottom.). We have discussed the perspective keeping in view its need for a serious study of the ramifications of rural society in India.

UNDERSTANDING SUBALTERN STUDIES

Ranjit Guha, the founder of the Subaltern Studies, is considered as the practitioner of a critical Marxist historiography, who sought an active political engagement with the postcolonial present, inspired by Gramsci and Mao (P. Chatterjee, 2009, 1–17). Guha, as founder and guiding spirit of Subaltern Studies, has provided a critique of both the colonialist and the nationalist historiographies of modern South Asia. He critically examined in the first volume of Subaltern Studies (1982) itself the two elitisms—the colonialist and the nationalist (P. Chatterjee, 2009, 12). David Arnold, Shahid Amin and Gyanendra Pandey joined Guha in England on debates on the two elitisms and the new path of historiography. In 1980, in India, Gautam Bhadra, Dipesh Chakrabarty and Partha Chatterjee joined him in the ongoing initial discourse on subalternity.

Partha Chatterjee (2009, 12–13) states that the early volumes of Subaltern Studies (1982–1989) were mostly concerned with the studies of peasant agitations during the nationalist movement. Guha's emphasis in these volumes was on the autonomy of peasant consciousness. The nationalist politics of the peasantry was not the same as that of the elite. Guha published his essay on this theme under the title *Dominance without Hegemony: History and Power in Colonial India* (1997). In Introduction to *A Subaltern Studies Reader 1986–1995* (1997, IX–XXII), and reproduced in Ranjit Guha (2009, 318–332), Guha argues that a hallmark of Subaltern Studies from the very beginning is insistence on a solidarity that would not reduce individual voice, styles and approaches to a flat undifferentiated uniformity. He writes:

> It is a strategy that is not without its risks, of course. It has opened us to attack from those party-liners, one horse riders, and other monists who had looked for the straight and the steady and the singular in our work only to find us wanting. But we have taken that risk in order to generate and continually renew a space that is vital to a project like ours. For its very existence, the concept as well as practice, depends on its ability to

negotiate the tensions of an irreducible non-coincidence within it—a stubborn reminder that is an essential condition of its creativity and the source of its energies. (Guha, 2009, 318)

The phenomenon of Subaltern Studies has its distinctive character and individuality. Human/social life, generation and community put together make a different history, compared to a simple chronology of individual lives studied in succession. Diversity and change can be studied more meaningfully by a multilateral approach. The incidences like the Naxalbari uprising and the emergency stimulated disillusionment and paved the way for Subaltern Studies. In the 1970s, two questions bothered Guha, and his anxiety to find answers to those questions were in the form of outcome of Subaltern Studies. These were:

1. What was there in our engagement with nationalism to land us in our current predicament—that is, the aggravating and seemingly insoluble difficulties of the nation-state?
2. How are the unbearable difficulties of our current condition compatible with and explained by what happened during colonial rule and our predecessors' engagement with the politics and culture of that period? (Guha, 2009).

Future-directedness was a consequence of a disillusionment of hope. 'A body of knowledge and interpretation relating to the past, which had been taken for granted and authorized academically as well as politically…. was now subjected to doubt in such a way as to lose its certainties' (Guha, 2009). Partha Chatterjee has aptly given the title *The Small Voice of History* to the essays edited by him (2009). In fact, Guha has tried to blow up the small voice to the big one. Such has been the impact of the Subaltern Studies that over the past three decades, hundreds of seminars and discussions have taken place on this theme, and a great amount of literature has been generated on the deprived and marginalized sections of society who had remained ignored during the colonial rule or even after India's Independence. However, in the post-globalization period, Subaltern Studies has lost the appeal which is reflected in the initial volumes. The publication of Subaltern Studies has ceased and this too has created a vacuum.

SUBALTERN STUDIES AS A CRITIQUE OF ELITISM OF COLONIALISTS AND BOURGEOISIE NATIONALISTS

Ranjit Guha thought of the subaltern people with a very clear perception that the Indian historiography was dominated by 'elitism' of colonialists and bourgeoisie-nationalists. Such a history ignored and undermined the incorporation of the poorest of the poor and the marginalized and therefore left them unnoticed. Twelve volumes of the Subaltern Studies appeared from the first volume in 1982 to the twelfth in 2005. The Subaltern Studies had the status of a global academic institution (V. Chaturvedi, 2000), though globalization–liberalization–privatization have slackened interest in subaltern studies in the post-globalization era.

Philosophically, and also considerably in practice, individualism is replacing humanism due to globalization. But that is undeniable that for nearly two decades, subaltern studies became a new creed in social sciences, it was considered a sort of an alternate to conventional approaches, namely, functionalism and Marxism. Subaltern approach overshadowed nationalist history writing, by declaring its ethos as colonialist and pro-bourgeoisie. Thus, subaltern studies has provided an appealing critique of the history of colonial India. It has provided a critical evaluation of the postcolonial theory and cultural studies in the West. So great has been the impact of the subaltern studies that in the 1990s, one could see the formation of the Latin American Subaltern Studies Group, and studies on subalterns in America, China, Ireland, Latin America and Palestine appeared as a significant development (V. Chaturvedi, 2000).

Since its inception, subaltern studies was intensely influenced by Marxism. With its increased significance, subaltern studies distanced from Marxism in general and the heterodox Gramscian Marxism in particular. The trajectory of subaltern studies has diverse roots. It is not simply confined to the volumes (1 to 12). We would analyse here the nature of coverage in the subaltern studies volumes.

A group of historians were associated with Guha in this endeavour. They had disaffection with historical interpretations of the freedom movement of India. The main criticism was that the nationalist historians made elite contributions in the making of the Indian nation at the neglect of 'politics of the people'. Therefore, the subaltern studies justified initially the following:

1. A historiographical 'negation, of a rigidly formulaic orthodox Marxism'; and
2. A denial of the 'Namierism' (history written by outsiders) of the Cambridge School in Britain.

The advocates of the subaltern studies were of the view that historiography and Namierism failed to account for the dynamic and improvisional modes of peasant political agency. Guha was anxious to know the relationships of politics to scholarship. In other words, scholarship had imprint of politics, and this inspired Guha to think of the subaltern studies, which would be influenced by 'politics'. As such, subaltern studies began as an attempt to transform the writings of colonial Indian history by drawing on the fluid concept of class articulated by Antonio Gramsci (1957). Such a beginning marked two things: (a) a break from the economic determinism of Orthodox Marxism; and (b) a commitment to the political agenda of Gramscian Socialism (Susobhan Sarkar, 1968; 1972, 1–18).

A STUDY OF PEOPLE FROM BELOW

Subaltern studies has popularized studies in social sciences from 'below', where the subaltern classes are the subjects in making of their own existence and history. The examples of the poor and marginalized communities are the Dalit women, hunters and food gatherers, bonded labourers, etc. For shaping an authentic politics of the people, subaltern studies has made a departure from the conventional social sciences. The following points may be noted in relation to the dialectic between Western Marxism and Indian political culture:

1. Ranjit Guha had an intellectual influence of Gramscian thought at the Presidency College, Calcutta.
2. The idea of Subaltern Studies emerged in Britain when Gramsci's writings were radically transforming the culture of English Marxism.

Around this time, Eric Hobsbawm had published *Primitive Rebels* (1971) and an essay, 'For a History of Subaltern Classes' (1960), from the Gramscian perspective. Hobsbawm tried to explain that 'primitive rebellions' did not belong to the categories of crime and backwardness. In fact, Ranjit Guha's seminal work was titled *Elementary Aspects of Peasant Insurgency in Colonial India*. Gramsci's concepts of state, popular culture and hegemony received experiences from worker's peasants and 'common people', with a view to have 'histories from below', to eliminate the perspective of the elite classes from the available traditional social history formed the focal theme of Guha's new milestone.

In the very first volume of Subaltern Studies (1932), Guha makes quite clear the objective of histories from below'. In one essay, Robert Brenner (1982), criticizes techno-economics determinism of Karl Marx. In another article, Partha Chatterjee (1982) provides a critique of 'political Marxism'. Chatterjee talks of 'community' as the organizing principle for subaltern studies. The Subaltern Studies reacted against the Marxist peasant insurgency of Naxalbari (which had begun in the 1960) and the Emergency (1975–1977). Subaltern studies emerged, in the wake of such a situation, as a new theory and policy. Guha theorized about the violent nature of subaltern ideology and consciousness. For Guha, a new epistemology was required to understand the antinomian dimensions of subaltern politics. Guha (1983) tried to disclose the otherwise concealed political character of peasant consciousness by reconstructing the vantage point, the spontaneous ideology of the peasant rebellion.

The subaltern studies approach was not liked by several critics. Many used secondary literature to argue against the Gramscian approach. They did not find new and revisionist ideas in the histories from below. There was a lot of imitation from British Marxist historians. The peasant rebellion themes of 1940s were not projected. Many Indian Marxists adhered to orthodox Marxism against the subaltern studies approach. Despite this, in the first four volumes, the peasant's rebellions were treated as an autonomous political subject in the making of his own history.

The second phase in the subaltern studies was marked by accommodation and reconciliation at the ideological level. By 1986, many, within the subaltern group, considered the tradition of historical materialism as a significant, and yet limited, resource for a project to contest a Eurocentric, metropolitan, and bureaucratic system of knowledge. Peasant consciousness was considered no longer an essential structure. This was considered as a 'post-structural moment' (Chaturvedi, 2000). In Europe, Marxism was underplayed due to post-structuralism and Foucauldian critiques. However, some continued to write 'histories from below' and some took post-Marxian stances.

THE EFFECT OF GLOBALIZATION ON SUBALTERN STUDIES

Globalization has affected a paradigm shift in social sciences. It has relegated Marxian approach into background. The role of state in relation to social welfare measures for the poor is no more as it used to be in the pre-globalization era. In the early 1990s, the question was: How to reimagine Marxism within the cultural logic of late capitalism? The answer to such a question lies in the presence of ideological differences and the lack of any clear 'subaltern theory'. The spirit of Marxism would always adorn subaltern studies. Subaltern studies would be more relevant for understanding the societies which are on the threshold of industrialization and liberalization and have a lot of deprived and marginalized peasant and workers. Subaltern studies has not picked up in America and Europe mainly for this reason. The subaltern has come as a wave in social sciences in India. In the twelve volumes, so far published, nearly one hundred case studies of the subaltern people, analysing their subjugation, deprivation, marginalisation, neglect, etc., have appeared. 'Spirit of Marx', negotiated Marxism and post-Marxist forms are reflected in most of the studies of the Indian Subalterns. The subaltern volumes are available in Bengali, Hindi and Tamil in India.

What would happen to subaltern studies in view of the present-day world economy and globalization? Our response is that so long as poor and deprived people remain, subaltern studies would be relevant. Caste, gender, poverty, unemployment and social divides would determine the future agenda of subaltern studies. Guha asks the question: Can subaltern studies help India go beyond its nationalist and colonial past? Guha's answer to this question lies in his view on historiography of colonial India. The following themes have been chosen by Guha (1982, 1983, 1984, 1985):

- Elitist domination;
- Colonialist elitism and bourgeoisie—nationalist elitism;
- Indian nationalism as a function of stimulus and response;
- Indian nationalism as an idealist venture;
- Structure of colonial state;
- No mass articulation of nationalism;
- Narrow and partial view of politics;
- Exclusion of the politics of the people;
- Ignoring horizontal mobilization of the people;
- No resistance to elite domination;
- No mention about exploitation of the subaltern classes;
- Failure of the Indian bourgeoisie to speak for the nation;
- Ignored role of the indigenous elite;
- Fragmentation of workers, peasants and the urban petty bourgeoisie; and
- Failure of nationhood as an identity.

Such a realization of the Indian nation, people, socio-political divides, politics, social mobilization, colonial hegemony, etc., inspired Guha to launch the subaltern studies, which has revealed the stark realities of social life, which had remained unexplored, often left ignored advertently by the colonial rulers and the indigenous elite of India. In the twelve volumes, 95 papers (case studies) have been published. The main themes are as follows:

- Agrarian relations, peasantry and peasant revolts and movements;
- Workers, trade unions, civil society;
- Gandhi, modes of power, bureaucracy, violence;
- Adivasis, moneylending consciousness, tribal uprisings;
- Gender, caste, religion, culture, community, race; and
- Diaspora, slaves, social orphans, etc.

REVISITING SUBALTERN AND SUBALTERN STUDIES

M. S. S. Pandian (2002), while acknowledging significance of counter-hegemonic projects in general, stresses on the understanding of the dominant reality of the subaltern classes, accepting the hegemony of the elite through such processes like deference to the elites and emulation of elite values. David Luden (2001), based on some selected essays, observes that the concept of 'subaltern' is significant in Indian historiography, but a couple of the contributors to subaltern studies sense that the idea behind 'subaltern' is restrictive as it stepped out of the history of Indian nationalism and moved into the cultural history of colonialism (Roy, 2002). However, most of them would agree that the subaltern studies aimed at the writing of the history of the poor in colonial and contemporary India. Roy writes: 'The concept was first applied in a specific context, peasant insurgency. The intention was to locate an autonomous field of peasant consciousness that expressed itself through resisting repression by the "elites"' (Roy, 2002). The concept of 'subaltern' has been used for writing the history of the underprivileged people. The concepts of 'subaltern' and 'subalternity' imply the construction of narratives from the below. In fact, 'subalternity' incorporates political, social and economic dimensions of the existence of the underprivileged. 'Protest' and 'Resistance' are common to all the subaltern studies. The genre does not explain factors such as market and resource conditions, which could weaken subordination. Subordination was considered as a characteristic feature of colonialism. However, repression and subordination have existed in the postcolonial world as well. In such a situation, a colonial state alone cannot be a genesis of repression.

Over the span of 12 volumes of the Subaltern Studies, several new themes have come up, beginning from repression and protest to civil society, marriage, family, religion, village community, etc. Luden (2001) argues that the purpose of his book is 'to provide a non-subaltern introduction to subaltern studies'. The essays included in Luden's book focus on disparities in reading 'subaltern'. Disparities may be due to local factors as well. Luden's volume analyses protest movements, power and colonial language, and colonial subject.

Tirathankar Roy (2002), in a critical review of Luden's edited volume (2001), finds that the contributors have no misgivings about the terms 'subaltern' and 'subalternity'. However, in his view, there is an intellectual history of subalternity outside the subaltern studies, and that the relationship between the two traditions tends to be underdeveloped and overlooked. Roy claims to develop an outsider's point of view. He recognizes the contribution of the term 'subaltern' in the specific context of revolt and resistance, but disputes its usefulness in a general theory of the 'below'. The term 'subaltern' is bound up with polarity, coercion, and resistance, and therefore as such, has been a limiting factor in the study of the underprivileged people in South Asia. In Roy's view, the term 'subaltern' refers to a fuzzy set of people. It is not clear whether the subaltern people are poor or victims of domination and repression, etc. The subaltern studies has not brought out clearly relationship between 'principals' and 'agents', or between the state and the subjects. Another point made by Roy is that 'subalternity' has propagated the idea that the non-elite must be studied via a repression–resistance narrative. This is an exercise in indoctrinating power, restricting analysis to the experience of the poor and a narrow meaning of economic history.

Gyanendra Pandey (2006), an insider of the subaltern studies, considers 'the subaltern as the subaltern citizen'. Pandey argues that 'subaltern citizen' refers to the subaltern's historical agency and belonging in a society and its self-construction. For nearly 200 years, the struggles of the subalterns may be seen 'as struggles for recognition as equals'. 'The history of these efforts appeared as a history of sameness' (Pandey, 2006). Later on, the struggle was for the demand for recognition of difference—the existence of a variety of differences that explained the diversity, density and richness of human experience (Pandey, 2006). The paradox lies in the construction of a subaltern citizen (struggle for equality) and for assertion of right to the recognition of difference. Pandey discusses this dilemma, but does not find a straightforward answer to this vexed question. However, Pandey observes: 'it is my belief that there is a critical and still largely unexplored relationship between dominance/subordination and the categorical attribution of difference' (Pandey, 2006). Difference is the mark of the subordinated or subalternized, because it is seen against the purported mainstream, the 'standard' or the 'normal'. Women, Muslims, tribals and Dalits are different vis-à-vis men, Hindus and non-tribals. Subalternity is a difference between differences. Difference is at the root of discrimination and subalternity. Caste, colour, sex or creed, and absence of freedom are the known bases of difference. 'Difference is not to be privileged, yet it must not be entirely denied' (Pandey, 2006).

An ardent supporter of subaltern studies, Partha Chatterjee (1984) divides politics into elite and subaltern domains in the colonial era. Though peasantry was engaged in organized political movements before Independence, yet remained distanced from the evolving forms of the postcolonial state. In the post-independence era, the subaltern classes have, however, come under the influence of the democratic process. It is a fact that in many parts of India, subalterns have neither been benefited nor politically integrated into the mainstream as a result of economic and political development. Based on an ethnographic study, Dayabati Roy (2008) reports that caste, class and gender continue as social impediments in Bengal. Divisions between the elite and the subaltern continue to exist in a complex form at the panchayat level. While reconstructing an anthropological history of Bastar (1854–2006), Nandini Sundar (2009) considers 'political power' as the key determinant of relations between subalterns (people) and sovereigns (kings). Rebellions in Bastar 'were very differently understood by subalterns and sovereigns, by the actors involved and those commenting on it at the time and later' (Sundar, 2009, 17). There were multiple histories and a polyphony of voices narrating pasts out of different presents. The histories were not strictly followed after a rebellion against the King. Sundar observes that there is no unitary insurgent consciousness in Bastar. She writes:

> In the process of individuals making collective choices of whom to support, what culture to adopt, when to rebel and when not to rebel— whether to organize under a 'traditional' system, whether to support a King or Communists, whether to represent themselves as indigenous people or as an exploited class or both, culture is redefined, sometimes in them are choices nonetheless. (Sundar, 2009)

Today, the subaltern groups such as plantation workers, industrial wage workers, agricultural labourers, sugarcane cultivators, makers and vendors of recycled goods in urban settings may not be accepted by the 'original inhabitants'. Migrants may not be liked by the natives. Locals do not accept themselves as 'strangers' in their own land.

MYTH AND REALITY OF SUBALTERN EXISTENCE AND CONSCIOUSNESS

Coming back to M. S. S. Pandian (2002), based on his understanding of the MGR (M. G. Ramachandran) Phenomenon, he relates culture and subaltern consciousness, despite the acceptance of the hegemony of the elite by the subaltern classes. Pandian observes that 'the "ascribed" consciousness and the "actual" consciousness of the subaltern classes do not produce the immediate consciousness of their existence, that their "actual" consciousness can be effectively mediated' (2002). Pandian observes that the elite produce consent among the subaltern classes (which is certainly not determined by the stark existential conditions of the subalterns). The subalterns have their own cultural mosaic, without having any necessary correspondence with their material lives. The fact is that dominant ideologies succeed in producing consent among the subaltern classes. MGR, himself, was a subaltern, and so were his roles as worker, peasant, boatman, cowherd velan, rickshaw puller, fisherman's friend, in various films. Such a message influenced consciousness of the subaltern fans of MGR. As an actor and later on as a political leader, MGR was no more in his childhood condition of misery and poverty. Thus, the MGR phenomenon is complex and multifaceted.

Pandian (2002) mentions that MGR's role as a subaltern hero fighting for justice reveals two aspects: (a) MGR appropriates of himself the right to dispense justice; and (b) he appropriates the right to employ physical violence. 'Both are in real life monopolies of the elite'. Thus, MGR fights oppression as an individual—though belonging to a subaltern class, as an individual adjudicator. MGR uses the instruments of oppression used by the sovereigns to help out the subalterns, in most of his films. Thus, subaltern consciousness is generated by using culture as a means of emancipation of the subalterns from the culture-bound dictates of the ruling classes.

A very clear view on the subalterns can be seen in Jan Breman's study of agricultural labourers in south Gujarat (2003). His argument is that 'the marginality of the subaltern class which existed earlier has been perpetuated or even become more pronounced in a pattern of both social and economic exclusion to which the rural proletariat is subjected' (2002, 3). The landlords, employers and rich people did not allow crystallization of class contradictions and demands for justice. No outside interference or arbitration was admitted and insistence was upon mutual consultation and harmony, which was a sort of diktat of the dominant classes.

Highly trained professionals like chartered accountants, lawyers and doctors with top incomes do not belong to subaltern classes. White collar employers also remain outside the exploited subaltern classes. In Ahmedabad, for example, Mahadevia (2001, 156) reports that the bosses, contractors and subcontractors, supervisors, jobbers, moneylenders and pawn brokers, commission agents and other brokers exploit the cheap labour power of the informal sector workers for their own gain. There are contracting work gangs, who exploit the army of casualized labour.

Another example of the role of culture in the lives of subaltern people is explained by Chakraborty (2003), based on her analysis of the film 'Lagaan'. Using 'Lagaan', Chakraborty argues that popular Bollywood films with their appeal to the mass audience of uprooted peasants, factory workers, the unemployed, uneducated and poor can decolonize the imagination of the Indian masses (2003). 'Lagaan' has created a debate regarding indigenization in a village in Awadh. The film brings out the presence of feudalism in conjunction with colonialism, showing supremacy of the latter on the former. Drought, exploitation, taxes, luxury of the British Officials and neglect of the misery of the rural folk are the main issues which make the film a subject of the understanding of the pathos of the subalterns. 'Lagaan' also brings out the role and significance of the struggle by the subalterns against the colonial rulers.

Consciousness is another means of understanding peasants and other subalterns. Arun Kumar (2001) in his study of peasant politics in terms of the 'cultural/religious/social/moral matrix of the lives of the peasantry explores peasant political consciousness and its political culture by exploring the everyday life of the *Kisans*. With reference of the peasant political consciousness in nineteenth century Bihar, Kumar uses 'the trope of language of politics'. Migration, crime, rumour, etc., are taken by Kumar as expressions of dissent and political consciousness. He argues that the peasant language of politics has essentially revolved around issues of caste identity and exploitation. The Congress and *Kisan Sabha* did not use/sense the lexicon of identity and exploitation.

Structural deprivation of the poor, tribals, rural masses, slum-dwellers, peasants, artisans, in terms of access to opportunities due to lack of capacity building is the dominant cause of the divide between the 'subalterns' and the 'sovereigns'. The state remains a silent spectator of the appalling condition of the subalterns. One of the important reasons is that the State is captivated by the rich and resourceful. The aged, single women and people with disability (Marder, 2008) suffer most in villages, for example, in Odisha, Rajasthan and Andhra Pradesh. A study of eight villages from these three states indicates that the enormity of human deprivation among the vulnerable and destitute is overwhelming. Living with hunger, as recounted by the sufferers, explains the meagre, uncertain and corruption-ridden intervention by the State; however, the subalterns have shown a great sense of dignity, courage and resilience. The study included a total of 474 persons, of whom 135 had disability, 194 were single women and 145 were old people. This study may be considered as a study of the subalterns, having the common problem of hunger, due to either disability or being a single woman or because of old age. The community and the state were both indifferent towards these people. Even these people had to beg for leftovers and rice-water. Such a human deprivation tells about the subalterns who are at the deep bottom of our society.

A similar analysis is given by Sengupta (2010). He provides a rationale for defining extreme poverty as a combination of income poverty, human development poverty and social exclusion. Sengupta finds three sets of people, suffering from anti-poverty programmes in the United States, European Union, Africa and Asia. He justifies the rights based perspective in a poverty reduction strategy, irrespective of a given country.

Here, it is pertinent to state that nowhere the subalterns are a homogenized entity. They are highly differentiated and hierarchical social block facing intra-caste distinction. Verma (2010) observes that there are elites among the *Dalit Bahujans* in Uttar Pradesh, and they extract advantage of their numbers in continuance of reservation benefits and affirmative action programmes without showing any inclination to pass them on to the marginalized. As such, it is necessary, as Verma argues, to transcend caste and address this 'class'. The marginalized and deprived ones constitute the true subaltern class of people.

CONCLUDING REMARKS

Subaltern Studies emerged as a reaction to the overshadowing of nationalism by colonialism, emplacing the need for a new historiography. The underscored and distorted narratives of the peasants, tribals, poor, oppressed and exploited people required rectification and fresh profiles. Autonomy of peasants remained unnoticed and un-understood. Subaltern Studies also called upon a re-examination of the classical/orthodox Marxist thought. Autonomy and self-consciousness of subaltern groups speak of such a Marxist revisionism. Influence of Gramsci, in particular, has been immense in most of the studies, beginning from Ranjit Guha to the contributors of the last few volumes.

Subaltern Studies has created a new space for historiography. It is to be seen as a fresh intervention and interpretation of the neglected sections of society. As O'Hanlon (2000) mentions Subaltern Studies is a project of restoring suppressed histories—of women, non-whites, non-Europeans—as well as the subordinate of colonial South Asia. The aim of the Subaltern Studies project is also the rejection of neo-colonialist, neo-nationalist and economistic Marxist modes of historiography. But then the question is: Will this not produce ethnocentric historicism, and ignore rationalist and universalizing historism 'other', that is, the colonial ruler. O'Hanlon questions the very nature of reconstruction and reconceptualization involved in Subaltern Studies.

He writes: 'My main concern here, however, is with the nature of the reconstruction attempted in the subaltern project' (O'Hanlon, 2000). In fact, the Western historicism or Western humanism emphasizing on the self-originating, self-determining individual, having a sovereign consciousness, based on reason and power of freedom, is not akin to Indian peasantry, women, tribals and backward sections of society. In O'Hanlon's view, Subaltern Studies, in essence, is overtaken by western intellectualism, and this he sees as a cognitive dissonance and incapability, regarding the study of the South Asian subordinate. In Subaltern Studies, it seems that there is more of a political/ideological commitment of the contributors.

Another point is that workers, peasants, tribals, women and rural poor are highly differentiated, and so are their consciousness, capabilities, engagement with political and social activities. Autonomy and undifferentiated consciousness/reason/freedom seem to be considerably hazy and much less in reality. Brass (2002) argues that neo-populist theory about peasant economy in Subaltern Studies misses politico-ideological dimension. Brass observes: 'To a large degree, this process is structured by the de-reconstruction effected as a result of postmodern epistemology' (Brass, 2002). Postmodernity is supportive of the 'middle peasant thesis', the 'moral economy' argument. Postmodernism does not recognize the universality of class and class struggle, collectivization and socialism as a consequence of class struggle. And postmodernism accepts the ideological pluralism of the subject, the autonomy of the individual, the political importance and acceptability of (self-defined) relativism as embodied in 'the cultural' (the 'tribal', the 'peasant'), the wholesale legitimacy of any/all 'everyday forms of resistance, and bourgeois democracy' (Brass, 2002). The popularity of Subaltern Studies attained such height that even some liberal academia joined and contributed to the volumes edited by scholars' other than Ranjit Guha. The array of themes and groups is today huge and vastly diversified. However, the zeal that was shown by Guha and his team in the 1980s is not visible. There could be an end number of reasons for the falling interest in Subaltern Studies, but the coming up of globalization and liberalization seem to be quite significant in the present situation. Subaltern Studies is, however, an enigma, a new enchanting paradigm in social sciences in general and in historiography in particular.

Chapter 15

Revisiting the Six Villages in Rajasthan After Half a Century

Before Independence, Rajasthan had 22 princely states, of which 19 were ruled by Rajput princes, 2 by Jat rulers, and 1 was a Muslim state. Feudalism in Rajasthan was so intense that it acquired a distinct mode of polity and economy. Feudalism subordinated all other institutions, including the caste system. Feudal hierarchy overshadowed the caste hierarchy. In Rajasthan, there were 45 types of *jagirs*, 175 log bags (cesses) and innumerable taxes, *begar* (forced labour), and arbitrary systems of land revenue assessment (Sharma, 1998a; Singh, 1964).

A number of malpractices of appropriation of human and material resources were in vogue. However, modes and practices of exploitation and punishment differed from caste to caste for the similar offences and violations. Feudal order was also a system of granting favours and positions of status and power to select families and individuals, including some from among the middle and lower castes. As such, this was incongruent with their lower caste ranks. At times, such people even dictated terms of the people of higher castes. In fact, a system of forced and structured dependence on the princes, *jagirdars* and other landlords was practiced without any restrictions. People had no freedom. There were no avenues and opportunities for migration and mobility. Education was neglected; healthcare was non-existent. Everything, including cultural activities, such as fairs, festivals, ceremonies, music, dance, dress, food, etc., was organized to glorify the princes and *jagirdars.* Despite such a domineering ambience of polity, there was also popular resistance (H. Singh, 1998) in terms of action from below (peasant movements). At the same time, such a resistance was often crushed by the rulers.

Hira Singh observes that feudalism coexisted with colonialism, and the latter (British rule) was supreme. Along with the below, and the 'above' lines of action, colonial rule always had a watchful eye on the princely states of Rajasthan. Further, H. Singh (1983) talks of three discourses: (a) the theory of the colonial mode of production; (b) the subaltern studies; and (c) the post-colonial Foucauldian discourse. He attempts to understand feudalism in terms of the colonial mode of historiography, and finds it akin to the subaltern studies perspective (Guha, 1988). Such was the existential reality of the rulers and the ruled in Rajasthan.

Some scholars, namely, Dudolph and Rudolph (1984, 7–25) and Narain and Mathur (1990, 1–58), observe that the legitimized ruler-ship in the princely states or the 'traditions of Rajput domination' (a *Kshatriya* model' of sanskritization) remained even after Independence. But such a continuity of the past in the post-Independence era is more of a myth than a reality (Sharma, 1998a, 168–184). Instead of referring to Rajputs as a ruling caste, more relevant was an analysis of the caste system as a system of socio-political and economic relations. Both Rudolphs and Narain and Mathur have inclination to glamour-ize the Rajput rule. Narain and Mathur (1990) state the Rajput rule as a 'remarkable continuity for nearly a thousand-years' of society and polity, ecology and sociocultural values in Rajasthan, and this also includes nearly four decades after Independence. The real changing face of Rajasthan before and after Independence remains ignored in these analyses in terms of 'the below' and 'the above' perspectives.

As discussed here in this chapter and in an earlier work (Sharma, 1974), the face of Rajasthan has undergone a tremendous change in the post-Independence era. Our revisit to the six villages (Narain and Mathur, 1990) in 2015–2016, after five decades, indicates that they are very different today from what they were in the mid-1960s, the time of our comprehensive study.

Immediately after Independence, the abolition of *Jagirdari* and *Zamindari* systems paved the way for *Khatedari* rights (ownership of land by the cultivators). This led to consolidation of socio-economic standing by tenants and peasants and other functionary castes, over a period of nearly two decades. In the meanwhile, in 1959, decentralization of power through Panchayati Raj Institutions (PRIs) initiated the process of empowerment of the rural people. Subsequent amendments in the PRIs have facilitated inclusion of women, the SCs/STs and the OBCs in sharing of power.

Besides such institutional initiatives for change, migration, education, adult franchise, elections, development programmes, non-farm sources of income, changing country–town nexus, etc., have transformed rural Rajasthan to a great extent. During the early post-Independence period, we have noted multiple contradictions and discontinuities, obverse structural processes of transformation, congruities and incongruities, and structurally induced and self-generating processes of change. Such a set of processes of change can be considered as the basis of reconstruction of Rajasthan. We have noticed such a change in the mid-1960s and again in 2015–2016 in our study of the six villages (Sharma, 1974, 2016). In 1965–1966, there was an overwhelming correspondence between various determinants of social status, and at the same time, significant cleavages between caste and class, caste and power, and power and class had also surfaced, implying remarkable effects of land reforms, adult franchise and Panchayati Raj Institutions. We had observed simultaneous occurrence of upward and downward mobility, indicating both gain and loss (Sharma, 1969, 1970, 1973). The formerly privileged people witnessed downward mobility as they lost legitimacy of their status and power. Such a loss benefited the deprived sectors, particularly the landless lower castes, artisans and the tenants-at-will, mainly coming from the intermediate castes.

Based on our comparative study of the six villages in the mid-1960s and in 2015–2016, we can convincingly say that a village is a mirror of differentiation and mobility in terms of caste, class, power, networks, education, employment and somewhat more egalitarian relations. However, to an extent, unevenness in the distributive shares, implying dominance of the new rural middle class, indicates a new social formation in making. Our comparative analysis is a clear evidence of a renewed construction of social formation in rural Rajasthan. Our double synchronic study paves a way for the following inferences:

1. The initial change was possible due to constitutional provisions.
2. The process of 'equalization' was set in motion in the 1950s and the 1960s. However, today, education, migration and mobility are playing more effective role in reshaping social relations.
3. Today, as we will describe later on, political power has become not only a decisive consideration in determination of social status, but power has become transposable in social, cultural and economic domains.
4. Agrarian hierarchy has become considerably hazy due to quantum jump in non-farm income, and also because of preference for government jobs, trade, and commerce, and longing for positions of power and authority.

Social inequality has, thus, acquired a new form. In this process of change, traditional uneven structures have not been totally eliminated. Traditional forces have receded to the background in the wake of the emergence of the new forces. We would not like to characterize such a situation as a 'mix' or 'synthesis' of tradition and modernity or of old and new phenomena. The present scene can be described as follows:

1. Downward mobility of the traditionally entrenched sections of rural society;
2. Upward mobility of tenants, peasants, artisans, agricultural workers and other deprived sections;
3. Non-farm income as a new source of status and social mobility (composite social status); and
4. Transformed country–town nexus, urban income, savings and surpluses as means of social mobility and change.

In 1965–1966, we observed initial trends of change in the villages, mainly emanating from the Indian State. In 2015–1916, the change is more due to various developments, schemes and programmes, and also due to efforts and aspirations of the people themselves. Today, the real face of Rajasthan can be seen in terms of rich, well off and poor families, rural–urban networks, non-farm sources of income, salaried government functionaries, education (particularly of girls), and presence of influential individuals and families. However, there are also weak, poor and resource-deprived families and individuals who have not seen much 'social break' in their existential conditions.

The above observations and inferences are based on our study of six villages in 1965–1966 and 2015–2016. A graphic description and analysis is presented here, not to make a claim for representing rural society in Rajasthan as rural India as a whole. However, the study shows a whole range of social change covering a span of seven decades, since Independence. Our effort is to describe the dynamics (Sharma, 1968, 1974), based on the study conducted in the mid-1960s and then the present re-study in 2015–2016.

K. L. Sharma's doctoral study, *The Changing Rural Stratification System (A Comparative Study of Six Villages in Rajasthan)* (1968, 1974), focused on multiple villages, implying a critique of single village studies of the 1950s and the early 1960s. Though earlier Ram Krishna Mukherjee (1957) and Yogendra Singh (1958) had conducted multiple village studies, Sharma's focus was on a comparative study and analysis based on criteria, such as sub-regional variations, dry/wet cultivation, caste composition, land-tenure system and proximity to urban centres. In the studies on the Indian village and caste system, earlier the main focus was on hereditary specialization, social (caste) hierarchy and reciprocal repulsion (Bougle, 1958; Dube, 1955; Hocart, 1950; Hutton, 1946/1963; Marriott, 1955; Mayer, 1960; Srinivas, 1952). However, in a couple of studies, emphasis was also on extra-caste considerations. Extra-caste approaches to social stratification do not make 'caste' as an all-inclusive basis of stratification, as the studies on caste stratification do. Economic position, lifestyle, education, occupation, personality attributes, etc., determine status and rank in relation to each other. As such, caste is one of the factors of social stratification. These factors tend to weaken the caste stratification. Studies of class relations, power structure and educational achievements in particular reveal that these factors also determine social status. However, these factors are also influenced by caste, and in turn affect caste.

It was reported that in a Tanjore village (Banks, 1960) the high social status of the Brahmins and the other twice-born castes had disappeared. The Vellala caste ritually speaking was no more dominant. At the sub-caste level, endogamy was an idea rather than a fact. In another study of a Tanjore village, Gough (1960) reported that the poor landless castes people thought of a political revolt against the old structures of the caste system. Ram Krishna Mukherjee (1957) explained the association of class groupings with caste hierarchy in a study of 12 Bengal villages (now in Bangladesh). The congruence of caste and class did not allow upward mobility for the people of the lower castes/classes and the scheduled castes. Economic hierarchy went alongside ritual hierarchy. Yogendra Singh (1961) found that in Uttar Pradesh villages, upper caste and class status coincided and upper castes continued to hold power. Beteille (1966), in his study of a Tanjore village, noted that the social system had acquired a much more complex and dynamic character and a tendency was for structural cleavages to cut across one another. Distribution of power created a sort of new hierarchy.

EXTRA-CASTE CRITERIA OF SOCIAL RANKING IN RURAL RAJASTHAN

The main focus in Sharma's study of the six villages in Rajasthan (1974) was on the extra-caste criteria of social ranking along with caste to have a deeper understanding of horizontal differences within various units of social ranking. Such a view implied that horizontal differences within the same caste negated homogeneity among the members of a caste/sub-caste. In other words, there were economic, political and cultural distinctions within the families and individual members of different castes. Such differences were a stark reality, despite a considerable congruence of caste, class and power in the six villages. The families of different castes which had maximum congruence of statuses on a higher plane were at the top of social hierarchy, even if some of them were ritually a little lower than Brahmins and other twice-born castes. Sharma had observed that some families with middle caste ranks, but with higher political and cultural statuses, were at the top of social stratification. Contrarily, some families with high caste ranks, but with correspondingly lower economic, cultural and political statuses played a deceive role in decision-making process. This did not mean that a family having merely a high caste rank, but with lower ranks in other domains had a decisive hand in the affairs of the village community. In the same way, an 'untouchable' caste member having high economic and educational status, could not have a decisive role in the village community. It was clearly visualized even in the 1960s by Sharma that caste did not function as a corporate group, and it was not a sole determinant of social status. Role of family of an individual was quite considerable, and it was undermined in most of the studies as mentioned earlier.

With a view to understand and analyse the congruence/incongruence syndrome relating to status and social stratification, Sharma studied six villages from Sikar, Jaipur and Bharatpur districts of Rajasthan on the basis of their economy, geography and cultural distinctiveness. The three districts in the 1960s comprised of dry cultivation, canal-irrigated and partly irrigated sub-regions. Two villages were chosen from each district, one near the district headquarters, and the other in a remote part. These six villages were selected to analyse the changing patterns of stratification in different situations in relation to urbanization, differentiation of roles, flexibility in ritual complex, migration, occupational mobility, functioning of Jajmani system and village and caste panchayats. Our purpose was also to see how the abolition of *jagirdari* and *zamindari* systems had brought about noticeable change in the selected villages.

THE SIX VILLAGES IN THE 1960s IN RAJASTHAN

A brief account of the six villages in the 1960s could be seen in terms of the role of caste, units of social ranking, namely, caste (group), class (economic status), family, and individual (achievement) in status determination. Ascription, including caste rank, inherited property and lifestyle, was the primary determinant of status in all the six villages. Since Rajasthan was an overwhelmingly a feudal formation, its values along with caste persisted. The hold of the upper castes was prevalent in all walks of life, including new occupations and positions of power and authority. The upper castes held superiority more in cultural domain than the middle and lower castes. There were significant indicators of the coming up of the middle castes in political and economic realms. Across all castes, there were differences among the families within their respective castes/sub-castes. We could see a class-differentiation in a given caste to some extent.

Ritual syndrome was the basis of caste stratification at the ground level. Often the higher castes claimed their cultural superiority over other castes despite their dwindling economic and political standing. To some extent, even intra-caste distinctions revealed ritual differences in terms of knowledge, literacy/education and Sanskrit praxis. The lower castes/sub-castes, who observed cultural ethos of Brahmin, claimed superiority over those who did not follow the Brahmin way of life.

The six villages had a class structure, comprising of former landlords, merchants, peasants and agricultural workers. These were concrete identifiable strata based on economic criteria. However, these groups were internally differentiated in terms of big and small landowners, petty shopkeepers and moneylenders, masons, artisans and agricultural workers, etc. Based on such differences, families and individuals were identified by the village people as well off, resourceful, influential and as poor, weak and voiceless. It was generally accepted that caste alone did not matter in status determination. Achievements through lucrative occupation, education and income were equally or even more decisive factors in real life.

THE IDEA AND PRACTICE OF 'COMPOSITE STATUS'

The idea of 'composite status' (Tumin, 1952) of each household was evaluated in our study of the six villages. Indices of caste, income, land-holding and type of house were taken up to construct a hierarchy of composite status system. A coincidence between caste, class and power was observed to a great extent. Since the study was carried out after less than two decades since India's Independence, caste and feudalism continued to play a domineering role in the six villages. Due to such a situation, the traditional forces were able to acquire social and political space for some time, despite the abolition of *Jagirdari* and *Zamindari* systems and introduction of Panchayati Raj. The upper castes/classes' people held formal offices of power, and some of them also exercised influence, informally. They formed a 'ruling minority'/'village aristoc-racy'. However, there were also some cleavages between caste, class and power. The change, that occurred during the first two decades after Independence, created divergences and cleavages which questioned the persisting 'summation of roles and statuses' in many instances.

For example, the former Jagirdars and Zamindars who managed to retain hold on substantial landholdings were quite influential, but those did/could not do so slid down in the status hierarchy. A couple of families from among Rajputs, Charans, Jats and Brahmins witnessed 'downward mobility'. On the contrary, the families, which were ben-efited by the post–Independence reforms and changes, moved up in social ladder. Thus, an obverse process of structural change in terms of losers and gainers or of downward and upward mobility occurred. It was a momentous period in the 1950s and the mid–1960s.

Land reforms brought about differentiation of institutional struc-tures, such as, the traditional village panchayat, caste panchayat, and division of landholdings. Nearly 20 per cent working people were engaged in secular or non–caste occupations. In different 29 new occupations, these people were engaged. Though 80 per cent of the people were pursuing traditional or caste-based occupations, however, they were dissociating from the *Jajmani* system. Commercialization of traditional occupations had made a little headway. Emergence of non-caste occupations, education and migration signified the new village scene. However, cumulative inequalities persisted to a considerable extent. The upper castes in general were more educated, resourceful and better off, and aspired for their continued dominance in the vil-lage community.

In the 1960s, two trends were quite conspicuous: (a) jubilation among the tenants and peasants' due to the abolition of landlordism, and (b) opportunity for education, migration and urban living. These factors were an onslaught on the traditional patron–client relation-ships, and these also created status rivalries/cleavages, innovation and new cultural ethos. However, the gap between the upper and the lower castes/classes took a new turn. When the upper castes lost their traditional hold in the community, they looked for new and greener grounds for status and honour. The lower castes/classes for quite some time continued to imitate the discarded lifestyle of the upper castes with a 'false' notion of enhancement of their status claiming 'equality' with the upper castes. A situation of 'transition' and continuity prevailed.

In all the six villages, we collected information about 1,160 households, including traditional occupations, non-caste occupations, caste background, *jajmani* relations, landholdings, caste–class nexus, income, education, migration, mobility, and political power. While analysing these aspects of social life in the six villages, we could say that the Indian village was not static and undifferentiated, country–town nexus existed, though in varying proportions in the six villages. As the villages were differentiated, so were the village people. The village had an urban face, and the town had accommodated rurality. Both structural and cultural factors had contributed to the process of change and transformation. However, 'remote villages', remained far more away from 'urbanity', and 'sub-urban villages' had more urban impact in terms of availability of means of transport (roads) and communication. Such a process of change and transformation was very different from what it is today.

THE VILLAGE AS A DIFFERENTIATED ENTITY

Over a period of time, different patterns of change have occurred. In some cases, economic development has been there without corresponding social change, and in other cases, social change has occurred without corresponding economic development (Epstein, 1962). It has been reported that discourse on development has changed from poverty, unemployment, illiteracy, etc., in a West UP village to the issues of dignity and honour (Kolenda, 1989). In other studies, country–town nexus (Sharma and Gupta, 1991), village networks (Shah, 1986, 1998), emergence of a new middle class in rural Gujarat (Shah, 1998), differentiated structures (Beteille, 1966), and downward social mobility (Sharma, 1973) have been analysed as trends of social change in rural India. Green revolution, empowerment of the depressed people, and adult franchise and the right to vote have also provided new grounds for social transformation. 'Structural-historical' perspective has substituted the culturological perspectives of the 1950s and the 1960s.

Gurcharan Das (2002, 187–203) talks of 'the ambiguous village', meaning thereby 'change' and 'no change' or 'partial change' in the village. For example, Haryana has made significant progress in agriculture by way of green revolution, and also in industry in recent years being a major constituent of the National Capital Region (NCR). Despite considerable economic growth, Haryana remains 'culturally backward'. Inter-caste marriages are considered as taboo, and violation of caste endogamy and class exogamy invites severe punishment, including death. The question is: What is rural/village? The Indian village is no more as B. R. Ambedkar remarked in the Constituent Assembly in 1948 (quoted from Gurcharan Das, 2002, 188). Ambedkar said: 'What is the village but a sink of localism, a den of ignorance, narrow-mindedness and communalism?' The village communities are also not 'the little republics' as observed by Charles Metcalfe in 1840s (quoted from Gurcharan Das, 2002, 188). Mahatma Gandhi also thought of village *swaraj*. Karl Marx commented on the Indian village as 'a blend of agriculture and industry' (handicrafts). Jawaharlal Nehru was of the view that Indian village was backward intellectually and culturally.

The Indian village is not monolithic. It has both cooperation and conflict, selfhood and collective identity, unity and factionalism, hierarchy and individualism/segmentation. All these are found in varying permutations and combinations in different parts of rural India. Even country–town nexus is of differing degrees. Some states have moved forward faster in taking forward the rural people in terms of development, empowerment and education. Our revisit to the six villages in Rajasthan brings out startling reality of social change, however, it does not imply that these villages are no more villages as such. Despite urbanization of the suburban villages, they retain 'village ethos', and the remote villages look like 'suburban' villages in terms of structural and cultural changes that have occurred over the past five decades. Now we may provide a brief description of the six villages.

ROOPGARH

In 1965, Roopgarh had a middle (upper primary) school, a branch post-office, an ayurvedic dispensary, a village panchayat, a credit cooperative society and the headquarters of Patwari and Village Level Worker (VLW). There were 215 households, and 1,495 persons in the village, including Tehtha (an adjoining hamlet). Out of 411 male workers, 163 were cultivators, 71 were agricultural and manual labourers, 60 were shoe-makers (Regars), and 43 were engaged in white-collar jobs, as teachers, clerks, officers, and peons. There was no female employed in government/private job. The rest of the male workers were masons, priests, artisans, etc. Nineteen Brahmin families out of 24 depended on income from outside the village. In all, 74 persons worked outside the village, and of them 35 were Brahmins. Brahmins also controlled the village panchayat and the cooperative society.

Today, Roopgarh has a Senior Secondary (10+2) School, with a strength of 600 students (both boys and girls). The other institutions in Roopgarh are: Primary Health Centre (PHC), Animal Husbandry Health Centre, two Anganbari Centres, a Private Ayurvedic Dispensary, a Bengali Doctor (Practitioner), Two Private Schools (One Secondary and other Senior Secondary), and one Private Industrial Training Institute, in addition to the Village Panchayat, Cooperative Society and Post-Office.

Now, Roopgarh is connected by a tarred road with Tehsil and District Headquarters. It is also connected with Jaipur (the capital of Rajasthan) by way of the State Transport (Bus Service), with twice to and fro service. According to the census of 2011, Roopgarh has a population of 2109 persons. Roopgarh is the headquarters of the Village Panchayat, comprising of other four villages, namely, Tehtha, Charanvas Tulika, Motipura and Bhawanipura. The total population of the Roopgarh Panchayat consists of 6,100 people. In 1965–1966, our focus was on Roopgarh and Tehtha and not on other smaller hamlets.

Only two Jain families were engaged in shop-keeping and money-lending. They were known as *Bohras* (moneylenders) and the borrowers were called as *Dhrias*. Such a relationship was like that of a patron and client as it was truly in the mould of *Jajmani* system (*Jajman-Kamin* relations). One Brahmin also owned a grocery shop, but he was not a successful endeavour. The Jain traders were more enterprising and dealt with all the needs of the people, including grocery, clothes and cash.

Generally, a Bohra was like a patron of his *Dhurias* (clients/borrowers), and was obliged to stand with his clients in situations arising out for expenses on birth, marriage, illness and death. The bazaar of Roopgarh of yesteryears is no more today a centre of mercantile and social activities. The shops owned by the Jain families have become depleted and ghost houses.

Today, amazing situation exists in Roopgarh. There are as many as 51 shops located on the roadside, whereas in the 1960s there were only 3 shops, 2 owned Jains and 1 by a Brahmin. In the 1980s, one Brahmin, one *Khati* (Carpenter), one *Gurjar* and one *Regar* ('untouchable') also ventured to start grocery shops within their residential premises, but after a couple of years, when the roadside shops mushroomed, those shops were shut down. In the old bazaar, for last few years, a Brahmin is engaged in shop-keeping. All other shops are on the roadside, where the School, Hospital, Gram Panchayat, Cooperative Society and other offices are situated. There was no tea stall in the village. Today, there are a couple of tea stalls and sweet-meat shops. Shops dealing with hardware, clothes, tailoring, shoes and *chappals,* animal food, electrical goods, flour mill, stationary goods, computer services, photo stating, sanitary goods, haircutting saloons have come up over the years. Trade and commerce is no more associated with Jains and Brahmins. Today, Brahmins, Gurjars, Kumawats, Jats, Naiks (ex-untouchables), Nais, Darjees, Swamis, Muslims, etc., are engaged in trade and commerce. As many as 9 Regars, 3 Naiks, 10 Gurjars, 2 Kumhars and 3 Nais are engaged in shop-keeping. Except one family, all Jain families migrated long ago to far off places, such as Kanpur, Ranchi, Raipur, Kolkata, Sambhar Lake for better opportunities. Not many Brahmins and Jats are engaged in shop-keeping. The only Jain family in Roopgarh is surviving on its inherited wealth and savings.

A lot of people have migrated to far off places, such as Delhi, Kolkata, Guwahati, Kanpur, Raipur, Ranchi, Mumbai, Hyderabad, Ahmedabad, Jaipur etc. Two persons have settled abroad, one in America and other in Finland. Some are working in the Gulf countries. Maximum people have migrated to Jaipur and Sikar, the state and the district headquarters, respectively. Their number is nearly 800. About

50 people are settled in the nearby small town—Danta–Ramgarh (tehsil headquarters).

Roopgarh has made significant strides in higher education. There are as many as 10 PhDs, and 18 engineers. All the PhDs are from the same extended Brahmin family. Even most of the Engineers are also from the same family, and three of them passed out from BITs, Pilani, one from MNIT, Jaipur, and one from Jai Narain Vyas University, Jodhpur. One boy is studying at IIT, Kanpur. There are 66 postgraduates, of which 21 are women, and one holds the dual degree of BTech and MSc from BITS, Pilani. One Engineer holds BTech degree from BIT, Mesra. Two hundred fourteen are graduates with BSc, BA, BCom and BEd degrees, and of them 52 are women. Twenty three persons have taken certificates from Industrial Training Institutes. As many as 296 are educated up to 10+2 schooling, and 88 of them are women. Nearly 350 persons are educated up to primary and upper primary levels. Only 73 men and 136 women are illiterate. A couple of young men and women are having training for school teaching at the lower and senior levels. The people in Roopgarh are engaged in as many as 62 diverse activities. Two boys, who belong to *Regar* caste, are pursuing MBBS at government medical colleges in Rajasthan. A couple of boys, who passed out recently BTech from some private engineering colleges are unemployed.

In 1960s, Roopgarh did not have even a bicycle. Today, there are at least 100 two-wheelers, 15 cars and jeeps and 3 buses, besides some tractors. Cultivation by use of bullocks, buffalos and camels is no more there. Being on the road route between district and tehsil headquarters; public and private transport facility has enhanced to a great extent. Drinking water is available through storage tank. Irrigation through tube wells is no more available as the tube wells have dried up. The village was electrified nearly 50 years ago. Even there are street lights in the village.

In the first 25 years, after Independence, Brahmins, Pareeks and Jains were dominant castes. After consolidation of their socio-economic standing, Jats asserted claim over statutory village panchayat, which commands funds and resources for development in the village. A Pareek and a Brahmin were Sarpanch of the village during the 1950s and 1960s.

Subsequently, only Jats have become Sarpanch, except ones when it was reserved for a SC women. Presently, an OBC (Jat) woman is Sarpanch, who is also a graduate. The SC woman Sarpanch was illiterate. Twice, Brahmin candidates for the post of Sarpanch were defeated by Jat candidates. Presently, a Jat from Roopgarh is Pradhan of the Panchayat Samiti, who is also educated, having MA, BEd degrees. One former Sarpanch, also a Jat, is also a government-approved contractor.

The village streets have cemented roads. Nearly 70 per cent houses have cooking gas, and also avail subsidy for this. Ten per cent houses had toilets even before the launch of the present scheme for *sauchalayas*. Under this scheme, people have received a subsidy of ₹2000/-. Nearly 60 per cent people are linked with the Prime Minister's *Jandhan Bima Yojana*. 80 per cent people are associated with Bhamashah schemes, and Bhamashah Health Card. However, only 2 per cent have received benefit from these schemes so far. Around 30 young men have received training under the Pradhan Mantri Kaushal Yojana. Anganwadi centres are run by the self-help group.

Inter-caste relations have nearly disappeared. Only for namesake people talk of *biradari*. *Jajmani* does not exist. *Nais*, *Kumhars*, Carpenters, Priests have commercialized their traditional activities. Apparently, there is no 'untouchability' or caste-based segregation, but on certain occasions it is observed in subtle ways. Many upper castes' people do not participate in functions organized by the lower (untouchable) castes. However, no unpleasant incidence of discrimination against the lower castes has occurred in Roopgarh.

Socio-economic transformation in Roopgarh (an interior village as per our study of the 1960s) indicates that today it is a different rural panorama than what it was half a century ago. It does not look like a remote village any more. Means of transport and communication, education, migration and mobility have made it more than a suburban village.

The changing village scene is evident on the basis of some facts relating to three former 'untouchable' castes, namely, *Regars*, *Balais* and *Naiks*. Of these three castes, *Regars* are numerically larger than *Balais* and *Naiks*. From among the *Regars*, as many as 24 persons are in government jobs, including one as Principal of a Senior Secondary School. One woman is a school teacher and four women are *Anganbari* workers. 14 male members are working in private sector and 10 male members are working in gulf countries as masons and artisans. One hundred three boys and 57 girls are pursuing studies at various levels. From among the *Balais*, 5 are in government jobs, 12 are salaried workers in private sector, and 8 are abroad like the *Regars*. Seventeen boys and 10 girls are studying at different levels. *Naiks* are the smallest of the three groups. Only 6 are in government jobs, and 6 are in private sector. But a good number of them are masons (4), tailors (10), and mechanics (8), and they are working in Delhi and Jaipur. Only 7 boys and 2 girls are pursuing studies.

We can infer that such a transformation has not only restructured social relations in Roopgarh, it has also reduced considerably social inequalities and cultural barriers between the upper and the lower castes. Adult franchise, participation in elections and reservation for the SCs, the STs and the OBCs and for women in the PRIs have recreated social matrix in the village. Those who have migrated and settled down in towns and cities, though do not participate in village affairs on a regular basis, but they are in contact with their family members, and relatives, living in the village. Some of them are often mentioned as 'reference groups'/'individuals', who occupy high positions as civil servants, professionals, businessman, etc.

SABALPURA

'Though Sabalpura is a "sandy" or desert village like Roopgarh, yet Sabalpura exhibits a number of distinct characteristics which are not found in Roopgarh', K. L. Sharma observed in 1965–1966 (1974, 37). The distinctive feature of Sabalpura was that it was situated on the fringe of Sikar town, and was linked by a pucca tarred road. It was at a distance of 5 kilometres from the district headquarters. A majority of the families depended upon employment and government services, particularly in police and army. Sharma also observed that the drift towards the township threw a severe blow to some institutions, particularly to the *Jajmani* system and hereditary occupations. However, caste remained a powerful pivot of hierarchical relations.

Sabalpura had Panchayat headquarters at a nearby village, Bharonpura. Sabalpura had a post office, a Primary School, and a Credit Cooperative Society. Other offices were located at Bharonpura. There were no grocery shops and tea stalls in Sabalpura, despite having a population of 1,772 people and 308 households. Brahmin, Rajput, Jat, Chamar and Muslim were the main castes and communities. Jats, Rajputs and Brahmins owned a major part of agricultural land. Like Roopgarh, Sabalpura was also a dry village. Education, white-collar jobs and political power were vested mainly among Brahmins, Rajputs and Jats. Out of 436 working male members, 165 were engaged mainly in government jobs. 174 persons were cultivators. The remaining ones were working at Sikar on daily wage as well on monthly salary basis.

Today, Sabalpura has geographically merged with Sikar town. It is linked by Jaipur-Churu state highway. Bharonpura continues its *Panchayat* headquarters. Many people from Sikar and other places have constructed houses in Sabalpura. Today, there are nearly 2000 households in the village. Now, there are 10 tea shops and nearly 150 grocery shops. Urban employment has enhanced enormously. In fact, in reality, Sabalpura is like a segment of Sikar town. The distance of 5 km between Sabalpura and Sikar has been abridged up by way of colonies, offices and institutions as a result of the expansion of Sikar town. The primary school has been upgraded as Senior Secondary School. One Kendriya Vidyalaya is also there. A College for Girls is there in the private sector. An NGO Grameen Vikas Society and the Govind Deo Mandir Committee also function in Sabalpura.

There are nearly 400 Muslim families, and several Muslims work in the gulf countries. One Muslim is a Superintendent Engineer, and one is a District Education Officer. A lot from among Rajputs are working in police and army, and some are also officers in CRPF and army. There are nearly 400 Rajput, 350 Brahmin, 150 Jat and 300 *Balai* families, besides 400 Muslim families. Though *Jajmani* system ceased to function long ago, yet caste hierarchy and segregation and discrimination prevail in the village. Inter-caste relations have given a strength to the persisting inter-caste hierarchical relations.

Even being effectively a part of Sikar town, generally people from Sabalpura have not made significant advance in having access to higher education, professions and civil services. Only three law graduates are in legal profession, and one of them leads a team of lawyers. Crime and quarrels have enhanced. Village is also faction–ridden on political party lines. There are factions having allegiance with Congress, BJP, BSP and CPI (M). Interestingly, no casteism is rampant as found elsewhere in the Shekhawati region.

Sabalpura has assimilated urbanity in many ways in several aspects of social life. Highways, Community Centre, Health Clinics, Private Schools and a Private College have created a sort of newness in the village itself. Urbanity is also reflected as people earn a lot from multiple sources, particularly by working in the Gulf Countries, high price of land, commercial activities by way of restaurants, marriage gardens, means of transport (taxies, etc.). Today, people are far more mobile and also go for outing as they have a lot of disposable income. There are more than 100 cars, and nearly 95 per cent of the people own two-wheelers. Marriage celebrations are on urban pattern, including buffet dinner, *barat* reception, decoration, dowry, etc. People have acquired assets in the form of plots of land, gold and from renting. A great amount of money has been brought to the village by the NRIs.

BHUTERA

In the 1960s, Bhutera was a remote village in a true sense as it was not linked with other villages and towns by either a kuccha or a pucca road or by a bus service. Nearest railway station was at a distance of 7 km, and the highway was at a distance of 15 km. Camels and bullock-carts were the only means of travel and transport. However, Bhutera had a primary school, a branch post office, a credit cooperative society, village panchayat, and the headquarters of *Patwari*. It was a multi-caste village like Roopgarh and Sabalpura of the Sikar district, and had segregated settlement pattern (houses), and agricultural land was mainly owned by Brahmins, Rajputs, Jats, *Ahirs* and *Kumar-Malis*. The lower castes led a life of poverty and suppression. In all, there were 210 houses, and a population of 1,217 persons.

The village, being physically and geographically isolated from other villages and towns due to formidable sand dunes and river basin, followed more rigidly norms relating to caste, joint family and rituals. There were only 10 persons educated up to High School. Only 56 persons worked outside Bhutera. 161 households had no income from outside the village. Agricultural was the main source of livelihood. Both Kharif and Rabi crops were grown. Water level was quite high (available at 30 feet). In Roopgarh and Sabalpura, water was down at 150 feet, and in Roopgarh today most of the tube wells have dried up. Irrigation in Roopgarh has come to an end. In Bhutera, out of 321 male workers, 189 were engaged in cultivation, 49 were agricultural and manual workers, 16 were priests, and 8 depended on begging. Jats in Bhutera were better off economically compared to even Brahmins, Rajputs and Banias.

Bhutera has witnessed tremendous socio-economic change over the past five decades. Its population has increased fivefold, from 1,217 in 1965–1966 to 5,800 in 2011. The primary school is now upgraded to Senior Secondary School, with science stream (biology). The riverbed, which kept the village cut-off, has now become a resource for providing water in abundance. Bhutera today supplies water to other villages of five Panchayats. Due to ample water for irrigation, Jats, an agricultural community, have multiplied in Bhutera, coming from nearby villages, up to 1,200 families. Brahmins have only 45 families. Approximately, there are 150 houses of *Regars* (shoe-makers). *Kumawats* have also made a space for themselves as 15 of them are local contractors.

In fact, Bhutera has witnessed enormous economic and social change. There are six school lecturers, and three of them are SCs. One SC is a college lecturer. At least 20 persons from the SCs are serving in Army, and 2 are in Rajasthan Police as Constables. One ST (Meena) is a Manager in the Thar Grameen Bank. A Jat, known for modern farming, is a *crorepati*. A *Kumhar* owns a furniture shop at Jaipur. A *Yadav/Ahir* is a Ration Shop dealer. A Brahmin is a contractor. Seven Jats are teachers, one is a *Gramsevak*, another is a tourist guide, working in Delhi. Nearly 100 engineers are there from Bhutera alone. There are two private 10+2 schools. A girl from the *Ahir* community has topped the Board examination (10th) in Jaipur district. One has been employed as a Forest Guard and another has cleared NEET.

One Bania (Agarwal) is a medical graduate (MBBS). After serving the government of Rajasthan for some time, he has started his own hospital/clinic at Sikar. His daughter, his son-in-law and son are also medical doctors. One of his brothers is a Chartered Accountant (CA), and three brothers are Engineers. They have now a factory of their own.

Bhutera has nearly 80 shops, dealing with clothes, grocery, welding, lathe machine, tea stalls (6), stationary goods, photo studio, beauty parlour, tent house, milk dairies (5 in public sector, 15 private ones), footwear, haircutting saloons, bangle store, medical store, poultry, etc. People of different castes are engaged in trade and commerce, including the SCs. No discrimination prevails in this regard.

Almost all houses own Bolero (jeep). Motorbikes, jeeps, cars are felt as a necessity. About 10 Boleros are available on hire. Roadways bus service is available for Jaipur. Supplies of water and electricity are there for the entire village. One Jat owns a Green House, turnover of which is nearly of ₹25 lacs. He is also a Social Worker. Land was donated by him for Gaushala. Nearly 60 per cent of people are benefited from MNEREGA. Even E-Mitra agency is there in Bhutera. *Sahakari Kraya-Vikraya Samiti* is also there to facilitate purchase and sale, keeping in view the rich agricultural base in Bhutera. Kisan Card system is also in practice. A veterinary dispensary to cater 6000 animals (cows, buffalos, goats) is also there. Artificial insemination is quite popular in regard to cows and buffalos. Besides this, there are one *Ausdhalaya* and ANM (female). *Atal Seva Kendra* is in place in Bhutera. There is also a solar energy plant in Bhutera.

Since agriculture is backbone of Bhutera's economy, *Jajmani* system persists. Intra and inter-caste relations are stronger than Roopgarh mainly due to intense engagement with agriculture. The elders of the village, drawn from different castes, resolve disputes among the people. Court cases are a rare phenomenon. Informal panchayat functions more as a counselling agency rather than a punishment awarding body. No thefts/dacoities have taken place in the village. Melas and *Sawamanis* (religious feasts) are also quite common in the village, which, in turn, promotes social networking and cohesion. *Gangaur mela* is ranked as the third biggest event in Jaipur district. There are also card play-groups. People also donate money for infrastructure in the school.

HARMARA

Harmara, being a peri-urban village, in the proximity of Jaipur, the capital of Rajasthan, and situated on national highway 11, was quite distinct in many ways even in the 1960s, compared to other five villages, particularly, the two suburban villages of Sikar and Bharatpur districts. *Tongas* and buses were available as means of transport from Jaipur to Harmara and back to Jaipur. The village had an upper primary school, a village panchayat, a police *chowki*, offices of *Patwari* and *Gramsevak*, and a post office. There were a few other organizations, such as a youth organization, credit cooperative society, milk cooperative society, quarry workers' union, and caste associations, namely, *Gautam Sabha* and *Maheshwari Sabha*. A lot of people used to commute to Jaipur as wage-workers or for selling their agricultural products.

There were as many as 18 castes and two Muslim families in Haryana. Spatial segregation among different castes was quite obvious *Charans*, a landowning caste (ex-*zamindars*), Brahmins and Banias were at the centre of the village. Other castes inhabited the periphery of the village. Inter-caste relations (*jajmani*) were not as rigid as observed in case of other villages of Sikar and Bharatpur districts. However, rules of marriage and commensal relations were intact. Occupational change was more in Harmara than other villages. Three factors could be noted: (a) an acute scarcity of agricultural land, (b) an easy accessibility to job opportunities in Jaipur (at a distance of 18 km), and (c) occupational diversification, affecting caste-based occupations.

Harmara had meagre means. There was a tea stall, a bicycle repairing shop, and a petrol pump, besides a police post, all on the roadside. There was no pucca road around 1950. Access to Jaipur by a pucca tarred road motivated the farmers to grow cash crops, particularly vegetables. There were around 30 wells, and approximately 250 acres of land was under irrigation. Cash economy had taken place with the coming of road, and it became more intense with introduction of electricity in 1969.

Harmara had 237 households and a population of 1,382 persons. The main castes were Brahmin, *Charan*, Bania, *Mali, Balai* and *Regar*. There were eight graduates, including one medical doctor and one engineer. Nearly 60 persons were educated up to middle and high school levels.

Occupational diversification in Harmara had occurred as a consequence of urban sources of income and work opportunities. Out of 351 male workers, 185 persons worked outside the village, mainly at Jaipur. Only 163 persons (less than 50%) worked in the village. Out of 231 households, 130 depended on income from outside the village. Only 43 persons were exclusively engaged in agriculture. There were 36 industrial workers and 138 were manual labourers. Some were also teachers, clerks, traders, shopkeepers, masons, artisans and village functionaries. A couple of people moved to Jaipur, opened tea shops, grocery shops, hair-cutting salons, and some worked as peons. However, despite occupational diversification and migration to Jaipur, the upper castes, namely, Brahmins, *Charans* and Banias were dominant and grabbed new jobs and opportunities.

In the past five decades, Harmara has lost its identity as a 'village'. The fact is that expansion of Jaipur has engulfed Harmara spatially and legally. Today, Harmara, the nearby Nindar-Benar and some other smaller villages and hamlets have been merged with Jaipur Municipal Corporation. The Corporation has carved out three wards out of Harmara and the allied villages. The old village forms one ward. Surrounding areas constitute the second ward, and the area beyond the flyover (Ajmer–Delhi Byepass) and Ninder are in the third ward. Between Jaipur and Harmara, the Vishwa Karma Industrial Area (VKIA) has filled up the distance with coming of industries, markets and residential colonies, including Murlipura on one side and Vidyadhar Nagar on the other. The VKIA has offered jobs to more than 50 per cent of adult workers of Harmara.

According to Ram Sahai Sharma, a 91 years old man, Harmara has become an extension of Jaipur, having a population of more than one lac. Most of the people have migrated to Harmara from Ganganagar, Jhunjhunu and some other districts. Sharma has mentioned that there are a lot of disputes and police cases. The tradition of mutual settlement is no more in vogue. There are more of impersonal relations. Mutual aid and cooperation, and the feeling of community/we have disappeared. Village level panchayat is no more in existence. 'Urbanization' and 'individualism' have swept the idea and practice of *bhaichara*. Sharma owns a shop, which he attends along with his wife. The next shop is owned by his son, who perhaps does not care for him. His other sons, who work elsewhere, visit him occasionally.

The face of the village is that of a crowded township. One can find almost all sorts of trade and commerce in Harmara. There are nearly 700 shops in Harmara as mentioned by the President of the *Vyapar Mandal*. Of these, there are at least 50 sweetmeat shops, 80 haircutting salons, 50 grocery shops, 50 medical stores, 4 shops for watch-repairing, photography 4, computer/cyber café 4, cooking gas agencies 3, banks 3, ATMs 5, etc. Besides these shops, there are also shops as follows:

1. Health clinics
2. Hardware
3. Building materials
4. Mobile (Oppo and Samsung)
5. Marble
6. Furniture
7. Clothes, Readymade garments (50)
8. Footwear
9. E-Mitra
10. Tent Houses
11. Decoration
12. Coaching Centres
13. Bakery
14. Alcohol
15. Gifts
16. Meat
17. Electronics
18. Tailoring
19. Beauty Parlours
20. Furnishing
21. Show Rooms (Cars, Two-wheelers, Tractors)

Harmara has not made a headway in higher education, even being a part of Jaipur. Since land has become a commodity by way of conversion of agricultural land into residential and commercial land, a large number of people are engaged in sale and purchase of land and construction activities. *Malis* have sold out a large part of their agricultural land for housing and commercial purposes, and today they are economically quite well off in Harmara. Only one Bania had education in medicine and served at the famous SMS Hospital in Jaipur. Currently, he has a clinic in Jaipur. One Bania is a gazetted officer working in Government of Rajasthan. One *Charan* is RTO. Another one owns a lot of plots of land and deals in sale/purchase of property. One Brahmin owns a shopping complex on the highway. Shopkeepers have formed associations and unions, such as *Vyapar Mandal, Sain Parivar Samiti*, etc.

The highway (both sides) is dominated by the upper castes and some well-off migrants from Shekhawati and nearby Chaumu town. Of the three *Nagar Nigam* Councillors, one is a *Brahmin* (BJP), educated up to 8th standard; other two are *Sainis* (independents), and graduates In general, *Charans,* Banias and Brahmins, and lately *Malis* are dominant communities. A large number of people have more inclination toward the BJP rather than the Congress party. One prominent BJP leader expressed his dissatisfaction with the top party leadership in Rajasthan.

The Senior Secondary School (10+2) in Harmara imparts education in all three streams, namely, science, commerce and arts. The school also provides training in vocational education, beauty and wellness. Nearly, 45 per cent are girls and 55 per cent are boys, and total strength is 1015 students. Uniform is compulsory. *Akshaypatra* has made arrangements for mid-day meals for both boys and girls from first to eight standard students.

The name Harmara remains despite its merger along with adjoining villages and hamlets in Jaipur Nagar Nigam. The old village has not changed such as houses and poor people continue to live in this part. However, the well-off people have shifted to the main highway and sideways and have been engaged in trade and commerce at the new sites.

BAWARI

Bawari was an interior village situated at a distance of 50 km from Bharatpur and 15 km from Bayana, the district and the tehsil head-quarters, respectively. The village was at a distance of nearly 3 km from Bharatpur–Dholpur road route. Bawari had a primary school and a credit cooperative society. There were only 105 households with a population of 590 people. Being a multi-caste village, caste hierarchy was intact. The residential pattern showed caste-based segregation and exclusiveness. Jats and Gurjars had houses in the centre of the village, whereas the houses of Jatavs and *Bhangis* were on the outskirts. The other intermediate and lower castes lived adjacent to the houses of Jats and Gurjars. Two houses of the Brahmins were close to that of the Jats. There was only one small grocery shop in the village, owned by a Bania, from the nearby village, Baroda.

Irrigation, Rabi crops, and fertile land were the salient features. Sugarcane was the main cash crop. In 1965, the land price ranged from ₹3000 to 4500 per acre, wherein the villages of Sikar and Jaipur districts, it was from ₹200 to 500. Out of 105 households, 101 depended on agriculture. Only 4 families depended mainly on government jobs. Out of 177 male workers, 129 were cultivators, 29 agricultural labourers, and 19 artisans and functionaries.

In all, only 10 persons were educated up to high school, and all of them were Jats and Gurjars. Out of 3 graduates, 2 were Jats and one was a Brahmin. Jats and Gurjars owned most of the agriculture land.

Today, Bawari is a completely transformed village, compared to its condition in 1965. In all, today there are 225 families, more than double. There is a middle (upper primary) school. ANM Health Centre is also there. An *Anganbadi* worker is there. A pucca link road is there connecting Bawari with main road of Bharatpur-Dholpur route. There are 10 shops, dealing with grocery, fruits and vegetables. The nearest towns are Rudawal and Bayana. Many of the facilities are available in Baroda, which is the headquarters of the village Panchayat. Ration shop is located in Baroda.

Despite a lack of civic facilities, higher education has become a fascination in Bawari. There are medical doctors, working as medical officers at Bharatpur, and has also started his own private clinic (ENT). Another person is in Rajasthan Administrative Service (RAS). All the three are Jats. Two Jats are veterinary doctors, one is in government service, and the other is a private practitioner. From the family of a former dominant Jat *zamindar*, Amrit Lal, Sinsinwal (Jat), is educated up to MCom, BEd and PGDM, and is associated with Jagannath University in Jaipur. A Jat woman is working as an Assistant Engineer. A *Gurjar* woman is working as a nurse. Both women are in government service. Earlier, a Brahmin was a Block Development Officer. Of the five influential persons in *Bawari*, two are Jats, two are Gurjars and one is a Brahmin. *Kumbhars* have also taken up government jobs. Three of them are in Indian Army, one is a clerk in postal department, and one is a Junior Engineer.

Jats are ahead of other castes. Besides, as mentioned earlier, one is working as a Secretary of the Cooperative Society, three are in Indian Army, three are teachers, one is under NDA training as Commissioned Officer, two are advocates, two are in Police, one is in Rajasthan Roadways, and one is working in Forest Department. Gurjars also, numbering ten, are in Indian Army, and two are in Merchant Navy, three are in Rajasthan Police, and one is working in Indian Railways. Since Jats and Gurjars are numerically larger groups, they have many people having salaried government jobs. But even Brahmins, who are only two families, have one lawyer, one compounder, one veterinary doctor, one Block Development Officer (BDO) and one clerk. Jatavs (SC) have five persons working as, one teacher, one in CRPF, two in Railways and one in State's Electricity Board. All these salaried people working outside in Rajasthan and elsewhere have constant contacts with the village and their kinsmen.

Agrarian scene is different from what it was half-a-century ago. Today, no sugarcane is grown. No canal irrigation is there. There is irrigation by tube wells. For drinking water, hand pumps are used. Village panchayat is not paying due attention to the problems of the village. There is no easy access to farm lands, as the government has not done land settlement for a very long time. Encroachments on land have been quite rampant.

The SCs have been benefited by the schemes like *Indira Awas Yojana* and MNREGA. Some people are engaged in animal husbandry, and supply milk to Cooperative Dairy at Bayana. Nearly twenty persons work in private schools and colleges at Bharatpur. A positive feature is that there is no exploitation, untouchability, child marriages, crime, abduction and rape in Bawari. However, women observe 'purdah', to some extent. Dowry exists, but education of girls has received momentum. Both Jats and Gurjars are considered 'equals' in socio-economic and political realms. Generally, people have more inclination for the BJP than the Congress Party.

Bawari was in limelight even before Independence as Captain Budha Singh was associated with the princely State of Bharatpur. His son was *Sarpanch* in the 1960s and was the biggest landowner in Bawari. His daughters received education at Bharatpur. In course of time, many people moved out for better opportunities. Today, a large number of people are not only outside the village, they are also in professions, such as medicine, law, teaching, administration, etc. Transformation of the village is quite comparable with the changes in the suburban villages, namely, Sabalpura, Harmara and Murwara.

MURWARA

Murwara, a suburban village in the vicinity of Bharatpur town, was a medium-sized village like Bawari. Number of households, population and caste structure were similar to that of Bawari, with minor differences. Distance from Bharatpur town was 4 km. There was no pucca road. Bicycles were the main means of transport. Almost every house had a bicycle. There were 110 households, a population of 621 people, distributed among eleven castes.

Murwara had a primary school, a credit cooperative society and a village panchayat. There were no post office and *ayurvedic* dispensary. The village did not have railway or bus facilities, but being close to Bharatpur, transport was not a big problem.

Numerically, the principal castes in Murwara were: Brahmins, Jats, *Malis, Gadarias* and Jatavs. Jats and Brahmins lived in the centre of the village. All the castes had clusters of houses, indicating spatial segregation and hierarchy.

The major crops were that of food-grains. Unlike Bawari, there were no cash crops. There was no sugarcane crop. Gram, wheat, barley, groundnut and mustard were grown without irrigation. Out of 110 families, 65 depended solely on agriculture and allied occupations. The remaining families depended on both agriculture and income from outside the village. Out of 173 male workers, 53 worked mainly at Bharatpur, and commuted daily. Only one small grocery shop, owned by a Brahmin, an ex-Lambardar, was there in Murwara. Of those who worked outside Murwara, 40 persons were engaged as industrial and white-collar workers.

Educationally Murwara was far behind than all other five villages. Only 12 persons had schooling up to eighth standard, 4 were educated up to high school, and 4 were graduates. All of them were Jats and Brahmins. Jats and Brahmins also possessed a large portion of agricultural land. Out of 804 acres of land, 364 acres was owned by 25 families of Jats, and 15 families of Brahmins owned 162 acres.

Influential families were also from Jats and Brahmins. A Jat was *Sarpanch* of the village panchayat, and a Brahmin was Secretary of the Cooperative Society. President of the *Nyay Panchayat* was also a Jat. Though agriculture was the nerve of the village economy, proximity to Bharatpur town impacted Murwara with urbanization and industrialization.

Murwara has not expanded much as people today prefer to settle down at Bharatpur. There are only 175 families, with a population of nearly 1200 people. Atal Seva Kendra is a new addition, and it is looked after by a Brahmin, a former *panch* of the village *Panchayat*. However, there are 7 grocery shops, 4 are owned, one each by a Jat, a Brahmin, a Mali and a Gadaria, and 3 are owned by Jatavs. There are no shops for vegetables and fruits, sweetmeats, and also no tea-stalls.

Problem of drinking water is acute, being full of salinity, and water-level has also gone down. Since, there is no drainage system, mud can be seen all-round, heaps of cow dung breed mosquitoes, which, in turn, cause vulnerability for malaria and other diseases in the village.

Another serious problem in Murwara is related to drug addiction. More than one hundred youth have become addicts of *Ganja* (opium). Ganja plants are grown in the village. One temple has become a site for the addicts. Two *Chilams* (sessions) cost ₹100.00. However, the drug addicts do not consume alcohol. Drug-addiction is even found among some adolescents. The problem has been acute also as there is no village-level effective leadership. People often mention that there are no more leaders of the standing of the late Niranjan Singh and Babu Singh, who commanded influence and respect in Murwara. Another problem is of factionalism and litigation. People do not have social solidarity and mutual cooperation as it was during the heydays of Niranjan Singh and Babu Singh.

Despite these problems, today, Murwara is linked with Bharatpur by a pucca road. Nearly 90 per cent houses are pucca. Many people have modern jobs. Niranjan Singh's one son is a retired Rajasthan Administrative Service (RAS) person, and another one was Director of District Cooperative Bank. Babu Singh's one son is a medical doctor. In a Brahmin family, one person is a retired Rly. Superintendent, the second one is a double A.O., one person is a Junior Engineer (JEN), and another one a school teacher. One BTech, from a Brahmin family, is preparing for Indian Engineering Service. One Brahmin is an engineering student in Jaipur. Nearly 55 persons are in government services, such as ammunition depot, army, CRPF, teaching, administration, forest department, railways, motor driving, engineering, electricity board etc. A large number of them are Jats, *Gadarias, Meenas,* Brahmins, *Malis,* Jatavs, etc. The ammunition depot located at Bharatpur has provided jobs to many people in Murwara.

The primary school of the yesteryears is now a secondary school, with a strength of 150 students. In a neighbouring locality (in municipal area), a private 10+2 school has 300 students. Parents prefer the private school or a school in Bharatpur proper. One person is pursuing PhD at Rajasthan University, Jaipur. Out of 13 teachers in the School, only one person is a male teacher. Women power is reflected also in regard to other positions held by women. *Sarpanch* is a Jatav (SC) woman. Secretary of the cooperative society is also a SC woman. Lower Division Clerk (LDC) is a ST woman. The Principal of the School is a woman (Jat). ANM Nurse is a Saini, married to a Brahmin.

Jatavs are no more engaged in their traditional occupations. More than 90 per cent of them have pucca houses like Brahmins and Jats. Nearly 400 motorcycles are there in the village, besides 2 auto-rickshaws and 7 cars. Nearly one hundred people are working in Bharatpura as daily wage-earners. No case of starvation has been there in the past.

The village is known for sports, particularly for Kho-Kho at the state level. Three girls have won laurels in this game. There has been a lot of awakening about health and education. But despite all this, in 2016, a woman was raped by a Jat.

In effect, Murwara is now a part of Bharatpur town, though technically it remains a village, with a statutory village panchayat and other offices and functionaries, like Sabalpura, a suburban village of Sikar district.

CONCLUDING REMARKS

Let us have a brief recount of the six villages. In the 1960s, in effect, the remote villages from all the three districts were 'remote' in terms of means of transport, communication, education, employment, migration and mobility. The suburban villages were also, in effect, 'suburban', and were not merged with the respective towns, namely, Sikar, Jaipur and Bharatpur. Sabalpura has practically merged with Sikar town, though it remains a part of Bharonpur village panchayat. In terms of housing, means of transport and communication, employment and education, it is like a segment of Sikar town. Harmara, a suburban village in the 1960s in Jaipur district, is no more a village technically as well as substantively, as it is merged with Jaipur town, and comprises of three municipal corporation wards. What one has/had in Jaipur, one can see the same in Harmara. The details mentioned regarding Harmara speak of its 'urbanity'. Murwara, a suburban village in Bharatpur district, is also, in reality, a part of Bharatpur town as seen in terms of its occupational matrix and dependence on Bharatpur town

Of the three 'remote' villages, Roopgarh in Sikar district shows maximum social change and occupational diversification. It is no more like a remote village, though higher education was more even earlier in this village, compared to other five villages. Bhutera, a suburban village in Jaipur district, has also witnessed a sea-change, but its main source of employment is availability of underground water for irrigation. Bawari, a suburban village in Bharatpur district, is also quite different today compared to its situation in the 1960s. Connectivity with tehsil and district towns has changed its sociocultural and economic scene. A number of people have moved out of the village also due to decline of the traditional crop of sugarcane, gram and spices. People have taken up a variety of government jobs, besides employment in private sector.

The narratives of the six villages clearly indicate a need for reconceptualization of the Indian village. Education, migration, mobility, occupational diversification, non-farm income, social networks and political power are the new determinants of social status. Though people often talk of castes/sub-castes, in terms of their numerical strength, education, occupation, etc., in day-to-day life caste hardly matters as social relations cut across caste boundaries. Intra-caste relations are not clearly visible, and inter-caste relations have disappeared, with the exception of Bhutera, a remote village, where agriculture has become a quite strong support for livelihood.

Thus, country-town nexus has taken a new shape, mainly due to basic macrostructural factors and cultural changes as a result of education and occupational mobility.

Conclusion
Emerging Matrix of Social Status and Change

The foregoing discussion suggests that inequality was never solely determined by the ideology of pure and impure as the main basis of the caste system. Caste was a system of social arrangements, and as such certain norms evolved in relation to each caste/sub-caste, and also in regard to relations between different castes. An exaggerated emphasis on the ideology of pure and impure was more of a political nature, and its legitimacy was created by religious beliefs and practices. The colonial rulers reinforced caste practices in the interest of the Raj, making the Indian people to believe that caste was a 'functional' institution as it ensured social division of labour to perform duties and responsibilities for the entire society. Such a make-believe situation was created to consolidate and perpetuate the colonial rule in India

The fact is that even in ancient India, people drew a line between 'sacred' and 'profane', and social mobility occurred in the profane activities quite distinctly. Caste too had these two aspects, the pure/sacred (priestly) and the profane/pragmatic (contra-priestly) functions. The lower functionary castes, such as carpenters, potters, barbers, sweepers, etc., performed priestly functions on occasions like birth, marriage, death and common village fairs and festivals. Thus, the lower (less pure/impure) people had an element of 'purity' and 'priestly' duties. In case, the functionaries were not duly rewarded for their services, they often took it to their caste councils and village elders for seeking justice. If such a course of action did not produce the expected results, sometimes they withdrew their services. Ultimately the patrons had to heed the demands of the functionaries by holding negotiations. No doubt, the upper caste patrons were at the top of social ladder, a structured hierarchy was in place, but there was interdependence, an element of 'equality', assertion of rightful demands and bargaining built into the system.

Let us make it clear here that all 'patrons' and 'functionaries' were not of the same calibre and capability. There were weak as well as strong patrons. Some functionaries often served the top-ranking patrons mainly, whereas others from their ranks, who were not so capable, served the weak patrons. Such distinctions were recognized and could be seen in everyday life. In-built flexibility and mechanisms of griev-ance redressal did not allow the caste system and its allied institutions from becoming 'absolutist' and hegemonic.

Inequality was certainly pronounced, but 'equality' was granted in certain respects, and this was so despite ascriptive ethos with regard to occupation, social interaction and marriage. A system of culture existed that was not reducible to group/sub-group (caste/sub-caste); it granted some amount of space to the lower strata, specific families and individuals, for realization of their worth in the society. Binary opposition (pure and impure) was magnified in terms of people and things at the extreme 'top' and the 'bottom' in the caste hierarchy of the Indian society. Homi K. Bhabha (1995, 13) observes about culture, though based on literary and philosophical notions, as follows:

> Private and public, past and present, the psyche and the social develop an interstitial intimacy. It is an intimacy that questions binary divisions through which such spheres of social experience are often spatially, opposed. These spheres of life are linked through an in-between temporality that takes the measure of dwelling at home, which produce an image of the world history.

India's national movement for freedom from the colonial yoke, besides questioning the Raj, created a socio-political consciousness, which, in turn, united Indians despite caste, class and religious differences. Families and individuals participated in the liberation movement ignoring caste-based norms of inclusion and exclusion. Attainment of Independence further enhanced the role and significance of individual and family through some provisions in the constitution of India. As we know, the backward sections of our society, namely, the SCs and the STs, were granted, under specific provisions, opportunities by way of reservations in educational institutions, government services, and in assemblies, parliament and civic bodies. The BCs were given reservations in education and jobs in 1993, based on the B. P. Mandal Commission Report. This was done based on the Census of 1931, conducted by J. H. Hutton, as it had a complete enumeration of all the castes/communities of India. Though 'caste' was the basis for reservations, its benefits have been cornered by specific families and individuals. A large section of the 'deprived' castes has remained devoid of the provisions of the policy of reservations. A 'creamy layer', a new middle class, and a miniscule elite have come up from such a policy.

Besides this, land records, Panchayati Raj institutions (PRIs) and the state-sponsored rural development programmes have too helped, though in varying measures, many families and individuals, drawn mainly from principal agricultural castes. The upper (twice-born) castes have not been benefited markedly by such a process of change and development. A large section of people have moved out for seeking alternative opportunities and better employment. Such a section of people, drawn from different social backgrounds, becomes a new status group entity in rural India. Besides such families and individuals, there are also people at the top, who are from the entrenched families and new status groups. There are groups at the middle level, and below them are several lower strata of cultivators, artisans, weavers, manual workers, etc.

At the centre of such a process of social and occupational mobility is the individual and his/her family. The question is not of a nuclear or joint/extended family. Concern and liking for joint family have almost faded out. Generally, people are concerned about their immediate families, and often their unmarried children. A strong tendency can be seen towards living separately after marriage, even within the village. Those who work in towns and cities do not leave their spouses in the village after marriage. Even the nature of 'functional jointness' has changed immensely. However, some lineal and collateral families can be found, particularly among those people who depend upon agriculture and entrepreneurship of some sort in the village itself. Such families too separate in course of time due to intra-family tensions. The cycle of family from nuclear to joint and joint to nuclear, although without the traditional gestalt, can be found in some cases.

Amartya Sen (2005, 1971–1974) talks of 'Three R's of Reform' for India as a whole, which could influence the lives of the Indian people. The three R's are: (a) Reach, (b) Range and (c) Reason. These apply to the rural people as well. The *reach* refers to the results to be achieved; the *range* implies the ways and means to be used; the *reason* indicates choosing the priorities people pursue. The three R's are person-oriented, and apply to everyone who can access to programmes of development and change sponsored by the state. Thus, rural people today look for improvement in their existential conditions by having the three R's as strategies. A new culture, not as a pre-given religious/caste-based dictate, but as a pragmatic objective, has emerged among the rural people. It is another thing that all people do not have the idea or capability to pursue the three R's. In this regard, Clifford Geertz's concept of culture (1973, 3–30) is quite useful. He says that culture is not an experimental science in search of law but an interpretive one in search of meaning. It is an explication, constructing social expressions. As such culture is *public*. Though culture is ideational, unphysical, it is not an occult entity. Geertz (1973, 12) writes: 'culture is public because meaning is'. Meaning is interpreted by people. As such culture is related to concrete social events and occasions, the public world of common life. Culture cannot be unrelated to the political, economic and stratificatory realities within which men are everywhere contained (Geertz, 1973, 30).

Rural India is engaged in reinterpretation of the criteria of status and power. People have been questioning the caste-based norms and practices for quite some time. Assertion for equality and dignity is quite visible. The educated salaried people from the lower and intermediate castes wish away or even ridicule the claim of the higher caste people for high ritual status. Right to vote has created a sense of equality among the former lower caste people. People prefer to vote as per their interests and concerns. People vote for multiple reasons, including extending support to their preferred candidates, ideological leanings, personal interests, and considering voting as a national duty. Adult franchise and voting have strengthened democracy in rural India, but India is far away from becoming a true republic.

In India, there is a strong tendency to sustain or even propagate 'democratic dynasties' (Chandra, 2016). During the past seven decades, *Panch, Sarpanch, Pradhan, Zila Pramukh*, MLA and MP have been elected from select families. Even political parties prefer dynastic candidates with a view to appropriate clout of the candidates, their families and kinsmen. Such a situation is indicative of a new pattern of power and its legitimation. Rivals divide the village people, not necessarily on the caste basis, but certainly in terms of political parties, ideologies, coalitions/alliances of castes and groups of families, and expectations of the people from the party leaders/power elite. All the power-seekers, power-wielders and their followers/supporters are a stratified segment of rural society. There are people whose families have been in politics for a very long time, and there are also political families. For the former, politics is a means of livelihood, and for the latter, it is a means of social mobility. In either case, power is the key to status and social mobility. What Barbara Hariss-White (2004, 103–131) talks about in 'family business and business families' also applies to the field of power-politics.

Differential access to resources such as quality education, gainful employment and participation in decision-making is the main factor in the persistence of inequality. Today, inequality is different from what it was before Independence Inequality is not a ritualistic phenomenon anymore; it is more structural, that is, differential shares of the people in resources of the state and society. Berreman (1979), while dismissing Louis Dumont's thesis of the idea of pure and impure as the basis of caste-based inequality, refers to inequality as deprivation and suffering of the inferior, who is at the bottom of the system. Berreman talks of a possibility of an egalitarian society in the future, without caste and class differences. Kolenda (2003, 415–431) has also briefly discussed both the concepts of 'equality' and 'inequality'.

The problem in rural India is that 'cultural equality' has increased, but correspondingly economic and political equality has not increased. In a new form inequality has enhanced. Rural people, in general, are at a disadvantage compared to the urban people, in regard to gender equality, education, employment, lifestyle, healthcare, etc. Despite a transformed country–town nexus, 'rural' remains rural. Role of parents, social background, and aspirations of individuals and families weaken inequality, and motivate people for social mobility. Ultimately social mobility is possible only when people are able to overcome the constraints. Fare distribution of shares is possible if most people are generally capable to have their due shares based on their performances.

We have emphasized on the creation of adequate spaces for both individual and family in overcoming of the caste-based rigidities and inequalities. The concept of *punush* (person), and not that of 'individual' or 'individualism', would recognize individual (person) and relate him/her with the state and society in harmony. A person is in family, and a family is in a person, and both are in the society and the society is in both of them. As a result of social mobility of individuals and families in rural India, we can see a fast-emerging middle class, drawn from different castes and communities and families. In one of the villages, reported in this volume, nearly 50 persons belonging to the SCs are in white-collar government jobs. Such is the story of other five villages. These persons and their families have become a 'class' by themselves, as they are distinct, compared to other persons and families who have remained deprived of such an upward mobility.

Education is another factor, besides migration and urban employment, that has transformed rural social scene. Education is pervasive among both the sexes, male and female. Quality education is not easily accessible even in nearby towns and cities. Both private mode and distance education mode are being adopted by those who are unable to afford education through a regular stream. Besides employment, education has also brought about social change by way of developing language skills, lifestyle changes, and sociocultural and political awakening.

While talking about rural economy we can see a vast change in the mode of agriculture and dependence on it as a main source of livelihood. Peasants are today a vague category. The 'middle peasants', as self-sufficient entity, have nearly disappeared. The landless and the poor ones have taken up other odd jobs rather than working for the rich peasants. Tractor has replaced the bullocks-managed cultivation. Use of modern technology in sowing, irrigation and harvesting is quite common. Green revolution has faded out long ago, replaced by new commercial crops with the advent of globalization and mega-marts in big towns and cities. Commercialization of agriculture has also caused suicides by farmers. Non-farm income has been cornered by the entrenched peasantry and even by the well-off people. Such a situation has further widened the divide among the peasants, and also among the rural people.

With regard to artisans and weavers, we have observed that generally arts and crafts and weaving are on decline. Family is at the centre of handicrafts and weaving. Low wages, middlemen and low technology keep weaving as a 'proto-industrial' economic activity. The artisans and weavers, of both Muslim and Hindu communities, have a miserable life. The role of the state and the cooperatives has also not done much to reduce the agony of the artisans and weavers. The binding with merchants and master-weavers has taken the shape of patron–client relationship.

Political institutions, such as adult franchise, elections, Panchayati Raj and cooperatives, are the most visible and engaging agencies in rural India. Despite lagging behind in industrialization, India is far ahead of even some advanced countries in the field of functioning of democracy and its allied institutions. In rural India, caste, religion family and other institutions have adapted to the challenges and demands of modern polity. Our 'pluralism' and 'toleration' are key to modern polity and democracy. We have been also a 'troubled democracy'; but we have stood by through thick and thin of the political march till today. Rural people talk maximum about political parties, leaders, factions, elections, candidates, corruption, etc. People vote with a realization that it is in their interest. Elections also reveal: Who is Who in Rural India?

PRIs are working since 1959 with a preamble of democratic decentralization of power. After the 73rd constitutional amendment, the PRIs have financial and legislative guarantee from the state at par with the state legislatures and parliament. Empowering of women, the SCs, the STs and the OBCs has also been made through this amendment.

To what extent women and weaker sections have become powerful through the PRIs? The stories of patriarchal hegemony and upper/upper middle castes' domination have been pouring in from different states. However, in some states like West Bengal, the success story of PRIs is quite encouraging in regard to empowerment of the rural people.

Lastly, regarding the caste system, we may have to raise some questions. Some people talk of the caste system, even though caste as a system has collapsed. Who are such people? What do they talk about caste? Why do they talk of the caste system, without its systemic ethos? Why people are allowed to appropriate caste for their vested political interests? Caste, and not the caste system, is discretionary, in terms of its use, misuse, abuse and non-use. 'Caste' in its new avatar is being used in terms of favours, discriminations, mobilizations and seeking of power.

Also at the end, it may be mentioned that the pattern of social stratification has changed due to new parameters, such as control of resources, assets, social networks, education, lucrative occupations, income and participation in PRIs. It is not that a given person/family must have all these criteria at the same time, but certain combination of these determinants would ensure status, prestige and power in the village. Such a matrix of status-determinants is known to the rural people. Caste is linked with the matrix, and it is not that caste determines the matrix. Caste may play some role, depending upon the achievements of some of its members and their networks within the village and outside it.

There are examples of upward social mobility from rags to riches, achieved by sheer efforts of the people through their education and/or entrepreneurial skills. In some cases, privileged parentage has proved to be a positive launching pad. But a large number of rural people have been benefited by macro-structural changes, such as adult franchise, land reforms, policies and programmes of the state. At the micro level, the infrastructural developments, including schools/colleges, healthcare, PRIs, road, transport, MNREGA, etc., have not only impacted all the villagers, though not uniformly, but have reshaped the Indian village with a new face. Such a process of social transformation has heightened the spirit for rivalry and competition among contenders for high status and power. Social tensions have also surfaced in everyday life and in regard to the functioning of the village institutions. Empowering of the PRIs has also added to the competitive uneasiness in rural life.

Thus, both cognitive and ontological bases of village life have changed immensely. Issues and dilemmas are not the same as we had on the eve of Independence. Development, power, dignity, capability and networks are the main considerations, and based on these considerations, a new system of stratification has emerged in Indian villages. The main dilemma is to have a *reach* to the available resources, and for that one needs to acquire capability, which is also the responsibility of the state, that is, to empower its citizens for an egalitarian social order.

We are not visualizing a uniform system of social stratification and change throughout rural India. Inter-district, inter-village variations and intra-district, intra-village variations have been observed. What we are arguing, is that the idea of 'status' and significance of 'power' are the valued considerations in status determination. For this, today, rural people strive, within the village and also outside it, by way of access to resources, education, migration and mobility for better living conditions, status, power and recognition in the society.

Bibliography

Abraham, Janaki, 2014, 'Contingent Caste Endogamy and Patriarchy: Lessons for Our Understanding of Caste', *Economic & Political Weekly*, Vol. 49, No. 2: 56–65.

Acharya, Shankar, 2007, *Can India Grow Without Bharat?* New Delhi, Academic Foundation.

Agarwal, Pawan, 2009, *Indian Higher Education: Envisioning the Future*, New Delhi, SAGE.

Aikara, Jacob, 2004, *Education: Sociological Perspective*, Jaipur and New Delhi, Rawat Publications.

Alaev, L. B., 1984, 'Non-Agricultural Production: (South India)', in Tapan Raychaudhuri and Irfan Habib (eds.), *The Cambridge History of India*, Vol. I, C., 1200–1750, New Delhi, Orient Longman, 315–317.

Alavi, Hamza, 1975, 'India and the Colonial Mode of Production', *Economic & Political Weekly*: 1235–1262.

Altbach, P.G., 2003, 'Globalization and the University: Myths and Realities in an Unequal World', *Journal of Educational Planning and Administration*, Vol. 17, No. 2: 227–247.

Ambedkar, B.R., 1946, *Annihilation of Caste*, Bombay, The Bharat Bhushan Press.

———, 1948, *The Untouchables: Who Were They and Why They Became Untouchables?* New Delhi, Amrit Book Company.

———, 1987, 'Revolution', in *Dr. Babasaheb Ambedkar Writings and Speeches*, Vol. 3, Bombay, Government of Maharashtra.

———, 2007 (1937), *Annihilation of Caste*, New Delhi, Critical Quest.

———, 2008, 'Who Were the Shudras?' in Valerian Rodrigues (ed.), *The Essential Writings of B.R. Ambedkar*, New Delhi, Oxford University Press.

Amin, Shahid, 1995, *Event, Metaphor, Memory: Chauri Chaura, 1922–92*, Delhi, Oxford University Press.

Amin, Shahid, and Dipesh Chakrabarty (eds.), 1996, *Subaltern Studies IX, Writings on South Asian History and Society*, Delhi, Oxford University Press. (Articles are by Ranjit Guha, Ajay Skaria, Gyan Prakash, Kamala Visweswaran, Shail Mayaram, Kancha Ilaiah, Vivek Dhareshwar and R. Srivatsan, and David Llyod).

Anderson, Perry, 2012, *The Indian Ideology*, Gurgaon, Three Essays, Collective.

Arnold, David, 2000, 'Gramsci and Peasant Subalternity in India', in Vinayak Chaturvedi (ed.), *Mapping Subaltern Studies and the Postcolonial*. London, New York, Verso, 24–49.

Arnold, David, and David Hardiman (eds.), 1994, *Subaltern Studies VIII, Essays in Honour of Ranjit Guha*, Delhi, Oxford University Press (Articles are by Partha Chatterjee, Dipesh Chakrabarty, David Hardiman, Gynendra Pandey, Shahid Amin and Gautam Bhakra).

Atal, Yogesh, 2007, *On Education and Development: Essays on the Sociology of Education*, Jaipur and New Delhi, Rawat Publications.

Babu, D. Shyam, 2011, 'An Eventful Journey: From the Real to the Comical', in D. Shyam Babu and R.S. Khare (eds.), *Caste in Life: Experiencing Inequalities*, New Delhi, Dorling Kindersley.

Baden-Powell, B.H., 1896, *The Indian Village Community*, London, Swan Sonnensc & Company.

———, 1899, *The Origin and Growth of Village Communities in India*, London, Swan Sonnensc & Company.

Bagchi, A., 1982, *The Political Economy of Underdevelopment*, Cambridge, Cambridge University Press.

Bailey, F.G., 1957, *Caste and the Economic Frontier*, Manchester, Manchester University Press.

———, 1959, 'For a Sociology of India', *Contributions to Indian Sociology*, No. III: 88–101.

———, 1963, 'Closed Social Stratification in India', *European Journal of Sociology*, Vol. 4, No. 1: 107–24.

Banaji, J., 1973, 'Mode of Production in Indian Agriculture', *Economic & Political Weekly*, Vol. 8, No. 4: 679–683.

———, 1975, 'India and the Colonial Mode of Production: A Comment', *Economic & Political Weekly*, Vol. 10, No. 49: 1887–1892.

———, 1977, 'Capitalist Domination and the Small Peasantry: Deccan Districts in the Late Nineteenth Century', *Economic & Political Weekly*, Vol. 12, Nos. 33 & 34: 1375–1404.

Banerjee-Dube, Ishita, 2008, *Caste in History*, New Delhi, Oxford University Press.

Banerjee, Mukulika, 2007, 'Sacred Elections', *Economic & Political Weekly*, Vol. 42, No. 17: 1556–1562.

———, 2014, *Why India Votes?* Delhi, Routledge.

Banerjee, Rahul, 2013, 'What Ails Panchayati Raj?' *Economic & Political Weekly*, Vol. 48, No. 30: 173–176.

Banks, Michael, 1960, 'Caste in Jaffna', in E.R. Leach (ed.), *Aspects of Caste in South India, Ceylon and North-West Pakistan*, Cambridge, Cambridge University Press, 61–77.

Barber, Bernard, 1968, 'Social Mobility in Hindu India', in James Silverbeg (ed.), *Social Mobility in the Caste System in India*, The Hague, Mouton Publishers.

Barnett, R., 1992, *Improving Higher Education: Total Quality Care*, London, SRHE/ Open University Press.

Barth, Fredrik, 1960, 'The System of Social Stratification in Swat, North Pakistan', in E.R. Leach (ed.), *Aspects of Caste in South India, Ceylon and North-West Pakistan*, Cambridge, Cambridge University Press.

Barth, Fredrik, 1969, 'Introduction', in Fredrik Birth (ed.), *Ethnic Groups and Boundaries*, London, George Allen and Unwin.

Baru, Rama, et al., 2010, 'Inequities in Access to Health Services in India: Caste, Class and Region', *Economic & Political Weekly*, Vol. 45, No. 38: 49–58.

Basant, Rakesh, and Gitanjali Sen, 2013, 'Who Participates in Higher Education in India? Rethinking the Role of Affirmative Action', in J.B.G. Tilak (ed.), *Higher Education in India: In Search of Equality, Quality and Quantity*, New Delhi, Orient BlackSwan, pp. 130–131.

Basole, Amit, and Dipankar Basu, 2011, 'Relations of Production and Modes of Surplus Extraction in India: Part I and II', *Economic & Political Weekly*, Vol. 46, Nos. 14 & 15: 41–58.

Basu, Aparna, 1991, 'Higher Education in Colonial India', in Moonis Raza (ed.), *Higher Education in India: Retrospect and Prospect*, New Delhi, Association of Indian Universities, 22–31.

Bayly, C.A., 1992, *Rulers, Townsmen and Bazaars, North Indian Society in the Age of British Expansion 1770–1870* (first Indian edition), New Delhi, Oxford University Press.

Bayly, Susan, 2000, *Caste, Society and Politics in India: From the Eighteenth Century to the Modern Age*, Cambridge, Cambridge University Press.

Berreman, Gerald D., 1967, 'Stratification, Pluralism and Interaction: A Comparative Analysis of Caste', in Anthony de Reuck and Julie Knight (eds.), *Caste and Race: Comparative Approaches*, London, J&A Churchill.

———, 1979, *Caste and Other Inequalities*, Delhi, Manohar.

———, 2002, *Caste and Race: Reservations and Affirmations* (mimeographed) (cited from Sukhadeo Thorat and Umakant (eds.), Caste, Race and Discriminations, Jaipur and New Delhi, Rawat Publications, p. XV.

Besley, Timothy, Rohini Pande, and Vijayendra Rao, 2007, 'Political Economy of Panchayats in South India', *Economic & Political Weekly*, Vol. 42, No. 8: 661–666.

Beteille, Andre, 1965/1966, *Caste, Class and Power: Changing Pattern of Stratification in a Tanjore Village*, Bombay/New Delhi, Oxford University Press.

———, 1966, 'Closed and Open Social Stratification in India', *European Journal of Sociology*, Vol. 7, No. 2: 224–246.

———, 1969a, Castes: Old and New, *Essays in Social Structure and Social Stratification*, New York, Asia Publishing House.

———, 1969b, 'Ideas and Interests: Some Conceptual Problems in the Study of Social Stratification in India', *International Social Science Journal*, Vol. 27, No. 7: 17–31.

———, 1974, *Studies in Agrarian Social Structure*, New Delhi, Oxford University Press.

———, 1991, 'The Reproduction of Inequality', *Contributions to Indian Sociology*, Vol. 25, No. 1: 3–28.

———, 1998, 'The Reproduction of Inequality: Occupation, Caste and Family', in P. Uberoi (ed.), *Family, Kinship and Marriage in India*, New Delhi, Oxford University Press, 435–451.

Beteille, Andre, 2002, *Equality and Universality: Essays in Social and Political Theory*, New Delhi, Oxford University Press.

———, 2003, 'Poverty and Inequality', *Economic & Political Weekly*, Vol. 38, No. 42: 4455–4463.

———, 2004, 'Race and Caste', in Sukhadeo Thorat and Umakant (eds.), *Caste, Race and Discrimination: Discourses in International Context*, Jaipur and New Delhi, Rawat Publications, 49–52.

———, 2005, 'The Reproduction of Inequaltiy', in Dipankar Gupta (ed.), *Anti-Utopia: Essential Writings of Andre Beteille*, New Delhi, Oxford University Press, 302-329.

———, 2006, 'On Individualsm and Equality: Reply to Louis Dumont', in R.S. Khare (ed.), *Caste, Hierarchy, and Individualism*, New Delhi, Oxford University Press, 110–119.

———, 2007, 'Classes and Communities', *Economic & Political Weekly*, Vol. 42, No. 11: 945–52.

———, 2010, *Universities at the Crossroads*, New Delhi, Oxford University Press.

———, 2012, 'The Peculiar Tenacity of Caste', *Economic & Political Weekly*, Vol. 47, No. 13: 41–48.

———, 2013, 'Does the Middle Class Have Boundaries?' in Surinder S. Jodhka (ed.), *Interrogating India's Modernity: Essays in Honour of Dipankar Gupta*, New Delhi, Oxford University Press, 79–98.

Beteille, Andre, 1966, 'Closed and Open Social Stratification in India', *European Journal of Sociology*, Vol. 7: 224–246. See also Louis Dumont, 1967, 'Caste: A Phenomenon of Social Structure or an Aspect of Indian Culture', in Anthony de Reuck and Julie Knight (eds.), *Caste and Race: Comparative Approaches*, London, J&A Churchill.

Beteille, Andre (ed.), 1969, *Social Inequality*, H. Middlesex, England.

Bettelheim, Charles, 1968, *India Independent*, London, Macgibbon & Kee, 1–7.

Bhabha, Homi K., 1995, *The Location of Culture*, London and New York, Routledge.

Bhadra, Gautam, Gyan Prakasha, and Susie Tharu (eds.), 1999, *Subaltern Studies X, Writings on South Asian History and Society*, Delhi, Oxford University Press. (Articles are by Sudesh Mishra, Kaushik Ghosh, Indrani Chatterjee, Ishita Banerjee-Dube, Sunder Kaali, Vijay Prasad, Christopher Pinney, and Rosemary Saying).

Bhaduri, Amit, 1973, 'An Analysis of Semi-feudalism in East-Indian Agriculture', *Frontier*, Vol. 6, 20 September.

Bhalla, G.S., and G.K. Chacha, 1983, *Green Revolution and the Small Peasant—A Study of Income Distribution among Punjab Cultivators*, New Delhi, Concept Publishing Co.

Bhambhri, C.P., 2005, 'Reservations and Casteism', *Economic & Political Weekly*, Vol. 40, No. 9: 806–808.

Bhatnagar, G.S., 1972, *Education and Social Change*, Calcutta, The Minerva Associates.

Bhattacharya, Sabyasachi, 1983, 'Introduction', in Dharma Kumar (ed.), *The Cambridge Economic History of India*, Vol. II, C. 1757–2003, pp. XXI–XLI.

Bhattacharya, Sukanta, 2003, 'Caste, Class and Politics in West Bengal: Case Study of a Village in Burdwan', *Economic & Political Weekly*, Vol. 38, No. 3: 242–246.

Bhattacharyya, Dwaipayan, 2011, 'Party, Society, Its Consolidation and Crisis: Understanding Political Change in Rural West Bengal', in Anjan Ghosh et al. (eds.), *Theorising the Present: Essays for Partha Chatterjee*, New Delhi, Oxford University Press.

Bhushan, Sudhanshu, 2009, *Restructuring Higher Education in India*, Jaipur and New Delhi, Rawat Publications.

Bohannan, P., 1963, *Social Anthropology*, New York, Holt, Rinehart and Winston.

Böröcz, József, 2005, 'Redistributing Global Inequality: A Thought Experiment', *Economic & Political Weekly*, Vol. 40, No. 9: 886–892.

Bose, Arun, 2006a, 'Indo-Hierarchy Theory', in R.S. Khare (ed.), *Caste, Hierarchy, and Individualism*, New Delhi, Oxford University Press.

———, 2006b, 'Louis Dumont on Individualism', in R.S. Khare (ed.), *Caste, Hierarchy, and Individualism*, New Delhi, Oxford University Press, 136–149 and 150–152.

Bose, N.K., 1975, 'Some Aspects of Caste in Bengal', in Milton Singer (ed.), *Traditional India: Structure and Change*, Jaipur, Rawat Publications.

Bose, Pradip Kumar, 2014, 'Abstract Individual, Concrete Person: Overcoming Individualism', in the Sociology of D.P. Mukerji, *Sociological Bulletin*, Vol. 63, No. 2: 185–205.

Bottomore, T.B. (ed.), 1983, *A Dictionary of Marxist Thought*, Oxford, Basil Blackwell Publishing.

Bottomore, T.B., and Maximilien Rubel (eds.), 1973, *Karl Marx: Selected Writings in Sociology and Social Philosophy*, H. Middlesex, England, Penguin Books, 137–154.

Bougle, C., 1958, 'The Essence of Reality of Caste System', *Contributions to Indian Sociology*, No. 2: 7–30.

———, 1971, *Essays on the Caste System*, Cambridge, Cambridge University Press (Originally Published in 1908).

Bourdieu, Pierre, 1984, *Distinction: A Social Critique of the Judgment of Taste*, London/Cambridge, MA, Routledge/Harvard University Press.

———, 1996, *The State Nobility: Elite Schools in the Field of Power*, (translated by Louretta C. Clough), Cambridge Polity Press.

Bourdieu, Pierre, and Jean-Claude Passeron, 1977, *Reproduction in Education, Society and Culture*, California, SAGE.

Brass, Paul R., 1990, *The Politics of India Since Independence*, Cambridge, Cambridge University Press, 138–147. Reprint in 2004 by Cambridge University Press, Cambridge.

———, 2014, 'How Political Scientist Experienced India's Development State', in L.I. Rudolph and John Kurt Jacobson (eds.), *Experiencing the State* (Reprint), New Delhi, Oxford University Press, 110–139.

Brass, Tom, 2000, 'Moral Economists, Subalterns, New Social Movements and the (Re-) Emergence of a (Post-) Modernized (Middle) Peasant', in Vinayak

Chaturvedi (ed.), *Mapping Subaltern Studies and the Postcolonial*, London, New York, Verso, 127–162.

Breman, Jan, 1974, *Patronage and Exploitation: Changing Agrarian Relations in South Gujarat*, Berkeley, University of California Press.

———, 1979, *Patronage and Exploitation: Changing Agrarian Relations in South Gujarat, India*, Delhi, Manohar Publications.

———, 1985, *Of Peasants, Migrants and Paupers, Rural Labour Circulation and Capitalist Production in West India*, Delhi, Oxford University Press.

———, 1997, 'The Village in Focus', in Jan Breman, Peter Kloss and Ashwini Saith (eds.), *The Village in Asia Revisited*, Delhi, Oxford University Press.

———, 2003, *The Labouring Poor in India: Patterns of Exploitation, Subordination, and Exclusion*, New Delhi, Oxford University Press.

———, 2007, *The Poverty Regime in Village India*, Oxford University Press.

Brenner, Robert, 1976, 'Agrarian Class Structure and Economic Development in Pre-industrial Europe', *Past & Present*, Vol. 70, February: 30–75, quoted from *Mapping Subaltern Studies and the Postcolonial*, edited by Vinayak Chaturvedi. London, New York, Verso, IV–XIX.

Brosius, Christiane, 2010, *India's Middle: New Forms of Urban Leisure Consumption and Prosperity*, New Delhi, Routledge.

Bukharin, N.V., 1969, *Historical Materialism: A System of Sociology*, Ann Arbor, University of Michigan Press.

Burghart, Richard, 1978, 'Hierarchical Models of the Hindu Social System', *Man*, Vol. 13.

———, 1983a, 'For a Sociology of India', *Contributions to Indian Sociology*, Vol. 17, No. 2.

———, 1983b, 'Renunciation in the Religious Traditions of South Asia', *Man*, Vol. 18.

Butler, David, Ashok Lahiri and Prannoy Roy, 1995, *India Decides: Elections 1952–1995*, New Delhi, Books & Things.

Byers, T.J., 1977, 'Agrarian Transition and the Agrarian Question', *Journal of Peasant Studies*, Vol. 4, No. 3: 258–274.

Carass, Mary C., 1972, *The Dynamics of Indian Political Factions*, London, Cambridge University Press.

Chakrabarti, Dalia, 2010, 'D.P Mukerji and the Middle Class in India', *Sociological Bulletin*, Vol. 59, No. 2: 235–255.

Chakraborty, Chandrima, 2003, 'Subaltern Studies, Bollywood and Legaan', *Economic & Political Weekly*, Vol. 38, No. 19: 1879–1884.

Chakravarti, Anand, 2001, *Social Power and Everyday Class Relations: Agrarian Transformation in North Bihar*, New Delhi, SAGE.

Chanana, Karuna, 2013, 'Globalization and Higher Education: Changing Subject Choices of Indian Women Students', in J.B.G. Tilak (ed.), *Higher Education in India: In Search of Equality, Quality and Quantity*, New Delhi, Orient BlackSwan, 408–429. Earlier published in *Economic & Political Weekly*, Vol. 41, No. 7: 590–598, 17 February 2007.

Chandra, Bipan, Mridula Mukherjee, and Aditya Mukherjee, 2000, *India After Independence* (1947–2000), New Delhi, Penguin Books, 1–19.

Chandra, Kanchan (ed.), 2016, *Democratic Dynasties, State, Party and Family in Contemporary Indian Politics*, New Delhi, Cambridge University Press.

Chandra, Nirmal, 1988, *The Retarded Economics: Foreign Domination and Class Relations in India and other Emerging Nations*, Bombay, Sameeksha Trust, Oxford University Press.

Chandra, Uday, and Kenneth Bo Nielsen, 2012, 'The Importance of Caste in Bengal', *Economic & Political Weekly*, Vol. 47, No. 44: 59–61.

Chatterjee, Ashoke, 2015, 'India's Handloom Challenge: Anatomy of a Crisis', *Economic & Political Weekly*, Vol. 50, No. 32: 34–38.

Chatterjee, Partha, 1982, 'Agrarian Relations and Communalism in Bengal, 1926–1935', in Subaltern Studies I, edited by Ranjit Guha. Delhi: Oxford University Press, 9–38.

———, 1984, 'Gandhi and the Critique of Civil Society', *Subaltern Studies III*, edited by Ranjit Guha. Delhi: Oxford University Press, 39.

———, 2000, 'The Nation and its Peasants', in Vinayak Chaturvedi (ed.), *Mapping Subaltern Studies and the Postcolonial*, London, New York, Verso, 8–23.

———, 2004, *Politics of the Governed: Reflections on Popular Politics in Most of the World*. Delhi: Permanent Black.

———, 2009, 'Editor's Introduction', in Ranjit Guha, *The Small Voice of History*, edited by Partha Chatterjee, Ranikhet, Permanent Black, 1–17.

Chatterjee, Partha, and Gyanendra Pandey (eds.), 1993, *Subaltern Studies VII, Writings on South Asian History and Society*. Delhi: Oxford University Press. (Articles are by Sudipta Kaviraj, Ranjit Guha, Saurab Dube, Amitav Ghosh, Terene Ranger and Upendra Baxi).

Chatterjee, Partha, and Pradeep Jeganathan (eds.), 2000, *Community, Gender and Violence*, New Delhi, Permanent Black. (Articles are by Aamir R. Mufti, Pradeep Jeganathan, Nivedita Menon, Flavia Agnes, Tejasvini Niranjana, Satish Deshpande, Qadri Ismail, David Scott and Gayatri Chakravorty Spivak).

Chattopadhyay, Soumen, 2013, 'The Market in Higher Education: Concern for Equity and Quality', in J.B.G. Tilak (ed.), *Higher Education in India: In Search of Equality, Quality and Quantity*, New Delhi, Orient BlackSwan, 430–448.

Chattopadhyay, Paresh, 1972, 'Mode of Production in Indian Agriculture', *Economic & Political Weekly*, Vol. 7, No. 13: A39–A46.

Chaturvedi, Sumit, 2014, 'Caste Publications: The Space for Upper Caste Sub-Culture Politics', *Economic & Political Weekly*, Vol. 49, No. 17: 33–37.

Chaturvedi, Vinayak (ed.), 2000, 'Introduction', in *Mapping Subaltern Studies and The Postcolonial*. London, New York, Verso, VII–XIX.

Chaudhuri, Maitrayee, 2010, 'Family and its Representation: From Indology to Market Research', in Yogendra Singh (ed.), *History of Science, Philosophy and Culture in Indian Civilization*, Vol. XIV, Part 2, Social Sciences: Communication, Anthropology, and Sociology, Delhi, Longman/Pearson, 363–389.

Chaudhuri, Maitrayee, 2013, 'Higher Education in "Global" India: The Need for Critical Sociology', in Ishwar Modi (ed.), *Education, Religion and Creativity*, Jaipur, Rawat Publications, 3–22.

Chauhan, B.R., 1957, *A Rajasthan Village*, New Delhi, Associated Publishing House.

———, 1974, 'Rural Studies: A Trend Report', in ICSSR (ed.), *Survey of Research in Sociology and Social Anthropology*, Bombay, Popular Prakashan.

———, 2009, *Rural Life: Grass Roots Perspectives*, New Delhi, Concept Publishing Company.

Chauhan, B.R., and A. Satyanarayana (eds.), 2012, *Changing Village India*, Jaipur, Rawat Publications.

Chauhan, Ramesh K., and S.N. Ghosh, 2009, 'Himachal Pradesh Elections 2007: A Post-Poll Analysis', *Economic & Political Weekly*, Vol. 44, No. 6: 46–47.

Chhapla, Hemali, 2016, 'New Entrants in India's Middle Class: Drivers, Carpenters, Pani Puri Vendors', *Times of India*, 25 July.

Chhiber, Pradeep, and Rahul Verma, 2014, 'An Ideological Consolidation of the Right', *Economic & Political Weekly*, Vol. 49, No. 39: 50–56.

Chitnis, Suma, 1972, 'Education for Equality: The Case of Scheduled Caste in Higher Education', *Economic & Political Weekly*, Vol. 7, Nos. 31–33: 1675–1682.

Chowdhry, Prem, 2011, *Political Economy of Production and Reproduction: Caste, Custom, and Community in North India*, New Delhi, Oxford University Press.

Cohn, B.S., 1968, 'Notes on the History of the Study of Indian Society and Culture', in Milton Singer and B.S. Cohn (eds.), *Structure and Change in Indian Society*, Chicago, IL, Aldine Publishing Company.

Cohn, B.S., 1987, *An Anthropologist Among Historians and Other Essays*, Delhi, Oxford University Press.

Cohn, Bernard S., 1969, 'Structural Change in Indian Rural Society': 1596–1885, in R.E. Frykenberg (ed.), 1969, 53–121. Also reproduced in Bernard Cohn, 1987, 343–421.

Coomaraswamy, Anand, 1905, *Borrowed Plumes*, Colombo, Manasa.

———, 1909, *The Indian Craftsman*, London, Probsthain.

———, 1912, *Art and Swadeshi*, Madras, Ganesh.

———, 1956, *The Christian and the Oriental, or True Philosophy of Art*, in *Christian and Oriental Philosophy of Art*, New York, Doner.

Cox, Oliver Cromwell, 1948, *Caste, Class and Race: A Study in Social Dynamics*, New York, Doubleday and Co. Press.

———, 1987, *Race, Class and the World System: The Sociology of Oliver C. Cox*, New York, Monthly Review Press.

Coxon, A.P.M., and C.L. Jones (eds.), 1975, *Social Mobility*, H. Middlesex, England, Penguin Books.

D'Souza, Victor S., 1967, 'Caste and Class: A Reinterpretation', *Journal of Asian and African Studies*, Vol. 2, Nos. 3 & 4.

———, 1967, *Social Structure of a Planned City—Chandigarh*, New Delhi, Orient Longmans.

Dahrendorf, R., 1969, 'On the Origin of Inequality among Men', in Andre Beteille (ed.), *Social Inequality*, H. Middlesex, England, 16–44.

Damle, Y.B., 1968, 'Reference Group Theory with Regard to Mobility in Caste', in James Silverberg (ed.), *Social Mobility in the Caste System in India*, The Hague, Mouton Publishers.

Damodaran, Harish, 2008, *India's New Capital: Its Caste, Business and Industry in a Modern Nation*, New Delhi, Palgrave Macmillan.

Das, Arvind N., 1983, *Agrarian Unrest and Socio-Economic Change in Bihar, 1900–1980*, Delhi, Manohar.

Das, Gurcharan, 2000, *India Unbound: From Independence to the Global Information Age*, New Delhi, Penguin Books.

————, 2002, *The Elephant Paradigm, India Wrestles with Change*, New Delhi, Penguin Books, 187–203. Reprinted in 2012 by Penguin Books, New Delhi.

Das, Veena, 1982, *Structure and Cognition: Aspects of Hindu Caste and Ritual*, Delhi, Oxford University Press.

Dasgupta, Biplab, 1975, 'A Typology of Village Socio-economic Systems from Indian Village Studies', *Economic & Political Weekly*, Vol. 20, Nos. 33–35 (SN).

———— (ed.), 1978, *Villages Studies in the Third World*, Delhi, Hindustan Publishing House.

Davis, Kingsley, and Wilbert E. Moore, 1945, 'Some Principles of Stratification', *American Sociological Review*, Vol. 10, No. 2: 242–249.

De Vos, George, 1967, 'Psychology of Purity and Pollution as Related to Social Self-identity and Caste', in Anthony de Reuck and Julie Knight (eds.), *Caste and Race: Comparative Approaches*, London, J&A Churchill, 292–315.

Desai, A.R., 1975, *State and Society in India (Essays in Dissent)*, Bombay, Popular Prakashan.

————, 1981, 'Relevance of the Marxist Approach to the Study of Indian Society', *Sociological Bulletin*, Vol. 30, No. 1: 1–20.

Desai, I.P., 1964, *Some Aspects of Family in Mahuva*, Bombay, Asia Publishing House.

Desai, Sonalde, and Amaresh Dubey, 2011, 'Caste in 21st Century India: Competing Narratives', *Economic & Political Weekly*, Vol. 46, No. 1: 40–49.

Deshpande, Ashwini, 2011, *The Grammar of Caste*, New Delhi Oxford University Press.

Deshpande, Ashwini, and Smriti Sharma, 2013, 'Entrepreneurship of Survival? Caste and Gender of Small Business in India', *Economic & Political Weekly*, Vol. 48, No. 28: 38–49.

Deshpande, Rajeshwari, and Suhas Palshikar, 2008, 'Occupational Mobility: How Much Does Caste Matter?' *Economic & Political Weekly*, Vol. 43, No. 34: 61–70.

Deshpande, Satish, 1997, 'From Development to Adjustment: Economic Ideologies, the Middle Class and 50 years of Independence', *Review of Development and Change*, Vol. 2, No. 2: 49–58.

————, 2003, *Contemporary India: A Sociological View*, New Delhi, Penguin Books.

————, 2006, 'Exclusive Inequalities: Merit, Caste and Discrimination in Indian Higher Education Today', *Economic & Political Weekly*, Vol. 41, No. 24: 2438–2444.

Deshpande, Satish (ed.), 2014, *The Problem of Caste*, New Delhi, EPW/Orient Black Swan.

Dewey, John, 2011, *Democracy and Education: An Introduction to the Philosophy of Education* (2nd Indian Reprint), Delhi, Aakar Books.

Dhanagare, D.N., 1983, *Peasant Movements in India: 1920–1950*, New Delhi, Oxford University Press.

Dirks, N.B., 2002, *Castes of Mind: Colonialism and the Making of Modern India*, Princeton, Princeton University Press. Reprinted in 2003 by Permanent Black, New Delhi.

Dirks, Nicholas B. (ed.), 1992, *Colonialism and Culture*, Ann Arbor, 175–208.

Djurfeldt, Goran, and J. Lindberg, 1975, *Behind Poverty: The Social Formation of a Tamil Village*, London/New Delhi, Curzon Press/Oxford and IBH.

Djurfeldt, Goran, and Staffan Lindberg, 1976, *Pills Against Poverty*, New Delhi, Oxford and IBH Publishing Co.

Doniger, Wendy, and Martha C. Nussbaum, 2015, 'Introduction', in Wendy Doniger and Martha C. Nussbaum (eds.), *Pluralism and Democracy in India: Debating the Hindu Right*, New York, Oxford University Press, 1–17.

Dreze, Jean, and Amartya Sen, 2013, *An Uncertain Glory: India and its Contradictions*, London, Allen Lane, an imprint of Penguin Books, Chapter 5, 107–142.

Dube, S.C., 1955, *Indian Village*, London/New York, Routledge and Kegal Paul/Cornell University Press.

———, 1968, 'Caste Dominance and Factionalism', *Contributions to Indian Sociology*, New Series, No. 2: 58–81.

Dumont, Louis, and D.F. Pocock, 1957, 'Village Studies', *Contributions to Indian Sociology*, No. 1: 7–64.

———, 1960, 'For a Sociology of India: A Rejoinder to Dr. Bailey', *Contributions to Indian Sociology*, No. 4: 82–89.

———, 1964, 'Nationalism and Communalism', *Contributions to Indian Sociology*, No. VII.

———, 1966a, 'A Fundamental Problem in the Sociology of Caste', *Contributions to Indian Sociology*, No. 9: 17–32.

———, 1966b, 'The Village Community from Munro to Maine', *Contributions to Indian Sociology*, No. IX.

———, 1967, 'Caste: A Phenomenon of Social Structure or an Aspect of Indian Culture', in Anthony de Reuck and Julie Knight (eds.), *Caste and Race: Comparative Approaches*, London, J&A Churchill, pp. 28–38.

———, 1970a, *Homo Hierarchicus*, London, Paladin Granda Publishing Ltd.

———, 1970b, '"The Village Community" from Munro to Maine', in Louis Dumont (ed.), *Religion/Politics and History and India*, Paris/The Hague, Mouton Publishers.

———, 1986, *Essays on Individualism: Modern Ideology in Anthropological Perspective*, Chicago, University of Chicago Press.

Dumont, L., 1987, 'On Individual and Equality', *Current Anthropology*, Vol. 5, No. 5: 669–672.

Dumont, L., 1999, (first published in 1970), *Homo Hierarchicus*, New Delhi, Oxford India Paperback.

Dumont, Louis, and D.F. Pocock, 2006, 'On Individualism and Equality', in R.S. Khare (ed.), *Caste, Hierarchy, and Individualism*, New Delhi, Oxford University Press, 225–230.

Durkheim, Emile, 1956, *Education and Sociology* (translated with an introduction by S.D. Fax), New York, The Free Press.

———, 1977, *The Evolution of Educational Thought: Lectures on the Formation and Development of Secondary Education in France* (translated by Peter Collins), London, Routledge & Kegan Paul.

Embree, Ainblie T., 1969, 'Landholding in India and British Institutions', in R.E. Frydenberg (ed.), *Land Control and Social Structure in Indian History* (2nd edition), New Delhi, Manohar Publications, 33–52.

———, 2013, 'Indian Civilization and Regional Cultures: The Two Realities', in Sudha Pai (ed.), *Handbook of Politics in Indian States (Regions, Parties, and Economic Reforms)*, New Delhi, Oxford University Press, 23–39.

Engel, Susan, and Brian Martin, 2015, 'Challenging Economic Inequality: Tactics and Strategies', *Economic & Political Weekly*, Vol. 50, No. 49: 42–48.

Entwistle, Horold, 1979, Antoni Gramsci: Conservative Schooling for Radical Politics, London, Routledge & Kegan Paul.

Epstein, T. Scarlett, 1962, *Economic Development and Social Change in South India*, Manchester/London, Manchester University Press/Oxford University Press.

Fanon, Frantz, 1963, *The Wretched of the Earth* (preface by Jean-Paul Sartre and translated by Constance Forrington), Harmondsworth, Penguin Books.

Fernandes, Leela, 2006, *India's New Middle Class: Democratic Politics in an Era of Economic Reform*, Minneapolis, University of Minneapolis Press. Reprinted in 2006 by Oxford University Press, New Delhi.

Fernandes, Sharon, 2016, 'When Caste Lines are Drawn Literally', *Times of India*, 7 February.

Firth, Raymond, 1951a, *Elements of Social Organization*, London, C.A. Watts.

———, 1951b, *Malayan Fisherman: Their Peasant Economy*, Routledge and Kegan Paul, cited from T. Shanin (ed.), 1971, 332–335.

Fletcher, Ronald, 2015, 'Vilfredo Pareto: The Social System—An Equilibrium of Psychological Forces', in *The Making of Sociology*, Vol. 2, Jaipur, Rawat Publications, 577–636.

Foster, G.M., 1965, 'Peasant Society and the Image of Limited Good', *American Anthropologist*, Vol. 2: 293–315.

———, 1967, 'Peasant Character and Personality', in J.M. Potter, M.N. Diaz and G.M. Foster (eds.), *Peasant Society: A Reader*, Little, Brown.

Foucault, Michel, and Jay Miskowiec, 1986, 'Of Other Spaces', *Diacritics*, Vol. 16, No. 1: 22–27.

Frankel, Z. Hasan, R. Bhargava, and B. Arova, 2004, 'The Elusive Mandate of 2004', *Economic & Political Weekly*, Vol. 39, No. 51: 5383–5398.

Freire, Paulo, 1973, *Pedagogy of the Oppressed (Reprint)*, Penguin Books.

Frenz, Margret, and Georg Berkemer, 2006, 'Colleges and Kings: Higher Education Under Direct and Indirect Rule', *Economic & Political Weekly*, Vol. 41, No. 13: 1261–1268.

Frykenberg, Robert Eric, 1969, 'Introduction' (viii–xx) and 'Village Strength in South India' (247–268) in R.E. Frykenberg (ed.), Land Control and Social, Structure in Indian History, Regents of the University of Wisconsin.

Furnivall, J.S., 1948, *Colonial Policy and Practice: A Comparative Study of Burma, Netherlands and India*, London, Cambridge University Press.

Gandhi, M.K., 1962, *Village Swaraj*, Ahmedabad, Navjivan Publishing House.

Gandhi, Rajmohan, 2015, 'Independence and Social Justice: The Ambedkar–Gandhi Debate', *Economic & Political Weekly*, Vol. 50, No. 15: 35–44.

Gardner, Peter M., 1968, 'Dominance in India: A Reappraisal', *Contributions to Indian Sociology*, New Series, No. 2: 83–97.

Geertz, Clifford, 1973, *The Interpretation of Cultures*, The USA, Basic Books, A Division of Harper Collins Publishers.

Gerth, H.H., and C.W. Mills (eds.), 1970, *From Max Weber: Essays in Sociology*, London, Routledge and Kegan Paul, 46–50.

Ghurye, G.S., 1932, *Caste and Race in India*, London, Kegan Paul & Co.

———, 1950, *Caste and Class in India*, Bombay, Popular Book Depot.

Goldthorpe, John H., 1987, *Social Mobility and Class Structure in Modern Britain*, Oxford, Clarendon Press.

Goode, William J., 1963, *World Revolution and Family Patterns*, London, Free Press of Glencoe.

———, 1964, *The Family*, Foundations of Modern Sociology Series, Englewood Cliffs, NJ, Prentice-Hall.

Gore, M.S., 1982, *Education and Modernization in India*, Jaipur, Rawat Publications.

———, 1994, *Indian Education: Structure and Process*, Jaipur and New Delhi, Rawat Publications.

———, 2002, *Unity in Diversity: The Indian Experience in Nation Building*, Jaipur, Rawat Publications.

Gough, Kathleen E., 1955, 'The Social Structure of a Tanjore Village', in McKim Marriott (ed.), *Village India. Studies in the Little Community*, Berkeley, University of California Press.

———, 1960, 'Caste in a Tanjore Village', in E.R. Leach (ed.), *Aspects of Caste in South India, Ceylon and North–West Pakistan*, London, Cambridge University Press, 11–60.

———, 1980, 'Modes of Production in Southern India', *Economic & Political Weekly*, Vol. 15, Nos. 5, 6 & 7: 337–364.

Gould, Harold A., 1967, 'Priest and Contra-Priest: A Structural Analysis of Jajmani Relations in the Hindu Plains and the Nilgiri Hills', *Contributions to Indian Sociology* (New Series), No. 1: 26–55.

———, 1988, *Caste Adaptation in Modernizing Indian Society*, New Delhi, Chanakya Publications.

Gramsci, Antonio, 1957, *The Modern Prince and Other Essays*, trans. Louis Marks, London, Laurence and Wishart.

Guha, Ramchandra, 2008, *India: After Gandhi,* New Delhi, Picador, 605–719.

Guha, Ranjit, 1982, *Subaltern Studies: Writings on South Asian History and Society* (5 Volumes), New Delhi, Oxford University Press. In all, there are 13 Volumes of the subaltern Studies, edited by different scholars.

———, 1983, *Elementary Aspects of Peasant Insurgency in Colonial India,* New Delhi, Oxford University Press.

———, 1988, 'The Prose of Counter Insurgency', in R. Guha and G.C. Spivak (eds.), *Selected Subaltern Studies,* New York, Oxford University Press, 123–131.

——— (ed.), 1982, *Subaltern Studies I, Writings on South Asian History and Society,* Delhi: Oxford University Press. (Articles are by Ranjit Guha, Partha Chatterjee, Shahid Amin, David Arnold, Gyan Prakash and David Hardiman).

———, 1983, *Subaltern Studies II, Writings on South Asian History and Society.* Delhi: Oxford University Press. (Articles are by Ranjit Guha, Gautam Bhadra, Gyar Pandy, Stephen Hennington, Arvind N. Das, N.K. Chandra, Dipesh Chakrabarty and Parth Chatterjee).

———, 1984, *Subaltern Studies III, Writings on South Asian History and Society.* Delhi: Oxford University Press. (Articles are by Shahid Amin, David Arnold, Dipesh Chakrabarty, Partha Chatterjee, David Hardiman, Gyanendra Pandey and Sumit Sarkar).

———, 1985, *Subaltern Studies IV, Writings on South Asian History and Society.* Delhi: Oxford University Press. (Articles are by David Aronld, Ramachandra Guha, Swapan Dasgupta, Tanika Sarkar, David Hardiman, Gautam Bhadra, Bernard S. Cohn, Gayatri Chakravorty Spivak and Dipesh Chakrabarty).

Gupta, Dipankar, 1984, 'Continuous Hierarchies and Discrete Castes', *Economic & Political Weekly,* Vol. 19, Nos. 46, 47 and 48.

———, 1988, Country-Town Nexus and Agrarian Mobilisation: Bhartiya Kisan Union as an Instance, *Economic & Political Weekly,* Vol. 23, No. 51: 2688–2696.

——— (ed.), 1991, *Social Stratification,* New Delhi, Oxford University Press.

———, 1992, 'Peasant Unionism in Uttar Pradesh: Against the Rural Mentality Thesis', *Journal of Contemporary Asia,* Vol. 22, No. 2.

———, 2000, *Interrogating Caste: Understanding Hierarchy and Difference in Indian Society,* New Delhi, Penguin Books.

———, 2004, 'Caste in Question: Identity of Hierarchy', *Contributions to Indian Sociology, Occasional Studies—12,* New Delhi, SAGE.

———, 2005a, 'Caste Today: The Relevance of the Phenomenological Approach', *India International Centre Quarterly,* Vol. 32, No. 1.

———, 2005b, 'Caste and Politics: Identity Over System', *Annual Review of Anthropology,* Vol. 34: 409–427.

———, 2005c, 'Wither the Indian Village: Culture and Agriculture in Rural India', *Economic & Political Weekly,* Vol. 40, No. 8: 751–758.

———, 2006, 'Continuous Hierarchicus and Discrete Castes', in R.S. Khare (ed.), *Caste, Hierarchy, and Individualism,* New Delhi, Oxford University Press, 120–131.

————, 2009, *The Caged Phoenix: Can India Fly?* New Delhi, Penguin/Viking/ Oxford University Press.

————, 2012, 'Rise of the Dalit Millionaire: A Low Intensity Spectacle', *Economic & Political Weekly*, Vol. 47, No. 50: 41–49.

Guru, Gopal, 2009, 'Archaeology of Untouchability', *Economic & Political Weekly*, Vol. 44, No. 37: 49–56.

Guru, Gopal, and S. Sarukkai. 2004, 'Publicly Talking about Caste: A Report on Jatisamvada in Prajavani', *Economic & Political Weekly*, Vol. 49, No. 1.

Habermas, Jurgen, 1991, *The Structural Transformation of the Public Sphere: An Inquiry into a Category of Bourgeois Society*, The MIT Press, quoted from Maitrayee Chaudhuri, op.cit.

Habib, Irfan, 1963, *Agrarian Systems of Mughal India*, Bombay, Asia Publishers.

————, 1974, 'Social Distribution of Landed Property in the Pre-British India: A Historical Survey', in R.S. Sharma (ed.), *Indian Society: Historical Probings*, New Delhi, People's Publishing House, 264–316.

————, 1995, *Essays in Indian History, Towards a Marxist Perception*, New Delhi, Tulika.

Haldipur, R.N., 1974, 'Sociology of Community Development and Panchayati Raj (Part I and II)', in *A Survey of Research in Sociology and Social Anthropology*, Vol. II, (edited by ICSSR), Bombay, Popular Prakashan.

Hardiman, David, 1987, *The Bhils and Sahukars in Eastern Gujarat*, *Subaltern Studies V*, Ranjit Guha (ed.). Delhi: Oxford University Press, 1–54.

————, 2000, *Feeding the Bania: Peasants and Usurers in Western India.* New Delhi: Oxford University Press.

Hardiman, Gautam Bhadra, 1997, *Dominance without Hegemony: History and Power in Colonial India.* Cambridge, Massachusetts, Harvard University Press.

————, 2009, *The Small Voice of History*, edited and with an introduction by Partha Chatterjee, Ranikhet, Permanent Black.

Hardiman, Gautam Bhadra (ed.), 1987, *Subaltern Studies V, Writings on South Asian History and Society.* Delhi: Oxford University Press. (Articles are by David Hardiman, David Arnold, Gayatri Chakravorty Spivak, Ranjit Guha, Shahid Amin, Asok Sen, Ajit K. Chaudhary, and Mahasweta Devi).

————, 1992, *Subaltern Studies VI, Writings on South Asian History and Society.* Delhi: Oxford University Press. (Articles are by Sumit Sarkar, Gautam Bhadra, Juile Stephens, Susie Tharu, Gyanendra Pandey, Partha Chatterjee, Ranjit Guha and Veena Das).

————, 1997, *A Subaltern Studies Reader 1986–1995*, Minneapolis, University of Minnesota Press.

Harper, E.B., 1968, 'Social Consequences of an 'Unsuccessful' Low Caste Movement', in James Silverberg (ed.), *Social Mobility in the Caste System in India*, The Hague, Mouton Publishers.

Harrison, Selig, 1960, *India, The Most Dangerous Decades*, Princeton, Princeton University Press.

Harriss, John, 1982, *Capitalism and Peasant Forming, Agrarian Structure and Ideology in Northern Tamil Nadu*, Bombay/Delhi, Oxford University Press.

Harriss-White, Barbara, 2004, *India Working, Essays on Society and Economy*, New Delhi, Cambridge University Press.

Hasan, Zoya, 2009, *Politics of Inclusion: Castes, Minorities and Affirmative Action*, New Delhi, Oxford University Press.

Haynes, Jeffrey, 2015, *Development Studies* (reprint), Cambridge, Polity Press, 106.

Hazari, R.K., 1966, *The Corporate Private Concentration: Ownership and Control*, Bombay, Asia Publishing House.

Hobsbawm, Eric, 1960, 'Por Lo Studio Delle Classi subalterni', *Soceita*, 16, quoted from *Mapping Subaltern Studies and the Postcolonial*, edited by Vinayak Chaturvedi, VII–XIX.

———, 1971, *Primitive Rebels*, Manchester: Manchester University Press.

Hocart, A.M., 1950, *Caste: A Comparative Study*, New York/London, Russel & Russell/Mathew & Co.

Hohendahl, Peter Uwe, 2005, 'The Transnational University and the Global Public Sphere', in Max Pensky (ed.), *Globalising Critical Theory*, Lanhan, Rowman and Littlefield Publications, 89–112.

Homans, George C., 1964, 'Bringing Man Back In', *American Sociological Review*, December.

Horowitz, Irving Louis, 1967, 'Mainliness and Marginals: The Human Shape of Sociological Theory', in Llewellyn Gross (ed.), *Sociological Theory: Inquiries And Paradigms*, New York, Harper & Row, 358–383.

Hosan, S. Nurul, 1969, 'Zamindars under the Mughals', in R.E. Frykenberg (ed.), 1969, 17–31.

Hutton, J.H., 1963, *Caste in India: Its Nature, Functions and Origin* (first published in 1946), New Delhi/Bombay, Oxford University Press.

Inden, Ronald, 1990, *Imagining India*, New Delhi, Oxford University Press.

India Rural Development Report, 2012–13, 2013, New Delhi, Orient Blackswan.

Iyer, Lakshmi, Tarun Khanna, and Ashutosh Varshney, 2013, 'Caste and Entrepreneurship in India', *Economic & Political Weekly*, Vol. 48, No. 6: 52–56.

Jacob, T.G., and P. Bandhu, 2009, *Reflections on the Caste Question: The Dalit Situation in South India*, Ootacamund, Odyssey.

Jafferelot, Christophe, 2010, Religion, Caste & Politics in India, New Delhi, Primus Books, 583–603.

Jaiswal, Suvira, 1998, *Caste: Origin, Function and Dimensions of Change*, Delhi, Manohar Publications.

Jal, Murzban, 2014, 'Asiatic Mode of Production, Caste and the Indian Left', *Economic & Political Weekly*, Vol. 49, No. 19: 41–49.

Jannuzi, F.T., 1974, *Agrarian Crisis in India: The Case of Bihar*, New Delhi, Sangam Books.

Jayaraj, D., 2013, 'Family Migration in India: 'Push' or 'Pull' or Both or What?' *Economic & Political Weekly*, Vol. 48, No. 42: 44–52.

Jayaram, N., 1977, 'Higher Education as a Statues Stabiliser: Students in Bangalore', *Contributions to Indian Sociology* (New Series), Vol. 2, No. 1: 169–91.

Jayaram, N., 1990, *Sociology of Education in India*, Jaipur, Rawat Publications.

————, 2013, 'The Decline of the University as a Public Institution in India', in Ishwar Modi (ed.), op. cit., 23–40.

Jha, P.S., 1980, *The Political Economy of Stagnation*, Delhi, Oxford University Press.

Jodhka, Surinder S., 2003, 'Agrarian Structures and Their Transformations', in Veena Das (ed.), *The Oxford Companion to Sociology and Social Anthropology*, New Delhi, Oxford University Press, Vol. 2, 1213–1242.

————, S., 2010, 'Dalits in Business: Self-Employed Scheduled Castes in North-West India', *Economic & Political Weekly*, Vol. 45, No. 11: 41–48.

————, 2015, *Caste in Contemporary India*, New Delhi, Routledge.

Jodhka, Surinder S., and Aseem Prakash, 2016, *The Indian Middle Class*, New Delhi, Oxford University Press.

Jodhka, Surinder S., and Tanvi Sirari, 2014, Rural and Agrarian Studies in India: A Survey of Contemporary Trends, in Yogendra Singh (ed.), *Indian Sociology*, Vol. I, New Delhi, Oxford University Press.

Joshi, Dhananjai, and Praveen Rai, 2009, 'Chhattisgarh 2008: Defeating Anti-Incumbency', *Economic & Political Weekly*, Vol. 44, No. 6: 38–41.

Joshi, P.C., 1975, *Land Reforms in India*, Bombay, Allied Publishers.

Joshi, Sanjay, 2010, *The Middle Class in Colonial India*, New Delhi, Oxford University Press.

Kak, Krishen, 2003, 'Culture Genocide?' *Seminar*, No. 523, *Celebrating Craft, a symposium on the State of Handicrafts*, 42–48.

Kalecki, M., 1972, *Essays on the Economic Growth of the Socialist and the Mixed Economy*, London, Unwin.

Kane, P.V., 1930–1962, *History of Dharmasastra*, 5 Vols., Poona, Bhandarka Oriental Research Institute.

————, 1990 (1930), *History of Dharmashastra*, Volumes I–V, Pune, Bhandarkar Oriental Research Institute.

Kapadia, K.M., 1955, *Marriage and Family in India*, London, Oxford University Press.

Kapoor, Radhika, 2013, 'Inequality Matters', *Economic & Political Weekly*, Vol. 48, No. 2: 58–65.

Kapur, Devesh et al., 2010, 'The Middle Class in India: A Social Formation or a Political Actor?' *Political Power and Social Theory*, Vol. 21: 215–240.

Karve, Iravati, 1953 (1965), *Kinship Organisation in India*, Bombay, Asia Publishing House.

Kaur, Ravinder, 2014, 'The "Emerging" Middle Class: Role in the 2014 General Elections', *Economic & Political Weekly*, Vol. 49, Nos. 26 & 27: 15–19.

Kessinger, Tom G., 1983, 'Regional Economy (1757–1857, North India)', in Dharma Kumar (ed.), *The Cambridge Economic History of India,* Vol. II, C. 1757–2003, 242–270.

Ketkar, S.V., 1909, *History of Caste in India*, Ithaca, New York, Cornell University Press.

Khosla, Rishab, 2011, 'Caste, Politics and Public Good Distribution in India: Evidence from NREGS in Andhra Pradesh', *Economic & Political Weekly*, Vol. 46, No. 12: 63–69.

Kolenda, Pauline, 1978, *Caste in Contemporary India: Beyond Organic Solidarity*, California, Benjamin Dimmings Publishing Co.

————, 1984, *Caste in Contemporary India* (Indian edition), Jaipur, Rawat Publications.

————, 1989, 'Micro Ideology and Micro Utopia in Khalapur: Changes in the Discourse on Caste Over Thirty Years', *Economic & Political Weekly*, Vol. 24, No. 2: 1833–1838.

————, 2003, *Caste, Marriage and Inequality, Essays on North and South India*, Jaipur and New Delhi, Rawat Publications.

Kosambi, D.D., 1958, *An Introduction to the Study of Indian History*, Bombay, Popular Book Depot.

————, 2002, 'Combined Methods in Indology', in B. Cattopadhyaya (ed.), *Combined Methods in Indology and Other Writings*, Delhi, Oxford University Press. See also 'D.D. Kosambi: A Special Issue', *Economic & Political Weekly*, July 26, 2008, Vol. XLIII, No. 30: 34–108; and A.J. Syed (ed.) 1985, D.D. Kosambi, Kosambi on History and Society and Problems of Interpretation, Bombay, University of Bombay.

Kothari, D.S., 1966, *Report of the Education Commission, 1964–66, under the Chairmanship of D.S. Kothari*, New Delhi, Government of India.

Kothari, Rajni (ed.), 1975, *Caste in Indian Politics*, Delhi, Orient Longman.

Kriedte, Peter, Hans Medick, and Jurgen Schlumbohm, 1981, *Industrialization before Industrialization (Rural Industry in the Genesis of Capitalism)*, Cambridge, Cambridge University Press.

Krishna, Anirudh, 2013, 'Making it in India: Examining Social Mobility in Three Walks of Life', *Economic & Political Weekly*, Vol. 48, No. 49: 38–49.

Krishna, Anirudh, and & Devendra Bajpai, 2015, 'Layers in Globalising Society and the New Middle Class in India: Trends, Distribution and Prospects, *Economic & Political Weekly*, Vol. 50, No. 5: 69–77.

Kulke, E., 1983, 'The Problems of the Educated Middle Class Harijans', in John P. Neelsen (ed.), *Social Inequality and Political Structures*, New Delhi, Manohar Publications.

Kumar, Ajay, 2012, 'Khap Panchayats: A Socio-historical Overview', *Economic & Political Weekly*, Vol. 47, No. 4: 59–64.

Kumar, Ajit, 2004, 'Politics in Three Villages: A Study in Nagpur District', *Economic & Political Weekly*, Vol. 39, No. 3: 228–233.

Kumar, Arun, 2001, *Rewriting Language of Politics: Kisans in Colonial Bihar*. Delhi: Manohar Publications.

Kumar, Arvind and Aryan Guha, 2014, 'Political Future of Caste in West Bengal', *Economic & Political Weekly*, Vol. 49, No: pp. 73–74.

Kumar, Nita, 1995, *The Artisans of Banaras: Popular Culture and Identity*, 1880–1986 (The Indian Edition), New Delhi, Orient Longman.

Kumar, Rajnish, Satendra Kumar, and Arup Mitra, 2009, 'Social and Economic Inequalities: Contemporary Significance of Caste in India', *Economic & Political Weekly*, Vol. 44, No. 50: 55–63.

Kumar, Sanjay, 2009, 'Delhi Assembly Elections: 2008', *Economic & Political Weekly*, Vol. 44, No. 6: 27–30.

Kumar, Sanjay, Anthony Heath, and Oliver Heath, 2002a, 'Changing Patterns of Social Mobility', *Economic & Political Weekly*, Vol. 37, No. 4: 4091– 4096. See also Anthony Heath, 1981, *Social Mobility*, London, Fontana.

———, 2002b, 'Determinants of Social Mobility in India', *Economic & Political Weekly*, Vol. 37, No. 29: 2983–2987.

Lal, S.K. (ed.), 1982, *Sociological Perspectives of Land Reforms*, New Delhi, Agricole Publishing Academy.

———, 1988, *Readings in the Sociology of Professions*, New Delhi, Gian Publishing House.

Lanjouw, Peter, and Abusaleh Shariff, 2004, 'Rural Non-Farm Employment in India: Access, Incomes and Poverty Impact', *Economic & Political Weekly*, Vol. 34, No. 4: 4429–4445.

Leach, E.R., 1960, 'Introduction: What Should We Mean by Caste?' in E.R. Leach (ed.), *Aspects of Caste in South India, Ceylon and North-West Pakistan*, London, Cambridge University Press, 1–10.

———, 1967, 'Caste, Class and Slavery: The Taxonomic Problem', in Anthony de Reuck and Julie Knight (eds.), *Caste and Race: Comparative Approaches*, London, J&A Churchill.

Leach, Edmund, 1971, '"Espirit" in Homo Hierarchicus', *Contributions to Indian Sociology*, No. V: 1–81.

Lewis, Oscar, 1958, *Village Life in Northern India*, Urbana, University of Illinois Press.

Lieten, G.K., 2003, *Power, Politics and Rural Development: Essays on India*, New Delhi, Manohar.

Lin, S.G., 1980, 'Theory of a Dual Mode of Production in Post-Colonial India', *Economic & Political Weekly*, Vol. 15, Nos. 10 and 11.

Lipton, Michael, 1977, *Why Poor People Stay Poor: A Study of Urban Bias in World Development*, London, Temple Smith.

———, 1993, Land Reforms as Commenced Business: The Evidence Against Stoppage, *World Development*, Vol. 11, No. 4: 641–657.

Lloyd I. Rudolph, and Susanne Hoeber Rudolph, 2008, *Explaining Indian Democracy, A Fifty-Year Perspective*, 1956–2006, Vol. II, New Delhi, Oxford University Press, 234–246.

Lodha, Sanjay, 2009, 'Rajasthan: Dissatisfaction and a Poor Campaign Defeat BJP', *Economic & Political Weekly*, Vol. 44, No. 6: 23–26.

Luden, David, 2001, *Reading Subaltern Studies: Critical History, Contested Meaning and the Globalization of South Asia*. Delhi: Permanent Black.

Lynch, Owen, 1968, 'The Politics of Untouchability: A Case from Agra, India', in M. Singer and B.S. Cohn (eds.), *Structure and Change in Indian Society*, Chicago, Aldine Publishing Company.

Madan, T.N., 1971a, 'Introduction', *Contributions to India Sociology*, No. V.

———, 1971b, 'On Understanding Caste', *Economic & Political Weekly*, Vol. 6, No. 34.

Madan, Vandana, 2002, 'Introduction', in Vandana Madan (ed.), *The Village in India*, New Delhi, Oxford University Press.

———— (ed.), 2004, *The Village in India* (paperback), Delhi, Oxford University Press.

Mahadevia, D., 2001, 'Informalisation of Employment and Poverty in Ahmedabad', in A. Kundu and A. N. Sharma (eds), *Informal Sector in India: Perspectives and Policies*, New Delhi, Institute for Human Development & Institute of Applied Manpower Research, 142–159.

Mahipal, 2005, 'Role of Social Capital in Haryana', *Economic & Political Weekly*, Vol. 40, No. 9: 822–825.

Maine, Henry Sumner, 1861, *Ancient Law*, London, John Murray.

————, 1871, *Village Communities in the East and West*, London, John Murray.

Majumdar, D.N., 1958, *Caste and Communication in an Indian Village*, Delhi, Asia Publishing House.

Majumdar, D.N. (ed.), 1955, *Rural Profiles*, Lucknow, Ethnographic and Folk – Culture Society.

Mamidipudi, Annapurna, Syamasundari B., and Wiebe Bijker, 2012, 'Mobilising Discourses: Handloom as Sustainable Socio-Technology', *Economic & Political Weekly*, Vol. 47, No. 25: 41–51.

Mandelbaum, David G., 1968, 'Family, Jati, Village', in Milton Singer and B.S. Cohn (eds.), *Structure and Change in Indian Society*, Chicago, Aldine Publishing Company.

————, 1970, *Society in India: Continuity and Change*, Vols. I & II, Berkeley, University of California Press.

————, 1972, *Society in India* (2 Volumes), Bombay, Popular Prakashan.

Mander, Harsh, 2008, Living with Hunger: Deprivation among the Aged, Single Women and People with Disability, *Economic & Political Weekly*, Vol. 43, No. 17: 87–98.

Maquet, J., 1961, *The Premise of Inequality in Ruanda*, London, Oxford University Press.

Marriott, McKim, 1955, 'Little Communities in an Indigenous Civilisation', in McKim Marrott (ed.), *Village India: Studies in the Little Community*, Berkeley, University of California Press.

————, 1959, 'Interactional and attributional Theories of Caste Ranking', *Man in India*, Vol. 34, No. 2: 92–107.

————, 1965, 'Caste Ranking and Community Structure in Five Regions of India and Pakistan', Poona, Deccan College, Poona.

————, 1968, 'Caste Ranking and Food Transactions: A Matrix Analysis', in Milton Singer and B.S. Cohn (eds.), *Structure and Change in Indian Society*, New York, Aldine Publishing Co.

Marriott, McKim, 1968b, 'Multiple Reference in Indian Caste Systems', in James Silverberg (ed.), *Social Mobility in the Caste System in India*, The Hague, Mouton Publishers.

Marriott, McKim, 1976, 'Hindu Transactions: Diversity without Dualism', in Bruce Kapferer (ed.), *Transaction and Meaning: Directions in the Anthropology of Exchange and Symbolic Behaviour*, Philadelphia, ISHI.

————, 1989, *India Through Hindu Categories*, New Delhi, SAGE.

Marriott, McKim (ed.), 1955b, *Village India: Studies in the Little Community*, Berkeley, University of California Press.

Marriott, McKim 1959, 'Interactional and Attributional Theories of Caste Ranking', *Man in India*, Vol. 39, No. 2: 92–107.

Marriott, McKim, and Ronald Inden, 1977, 'Towards an Ethno Sociology of South Asian Caste Systems', in Kenneth David (ed.), *The New Wind: Changing Identities in South Asia*, The Hague, Mouton.

Martin, Nicolas, 2015, 'Rural Elites and the Limits of Scheduled Caste Assertiveness in Rural Malwa, Punjab'. *Economic & Political Weekly*, Vol. 50, No. 52: 37–44.

Marx, Karl, 1954, *Capital*, Volume I, Moscow, Progress Publishers.

————, 1964a, *Pre-Capitalist Economic Formations*, London, Lowrence and Wishwart.

————, 1964b, *The German Ideology*, Moscow, Progress Publishers.

————, 1975, *Manifesto of the Communist Party*, Moscow, Progress Publishers.

Mathew, George, 2003, 'Panchayati Raj Institutions and Human Rights in India', *Economic & Political Weekly*, Vol. 38, No. 2: 155–162.

Mathur, Kuldeep, 2013, *Panchayati Raj*, Oxford India Short Introductions, Delhi, Oxford University Press.

Mayaram, Shail, M.S.S. Pandian, and Ajay Skaria (eds.), 2005, *Subaltern Studies XII, Muslims, Dalits, and the Fabrications of History*. Delhi: Permanent Black. (Articles are by Shahid Amin, M.T. Ansari, Faisal Fatehali Devji, Milind Wakankar, Anupama Rao, Preveena Kodoth, and Rashmi Dube Bhatnagar, Renu Dube and Reena Dube).

Mayer, Adrian C., 1960, *Caste and Kinship in Central India*, Berkeley, University of California Press.

Medick, Hans, 1981, 'The Proto-Industrial Family Economy', in P. Kriedte, Hans Medick and Jurgen Schlumbohm, *Industrialization before Industrialization (Rural Industry in the Genesis of Capitalism)*, Cambridge, Cambridge University Press, 38–73.

Mehrotra, Nilika, 2011, 'Picture of Haryanvi Society', Review of Prem Chowdhry's book (2011), op. cit., *Economic & Political Weekly*, Vol. 46, No. 28: 36–37.

Mehrotra, Santosh 2006, 'Well-Being and Caste in Uttar Pradesh: Why UP is Not Like Tamil Nadu', *Economic & Political Weekly*, Vol. 41, No. 40: 4261–4271.

Mehta, Asoka, 1978, *Report of the Committee on Panchayati Raj Institutions*, New Delhi, Ministry of Agriculture and Irrigation, Government of India.

Mehta, Balvantray, 1957, *Report of the Team for the Study of Community Projects and National Extension Service*, Vol. I, New Delhi, Planning Commission, Government of India.

Mehta, Deepak, 1992, 'The Semitics of Wearing: A case Study', *Contributions to Indian Sociology*, Vol. 26, No. 1: 77–113.

Meillassoux, Claude, 1973, 'Are There Castes in India?' *Economy and Society*, Vol. 3, No. 1: 89–111.

Mencher, Joan P., 1974, 'Conflicts and Contradictions in the Green Revolution: The Case of Tamil Nadu', *Economic & Political Weekly*, Vol. 9, Nos. 6, 7 and 8: 309–323.

———, 1991, 'The Caste System Upside Down', in Dipankar Gupta (ed.), *Social Stratification*, Delhi, Oxford University Press.

Mendelsohn, O., 1986, '"A Harijan Elite?" The Lives of Some Untouchable Politicians', *Economic & Political Weekly*, Vol. 21, No. 12: 501–509.

Metcalf, Thomas R., 1979, *Land, Landlords, and the British Raj: Northern India in the Nineteenth Century*, Cambridge, Cambridge University Press.

Mines, Mattison, 1984, *The Warrior Merchants: Textiles, Trade and Territory in South India*, Cambridge, Cambridge University Press.

Misra, B.B., 1961 (1983), *The Indian Middle Classes: Their Growth in Modern Times* (2nd impression, paperback), New Delhi, Oxford University Press.

Modak, Savita, 2006, 'Weaving Customers' Dreams', *Economic & Political Weekly*, Vol. 41, No. 31: 5367–5368. See also other articles in this issue, 3369–3398.

Mohanty, Mritiunjay, 2006, 'Social Inequality, Labour Market Dynamics and Reservation', *Economic &Political Weekly*, Vol. 41, No. 35: 3777–3789.

Moore, Barrington, 1966, *Social Origins of Dictatorship and Democracy (Land and Peasant in the Making of the Modern World)*, H. Middlesex, Penguin Books.

Mooreland, W.H., 1920, *India at the Death of Akbar*, London. Cited from B. Moore, op. cit., Chapter 6.

———, 1929, *The Agrarian System of Moslem India*, Cambridge, Cambridge University Press.

Morgan, D.H.J., 1975, *Social Theory and the Family*, London, Routledge and Kegan Paul.

Morton, Klass, 1980, *Caste: The Emergence of the South Asian Social System*, New Delhi, Manohar Publications.

Mukerji, D.P., 1942 (1948), *Modern Indian Culture: A Sociological Study* (2nd edition), Hind Kitabs (reprinted as Indian Culture: A Sociological Study, New Delhi, Rupa & Co., 2002).

———, 2002 (1958), *Diversities: Essays in Economics, Sociology and Other Social Sciences*, New Delhi, Manak Publications, Chapter 4, 28–76.

———, 2004 (1932), *Personality and the Social Sciences*, Kolkata, Rupa & Co.

Mukherjee, Ramkrishna, 1957a, *Six Villages of Bengal: A Socio-Economic Survey*, Calcutta, Asiatic Society of Bengal.

———, 1957b, *The Dynamics of a Rural Society*, Berlin, Academie-Verlag.

Munro, T., 1886, *Writings of Sir Thomas Munro*, Madras, Higginbotham & Co., cited from Robert Eric Frykenberg (ed.), 1969, *Land Control and Social, Structure in Indian History*, New Delhi, Manohar, 247–267.

Myrdal, Gunnar, 1968, *Asian Drama*, Vol. I, New Harmondsworth, Penguin Books.

Nadel, S.F., 1954, 'Caste and Government in Primitive Society', *Journal of the Anthropological Society of Bombay*, Vol. 8 (cited from de Reuck and Knight (eds.) op.cit.)

Nadkarni, M.V., 2003, 'Is Caste System Intrinsic to Hinduism? Demolishing a Myth', *Economic & Political Weekly*, Vol. 38, No. 45: 4783–4793.

Narain, Iqbal, and P.C. Mathur, 1990, 'The Thousand Year Raj: Regional Isolation and Rajput Hinduism in Rajasthan before and after 1947', in Francine R. Frankel and M.S.A. Rao (eds.), *Dominance and State Power in Modern India: Decline of A Social Order*, Vol. II, Delhi, Oxford University Press, 1–58.

Natrajan, Balmuri, 2013, 'Punctuated Solidarities: Caste and Left Politics', *Economic & Political Weekly*, Vol. 48, No. 6.

Navlakha, Suren, 1989, *Elite and Social Change: A Study of Elite Formation in India*, New Delhi, SAGE.

Nayyar, Deepak, 2013, 'Globalization: What Does It Mean for Higher Education'? In J.B.G. Tilak (ed.), *Higher Education in India: In Search of Equality, Quality and Quantity*, New Delhi, Orient BlackSwan, 461–471.

Nehru, Jawaharlal, 1981 (1946), *The Discovery of India*, New Delhi, Oxford University Press.

Nesfield, J.C., 1885, *Brief View of the Caste System of the North-West Provinces and Oudh*, Allahabad, Government Printing Press.

Niranjana, Seemanthini, Annapurna M., B. Syamasundari, Latha Tummuru and Uzramma, 2006, 'Marketing Handlooms', *Economic & Political Weekly*, Vol. 41, No. 31: 3361–3365.

O'Hanlon, Rosalind, 2000, 'Recovering the Subject: Subaltern Studies and the Histories of Resistance in Colonial South Asia', in *Mapping Subaltern Studies and the Postcolonial* edited by Vinayak Chaturvedi, 72–115.

Omvedt, Gail, 1982, *Land, Caste and Politics in India*, Delhi, Authors Guild Publications.

Oommen, T.K., 2004, 'Race and Caste: Anthropological and Sociological Perspectives', in Sukhadeo Thorat and Umakant (eds.), *Caste, Race and Discrimination: Discourses in International Context*, Jaipur and New Delhi, Rawat Publications, pp. 97–109.

Opler, M.E., 1956, 'The Extensions of an Indian Village', *Journal of Asian Studies*, Vol. 16, No. 1.

Ostor, A., 1984, *Culture and Power, Legend, Ritual, Bazaar and Religion in a Bengali Society*, New Delhi, SAGE.

Pal, Mahi, 2004, 'Panchayati Raj and Rural Governance: Experience of a Decade', *Economic & Political Weekly*, Vol. 39, No. 2: 137–143.

Palshikar, Suhas, 2015, 'Ambedkar and Gandhi Limits of Divergence and Possibilities of Conservation', *Economic & Political Weekly*, Vol. 50, No. 15: 45–50.

Palshikar, Suhas, and Sanjay Kumar, 2004, 'How Broad Based is the Participatory Norm?' *Economic & Political Weekly*, Vol. 39, No. 51: 5412–5417.

Palshikar, Suhas, and K.C. Suri, 2014, 'Critical Shifts in the Long-Term Caution in the Short Term', *Economic & Political Weekly*, Vol. 49, No. 39: 39–41.

Pandey, Gyanendra, 1984, 'Encounters and Calamities: The History of North Indian Qasba in the Nineteenth Century', in *Subaltern Studies III*, edited by Ranjit Guha, Delhi, Oxford University Press, 231–270.

———, 1990, 'The Biogoted Julaha', in *The Construction of Communalism in Colonial North India*, New Delhi, Oxford University Press, 66–108.

———, 2006, 'The Subaltern as Subaltern Citizen', *Economic & Political Weekly*, Vol. 41, No. 46: 4735–4741.

Pandian, M.S.S., 2002, Culture and Subaltern Consciousness: An Aspect of the MGR Phenomenon, in Chatterjee (ed.), *State and Politics in India (4th impression)*, Partha, New Delhi, Oxford University Press, 367–389.

Panikkar, K.M., 1955, *Hindu Society at the Crossroads*, Bombay, Asia Publishing House.

Pareto, V., 1935, *The Mind and Society*, 4 Volumes, New York and London.

Parry, Jonathan, 2013, 'The "Embourgeoisement": A "Proletarian Vanguard?"' in Surinder S. Jodhka (ed.), *Interrogating India's Modernity, Essays in Honour of Dipankar Gupta*, New Delhi, Oxford University Press.

Parsons, Talcott, 1954, 'An Analytical Approach to the Theory of Social Stratification', and 'A Revised Analytical Approach to the Theory of Social Stratification', in his book–*Essays in Sociological Theory*, Glencoe, The Free Press.

Patnaik, Utsa, 1972, 'On the Mode of Production in Indian Agriculture', *Economic & Political Weekly*, Vol. 7, No. 40: A-145–A-151.

———, 1976, 'Class Differentiation within the Peasantry: An Approach to Analysis of Indian Agriculture', *Economic & Political Weekly*, Vol. 11, No. 39: A82–A101.

Picketty, Thomas, 2014, *Capital in the Twenty-First Century*, Cambridge, The Belknap Press of Harvard University Press.

Polanyi, Karl, 2001, *The Great Transformation: The Political and Economic Origins of our Time*, Boston, Beacon Press, vii-viii. First printed in 1957 by Beacon Press, Boston.

Poliakov, L., 1967, 'Racism in Europe', in Anthony de Reuck and Julie Knight (eds.), *Caste and Race: Comparative Approaches*, London, J&A Churchill.

Potter, J.M., M.N. Diaz, and G.M. Foster (eds.), 1967, *Peasant Society: A Reader*, Little, Brown.

Pouchepadass, Jacques, 1980, 'Peasant Classes in Twentieth Century Agrarian Movements in India', in E.J. Hobsbawn et al. (eds.), *Peasants in History: Essays in Honour of Daniel Thorner*, Calcutta, Oxford University Press.

Pradhan, Kanhu Charan, 2013, 'Unacknowledged Urbanisation: New Census Towns of India', *Economic & Political Weekly*, Vol. 48, No. 36: 43–53.

Prasad, Chandra Bhan, and Milind Kamble, 2013, 'Manifesto to End Caste: Push Capitalism and Industrialistation to Eradicate this Pernicious System', *The Times of India*, 23 January.

Prasad, N. Purendra, 2015, 'Agrarian Class and Caste Relations in 'United' Andhra Pradesh, 1956–2014', *Economic & Political Weekly*, Vol. 50, No. 16: 77–83.

Prasad, Pradhan H., 1979, 'Caste and Class in Bihar', *Economic & Political Weekly*, Vol. 14, Nos. 7 & 8.

————, 1980, 'Rising Middle Peasantry in North India', *Economic & Political Weekly*, Vol. 15, No. 4.

Purakayastha, Anindya Sekhar, and Saswat Samay Das, 2015, 'Homo Heirarchicus and Liberalisation', *Economic & Political Weekly*, Vol. 50, No. 9: 189.

Puri, Ellora, 2009, 'Understanding the Paradoxical Outcome in Jammu and Kashmir', *Economic & Political Weekly*, Vol. 44, No. 6: 31–34.

Rai, Praveen, 2009, 'Issues in Election 2009', *Economic & Political Weekly*, Vol. 44, No. 39: 80–82.

Rajagopal, V., 2011, 'The Leading Natives: A Review of the Middle Class in Colonial India', in Sanjay Joshi (ed.), 2010, New Delhi, Oxford University Press, reviewed in *Economic & Political Weekly*, Vol. 46, No. 6: 39–41.

Ram, Nandu, 1988, *The Mobile Scheduled Castes: Rise of a New Middle Class*, New Delhi, Hindustan Publishing Corporation.

Raman, Vasanthi, 2010, *The Warp and the Weft*, (Community and Gender Identity among Banaras Weavers), New Delhi, Routledge.

Ramaswamy, Vijaya, 1985, *Textiles and Weavers in Medieval South India*, New Delhi, Oxford University Press.

————, 2003, 'Through History', *Seminar*, No. 523, 48–53.

Rao, P.H.S., and M.N. Palsane, 1994, *Training for Higher Education*, Jaipur and New Delhi, Rawat Publications.

Rawls, J., 1999 (revised), *A Theory of Justice*, Oxford, Oxford University Press (first published in 1971 by Harvard University Press, Cambridge, MA).

Raychaudhuri, Tapan, 1983, 'The Mid-Eighteenth Century Background' (The Land and The People), in Dharma Kumar (ed.), *The Cambridge Economic History of India*, Vol. II, New Delhi, Orient Longman, 3–35.

————, 1984, *Non-Agricultural Production* (Mughal India), Tapan Raychaudhuri and Irfan Habib (eds.), *The Cambridge History of India*, Vol. I, C. 1200–1750, New Delhi, Orient Longman.

Redfield, Robert, 1941, *The Folk Culture of Yucatan*, Chicago, Chicago University Press.

————, 1955, *The Little Community: The Viewpoints for the Study of a Whole*, Chicago, The University of Chicago Press.

————, 1956, *Peasant Society and Culture*, Chicago, The University of Chicago Press.

Redfield, Robert, and Milton Singer, 1955, 'Foreword', in McKim Marriott (ed.), *Village India: Studies in the Little Community*, Berkeley, University of California Press.

Reuck, Anthony de, and Julie Knight (eds.), 1967, *Caste and Race: Comparative Approaches*, London, J&A Churchill.

Right to Education (RTE) Act, 2009, New Delhi, Government of India.

Risley, H.H., 1969, *The People of India* (2nd edition), New Delhi, Orient Books (first published in 1909 by Thacker & Co., London).

Rowe, William L., 1968, 'The New Cauhans: A Caste Mobility Movement in North India', in James Silverberg (ed.), *Social Mobility in the Caste System in India*, The Hague, Mouton Publishers.

Roy, Dayabati, 2008, '"Wither the Subaltern Domain?"—An Ethnographic Enquiry', *Economic & Political Weekly*, Vol. 43, No. 23: 31–38.

Roy, Kumkum, 2008, 'Kosambi and Questions of Caste', *Economic & Political Weekly*, Vol. 43, No. 30: 78–84.

Roy, Sarat Chandra, 1927, Caste, Race and Religion in India, as referred in Louis Dumont, 1970, *Homo Hierarchicus*, London, Paladin, 317fn 14b.

Roy, Tirthankar, 1993, *Artisans and Industrialization* (Indian Weaving in the Twentieth Century), New Delhi, Oxford University Press.

———, 2002. Subaltern Studies: Questioning the Basics, *Economic & Political Weekly*, Vol. 37, No. 23: 2223–2228.

Rudolph, Lloyd I., and Susanne Hobber Rudolph, 1967, *The Modernity of Tradition: Political Development in India*, Chicago, Chicago University Press.

———, 1987, *In Pursuit of Lakshmi: The Political Economy of the Indian State*, New Delhi, Orient Longman Ltd.

———, 1967, 'Para Communities: The Sociology of Caste Associations', in L.I. Rudolph and S.H. Rudolph (eds.), *The Modernity of Tradition*, Chicago, Chicago University Press.

Rudolph, Lloyd I., and John Kurt Jacobson (eds.), 2014, *Experiencing the State* (Reprint), New Delhi, Oxford University Press.

Rudolph, Susanne Hoeber, and Llyod I Rudolph (ed.), 1972, *Education and Politics in India*, Delhi, Oxford University Press.

———, 1984, *Essays on Rajasthan*, New Delhi, Concept Publishing Company.

Rudra, Ashok, 1978, 'Class Relations in Indian Agriculture-I', *Economic & Political Weekly*, Vol. 13, No. 22: 916–923.

———, 1989, 'Emergence of the Intelligentsia as a Ruling Class', *Economic & Political Weekly*, Vol. 24, No. 3.

Saavala, M., 2001, 'Low Caste but Middle Class: Some Religious Strategies for Middle Class Identification in Hyderabad', *Contributions to Indian Sociology*, Vol. 35, No. 3: 295–318.

Saberwal, Satish, 1976, *Mobile Men: Limits to Social Change in Urban Punjab*, New Delhi, Vikas Publishing House.

Sabharwal, Gopa, 2006, *Ethnicity and Class*, Delhi, Oxford University Press.

Sachidananda, 1974, *The Harijan Elite,* New Delhi, Thompson Press.

Sahai, Nandita Prasad, 2006, *Politics of Patronage and Protest: The State, Society, and Artisans in Early Modern Rajasthan*, New Delhi, Oxford University Press.

Sahay, Gaurang Ranjan 1998, Caste System in Contemporary Rural Bihar: A Study of Selected Villages, *Sociological Bulletin*, Vol. 47, No. 2: 207–220.

———, 2002, 'Caste and Agrarian Economic Structure: A Study of Rural Bihar', *Sociological Bulletin*, Vol. 51, No. 2: 195–216.

Sahlins, Marshall, 1981, *Historical Metaphors and Mythical Realties*, London, Oxford University Press, Quoted from Nita Kumar, op.cit., 6fn.

Samarendra, Padmanabh, 2011, 'Census in Colonial India and the Birth of Caste', *Economic & Political Weekly*, Vol. 46, No. 33: 51–58.

Sarkar, Sumit, and Tanika Sarkar (eds.), 2015, *Caste in Modern India* (paperback), New Ramkhet, Permanent Black.

Sarkar, Susobhan, 1968, The Thought of Gramsci, Mainstream, November 2. See also Susobhan Sarkar, 1972. 'General President's Address', Indian History Congress, Proceedings of the Thirty Third Session, Muzaffarpur. Also published by Sudha Publications, New Delhi, 1–18.

Sau, Ranjit, 1973, 'On the Essence and Manifestation of Capitalism in Indian Agriculture-I', *Economic & Political Weekly*, Vol. 8, No. 13: A27–A30.

Searle-Chatterjee, Mary, and Ursula Sharma (eds.), 2003, *Contextualising Caste, Post-Dumontian Approach*, (Indian Edition), Jaipur, Rawat Publications.

Sen, Amartya, 1995, *Inequality Reexamined*, New Delhi, Oxford University Press.

———, 2000, *Development as Freedom*, New Delhi, Oxford University Press.

———, 2005a, *The Argumentative Indian (Writings on Indian Culture, History and Identity)*, London, Penguin Books.

———, 2005b, The Three R's of Reform, *Economic & Political Weekly*, Vol. 40, No. 19: 1971–1974.

———, 2013, 'The Crisis in Indian Education', in R.K. Mishra (ed.), *India: Leading Issues in Economic Development*, New Delhi, Academic Foundation, 129–162.

Senart, Emile, 1930, *Caste in India: The Facts and the System* (first published in 1894 in French), London, Metheun & Co.

Sengupta, Arjun, 2010, Subaltern Studies: Questioning the Basics, *Economic & Political Weekly*, Vol. 15, No. 17: 85–93.

Sengupta, Nirmal, 1982, 'Background of the Jharkhand Question', in Nirmal Sengupta (ed.), *Fourth World Dynamics: Jharkhand*, Delhi, Shankar Printing Service.

Seth, Suhel, 2015, *Mantras for Success*, New Delhi, Rupa Publications.

Shah, A.M., 1964, 'Basic Terms and Concepts in the Study of the Family in India', *Indian Economic and Social History Review*, Vol. 1: 1–36.

———, 1973, *The Household Dimension of the Family in India: A Field Study in a Gujarat Village and a Review of Other Studies*, New Delhi, Orient Longman.

———, 1991, 'The Rural-Urban Networks in India', in K.L. Sharma and Dipankar Gupta (eds.), *Country-Town Nexus*, 11–42, Jaipur, Rawat Publications.

———, 2005, 'Family Studies: Retrospect and Prospect', *Economic & Political Weekly*, Vol. 49, No. 1: 19–22.

———, 2005, 'Sanskritization Revisited', *Sociological Bulletin*, Vol. 54, No. 2.

———, 2007, 'Caste in the 21st Century', *Economic & Political Weekly*, Vol. 42, No. 44: 109–116.

———, 2013, 'Higher Education and Research: Roots of Mediocrity', in Jandhyala B.G. Tilak (ed.), *Higher Education in India: In Search of Equality, Quality and*

Quantity, New Delhi, Orient BlackSwan, 184–203. Earlier published in *Economic & Political Weekly*, Vol. 40, Nos. 22–23: 2234–2242, 28 May 2005.

Shah, A.M., 2014, *The Writings of A.M. Shah: The Household and Family in India*, New Delhi, Orient Black Swan.

Shah, A.M. (ed.), 2007, *The Grassroots of Democracy: Field Studies of Indian Elections*, Delhi, Permanent Black.

Shah, A.M., and I.P. Desai, 1988, *Division and Hierarchy: An Overview of Caste in Gujarat*, Delhi, Hindustan Publishing Corporation.

Shah, B.V., and K.B. Shah, 2006, *Sociology of Education* (reprint), Jaipur and New Delhi, Rawat Publications.

Shah, Ghanshyam, 1986, 'Caste Sentiments, Class Formation and Dominance in Gujarat', in K.L. Sharma (ed.), *Caste and Class in India*, Jaipur, Rawat Publications.

———, 1986, 'Stratification among the Scheduled Tribes in the Bharuch and Panch Mahals Districts of Gujarat', in S.C. Malik (ed.), *Dynamics of Social Status in India*, Delhi, Moti Lal Banarsidas, 149–183.

———, 1998, 'Caste Sentiments, Class Formation and Dominance in Gujarat', in K.L. Sharma (ed.), *Caste and Class in India* (reprint), Jaipur, Rawat Publications.

Shanin, Teodor (ed.), 1971, *Peasants and Peasant Societies*, H. Middlesex, England, Penguin Books.

Shankar, Ram, and Yatindra Singh Sisodia, 2009, 'Madhya Pradesh: Overriding the Contours of Anti-Incumbency', *Economic & Political Weekly*, Vol. 44, No. 6: 35–38.

Sharma, A.N., 2005, 'Agrarian Relations and Socio-economic Change in Bihar', *Economic & Political Weekly*, Vol. 40, No. 10: 960–972.

Sharma, K.L., 1968a, 'Occupational Mobility and Class Structure', *Man in India*, Vol. 48, No. 2.

———, 1968b, *The Changing Rural Stratification System: A Comparative Study of Six Villages in Rajasthan*, Jaipur, PhD thesis, University of Rajasthan.

———, 1969a, 'Patterns of Occupational Mobility: A Study of Six Villages in Rajasthan', *The Indian Journal of Social Work*, Vol. 30, No. 1, April.

———, 1969b, 'Stresses in Caste Stratification: A Study of Six Villages in Rajasthan', *Economic & Political Weekly*, Vol. 4, No. 3: 217–222.

———, 1970a, 'Caste and Class Consciousness in Rural Rajasthan', *Sociology and Social Research*, Vol. 54, No. 3.

———, 1970b, 'Changing Class Stratification in Rural Rajasthan', *Man in India*, Vol. 50, No. 3.

———, 1970c, 'Modernization and Rural Stratification: An Application at the Micro-level', *Economic & Political Weekly*, Vol. 5, No. 3: 1537–1543.

———, 1973, 'Downward Social Mobility: Some Observations', *Sociological Bulletin*, Vol. 22, No. 1: 116–134. Also reproduced in K.L. Sharma (ed.), 2014, *Sociological Probings in Rural Society*, New Delhi, SAGE.

Sharma, K.L., 1974. *The Changing Rural Stratification System (A Comparative Study of Six Villages in Rajasthan, India)*, New Delhi/Jaipur, Orient Longman/Rawat Publications.

———, 1982, 'Land Tenure Systems, Social Structure and Change: Some Reflections on Land Reforms in Rajasthan', in S.K. Lal (ed.), *Sociological Perspectives of Land Reforms*, New Delhi, Agricole Publishing Academy.

———, 1983, 'Agrarian Stratification: Old Issues, New Explanations and New Issues, Old Explanations', *Economic & Political Weekly*, Vol. 18, Nos. 42 & 43, 15 and 22 October.

——— (ed.), 1986, *Social Stratification in India*, New Delhi, Manohar Publications.

———, 1991, 'The Country–Town Nexus in India: A Macro-View', in K.L. Sharma and Dipankar Gupta (eds.), *Country–Town Nexus (Studies in Social Transformation in Contemporary India)*, Jaipur, Rawat Publications.

———, 1994, *Social Stratification and Mobility*, Jaipur, Rawat Publications.

———, 1996, 'Conceptualisation of Caste-Class Nexus as an Alternative to Caste-Class Dichotomy', in A.R. Momin (ed.), The Legacy of G.S. Ghurye: A Centennial Festschrift, Bomby, Popular Prakashan. pp. 130–146.

———, 1997a, 'Changing Aspects of Merchants, Markets, Moneylending and Migration: Reflections Based on Field Notes from a Village in Rajasthan', in Philippe Cadene and Denis Vidal (eds.), *Webs of Trade, Dynamics of Business Communities in Western India*, New Delhi, Manohar, 174–194.

———, 1997b, *Rural Society in India*, Jaipur, Rawat Publications.

———, 1997c, *Social Stratification in India: Issues and Themes*, New Delhi, SAGE.

———, 1998a, *Caste, Feudalism and Peasantry: The Social Formation of Shekhawati*, Delhi, Manohar Publications, 26–43.

———, 1998b, 'Changing Aspects of Merchants, Markets, Moneylending and Migration: Reflections Based on Field Notes from a Village in Rajasthan', in Philippe Cadene and Denis Vidal (eds.), *Webs of Trade*, New Delhi, Manohar Publications.

———, 1999, Chanderi: 1990–1995, Vol. 2, Paris, Edition-Diffusion De Boccard.

———, 2001, *Reconceptualising Caste, Class and Tribe*, Jaipur–New Delhi, Rawat Publications, 17–43.

———, 2003, 'The Social Organization of Urban Space: A Case Study of Chanderi, a Small Town in Central India', *Contributions to Indian Sociology*, Vol. 37, No. 3: 405–427.

———, 2007a, 'Caste, Class and Globalization: Continuity and Change', in Kameshwar Choudhary (ed.), *Globalization, Governance Reforms and Development in India*, New Delhi, SAGE, 241–258.

———, 2007b, *Rural Society in India*, Jaipur, Rawat Publications.

Sharma, K.L., 2007c, *Social Structure and Change in India*, Jaipur and New Delhi, Rawat Publications.

———, 2010, *Perspectives on Social Stratification*, Jaipur and Delhi, Rawat Publications.

Sharma, K.L., 2011, *Culture, Stratification and Development* (see Chapter 9 on Some Reflections on Higher Education, State and Social Hierarchy in India), Jaipur and New Delhi, Rawat Publications, 199–214.

———, 2012, 'Is There Today Caste System or There Is Only Caste in India?' *Polish Sociological Review*, Vol. 2, No. 178: 245–264.

———, 2013a, 'Education and Social Stratification in India: Systematic Inequality', in *Handbook on Social Stratification in the BRIC Countries: Change and Perspective*, co-authored by Li Peilin, M.K. Gorshkov, Celi Scalon and K.L. Sharma, Singapore, World Scientific, 549–568.

———, 2013b, *Handbook on Social Stratification in the BRIC Countries* (with co-authors Li Peilin, M.K. Gorshkov and Celi Scalon), Singapore, World Scientific, 201–219.

———, 2014a, 'Caste: Continuity and Change', in Yogendra Singh (ed.), *Indian Sociology*, Vol. I, *Emerging Concepts, Structure, and Change* (ICSSR Research Surveys and Explorations), New Delhi, Oxford University Press.

———, 2014b, 'Introduction: Reconceptualising the Indian Village', in K.L. Sharma (ed.), *Sociological Probings in Rural Society*, Vol. 2, New Delhi, SAGE, XXI–XL.

———, 2016, *Field Notes based on our Restudy of the Six Villages in Sikar, Jaipur and Bharatpur Districts of Rajasthan.*

Sharma, K.L., and Dipankar Gupta, 1991a, *Country-Town Nexus (Studies in Social Transformation in Contemporary India)*, Jaipur, Rawat Publications.

———, 1991b, 'Introduction', in K.L. Sharma and Dipankar Gupta (eds.), *Country-Town Nexus*, Jaipur, Rawat Publications.

———, 1997, 'Changing Aspects of Merchants, Markets, Moneylending and Migration: Reflections Based on Field Notes from a Village in Rajasthan', in Philippe Cadene and Denis Vidal (eds.), *Webs of Trade*, New Delhi, Manohar Publications.

———, 2016, *Revisiting the Six Villages in Rajasthan*, included in the ms.

——— (ed.), 2014, *Sociological Probings in Rural India* (Vol. 2), New Delhi, SAGE.

Sharma, K.N., 1963, 'Panchayat Leaders and Resource Groups', *Sociological Bulletin*, Vol. 12, No. 1: 45–52.

———, 1969, 'Resource Groups and Networks in the Social Structure', *The Eastern Anthropologist*, Vol. 22, No. 1.

Sharma, Kavita A., 2013, *Sixty Years of the University Grants Commission, Establishment, Growth and Evolution*, New Delhi, University Grants Commission.

Sharma, R.S., 2001, *Early Medieval Indian Society*, Kolkata, Orient Longman.

Sharma, Surendra, 1985, *Sociology in India*, Jaipur, Rawat Publications.

Shastri, Sandeep, and B.S. Padmavathi, 2009, 'Karnataka: The Lotus Blooms… Nearly', *Economic & Political Weekly*, Vol. 44, No. 6: 42–45.

Sheth, D.L., 2004, 'Caste in the Mirror of Race', in Sukhadeo Thorat and Umakant (eds.), *Caste, Race and Discrimination: Discourses in International Context*, Jaipur and New Delhi, Rawat Publications, pp. 85–96.

Silverberg, James (ed.), 1968, *Social Mobility in the Caste System in India*, The Hague, Mouton Publishers.

Singer, Milton, and B.S. Cohn (eds.), 1968, *Structure and Change in Indian Society*, New York, Aldine Publishing Co. Reprint in 1996 by Rawat Publications, Jaipur and New Delhi.

Singh, Archana, 2014, 'Middle Class in India', in Yogendra Singh (ed.), Indian Sociology, Vol. I, *Emerging Concepts, Structure and Change*, New Delhi, Oxford University Press, 307–333.

Singh, Avinash Kumar, 2016, 'Introduction: Education and Empowerment in India: Policies and Practices', in Avinash Kumar Singh (ed.), *Education and Empowerment in India: Policies and Practices*, London and New York, Routledge, 1–19.

Singh, Dool, 1964, *Land Reforms in Rajasthan (A Study of Evasion, Implementation and Socio-economic effects of Land Reforms)*, New Delhi, Planning Commission of India.

Singh, Hira, 1983, *The Decline of Feudalism in India*, PhD thesis, Delhi, University of Delhi.

———, 1998, *Colonial Hegemony and Popular Resistance: Princes, Peasants and Paramount Power*, New Delhi, SAGE.

Singh, R.P. (ed.), 1998 *Indian Universities: Towards Nation Building*, New Delhi, University Grants Commission.

Singh, Yogendra, 1958, *The Changing Pattern of Socio-Economic Relations in the Countryside: A Survey of Selected Villages in Eastern Uttar Pradesh*, PhD Thesis, University of Lucknow.

———, 1961, 'The Changing Power Structure of Village Community – A Case Study of Six Villages in Eastern U.P.', in A.R. Desai (ed.), *Rural Sociology in India*, Bombay, The Indian Society of Agricultural Economics, 669–688.

———, 1973, *Modernization of Indian Tradition: A Systematic Study of Social Change*, Delhi/Faridabad, Thompson Press.

———, 1984, *Image of Man: Ideology and Theory in Indian Sociology*, Delhi, Chanakya Publications, 23–75.

———, 2009, 'Social Praxis, Conceptual Categories and Social Change: Observations from a Village Study', *Sociological Bulletin*, Vol. 58, No. 2: 178–195.

Singhi, N.K., 1979, *Education and Social Change*, Jaipur, Rawat Publications.

Smaje, Chris, 2000, *Natural Hierarchies: The Historical Sociology of Race and Caste*, Oxford, Blackwell Publishers Ltd.

Smart, Barry, 1976, *Sociology, Phenomenology and Marxian Analysis*, London, Routledge & Kegan Paul.

Smith, M.G., 1960, 'Social and Cultural Pluralism', in *Social and Cultural Pluralism in the Caribbean*, Annals of the New York Academy of Sciences, Vol. 83.

Smith, M.G., 1965, *The Plural Society in the British West Indies*, Berkeley, University of California Press.

Smith, Vincent A., 1923, *Oxford History of India*, Oxford University Press.

Society for Rural, Urban and Tribal Initiative (SRUTI), 1995, *India's Artisans: A Status Report*, Sponsored by CAPART, New Delhi.

Solanki, S.S., 2002, 'Migration of Rural Artisans: Evidence from Haryana and Rajasthan', *Economic & Political Weekly*, Vol. 37, No. 35: 3579–3580.

———, 2003, 'Reaching the Unreached: The Missing Links—A Case Study of Rural Artisans of Haryana and Rajasthan', *Man and Development*, Vol. 25, No. 2: 33–47.

———, 2008, 'Sustainability of Rural Artisans', *Economic & Political Weekly*, Vol. 43, No. 19: 24–27.

Sorokin, P.A., 1927, *Social and Cultural Mobility*, New York, Harper & Brothers. This is one of the four volumes and one chapter from Volume IV. Sorokin had published earlier Four Volumes – Social and Cultural Dynamics.

Spate, O.H.K., 1960, *India and Pakistan*, London, Methuen.

Spivak, Gayatri Chakravarty, 2000, 'The New Subaltern: A Silent Interview', in Vinayak Chaturvedi (ed.), *Mapping Subaltern Studies and the Postcolonial*, pp. 324–340.

Srinivas, Gurram, 2016, *Dalit Middle Class: Mobility, Identity and Politics of Caste*, Jaipur, Rawat Publications.

Srinivas, M.N., 1952, *Religion and Society among the Coorgs of South India*, London/ Oxford, Oxford University Press/Clarendon Press.

———, 1954, 'A Caste Dispute among Washer man of Mysore', *Eastern Anthropologist*, Vol. 7: 149–168.

———, 1962, *Caste in Modern India and Other Essays*, Bombay/New Delhi, Asia Publishing House/ Oxford University Press.

———, 1966, *Social Change in Modern India*, Berkeley, University of California Press.

———, 1978, *The Remembered Village* (paperback), Delhi, Oxford University Press. First published in 1976.

———, 1987, *The Dominant Caste and Other Essays*, Delhi, Oxford University Press.

———, 1995, *Social Change in Modern India*, Delhi, Orient Longman.

———, 1998, *Village, Caste, Gender and Method: Essays in Indian Anthropology*, New Delhi, Oxford University Press.

———, 2003, 'An Obituary on Caste as a System', *Economic & Political Weekly*, Vol. 38, No. 5: 455–459.

Srinivas, M.N. (ed.), *India's Villages*, London, Asia Publishing House.

———, 1996, *Caste: Its Twentieth Century Avatar*, New Delhi, Viking/Penguin.

Stein, Burton, 1968, 'Social Mobility and Medieval South Indian Sects', in James Silverberg (ed.), *Social Mobility in the Caste System in India*, The Hague, Mouton Publishers.

Stein, Burton, 2012, *A History of India (Tenth impression)*, New Delhi, Oxford University Press.

Stern, Robert W., 2003, *Changing India: Bourgeois Revolution on the Subcontinent* (2nd edition), Cambridge, Cambridge University Press.

Stokes, Eric, 1978, *The Peasant and the Raj: Studies in Agrarian Society and Peasant Rebellion in Colonial India*, Cambridge, Cambridge University Press.

Subramaniam, A., and D. Jayaraj, 2015, Growth and Inequality in the Distribution of India's Consumption Expenditure: 1893 to 2009–10 *Economic & Political Weekly*, Vol. 50, No. 32.

Sundar, Nandini, 2009. *Subalterns and Sovereigns: An Anthropological History of Bastar (1854–2006)*, (2nd impression), New Delhi, Oxford University Press.

Suri, K.C., 2006, 'Dimensions of Agrarian Distress in Andhra Pradesh', *Economic & Political Weekly*, Vol. 41, No. 6.

Teltumbde, Anand, 2010, *The Persistence of Caste*, New Delhi, Navayana Publishing.

———, 2011, 'Dalit Capitalism and Pseudo Dalitism', *Economic & Political Weekly*, Vol. 46, No. 10: 10–11.

Thakur, Manish, 2014, *Indian Village: A Conceptual History*, Jaipur, Rawat Publications.

Thapar, Romila, 1974, 'Social Mobility in Ancient Indian Society', in R.S. Sharma (ed.), *Indian Society: Historical Probings* (In Memory of D.D. Kosambi), New Delhi, People's Publishing House.

The Report of the World Commission on the Social Dimension of Globalisation (2004). *The Times Higher Educational Supplement*, 2011, 2012, 2013.

Thompson, E.P., 1974, 'Patrician Society, Plebeian Culture', *Journal of Social History*, Vol. 7: 382–405.

———, 1984, *The Making of the English Working Class* (Reprint, paperback), H. Middlesex, England, Penguin Books, Chapter 9 on Weavers, 297–346.

Thorat, Sukhdeo, 2012, 'Caste Identity and Economics', Review of the book. *The in Grammar of Caste* by Aswani Deshpande, 2011, Delhi, Oxford University Press, *Economic & Political Weekly*, Vol. 47, No. 9: 4121–4124.

Thorat, Sukhdeo, and Katherine S. Newman, 2007, 'Caste and Economic Discrimination: Causes, Consequences and Remedies', *Economic & Political Weekly*, Vol. 42, No. 41.

Thorat, Sukhdeo, and Nidhi Sadana, 2009, 'Caste Ownership of Private Enterprises', *Economic & Political Weekly*, Vol. 41, No. 23: 13–16.

Thorat, Sukhadeo, and Umakant, 2004, 'Introduction' in Sukhadeo Thorat and Umakant (eds.), pp. XIII–XXXV. *Caste, Race and Discrimination: Discourses in International Context*, Jaipur and New Delhi, Rawat Publications.

Thorner, Alice, 1982, 'Semi-feudalism or Capitalism? Contemporary Debate on Classes and Modes of Production in India', *Economic & Political Weekly*, 4: 1961–1968, 1993–1999, 2061–2066, 11 and 18 December.

Thorner, Daniel, 1956, *Agrarian Prospect in India*, Delhi, Delhi University Press.

———, 1962, *Land and Labour in India*, Bombay, Asia Publishing House.

Thorner, Daniel, and Alice Thorner, 1962, *Land and Labour in India*, Bombay, Asia Publishing House.

Tilak, J.B.G., 2004, 'Absence of Policy and Perspective in Higher Education', *Economic & Political Weekly*, Vol. 34, No. 21: 2159–2164.

Tilak, J.B.G., 2005, 'Higher Education in Trishanku: Hanging between State and Market', *Economic & Political Weekly*, Vol. 40, No. 37: 4029–4037.

———, 2013, 'Introduction', in Jandhyala B.G. Tilak (ed.), *Higher Education in India: In Search of Equality, Quality and Quantity*, New Delhi, Orient BlackSwan, 1–18.

Timberg, T.A., 1978, *The Marwaris: From Traders to Industrialists*, New Delhi, Vikas Publishing House.

Trawick, Margaret, 2003, 'The Person Beyond the Family', in Patricia Uberoi (ed.), op. cit.

Tumin, Melvin M., 1953, 'Some Principles of Stratification', *American Sociological Review*, Vol. 18, August.

———, 1952, *Caste in a Peasant Society*, Princeton, Princeton University Press.

Turner, R.H., 1960, 'Sponsored and Contest Mobility and the School System', *American Sociological Review*, Vol. 25: 855–867.

Uberoi, Patricia, 2003, 'The Family in India: Beyond the Nuclear Versus Joint Debate', in Veena Das (ed.), *The Oxford India Companion to Sociology and Social Anthropology*, Vol. 2, New Delhi, Oxford University Press.

Udupa, Sahana, 2013, 'World Class Aspirations: The New Middle Class of India', *Economic & Political Weekly*, Vol. 48, No. 15: 29–31.

Vaidyanathan, Anand, and R. Srinivasan, 2015, 'Changing Characteristics of Villages in Tamil Nadu', *Economic & Political Weekly*, Vol. 50, No. 52: 65–73.

Varma, Pavan K., 1998, *The Great Indian Middle Class*, New Delhi, Penguin Books.

———, 2010, *Becoming Indian*, New Delhi, Penguin Book, pp. 64–87, on Macaulay's Legacy.

———, 2013, 'India's Middle Class Awakes', *Times of India*, November 23.

———, 2014, 'Middle Class Comes of Age', *Times of India*, May 10.

Veblen, Thorstein, 1984, *The Theory of the Leisure Class*, London, Macmillan Co.

Venkatarangaiya, M., 1962, *Welfare State and Socialist State*, Madras, Triveeni Publishers. Cited from A.R. Desai, 1975, *State and Society in India (Essays in Dissent)*, Bombay, Popular Prakashan.

Venkatesan, Soumhya, 2009, *Craft Matters: Artisans, Development and the Indian Nation*, New Delhi, Orient BlackSwan.

Verma, A. K., 2010, Subalterns in Uttar Pradesh, *Economic & Political Weekly*, Vol. 45, No. 48: 11–14.

Verma, Rahul, and Shreyas Sardesai, 2014, 'Does Media Exposure Affect Voting Behaviour', *Economic & Political Weekly*, Vol. 49, No. 39: 82–88.

Vidyarthi, L.P., 1961, *The Sacred Complex of Hindu Gaya*, Bombay, Asia Publishing House.

Vijay, R., 2012, 'Structural Retrogression and Rise of "New Landlords" in Indian Agriculture: An Empirical Exercise', *Economic & Political Weekly*, Vol. 47, No. 5: 37–45.

Vijayagopalan, S., 1993, *Economic Status of Handicraft Artisans*, New Delhi, National Council of Applied Economic Research.

Van den Berghe, Pierre L., 1964, *Caneville: The Social Structure of a South African Town*, Middletown, Connecticut: Wesleyan University Press. (Referred from Anthony de Reuck and Julie Knight (eds.), op. cit.)

Weber, Max, 1957, *The Theory of Social and Economic Organization*, Glencoe, The Free Press.

Wedderburn, Dorothy, 1965, *The Socialist Register*, London, The Merlin Press, cited from A.R. Desai, 1975, *State and Society in India (Essays in Dissent)*, Bombay, Popular Prakashan.

Weiner, Myron, 1978, *Sons of the Soil, Migration and Ethnic Conflict in India*, Princeton, Princeton University Press.

———, 2001, 'The Struggle for Equality: Caste in Indian Politics', in Atul Kohli (ed.), *The Success of India's Democracy*, New York, Cambridge University Press.

Wiser, W.H., 1936, *The Hindu Jajmani System*, Lucknow, Lucknow Printing House.

Wiser, W.H., and C.W. Wiser, 1964, *Behind Mud Walls: 1930–1960*, Berkeley and Los Angeles, University of California Press. The First Edition was published in 1930.

Wolf, Eric, 1966, 'Closed Corporate Peasant Communities in Meso–America and Central Java', *South–Western Journal of Anthropology*, Vol. 13, No. 1.

———, 1971, *Peasant Wars of the Twentieth Century*, London.

World Bank, 2004, cited from Anand Kumar, 2014, 'People, Power and Paradigm Shift', in Yogendra Singh (ed.), *Indian Sociology*, Vol. I, New Delhi, Oxford University Press, 377–380.

Yadav, Yogendra, 2000, 'Understanding the Second Democratic Upsurge: Trends of Bahujan Participation in Electoral Politics in the 1990s', in E.R. Frankel, Z. Hasan, R. Bhargava, and B. Arova (eds.), *Transforming India: Social and Political Dynamics of Democracy*, New Delhi, Oxford University Press, 120–145.

Yadav, Yogendra, and Suhas Palshikar, 2009a, 'Between Fortune and Virtue: Explaining the Congress' Ambiguous Victory in 2009', *Economic & Political Weekly*, Vol. 44, No. 39: 33–46.

———, 2009b, 'Principal State Level Contests and Derivative National Choices: Electoral Trends in 2004–09', *Economic & Political Weekly*, Vol. 44, No. 6: 55–62.

Index

About the Author

K. L. Sharma is Pro-Chancellor at Jaipur National University, and Vice-Chairman of Institute of Development Studies (ISD), Jaipur. Formerly, Dr. Sharma was Professor of Sociology and Rector (pro-Vice-Chancellor) at Jawaharlal Nehru University, New Delhi. He was Vice-Chancellor at the University of Rajasthan during 2003–2005 and also Vice-Chancellor at Jaipur National University, Jaipur, from 2007 to 2014. K. L. Sharma earned his Master's and Ph.D from the University of Rajasthan, Jaipur.

K. L. Sharma was invited as visiting faculty by College de France, Paris, for five terms from 1991 to 2005. In 2002, the University Grants Commission of India honoured him with the Pranavananda Saraswati Award. He has also served on several committees and commissions as an expert member. The Indian Council of Social Science Research, New Delhi, bestowed him with a National Fellowship (2014–2016).

During his nearly half-century-long academic career, Sharma has published 26 books and 90 research papers. His main areas of interest include rural sociology, caste and class, social stratification and mobility, agrarian and tribal movements, etc. Presently, he also writes on current issues for a well-known Hindi daily, for the benefit of the common people. Sharma's writings are widely read by students, researchers and faculty of social sciences, and other concerned people.